Casseroles, Can Openers, and Jell-O

Casseroles, Can Openers, and Jell-O

American Food and the Cold War, 1947–1959

Elizabeth Aldrich

The recipes in this book may not employ current cooking procedures and the reader is encouraged to exercise caution and to utilize up-to-date food safety practices.

Published by State University of New York Press, Albany

© 2023 State University of New York

All rights reserved

Printed in the United States of America

No part of this book may be used or reproduced in any manner whatsoever without written permission. No part of this book may be stored in a retrieval system or transmitted in any form or by any means including electronic, electrostatic, magnetic tape, mechanical, photocopying, recording, or otherwise without the prior permission in writing of the publisher.

For information, contact State University of New York Press, Albany, NY
www.sunypress.edu

Library of Congress Cataloging-in-Publication Data

Name: Aldrich, Elizabeth, 1947– author.
Title: Casseroles, can openers, and Jell-O : American food and the Cold War, 1947–1959 / Elizabeth Aldrich.
Description: Albany, NY : State University of New York Press, [2023] | Includes bibliographical references and index.
Identifiers: LCCN 2022037705 | ISBN 9781438493060 (hardcover : alk.paper) | ISBN 9781438493084 (ebook) | ISBN 9781438493077 (pbk. : alk. paper)
Subjects: LCSH: Gastronomy—United States—History—20th century. | Dinners and dining—United States—History—20th century. | Cold War—Social aspects—United States. | United States—Social life and customs—20th century. | Food—United States—History—20th century. | Cooking, American.
Classification: LCC TX633 .A43 2023 | DDC 641.5/40973—dc23/eng/20220812
LC record available at https://lccn.loc.gov/2022037705

10 9 8 7 6 5 4 3 2 1

*I dedicate this book to my mentor and faithful advisor,
Claude B. Conyers (1934–2019),
and to my dear friend and trusted colleague,
Victoria Phillips.*

I believe that one of the most dignified ways we are capable of, to assert and then reassert our dignity in the face of poverty and war's fears and pains, is to nourish ourselves with all possible skill, delicacy, and ever-increasing enjoyment. And with our gastronomical growth will come, inevitably, knowledge and perception of a hundred other things, but mainly of ourselves. Then Fate, even tangled as it is with cold wars as well as hot, cannot harm us.

—M. F. K. Fisher (1942)

Contents

LIST OF ILLUSTRATIONS xi

ACKNOWLEDGMENTS xix

INTRODUCTION 1

Part I.
Setting the Table

CHAPTER 1
Food Is a Weapon 13

CHAPTER 2
From the Factory to the Suburbs: New Social Roles for Women 33

CHAPTER 3
Little Girls Make Fluffy Jell-O Desserts: Little Boys and Their Fathers Grill Steaks 45

Part II.
Sitting Down and Unfolding Our Napkins

CHAPTER 4
"If I Knew You Were Comin', I'd Have Baked a Cake": Cookbooks, Cooks, and Cooking 67

CHAPTER 5
"Honey, I'm Home. What's for Dinner?": The 1950s American Diet, Part I 91

CHAPTER 6
SPAM® and Jell-O Tell Their Stories While We Sit Back and Enjoy a Cola: The 1950s American Diet, Part II 115

CHAPTER 7
Fancy Appetizers, Beef Stroganoff, and an Atomic Cocktail: Fun and Elegant Entertaining in the Suburbs, Part I 139

CHAPTER 8
More Parties, the Cult of the Chafing Dish, and the Suburban Luau: Fun and Elegant Entertaining in the Suburbs, Part II 163

CHAPTER 9
Foreign Foods? Chop Suey, Tamale Pie, Chef Boy-Ar-Dee, and Some Curry 187

Part III.
Indigestion

CHAPTER 10
Selling Plymouths to Men, Electric Can Openers to Women, and Televisions for All 217

CHAPTER 11
Step Away from the Donuts: The Importance of Staying Healthy (in Case the Cold War Turns Hot) 245

Part IV.
Watching History Unfold with an After-Dinner Drink

CHAPTER 12
The Kitchen Debate: Vice President Richard M. Nixon and Soviet Premier Nikita Khrushchev Meet in a Lemon-Yellow Kitchen, July 24, 1959 273

Epilogue	293
Notes	305
Index	347

Illustrations

Figure I.1	"Stay slim and trim." Domino Sugar magazine advertisement, 1950s.	7
Figure 1.1	World War II poster to discourage food waste.	15
Figure 1.2	A crowd of Berliners watch as an American aircraft lands with food and supplies during the Berlin Airlift (1948–1949).	27
Figure 1.3	*Operation Vittles*, a book of recipes compiled in 1949 during the Berlin Airlift.	29
Figure 2.1	World War II poster to recruit women into war production work.	35
Figure 2.2	WASPs at Laredo Airforce Base, Texas, 1944.	37
Figure 2.3	Living the American way of life: a house in the suburbs, 1950s.	40
Figure 2.4	A mother proudly presents a dish to her appreciative husband and children, 1950s.	43
Figure 3.1	Wearing an apron identical to her mother, a young girl learns about baking cakes.	46
Figure 3.2	Wearing a chef's hat, a young boy cooks while his sisters and the family dog watch.	47
Figure 3.3	Little boys and their fathers grill steaks and the women present side dishes, 1950s. 7 Up magazine advertisement.	57

xiv | Illustrations

Figure 3.4	A woman displays her impressive collection of Tupperware, c. 1955.	58
Figure 3.5	Cooking meat over a fire on a raised platform was a traditional method employed by Native Americans. In this illustration, the Timucuan from central and northeastern Florida grill alligators. From *Brevis narration eorum quae in Florida Americae provi[n]cial Gallis acciderunt*, published in Frankfurt, Germany, 1591.	59
Figure 4.1	Four women and two cookbooks collaborate to bake a cake.	71
Figure 4.2	Magazine advertisement in 1959 for Betty Crocker's Yellow Cake Mix.	79
Figure 5.1	A billboard in Los Angeles, advertising Libby's Canned Peaches, c. 1955.	93
Figure 5.2	A 1950s magazine advertisement for Birds Eye frozen vegetables.	100
Figure 5.3	A woman proudly shows off her Pillsbury Cake Mix creation.	102
Figure 5.4	1950s Reddi-Wip magazine advertisement.	105
Figure 6.1	Canned luncheon meat is elevated to a fancy meal in "Crown Roast Dinner." The center of the roast is potatoes rolled in parsley. The roast is flanked with asparagus, covered in a quick hollandaise sauce. Slices of pineapple topped with strawberries are tucked between the asparagus. *Better Homes and Gardens New Cook Book*, 1953. Used by permission of Meredith Corporation.	118
Figure 6.2	Teens ordering food from a drive-through restaurant, magazine advertisement for Coca Cola, c. 1959.	130
Figure 6.3	Nikita Khrushchev enjoys a Pepsi Cola, poured by the Pepsi-Cola Company chairman Donald M. Kendall. Vice President Richard Nixon intently looks on. American National Exhibition, Moscow, 1959.	132

Illustrations | xv

Figure 6.4	Canada Dry Ginger Ale and Club Soda are advertised to adults as mixers for alcoholic beverages, c. 1950s.	134
Figure 7.1	Downtown Las Vegas, Nevada, 1950s. A cloud from a recent atomic test can be seen in the background. The Nevada Test Site was a mere sixty miles north of Las Vegas. Courtesy of Nevada National Security Site, Nuclear Testing Archive, Las Vegas, Nevada.	151
Figure 7.2	"Wilbur Clark's Desert Inn, Las Vegas, Nevada," 1951 postcard. The glass enclosed Sky Room Cocktail Lounge was located just under the "Desert Inn" sign. In 1951 the hotel was the tallest structure in Las Vegas and a popular gathering spot to watch the nuclear bomb tests from the Nevada Test Site.	152
Figure 7.3	An elegant buffet dinner consisting of Veal with Wine and Mushrooms over rice, broccoli, and a Chocolate Sponge Mold with Eggnog Sauce. *General Foods Kitchen Cookbook*, 1959. Used by permission Kraft Heinz Foods Company.	154
Figure 8.1	"Come for tea," *General Foods Kitchen Cookbook*, 1959. The teapot and matching cup and saucer, along with an assortment of toast, jam, desserts, and sandwiches, are set on an elegant tray, with a warm, inviting fireplace as background. Used by permission of Kraft Heinz Foods Company.	168
Figure 8.2	"The prettiest party of the season is the one you give." The centerpiece is a baked ham, glazed with a mixture of herbs, vinegar, and lemon Jell-O. It is decorated with scallion tops, stuffed olives, and cucumber rounds. The ham sits on a base of Jell-O cubes, surrounded by sweet potato rosettes. A chafing dish (*top left*) holds the dessert of cherries jubilee. *General Foods Kitchen Cookbook*, 1959. Used by permission of Kraft Heinz Foods Company.	172

Figure 8.3	Movie poster for *She Gods of Shark Reef* (1958). Directed by Roger Corman, the movie centers on two brothers (one wanted for murder), who find themselves shipwrecked on an island inhabited by attractive young women.	178
Figure 8.4	Thor Heyerdahl's raft, Kon Tiki, 1947.	179
Figure 8.5	Mitzi Gaynor as Ensign Nellie Forbush in the 1958 film adaptation of Rodgers and Hammerstein's Broadway hit musical *South Pacific*.	180
Figure 8.6	A 1950s magazine advertisement for Dole canned Hawaiian pineapple juice.	182
Figure 9.1	"For something to surprise." Magazine advertisement for Chun King's Canned Chicken Chow Mein, c. 1950s. Courtesy ConAgra.	204
Figure 9.2	"For a fiesta of good eating." Magazine advertisement for Van Camp's canned Mexican-style foods, c. 1950s. Courtesy ConAgra.	208
Figure 9.3	A magazine advertisement for French's Currie Powder, 1950s.	211
Figure 10.1	A late 1940s billboard in Dubuque, Iowa.	218
Figure 10.2	Crowds in Iowa protest the fall 1959 visit of Soviet Premiere Nikita Khrushchev. Photograph by Thomas J. O'Halloran.	219
Figure 10.3	A 1950s magazine advertisement for Aunt Jemima Pancakes, featuring the face of spokesperson Anna Robinson.	222
Figure 10.4	An elegantly attired couple prepare for a ride in their big-finned Plymouth, 1950s magazine advertisement.	224
Figure 10.5	A woman cooks in her electric broiler.	226
Figure 10.6	A happy couple welcomes a new Motorola television into their lives.	232

Illustrations | xvii

Figure 10.7	A man stands next to a large billboard advertising Philadelphia Cream Cheese and a dip for potato chips (perhaps the popular, Kraft Clam Appetizer Dip).	234
Figure 10.8	The Oscar Mayer Wienermobile appears in the Philadelphia Thanksgiving Day Parade, 1951.	238
Figure 10.9	Religion was an important component in the American way of life, often reflected in the era's popular sitcoms. Here, the Anderson family prays together before a meal: (*left to right*) Lauren Chapin, Billy Gray, Robert Young, Jane Wyatt, and Elinor Donahue in the television series *Father Knows Best*.	242
Figure 11.1	During World War II rationing in the US, many recipes circulated to encourage food conservation. This is a Baked Bean Loaf, described as a "healthy and nourishing meat substitute."	246
Figure 11.2	The oldest McDonald's still in operation, located in Downey, California. Opening in 1953, it is an example of the 1950s architectural style used for McDonald's restaurants.	253
Figure 11.3	Identically dressed mother and daughter show off their tiny waists in a 1950s Post Grape Nuts magazine advertisement.	255
Figure 11.4	A young girl tries to exercise via television in a 1950s Jell-O magazine advertisement.	256
Figure 11.5	Exercise and health guru Jack LaLanne poses in handcuffs for his 1955 swim from Alcatraz to San Francisco's Fisherman's Wharf.	266
Figure 12.1	Cover, official USSR booklet for the 1959 exhibition in New York, 1959.	276
Figure 12.2	Russians view American television sets at the American National Exhibition, Moscow, 1959.	279

| Figure E.1 | "You don't need to wear armor to be a charmer." Magazine advertisement in the 1950s for Warner's bras, girdles, and corselettes. | 294 |
| Figure E.2 | "If he discovers you're still taking chances on getting flat, stale coffee, woe be unto you!" Chase and Sanborn magazine advertisement, 1950s. | 295 |

Acknowledgments

This book was written during the early years of the COVID-19 pandemic, when trips to archives and libraries became impossible. I am grateful to the librarians at the Apache Junction Public Library who cheerfully helped me obtain additional research materials from interlibrary loan. I also am indebted to the various organizations, both private and governmental, that have continued to curate and digitize materials in their archives. During these difficult times, I found these materials to be enormously helpful.

My assistant, Jonathan Cohn, negotiated the ins and outs of recipe and illustration permissions, and I cannot thank him enough for his noble efforts. We are particularly grateful for the rapid responses and cooperation of Patty Bellus from Meredith Publishing, Kristen Stalling from the Harry S. Truman National Historic Site/Independence Multi-Park Facility, Linda K. Smith from the Eisenhower Presidential Library and Museum, and Lindsay Passet from Alamy Stock Photo, who patiently guided me through the process of obtaining photos. Russian specialist and former University of New Mexico colleague Eric Newton reviewed and commented on a chapter, and Stacey Prickett and Victoria Phillips read and critiqued every chapter—sometimes more than once. I am grateful to Richard Carlin, senior acquisitions editor in music, education, and New York State history and culture, for having faith in this project and to Susan Geraghty, production editor, for providing invaluable support during the last phases of manuscript preparation.

In our memories, exceptional meals are evoked on many sensory and emotional levels, and although good meals can be enjoyed without the company of others, most memorable meals are those shared with friends or family. Over the years, I have been fortunate to share wonderful meals with good friends, for example, Kathryn and Frank Krogh in Virginia; Peggy Bulger and Doug Leatherbury in Florida; Pam Arth and Gary Seale in Annapolis at restaurants Grapes and Vin; and Madeline Ritter and Peter

Legermann, cooking in Berlin. I lived for some time on the coast of Chile, and I have very fond memories of dinners and long lunches with our small community in Tunquén, including Ximena Fernandez and Pedro Salas (d. 2022), Ricardo Salas (d. 2021) and Leonora Calderón, Alvaro Rosas (d. 2021) and Brenda Ferrer, and my longtime friends Pedro Sánchez and Daniela Muller. Often, we were joined by Lorena Barba or we might gather at her fabulous restaurant Pezcadores, located in Quintay. France brings memories of a Thanksgiving dinner with lots of foie gras and good friends Joan Greenfield and Dominique Singer and, on another trip, an incredible dinner at La Récréation in Les Arques, where I experienced the most glorious appetizer of lobster ravioli (the pasta was so thin that I could see the tantalizing morsels of lobster). While working at the Library of Congress, Susan Manus, Carol Lynn Ward-Bamford, Robin Rausch, and I often joined for Ladies' Lunch, and music division colleague Kevin LaVine and I would frequent the Banana Café. Memories of these remarkable meals and especially the good fellowship always make me smile.

In 1994, Claude B. Conyers, editorial director of Scholarly and Professional Reference, hired me to be the managing editor of the six-volume *International Encyclopedia of Dance* (Oxford University Press, 1998). Claude also loved food and was an excellent cook. (In 2016 he published his own cookbook, *A Miscellany for Cooks: Tantalizing Recipes from My Southern Family and Friends from Faraway Places*.) Claude also edited the very first iteration of this volume—a short syllabus for a class in Cold War culture—and he often inserted some of his wry humor. After he retired and moved to his upstate New York house, former Oxford alums and partners would gather for lots of good food, wine, and a round of cutthroat Monopoly. Included in these annual excursions were Marion Osmun, Jeff Edelstein, Joan Greenfield, Dominique Singer, and Mark Finley. Claude provided unwavering friendship and support of my work and I will forever be grateful for knowing him.

During the fall and winter of 2018–2019, my dear friend Victoria Phillips allowed me to stay in her beautiful Long Island home. There I cemented my thoughts, continued the research, and outlined chapters and contents. Victoria and I have curated exhibitions together, attended conferences, and searched archives throughout the United States and Europe. Victoria also encouraged me to look beyond the confines of my work, which had been centered on historical dance. Without her encouragement and support, I never would have had the courage to write this book. I thank her for many things but especially for opening my eyes to the greater world of food and history.

Introduction

My mother was a terrible cook, and my earliest memories of food center around her indescribable home-cooked meals during the 1950s and early 1960s. She was a popular public school music teacher and a talented pianist, but she could not cook. She baked roasts in a hot oven until they resembled shoe leather; she boiled broccoli for nearly an hour.

Both my parents worked, which did not conform to the idealized nuclear family of the 1950s; however, my mother was part of the middle-class audience targeted by the expanding advertising industry. She embraced processed foods with a vengeance: birthday cakes originated with a Betty Crocker or Duncan Hines box mix and Cheez Whiz on Ritz Crackers snacks. She served SPAM® in every conceivable manner. Tuna noodle casserole, based on a foundation of a can of tuna and a can of Campbell's Cream of Mushroom Soup, was on the family menu at least once a week. When she arrived home later than expected, we chose Swanson frozen dinners from the freezer. My mother's Jell-O creations were not the colorfully illustrated towering results found in cookbooks and magazines. Her designs utilized an excess of shredded carrot, miniature marshmallows, and canned pineapple, all crammed within the confines of bilious green lime gelatin. Of course, as was the practice, my mother topped this with a dollop of mayonnaise and a maraschino cherry.

Beliefs and notions about food are tangled into a perplexing web of social issues and politics, both domestic and global. During the 1950s, the increasing sophistication of the advertising industry through print, radio, and television played a fundamental role in exploiting food to reaffirm social and political ideologies and promote traditional, prewar gender roles. Food also is profoundly political, often found at the center of government policies. Supplying it can be a supportive reward for allies and withholding it can be a crippling hindrance to enemies. This volume touches on examples of the United States using food in its domestic and foreign policy. As we look back at government-sponsored international programs through the lens of more than seventy years, one can use these initiatives to demonstrate that the US was a noble, caring nation. However, these programs also represented pragmatic, political decisions to assure the US that hungry nations would not look to the Soviet Union for assistance. Industry wanted new markets. US domestic policy made it clear that postwar rationing and agricultural programs also would support struggling European countries and prevent them from falling into the sphere of communism.

Following the years of austerity during World War II, most Americans were once again enjoying an abundance of food by the beginning of the Cold War. The nation recovered its economic health and began to prosper with new growth in agriculture and industry. Food in the 1950s was part of a growing commercial, industrial complex, which in turn heavily influenced what we ate, dictated a delivery system, and ultimately determined how food tasted, looked, and smelled.

The transference of industrial manufacturing from war materials to the creation of commodities for the domestic sphere, aided by improved technologies in food production and processing (freezing, canning, dehydrating), placed a renewed emphasis on women and the kitchen. As the economy expanded, many Americans moved to newly built suburbs, spiking the development of fast-food chains, such as McDonald's and Dunkin' Donuts.

Most women's lives changed drastically during World War II when high-paying jobs attracted women of all races and classes to work as part of the US war effort. While it was considered a woman's patriotic duty to work for the war effort, government publications reminded women that their husbands and sons were fighting for an elusive idea: the "American way of life," sometimes defined as the "American dream." Although most women admitted that their wartime jobs had been rewarding, both monetarily and emotionally, returning soldiers needed these jobs to support their families in the new economy. The early Cold War years forced different gender issues on men and women. Thus began the gender split that advertisers and industries pushed throughout the 1950s. Men worked to provide food and material goods for their families, and women were responsible for the requirements of running a household, including cooking all the family meals. Many new transplants to the suburbs were men and women, separated from close family members and friends, uprooted to a truly isolating landscape.

Television was the most important consumer innovation of the 1950s. With a captive audience focused on a flickering black and white image, food and appliance advertisers reinforced the importance of a new consumer world. Alongside family-friendly programs, such as *Father Knows Best*, *The Donna Reed Show*, and *Leave It to Beaver*, advertisers were able to encourage the purchase of products while supporting the ideals of the 1950s family unit.

Madison Avenue advertising agencies pushed processed foods in cans and boxes and electric kitchen appliances—skillets, mixers, coffee makers, and can openers—all intended to make cooking fun and entertaining, fast, and easy. Advertising directors assumed that women would leave their wartime work and return to their roles as contented, productive housewives. As the 1950s progressed, more women entered (or reentered) the workforce—despite persistent campaigns that encouraged them to remain exclusively in the domestic sphere. Without missing a beat, advertisers turned their attention to this demographic, including my mother, by promoting time-saving gadgets and foods to liberate the modern working woman. But while the advertising industry was courting the white middle class, others mostly remained invisible: African Americans, immigrants, rural people, and Native Americans.[1]

A primary focus of the Cold War centered around a perceived and looming threat of communism. International programs, such as the Marshall Plan, were designed to support democracy by discouraging countries from favoring the USSR. Domestic anxieties over communism culminated in Wisconsin Senator Joseph McCarthy's House Un-American Activities Committee. Civil rights organizations, always under suspicion of subversion, had to clarify "that their reform efforts were meant to fill out the contours of American democracy, and not to challenge or undermine it."[2] A politically charged racial climate in the US damaged the image of a freedom-respecting American democracy as the world consumed newspaper articles and watched newsreels that covered the struggles of America's people of color.

African Americans held the most prominent presence of any other minority group of Americans in advertising. Still, the images were patronizing and reinforced stereotypes—stereotypes either expected or not recognized by the white audience. The illustrations of Uncle Ben (rice products), Rastus (Cream of Wheat and Cream of Rice), and an "apron-clad plantation mammy named Aunt Jemima"³ all harkened to the days of slavery.

Publisher's Weekly announced a "cook book boom" in 1947 when *The Good Housekeeping Cook Book*, first published in 1944, sold over a million copies. During the 1950s, publishers, as well as food product manufacturers, released a cascade of cookbooks. Some assisted the housewife in her quest to be a modern woman. Still, perhaps more importantly, they acted as a support for the many new suburban women who no longer had easy access to their mothers' or grandmothers' culinary advice. Cookbooks came forth from commercial publishers and manufacturers, and others were issued informally by church groups and charitable organizations. Throughout the 1950s, readers purchased cookbooks that brimmed with color photographs bound between visually unique covers. Recipe books became splashier, more extensive, and elaborately illustrated.⁴ Recipes for fruity Jell-O molds, casseroles galore, sandwich loaves, sauces, creams, and frostings proliferated throughout the cookbook world. Simultaneously, many of the recipes in these books became simpler, assuring the reader that she could save time by using more processed foods to create culinary masterpieces.

Betty Crocker's Picture Cook Book is, without doubt, the most famous cookbook of the era. Published in 1950 and known as Big Red because of its vivid red and white cover, it quickly became a bestseller. In 1945 *Fortune* magazine recognized Betty Crocker as "America's First Lady of Food" and declared her to be the second most popular woman in America (former first lady Eleanor Roosevelt placed first). Three years later, President Harry S. Truman (1884–1972) acknowledged Betty Crocker as Women's National Press Club Woman of the Year, and in 1949, the Advertising Federation of America named Betty Crocker Advertising Woman of the Year. But Betty Crocker was an illusion; she was not a real woman but an entity created in 1921 within the walls of the Washburn-Crosby Company (later to become General Mills).

The 1950s produced a plethora of cookbooks that provided recipes and helpful hints for the use of canned and frozen foods and advice on how to make quick, one-dish casseroles. Poppy Cannon (1905–1975), the author of *The Can-Opener Cook Book*, exclaimed with pride: "At one time a badge of shame, hallmark of the lazy lady and the careless wife, today the can opener is fast becoming a magic wand."⁵ Cannon's book presents can-opener-friendly recipes ranging from Five Minute Louisiana Gumbo to California Chili (requiring only cans of chili con carne and red kidney beans).

I have no recollection that my mother owned any cookbooks, and I only remember watching as she read the directions given on the back of a package. When I married in the late 1960s, I received a copy of *Betty Crocker's New Picture Cookbook*, published in 1961—ironically, a gift from my mother. One can only imagine my pride after producing a picture-perfect pineapple upside-down cake. Eventually, I conquered many more uncomplicated recipes, utilizing all the canned and frozen items I could find. I suddenly felt like a grown-up woman (an illusion shattered a few years later when I realized that all my friends had exchanged their sad Betty Crocker cookbooks for Julia Child's *Mastering the Art of French Cooking*).

During the 1950s, cooking outdoors on the barbecue proved to be men's territory: "Husbands become the experts and do the barbecuing."[6] Women were not welcome in the barbecue world. With the production of George Stephen's kettle-shaped covered grill, later sold under the name Weber kettle, charcoal briquettes and manly barbecue accessories soon became the rage. The backyard barbecue became an influential family and community event with cooking reserved for men. During the 1950s, men were encouraged by social scientists and psychologists to establish a masculine authority to counter a perceived notion that their sons spent too much time under the feminine influence of their mothers. The popular opinion was that these young boys might grow up to become homosexuals, juvenile delinquents, or even communists without a father's input. Illustrated print advertisements from this era reinforced this male gender role. For example, popular illustrations represent the suburban family and community spirit by depicting groups of men and boys busy at work grilling steaks and hot dogs. The women are in the background, presumably ready to present the side dishes.

The US has always been considered a melting pot of culinary experiences, encompassing many worldwide flavors. Or, as American historian Arthur M. Schlesinger Sr. astutely noted, "The melting pot was also a cooking pot."[7] Latin Americans, particularly Mexicans, contributed foods to the American diet, as much of the Southwest was initially Mexican territory, creating dishes infused with the rich culinary heritage of Native Americans. During the nineteenth century, Chinese immigrants arrived in the US to work in mines and on the western branch of the first transcontinental railroad. When not performing manual labor, many of these immigrants became known for their cooking skills. Thus, in addition to the English and Scots-Irish cuisines of early American settlers,[8] French,

Chinese, and Mexican foods have also long been a part of US culinary traditions. Germans, Poles, Scandinavians, Italians, Greeks, and people from other European and Asian nations followed, bringing their recipes and cooking techniques. The 1936 edition of *The Joy of Cooking*, by Irma S. Rombauer (1877–1962), included Chinese, Mexican, and Italian dishes. However, while the recipes themselves may have had foreign-sounding names, following the examples of other contemporary cookbooks, most recipes were stripped of their foreignness by reinterpretation and utilization of already familiar ingredients, including the reduction or elimination of herbs and spices, a practice that continued into the 1950s.

The casserole was the favorite meal that often connected the American family to foreign, exotic locations. Never calling for fully authentic ingredients, foreign-inspired dinner casseroles from one 1958 cookbook included a Mexicali Spaghetti Bake, which contained spaghetti, ground meat, and cans of tomatoes, cream-style corn, and pitted olives. Likewise, a recipe for Ham Ling Lo had no ingredient associated with Asian cooking but consisted of some mashed potatoes, two cans of coarsely grated luncheon meat (most likely SPAM®), and a can of pineapple slices.[9] If these recipes proved to be elusive, one could always use cookbook author Poppy Cannon's "magic wand" and open a can of Chef-Boy-Ar-Dee Spaghetti, one of Van Camp's Mexican-style foods, or a can of Chun King Chop Suey.

The newly processed foods of this era, and the rise of fast-food restaurants that encouraged consumption of fatty foods such as hamburgers and fried foods, led to obesity. Medical experts also agreed that American children were clearly overweight and physically unfit. In 1953, the *Journal of the American Association for Health, Physical Education, and Recreation* published a report outlining the physical deficiencies of American children compared with European children. Alerted to this report, and following the President's Conference on Fitness of American Youth, President Dwight D. Eisenhower (1890–1969) created the President's Council on Youth Fitness (with cabinet-level status) in 1956, chaired by Vice President Richard M. Nixon (1913–1994). Eisenhower supported the idea that it was entirely appropriate for the federal government to be concerned about the health of its young people, especially young men. With the constant threat that the Cold War might turn hot, the nation needed strong and healthy soldiers.

An early pioneer in fitness and health, Jack LaLanne (1914–2011) also focused on the unhealthy effects of popular fatty, processed foods, including salt-ladened canned fruits and vegetables, and the substantial amounts of refined sugar and flour found in the cereals and celebrated desserts of the 1950s. In a first for television, and years before the world discovered Jane Fonda's televised exercise program, LaLanne created his fifteen-minute program, which targeted the housewife and encouraged her to exercise. He often utilized everyday household items, such as chairs or brooms, as makeshift gym equipment.

Industrial food producers and advertisers took note of the burgeoning health-concerned trends of the time. Kellogg's issued Special K, marketed as a low-fat cereal aimed at consumers desiring to lose weight. Not wishing their products to fall in popularity, food lobbies recruited advertising agencies to tout their foods as healthy and suitable for diets. One such lobby, Sugar Information Inc., asked consumers, "Are you getting enough sugar to keep your weight down?" Post Grape-Nuts cereal and even Pepsi-Cola joined the chorus by proclaiming their products to be the perfect foods for losing weight.

Figure I.1. "Stay slim and trim." Domino Sugar magazine advertisement, 1950s. Source: Retro AdArchives/Alamy Stock Photo.

8 | Casseroles, Can Openers, and Jell-O

The gastronomic 1950s dramatically ended on July 24, 1959, during the "Kitchen Debate" between the US vice president Nixon and the Soviet premier Nikita Khrushchev (1894–1971). The leaders of the two most powerful countries in the world stood in the kitchen of a model home, decorated in a lemon-yellow, and debated the merits of capitalism and communism. For Nixon, the American kitchen—the heart of a tranquil, middle-class home, with its time-saving gadgets and colorful, modern appliances—clearly demonstrated the superiority of the US and democracy. Historians have portrayed this as a decisive moment in the Cold War; the US had presented a modern, streamlined kitchen as the most persuasive weapon against the communist threat. Perhaps the most ironic part of this debate was that the kitchen itself was a model and not even real. It was part of an imaginary American model ranch house, sitting like a duck out of water in Moscow's Sokolniki Park. Barricaded and cut in half, the kitchen was an illusion, a room designed only for spectators.

In the broader social spectrum of house and home and family life, the 1950s was a time of revolution in the American kitchen, with new technologies for refrigerators, stoves, and small electric appliances. The food industry introduced new products, and snack foods became popular. Although not to everybody's tastes, the canned, frozen, and dehydrated foods of the 1950s, frequently jammed into Jell-O molds or one of the decade's famous casseroles, are now often described as comfort food: a handful of chips or popcorn as we watch our favorite television shows (now more than likely downloaded or streamed); chips and dip, which entered our snack vocabulary in the 1950s; the ubiquitous little Vienna sausages in mystery sauce or pigs in a blanket that appear at birthday or anniversary parties; casseroles prepared by our mothers or grandmothers, perhaps one of President Truman's favorite meals—the ultimate comfort food, Tuna Casserole. The following recipe was created by his wife, Bess Truman (1885–1982).

Tuna Casserole

Harry S. Truman National Historic Site, U.S. Department of Interior, National Park Service Museum Collection[10]

Directions

Cook elbo mac [elbow macaroni] for 20 min.

Drain good.

Stir in tuna packed in water (DRAIN), 1 c. [cream] of celery soup and less than ½ c. milk

Sprinkle with cheddar cheese & bread crumbs

Bake at 350° for about 20 min. or until bubbles.

Slice hard boiled egg on top.

In a 2012 *Time* magazine article, Jeffrey Kluger asked, "Is there anything sadder than the foods of the 1950s? Canned, frozen, packaged concoctions served up by the plateful, three meals per day. We knew far less of flavor or freshness or artisanal excellence than we do now. We were culinary rubes and too clueless even to know it. [The food] was easy to prepare and it was always there. You loved it as a kid, and, be honest, you still love it a lot now."[11]

Often, one views the 1950s as a time of petal pink or cadet blue refrigerators, SPAM® sandwiches, big-finned Buicks, poodle skirts, or the change in popular music due primarily to a singer named Elvis. Some think of the 1950s as an era of domestic bliss, represented in television sitcoms. Although it was a time of abundance in the US, it was also a time of societal transition. Now, after nearly seventy years, we look back at the 1950s as the golden era, a time when the American dream was within reach of the average American family. It was an illusion for many, particularly anybody who was not white or middle class. Today, many describe the 1950s as nostalgic—a time of conformity, consumerism, and a simpler life. It was a time to celebrate the nuclear family—husbands and wives defending their homes from real or illusive dangers within utopian suburban communities. Advertisements for food, refrigerators, coffee makers, and soda pop all hawked their goods in the context of this perfect nuclear family. This image was inescapable, "scattering its potent assumptions of family deep into our collective psyches."[12]

In her foreword to *The Gastronomical Me*, food writer M. F. K. Fisher (1908–1992) noted, "People ask me: Why do you write about food, and eating and drinking? Why don't you write about the struggle for power and security, and about love, the way others do?" I, too, am often asked why I am immersed in the food of my childhood after starting my adult life as a professional musician and then becoming a dance historian. Fisher responds, "Like most other humans, I am hungry. But there is more than that. It seems to me that our three basic needs, for food and security and love, are so mixed and mingled and entwined that we cannot straightly think of one without the others."[13] I echo Fisher's response and have written this volume to address some of the issues I have been thinking about for a long time. For example, I am intrigued by my mother's choices in meals and honor the many women who have shaped our likes (and dislikes) about food and the generations of women who have provided comfort and love through food, often while juggling full-time employment. I am interested in and often horrified by how government policies use food as a source of incredible power. Why have so many people been left out of food conversations: African Americans, immigrants, and Native Americans? Even in the 1950s and earlier, American food would not have been as vibrant and varied without these influences.

On the other hand, how do we reconcile food authenticity or appropriation today when examining the 1950 versions of the foods of different cultures? Today many consumers are knowledgeable about organic foods and often inquire about the source of food they eat, fueling the farm-to-table movement. However, most do not think about the origins of food—whether that is Africa, the Caribbean, Europe, North or South America—nor do they think much about appropriation, accepting Schlesinger's "melting pot as cooking pot" explanation.

Finally, I am fascinated by the extraordinary power held by the advertising and manufactured food industries that shaped ideas about the taste, smell, texture, and appearance of the food we ate. Advertising created the packaging on cans, jars, and frozen food containers that cried out "Choose me" to our mothers in grocery stores across our country. Finally, and most importantly for me, I am interested in how food ties families and communities together, often uniting opposites in sharing precisely what Fisher sees: love.

Part 1
Setting the Table

Chapter 1

Food Is a Weapon

> That we sentence 1.2 million Jews to die of hunger should be noted only marginally.
>
> —Governor-General Hans Frank,
> German-occupied Poland (1939–1945)[1]

Bullets and bombs were not the deadliest weapons of World War II. The most potent weapon in any combatant country's arsenal was death through starvation. While it is impossible to know the actual number of World War II casualties, military deaths are estimated at 19.5 million, while more than twenty million succumbed to famine.[2] Control of the world's food supply is often at the core of international conflict, and when used as a weapon, its effects can be as lethal as military action.

Fear of Hunger Leads to World War II

After World War I, Germany and Japan anticipated future problems feeding their urban populations. Other countries, such as Britain, could import large quantities of food, but Germany and Japan felt disadvantaged by an international economy dominated by the United States and Britain. The solution was to expand their empires; the Japanese moved into China while Germany looked to the East.

With little arable land, the Japanese needed to find other sources for food and natural resources. In 1931 they invaded the Chinese province of Manchuria, which was rich in coal and iron and agricultural land. In a grandiose plan known as the Japanese Settlement of One Million Households, in 1932 the Japanese began evicting Manchurian farmers in order to resettle their farmers to provide food for the mainland. In 1945, these Japanese colonists—mostly older women and children—were caught in the Soviet invasion. Of the two hundred thousand settlers sent from Japan, over seventy-eight thousand perished from attacks and starvation.[3]

Nazi Germany's Hunger Plan, well-advanced in development by May of 1941, was designed by Herbert Friedrich Wilhelm Backe (1896–1947), state secretary and minister in the Reich Ministry of Food and Agriculture. The calculated extermination by starvation was a centerpiece of the National Socialists' proposed wartime food supply. The intention of the Hunger Plan was to murder, by starvation, millions of Slavic and Jewish "useless eaters." Germany needed food at any cost. As well as securing food, the Germans envisioned an expansion of their empire by populating the newly acquired lands—now rid of Slavs, Poles, and Jews—with Aryan German families.

After surviving hunger in the US during the economic depression, in the early 1940s as World War II was waged in Europe, Americans were encouraged by the US Department of Agriculture to plant "victory gardens," as was practiced during World War I. It was argued that the produce from such gardens would help lower the cost of vegetables needed by the US War Department to feed the troops, thus saving money for other military needs. In 1917, a widely distributed poster urged the public to "plant the seeds of victory"; in 1942, a poster reassured gardeners that "our food is fighting." Growing vegetables also meant that a ration card would go further. By 1944, more than twenty million victory gardens had been established throughout America, producing an estimated eight million tons of food and 40 percent of all the fresh vegetables consumed in the United States.[4] Because of civilian efforts and a technologically advanced agricultural and delivery system, the military was well fed. Even with rationing in place, American civilians fared far better than people of most other countries during World War II.

Figure 1.1. World War II poster to discourage food waste. Source: CBW/Alamy Stock Photo.

> You can find anything in the list of things that were eaten during the blockade, from the hempseed in bird food, to the canaries themselves. People scraped flour paste off the wallpaper, extracted it from bookbindings, boiled down driving belts, ate cats, dogs, crows, used all kinds of industrial oil or grease. One woman cut up, boiled, and then ate a coat made from gopher fur.
>
> —Ales Adamovich and Daniil Granin (1983)[5]

The siege of Leningrad is considered one of the great atrocities of World War II. In September 1941, the siege began when the Wehrmacht, led by General Field Marshall Wilhelm von Leeb (1876–1956), severed the last road into Leningrad, and it ended 872 days later on January 27, 1944. Simply occupying the city was not an option because the Germans would be responsible for feeding Leningrad's citizens. Instead, the Germans decided to starve Leningrad's population and eventually destroy the city. Approximately 1.1 million Soviet civilians died during the siege.

Poland's Warsaw ghetto contained one of the largest Jewish populations in Nazi-occupied Europe. In 1940, over four hundred thousand Jews were forced into an area of just over one square mile. Residents of the ghetto were given ration cards and allowed only three hundred calories worth of food daily. (Some accounts state the number of calories as 180.)[6] "The basic provisioning of the Jewish Residential District must be less than the minimum necessary for preserving life, regardless of the consequences."[7] By July 1942, the time of the "Grossaktion Warsaw" or the mass deportation of Jews from the ghetto to Treblinka, an estimated one hundred thousand had already died of starvation or disease. By September 1942, more than two hundred and fifty thousand of the remaining residents had been sent to Treblinka.[8]

Food Shortages during World War II

Food shortages in other parts of China were also a result of Japanese occupation. Still, after the Chinese Nationalist government decided to focus on the food requirements of its army in fighting the Sino-Japanese War, some two to three million peasants died of famine in Henan province from 1932 to 1933. In Vietnam, insensitive food requisitioning policies by the French Vichy colonial government and the occupying Japanese were directly responsible for a famine that killed at least two million Vietnamese people from 1944 to 1945.[9] Between 1943 and 1945, estimates for deaths in Java due to famine range from 1.3 million to 2.4 million.[10] Blockades further exasperated the food crisis, including blockades by the Japanese on nationalist China, the United States on Japan, and the British blockade that surrounded occupied Europe. Meanwhile, the Germans waged a U-boat war on Allied shipping.

British colonies supplied crops in return for badly needed food imports, but at the start of World War II, the colonies were suddenly compelled to become as self-sufficient as possible. In contrast, their cash crops were requisitioned for Allied military needs. For example, in India, the economy was pushed beyond its limits. The British feared a Japanese invasion via the eastern border of Bengal, and in March 1942, the British launched a scorched-earth program to block the Japanese from obtaining food supplies and other resources. By 1943, these actions resulted in the starvation of three million people in Bengal.[11] British diplomat Leo Amery, secretary of state for India, commented that the famine was "the worst blow we have had to our name as an Empire in our lifetime."[12]

Peter Lewis, British soldier and journalist, noted:

> We had never seen anything like it. Massive, well-fed men marching sloppily through our streets with enormous bottoms wagging. They showed generosity with Hershey chocolate bars and chewing gum. Here was the best-fed army in the world. For them the war was "the good war" which pulled their farms and industries out of recession and into unprecedented prosperity. They were fighting for "The American Way of Life." It seemed mainly to consist of enormous amounts to eat.[13]

Feeding the Military Machine

Japanese soldiers were issued only a minimum amount of food as they went into battle. If food supplies ran out, soldiers took from the enemy, and if the enemy did not have enough food, the soldiers grew it themselves. With little attention paid to supply lines and the tightening of the American embargo, food became a critical issue. Author Lizzie Collingham wrote that soldiers "found themselves fighting on the front line on a diet of wild grasses."[14] Japan's military commanders suggested that soldiers only needed *bushido* ("way of the warrior") to survive. (Tenets of *bushido* emphasized honor, courage, loyalty to a warrior's master, respect, and self-control. A follower of this ethical system was supposed to be immune from the fear of death.)[15] In the end, 60 percent of Japan's 1.74 million military deaths were due to starvation, not combat.

The German military was fed on a diet based on science and high in calories and protein. Each soldier received a daily supply of canned meat and hard bread. Rations often included a dehydrated soup compressed into a pellet, which was crushed and placed in boiling water, or part water and part canned condensed milk (when it was available). The SS had its version of rations, consisting of rye bread, canned sausage, canned vegetables, a half-ounce of butter or margarine, and actual or ersatz coffee and sugar.

German field kitchens (*Gulaschkanone*) proved to be an efficient means of providing large quantities of hot meals, including stews, potato soup, or pea and ham soup. Bread or biscuits regularly accompanied meals. The American approach to field kitchens required trucking in all foodstuffs. The Germans, however, relied on acquiring all supplies in occupied countries, primarily through confiscation, thus contributing to the eventual starvation of many locals. The Nazis depleted conquered territories of resources to feed the German war machine. Industries and agriculture in France, Belgium, the Netherlands, Denmark, and Norway were forced to produce goods, especially food, to meet German demands.[16] Despite its otherwise well-organized feeding plans, the German military relied on horse-drawn woodburning stoves when it was impossible to use its field kitchen cooking ranges. Toward the end of the war, the entire system began to break down when the Germans could not deliver hot meals without air cover.

In its push to capture land and resources in the East, the German army did not consider the poor roads, subsequent fuel shortages, and issues with rail transport (German and Soviet train track gauges were different, and it took some time for the Germans to rebuild the tracks). Thus, a large portion of the German army could not avail itself of rations or field kitchens but was forced to live off occupied lands, often a futile effort as the locals preferred to destroy their crops rather than turn them over to the enemy.[17]

Compared to the rest of World War II soldiers, American soldiers were the most well-fed. Because of a thriving agricultural and industrial complex, the food requirements of the 11.5 million US servicemembers were easily met with rationing that had less impact on American citizens than in any other country. "The American way of life," an often-quoted phrase by Madison Avenue throughout the war and ensuing Cold War, became a potent slogan that demonstrated America's dominance to both its friends and foes.

The US military created menus similar to American school lunches and represented typical Anglo-Saxon preferences of meat, potatoes, a vegetable, and a sweet dessert. Offerings were bland but filling and nutritious. "The recruits from diverse regional, religious and ethnic backgrounds found themselves eating the innocuous food of democracy. Their taste buds were moulded into conformity."[18] As dull as the diet might have been, it made a significant impression on Allied soldiers. For example, newly liberated British prisoner of war Eric Barrington observed, "How those dough boys do feed, porridge and cream and peaches, white bread and jam, pancakes, and syrup, and bacon and pukka coffee."[19]

US military field kitchens could be set up in a matter of minutes, as close to the battlefront as possible. Although serving basic meat and potatoes, cooks were able to source fresh foods from locals. However, most of the food shipped from the United States came in dehydrated or canned form. Designed to feed between 150 and 200 soldiers, all food, gasoline, and water for each kitchen was trucked from location to location. Each kitchen had one or more M19-range stoves powered by gasoline, and these stoves could cook anything that a conventional, domestic home range of the time was able to cook. Field kitchens served two meals: breakfast and dinner (both served in the dark, for security reasons). A third meal, lunch, was a K ration. According to military standards, two hot meals a day were essential for nutrition; also, a hot meal proved to be a morale booster. After being prepared in the kitchen, the hot meals were packed into five-gallon metal cans and trucked to the front line. Based on the superior organization of these field kitchens, it is easy to see why the US military was the best fed in the world.

In 1942 the military adopted the type K ration, with contents that evolved over time. The ration consisted of three separate meals: breakfast, lunch, and dinner and contained 2,830 calories, lower than the requirement for active duty. As an "assault" ration, K rations were intended for minimal use of no more than a few days. However, this proved to be impractical, and soldiers often ate them for many days or weeks, especially in heavy combat, which precluded the presence of a field kitchen. While the early boxes were contained in brown card stock, later versions made it easier to select the proper meal: brown packaging for breakfast, green for lunch, and blue for dinner. A typical breakfast consisted of a canned meat product, eggs, biscuits, a cereal bar, powdered coffee, a fruit bar, water purification tablets, cigarettes, chewing gum, sugar (granulated, cubed, or compressed), and a packet of toilet paper. Lunch included canned processed cheese, biscuits, five caramels, sugar, a salt packet, cigarettes, a matchbook, chewing gum, and a powdered beverage packet (lemon in 1940, orange in 1943, and grape in 1945). Dinner was canned meat (beef and pork), biscuits, an emergency chocolate bar, coffee, sugar, toilet paper, cigarettes, chewing gum, and a cubed or powdered bouillon packet. Because carrying mess kits was impractical—they made too much noise and there were no cleaning facilities—each meal packet contained a can opener and a wooden spoon. At the height of the war, the US produced more than 105 million K rations.[20]

Military and Humanitarian Chocolate

Chocolate was often given out in the towns and cities liberated by US troops, and numerous photographs of this humanitarian effort permeated American periodicals and newsreels. Created by Milton Hershey, the Hershey Bar is a milk chocolate candy bar first launched for five cents in 1900. The Hershey Company is the most well-known chocolate producer in the US and its chocolate bars are considered a quintessentially American product. Chocolate also made a substantial impression because of its association with American soldiers, World War II, and the Cold War.

Sugar is a central ingredient in creating chocolate. Sugar shortages were first felt in the US in early 1942—a result of the Japanese invasion of the Philippines, which had been a major supplier. Cargo ships that brought sugar from Hawaii and the Americas were reduced by half as vessels were redirected for military use, straining the supply. To guarantee supplies for the military, sugar was the first food to be rationed in April of 1942 (and the last food to be taken off the ration list in June 1947). Sugar was rationed for domestic use but certain candy makers such as Hershey and Mars were exempted. When Congress deemed these industries to be nonessential for the war effort and suggested the manufacture of candy and beverages be declared illegal, the Hershey company persuaded Congress that chocolate was necessary as a morale booster. "It would remind the boys of home and what they were fighting for."[21]

In the late 1930s, the US Army asked the Hershey Company to manufacture a special chocolate bar for its emergency rations. The D ration was created in 1937, utilizing Hershey's newly formulated "military chocolate," a high-energy ration bar meant for emergencies. This chocolate was different from the regular Hershey's candy bar. Rather than the thin bar of creamy milk chocolate known and loved throughout the US, this was a thick, rectangular bar, a mixture of chocolate, sugar, oat flour, cocoa fat, skim milk powder, and artificial flavoring. It was flavored explicitly so troops would not be tempted to consume the bars before they were needed. In other words, they did not taste very good. Bitter and brutal on the digestive system, the density of the bars also meant that they were tough to chew. Per military instructions, the chocolate bar was high in energy and withstood heat up to 120°F without melting. In 1944, the Hershey Company produced a pamphlet that described the various ways the military used its chocolate, including as an aircraft snack ration to "provide extra energy on long flying missions"; as the US Navy life raft emergency ration, created to "sustain life in case of shipwreck"; and as a prisoner of war package, "a gift of the American Red Cross supplied to those of our fighting forces who have fallen into enemy hands."[22] The Hershey Company produced more than forty million chocolate bars for the military during World War II.

The Mars Company also provided chocolate to the military, and the ever-popular M&M's candies were exclusively manufactured as a snack for troops during World War II. The signature sugar-coated shells helped keep the candy from melting in warmer, war-zone climates. (They also would not melt in your hands.) M&M's were so popular with the troops that Mars introduced the candy into the domestic market in 1948.

After World War II

> Food is a vital factor in our foreign policy. And the attitude of Americans toward food can make or break our efforts to achieve peace and security.
>
> —Secretary of State George C. Marshall (1947)[23]

After supplying the allies with food during World War II, the postwar US government formed new alliances with private corporations to provide food and other commodities to countries as they rebuilt their infrastructures and economies. These alliances allowed the US to continue to promote itself as a benevolent savior to hungry people worldwide while expanding international markets and maintaining profits for industry. The hungry included much of war-torn Europe and European colonies in Africa and Asia, as the US perceived all to be vulnerable to Soviet domination.

In one of the first postwar uses of food as a tool of domestic government policy, Americans were called upon to conserve food for Europe in order to "help prevent starvation and distress among our fellow men in other countries."[24] Consequently, President Truman issued a call for "meatless Tuesdays" in an address televised to the nation on October 5, 1947. (This was the first nationally televised presidential address.) Truman's press secretary later noted in his memoirs, "The new program of the president called for four main points—meatless Tuesdays, no eggs or poultry on Thursdays, saving a slice of bread every day, and the serving of bread and better in public eating places only on request."[25] In his televised speech, Truman remarked, "If the peace should be lost because we failed to share our food with hungry people there would be no more tragic example in all history of a peace needlessly lost."[26] In an October 7, 1947, letter to his wife, Bess, Truman complained, "The Catholics are all mad because we asked for Tuesday for meatless day instead of Friday. The turkey growers are all mad because three holidays come on Thursday. But, I suppose we can eat turkey on those days."[27] Consuming poultry was allowed on Thanksgiving, Christmas, and New Year's. However, pumpkin pie, which requires eggs, was discouraged.

As humanitarian as the program sounded, the point was to keep Europe from leaning toward the sphere of the Soviet Union. Secretary of State George C. Marshall (1880–1959) bluntly stated, "Our foreign policy has entered the American home and taken a seat at the family table." He asked Americans "to tighten our belts—clean our plates—push ourselves away from the table." Marshall declared that if Americans heed his words, we "can save Europe from collapse."[28]

To promote the program, the White House issued Truman's menus for his first "meatless Tuesday" and first "poultry-less, eggless Thursday." Tuesday's lunch consisted of grapefruit, cheese soufflé, buttered peas, grilled tomatoes, and chocolate pudding. Dinner started with chicken soup, followed by salmon with scalloped potatoes, string beans, sautéed eggplant, Perfection Salad, and sliced peaches. Thursday lunch was corn soup, pepper stuffed with rice and mushrooms, lima beans, glazed carrots, and baked apples. The dinner menu consisted of baked ham, sweet potatoes, asparagus and cauliflower, a green salad, and Coffee Mallow for dessert.[29]

COFFEE MALLOW

Public Papers of the Presidents of the United States, Harry S. Truman[30]

16 marshmallows
½ cup hot coffee
1 cup heavy cream
½ tsp. vanilla

Cut marshmallows in quarters with wet scissors. Add coffee. Cook in double boiler until melted. Cool. When beginning to thicken, fold in cream, beaten stiff and add vanilla. Mold in dessert glasses. Serves 6

Although the Truman White House enthusiastically threw its support behind meatless Tuesdays, it was mostly a symbolic gesture. Many of the nation's restaurants and shoppers ignored the call, and meatless Tuesdays quietly disappeared by the end of the year. *The New York Times* postmortem was merciless, suggesting that the policy was "a colossal misappraisal of human nature."[31]

The European Recovery Program (April 1948–December 1951)

> What is Europe now? It is a rubble-heap, a charnel house, a breeding ground of pestilence and hate.
>
> —Winston Churchill (1947)[32]

The months and early years in post–World War II Europe, known as the Age of Austerity in Britain, were dark and miserable for many. British citizens faced endless lines and ration books for essentials such as food and gasoline, and even with ration cards, food had fallen below wartime allowances. France was facing Communist-inspired strikes, and in Germany, the population struggled to survive on about one thousand calories per day.

Officially called the European Recovery Program, the Marshall Plan was an initiative of the US designed to rebuild postwar Europe. The program was named after Secretary of State George C. Marshall, who outlined problems plaguing postwar Europe in a speech at Harvard University on June 5, 1947. In his remarks, Marshall noted that the US should do what it can "to assist in the return of normal economic health to the world, without which there can be no political stability and no assured peace."[33] These issues included widespread hunger (millions were said to be on the verge of starvation), the need to rebuild industry, and solving economic problems that resulted from the scarce foreign exchange required for the purchase of goods. When the program began in 1948, one of the first requests from participating countries was for food. Thus, American Hershey chocolate and cans of SPAM® were included in goods delivered to war-torn Europe as part of the Marshall Plan.

Marshall suggested that the European countries create a cooperative program for recovery and invited twenty-two nations to join in a conference held in Paris in July 1947. Sixteen nations agreed to participate (West Germany and the territory of Trieste joined in 1949). An invitation was extended to the Soviet Union, but it refused and denounced the plan as an American plot to subjugate Western Europe. None of the countries under Soviet domination were allowed to participate.

Fueled by a fear of communism and the precipitous decline of the European economy, in 1948, the US Congress passed the Economic Cooperation Act. From 1948 to 1951, the US government contributed more than $12 billion to supply food and tools required by Europe to reactivate its economy. While the Marshall Plan did help in the recovery of Europe's industry and helped return butter and eggs to stores, it also energized and created markets for American goods. It established the entry of Western Europe into the consumer age. For example, in 1951, Marshall Plan organizers planned an industrial fair that provided Europe with its first preview of color television. Several open-air TV screens were erected close to the East Berlin border, giving clear views into the Soviet sector. In exploiting the propaganda possibilities, a Marshall Plan press release noted, "Free Berlin exhibits draw communist youths," and further remarked that "a steady flow of wide-eyed visitors, some who had come to Berlin from many parts of the world 'played hooky' from the phony-peace propaganda of the East."[34]

The passage of the Smith-Mundt Act (Public Law 402) in early 1948 authorized the US Department of State "to promote a better understanding of the United States in other countries and to increase mutual understanding between the people of the United States and the people of other countries." The Act also encouraged the Department to utilize "to the maximum extent practicable, the services and facilities of private agencies, including existing American press, publishing, radio, motion picture and other agencies."[35] The Department of State crafted the Private Enterprise Unit, which was responsible for undertaking projects including the distribution of commercially-prepared materials, book donations, training for businesses in how to advertise American policies, and traveling exhibits that showcased American cultural and industrial progress. The Advertising Council was a significant player in these efforts.

The Advertising Council's 1948 report titled "A Year of Cold War. Advertising Faced it Realistically" notes that "the Cold War overshadowed all other national and international developments—and mass information campaigns directly or indirectly connected with it formed an important part of The Advertising Council's work." Some of the Council's projects included the Freedom Train, designed "to make Americans more conscious of their hard-won rights and freedoms," and the creation of an emblem for the Marshall Plan, a design of a red, white, and a blue shield bearing four stars and thirteen red-and-white stripes. The words "For European recovery, supplied by the United States of America" appeared across the shield. The Council also issued a campaign guide for American business firms that advertised overseas to assist in dispelling communist misconceptions and to explain the "true motives behind Marshall Plan aid—the first participation of advertising in the Cold War overseas." Finally, the Council launched a campaign known as the Miracle of America to increase understanding of America's economic system.[36] The primary goal of marketing and advertising was to promote the cause of freedom and to stimulate the sales of American products. Advertising became a weapon of the Cold War.

The Soviet Blockade of West Berlin: The First Major Crisis of the Cold War (1948–1949)

Hell's fire, we're hauling grub. Call it Operation Vittles.

—Brigadier General Joseph Smith (1948)[37]

Germany was organized into four parts at the end of World War II, controlled by the United States, Great Britain, France, and the Soviet Union.

The capital, Berlin, was in the Soviet-controlled, eastern half of Germany, and it too was divided into four parts. Thus, it was necessary to plan for a supply link from the American zone of Germany to Berlin. All agreed that the British and American forces in Berlin had the use of one railway and one highway from Magdeburg, Germany, to Berlin. A twenty-mile-wide air corridor into Berlin was open to American and British planes. To force the Western powers out, beginning in April 1948, Joseph Stalin (1878–1953) ordered measures that eventually led to the blockade of West Berlin. These measures started with traffic disruption in the agreed-upon road and railway routes. Travel in and out of the Soviet sector depended on obtaining the applicable permits, subject to Soviet interpretation. On April 3, the Soviets denied the right to "free and unrestricted use of the established corridors." During the following weeks, measures were sufficiently effective to lessen east-west traffic.[38] On April 25, the Soviet military administration halted all passenger and freight traffic to and from Berlin. Further, they announced that West Berlin would have electricity only between 11 p.m. and 1 a.m.

The US had options: withdraw from Berlin, remain in Berlin at all costs, or postpone the decision to withdraw until it became necessary. Berlin was located deep inside Soviet-controlled Germany. Militarily, "the United States maintained approximately two divisions in Europe. In ground strength, Stalin held the trump cards."[39] Representatives of the military and the Central Intelligence Agency (CIA) both weighed in, expressing concern that US interests would be compromised if action was not taken. The CIA warned that if "friendly Germans cannot move freely to and from the Soviet zone or within the city, the U.S. cannot as before, support anti-communism within the Soviet zone."[40] Even the American Federation of Labor expressed alarm. "The immediate future of Germany and Western Europe depends upon sure firmness in maintaining our policy which alone can assure freedom of the people. We know only too well that communist desire for domination will not stop at either ocean. We urge firmness, now, before the tide of conflict reaches our own country."[41] Anti-communist rhetoric resonated in the United States.

The military estimated that it would require 2,000 tons of coal and over 1,500 tons of food per day to meet the minimum basic needs of West Berlin's two million inhabitants, far from the standard requirements of 13,500 tons a day.[42] This massive amount of food, which represented only 1,800 tons, included 646 tons of flour and wheat, 125 tons of cereal, 64 tons of fat, 109 tons of meat and fish, 100 tons of dehydrated potatoes, 180 tons of sugar, 11 tons of coffee, 19 tons of powdered milk, 5 tons of whole milk for children, 3 tons of fresh yeast for baking, 144 tons of dehydrated vegetables, 387 tons of salt, and 10 tons of cheese.

On June 26, 1948, Operation Vittles commenced when thirty-two US C-47 aircrafts landed at Templehof Airport (in the US sector of West Berlin), carrying eighty tons of food from the airbase in Wiesbaden, West Germany. Eventually, the operation utilized airports in the British (Gatow) and French (Tegel) sectors. Proudly describing the efficiency of the operation, Transportation Officer Colonel Donald C. Foote enthusiastically bragged that on April 16, 1949, between 11 a.m. and 1:45 p.m. (165 minutes), ninety-one planes landed at Templehof. "A plane every minute and a half! Yet our support phase operated so efficiently that as many as 18 planes were awaiting take-off or return to Wiesbaden or Rhine-Main. Think of it! Nearly 1,000 tons of precious coal and food were landed and handled on one field in 165 minutes—over 6 tons a minute."[43]

Figure 1.2. A crowd of Berliners watch as an American aircraft lands with food and supplies during the Berlin Airlift (1948–1949). Source: World History Archive/Alamy Stock Photo.

US Air Force Colonel Gail Seymour Halvorsen (1920–2022), known as the Berlin Candy Bomber or Uncle Wiggly Wings, became a local folk hero for his candy dropping to children during the Berlin Airlift. As the public became aware of Halvorsen's goodwill efforts, corporations began to donate large amounts of chocolate and other candy for the effort. Ultimately, Uncle Wiggly Wings dropped twelve tons of sweets for the children of West Berlin.

Soviet forces often harassed but did not directly attack the airlifts. By the spring of 1949, it was clear that Soviet tactics had not deterred the Americans nor the British (who had been joined by France, New Zealand, and other Allied countries). As a result, the Soviet Union signed an agreement in early May 1949 and lifted the blockade. However, the airlifts lasted until the end of September 1949 to build up reserves in case of a future blockade. "The tallies for 321 days of operation were a total of 227,655 passengers flown either in or out of Berlin and 2,323,067 tons of food and coal delivered."[44]

The Western powers created the Federal Republic of Germany in September 1949, and a month later, the Soviets formed the German Democratic Republic in their occupation zone.

A Cookbook Is Created in Blockaded Berlin

Despite the uncertainty of living in the American-occupied sector of Berlin, over 1,700 American women and children joined their husbands. They found themselves participants in the first major crisis of the Cold War. The *Chicago Tribune* noted that by staying in Berlin, the women were "encouraging Berliners frightened by the prospect of Russia taking full control of the city."[45]

In January 1949, the American Women's Club of Berlin compiled a cookbook called *Operation Vittles Cook Book*. As well as recipes from members of the Women's Club, other contributions came from West Berlin's military missions and governments, such as Australia (Sherry Chocolate Cake), England (Toad-in-the-Hole), Canada (French Canadian Pea Soup), China (Spring Rolls), Czechoslovakia (Carp in Jelly), France (Cherries à l'Eau de Vie), and Greece (Moussaka).

Five pages of black-and-white photographs precede the recipes and show military aircraft and groups of children gazing at the incoming planes. The last five pages are examples of children's artwork depicting life during the airlift (including one that illustrates aircraft dropping chocolate). Recipes range from all-American favorites such as Chocolate Cake, Sugar Cookies, and Italian Meatballs to Polish Golabki, Mexican Hominy, and Baked Sauerkraut. They often represented a range of choices, from the straightforward, such as Cheese Toasties, that required only three ingredients easily obtained during the blockade to more elaborate dishes that required items not accessible during the crisis, such as Deep-Dish Gooseberry Pie, Clam Chowder, and Fillet of Sole. Some of the recipe titles are whimsical, including Heaven-Knows-What Chicken and Block-Ade, a potent beverage that served seventy-five in a mixture of canned fruit cocktail, sugar, and twenty bottles of alcohol (cognac, red and white wine, and champagne). Perhaps in an attempt to hide its Russian origins, the book provides a recipe for a popular American dish, beef stroganoff, but here it is called Beef Strageneuff.

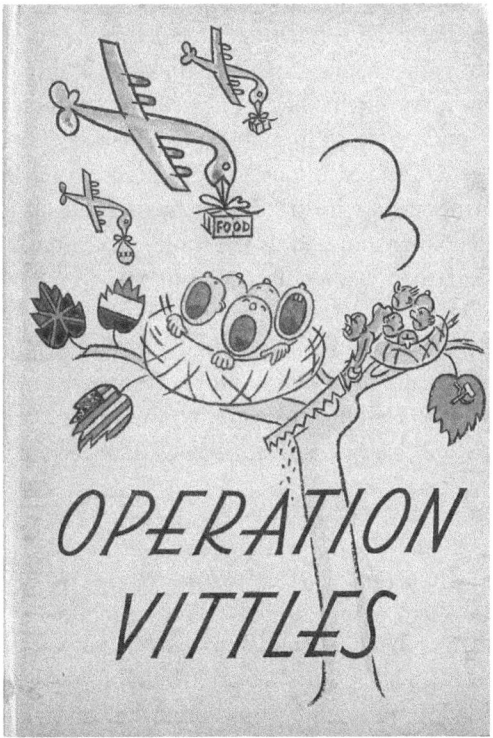

Figure 1.3. *Operation Vittles*, a book of recipes compiled in 1949 during the Berlin Airlift. Source: Author's collection.

The preface notes that the cookbook is "dedicated to the happy group of wives who attempted to obtain American meals by slaying the dragons of language, old utensils, ovens sans thermometers, conflicting opinions, etc., ad infinitum, and to the many excellent cooks who bore with the puzzling variety in the American diet—the endless series of *'Immer was neu ist!'* "[46] Each recipe is signed by its contributor and includes an anecdote about life as an American housewife in occupied Berlin. Many of the stories demonstrate difficulty with language and others "all too often cast 'the many excellent [German] cooks' they encountered as culinary conservatives, simpletons who complained about 'the puzzling variety in the American diet and its tendency for newness.' "[47] As well as callously poking fun at their hosts' preference for cold foods, which might well have been because of wartime conservation, one contributor noted, "There are no egg custards in Germany, so German cooks and on-lookers in the kitchen were completely dubious as to the thickening ability of the egg. When the thin soupy mixture, 'No cornstarch? No flour?'—emerged from the oven perfect, the resultant expressions were well worth seeing!" Another quipped, "The all-time saddest chicken we've seen was a roasted job produced by a cook who had confused the ingredients and stuffed it with one cup poultry seasoning and one tablespoon bread crumbs!"[48]

Authors Lieffers and Mills observed, "*Operation Vittles* is a testament to a group of Americans who tried to make do and do good. The quotidian work of cooking and eating was political action during the Cold War, holding more than just a culinary front against a Soviet menace." At the same time "in taking large responsibility for a free West Berlin and a free world, American soldiers and their families shouldered much of the burden of constructing a liberal global framework. But this postwar order, so essential for European prosperity, would also carry the seeds of American hubris and exceptionalism that we still reckon with today."[49]

Mary's Cornbread

Operation Vittles Cook Book (1949)[50]

Our joy that we have persuaded a few Germans to the edibility of corn, which they had always thought was intended for horses and American Indians, is somewhat diminished when we consider the small proportion thus influenced.

1¼ C flour
¾ C cornmeal
2 T sugar
2½ t baking powder
½ t salt
1 C milk
1 egg (slightly beaten)
2 T shortening (melted)

Sift dry ingredients together. Add milk to egg. Add to flour mixture. Add shortening. Pour into greased baking dish. Bake. Oven: 350° Time: 25 Minutes

In December 1948, one of America's most famous songwriters, Irving Berlin, joined comedian Bob Hope for a special show in Berlin to honor the American military. For this occasion, Irving Berlin composed the song "Operation Vittles," which he performed with a chorus of military corpsmen. (As part of the show, Berlin jokes with Bob Hope that he has changed his last name to Jones because every time someone says "Berlin," another person tries to divide him up into four parts.)

1953: Nobel Peace Prize for Marshall

In acknowledgment of the success of the Marshall Plan, George C. Marshall received the Nobel Peace Prize in December 1953 for his role in designing and executing the Marshall Plan. During the ceremony in Oslo, communists dropped leaflets from the balcony, shouting, "We protest!" However, Norwegian King Haakon VII led the audience in applause for Marshall.[51] Yet, the Marshall Plan had long-term ramifications for the US as it "institutionalized and legitimized the concept of U.S. foreign aid programs, which have become an integral part of U.S. foreign policy."[52]

Author Tom Standage wrote that food is "literally the fuel of war."[53] A military victory in war is always interwoven with domination over a nation's food supply. After the war, the world was characterized less by peace accords and newly drawn borders and more by the challenges of hunger. The US responded with a continuation of selected domestic rationing, the Marshall Plan, and the Berlin Airlift. It can be argued that the benefits of the propaganda may have outweighed humanitarian returns; it cannot be disputed that these programs enabled millions of hungry Europeans to fill their stomachs and have the strength to rebuild their lives and economies.

Chapter 2

From the Factory to the Suburbs

New Social Roles for Women

> The War Department must fully utilize, immediately and effectively, the largest and potentially the finest single source of labor available today—the vast reserve of women-power.
>
> —Secretary of War Henry L. Stimson (1943)[1]

In April 1942, President Franklin D. Roosevelt (1882–1945) signed an executive order creating the War Manpower Commission (WMC).[2] The Women's Bureau, an established agency within the Department of Labor, fiercely lobbied WMC's chairman Paul V. McNutt to have a seat at the table.[3] McNutt rejected the addition of women as part of his all-male commission. Instead, he created a separate Women's Advisory Committee (WAC) one year later. Beyond a per diem and transportation funds, the WAC had no support staff or budget. Any recommendations emanating from the WAC first passed through the Management-Labor Policy Committee. If the Management-Labor Policy Committee approved a WAC recommendation, it went to the WMC. Even with this unwieldy bureaucratic pipeline, there were no women on the Management-Labor Policy Committee, and it was difficult to enact policies regarding women's employment. Without an invitation to join the table, women workers had no voice, but they would have concerns.

Harold W. Metz, the author of *Is There Enough Manpower?*, somberly noted, "We might bring into war production all of the nonfarm homemakers who are under 45 and without young children."[4] Would childcare for older children be available at the factories? With projected forty-eight-hour weeks, when or where would women do grocery shopping or have time to clean their homes? Would training programs be offered? How would factories address safety and hygiene matters? Many needed transportation to get to the factories, but automobile travel proved challenging with rationed gasoline and rubber for tires virtually unavailable. Housing, especially for women of color, was hard to come by. In *Womanpower Committees During World War II* (a report published in 1953), the Women's Bureau noted that it seemed reasonable for women to have had a voice. The report observed that women, who represented one-third of the civilian working population, carried "a far greater proportion of responsibility for the maintenance of family and community welfare."[5] Metz confirmed, "The greatest reservoir of additional manpower is the 29.8 million women who are classified as homemakers." The war effort needed women workers, and they were willing to serve, even without a voice at the table.

On June 13, 1942, Roosevelt established the Office of War Information (OWI), which created information programs to "promote, in the United States and abroad, an understanding of the status and progress of the war effort and war policies, activities, and aims of the U.S. government."[6] As a propaganda office, the OWI worked closely with a powerful non-government agency, the Advertising Council. One year later, the Council changed its name to the War Advertising Council to support the OWI through advertising campaigns in all forms of print media, radio, and film.

This powerful combination of government and the advertising industry created one of the most effective recruitment campaigns in American history, the Women in War Jobs, led by the fictional character Rosie the Riveter—a World War II icon. By mid-1943, Women in War Jobs recruited more than two million women into the workforce by encouraging them to join the war effort as a patriotic responsibility.

Government advertising campaigns and popular magazines such as *Life* emphasized the importance of women's participation in World War II. "If the women of America will take on this war, thoroughly and relentlessly, then this country would begin to look like a real war machine,"[7] advised *Life*, published by the famed Henry Luce. Albert Perry proclaimed that women were America's secret weapon in the 1942 government pamphlet *What Women Can Do to Win the War*. "The Axis forces often boast of a 'secret weapon.' America's secret weapon is its millions of trained, wide-

Figure 2.1. World War II poster to recruit women into war production work. Source: CBW/Alamy Stock Photo.

awake women, who stand ready to take their places, shoulder to shoulder, with the men of America until the world is again made free for all men and all women—and all children—everywhere."[8] Thus women were expected to work on behalf of the war to be considered loyal Americans. Approximately six million women entered the paid workforce for the first time to help win World War II, accepting jobs reserved for men. Simultaneously, the government also reminded these patriotic women that their homes should be "stable, unified, healthy, and ready to wage battle."[9]

Before the US entry into World War II, there was a pushback against any change in women's traditional roles. During the Great Depression of the 1930s, when jobs were scarce, numerous states passed legislation that discouraged married women from seeking employment. William H. Chafe noted that over 80 percent of Americans opposed the idea of working married women, and many people, including women, seemed disinterested in changing the accepted gender roles.[10] In 1940, the number of women with jobs outside the home was just about the same as what it had been in 1910.

A major transition for women began with the bombing of Pearl Harbor on December 7, 1941, and the US declaration of war against the Axis powers, which had repercussions for every American family. Production of consumer goods quickly took a back seat to military supplies, and nationwide rationing of certain goods started within a few months. In May 1942, the US Office of Price Administration froze the prices of most everyday goods, starting with sugar and coffee. War ration books containing coupons were issued to each American household, dictating just how much gasoline, meat, butter, and other commodities in short supply any one person could buy. Rationing was the only way to ensure that everyone got a fair share. Men left their factory or industry jobs to join the armed services or take up wartime work in other cities. Urged by government and advertising agencies, women swarmed to take high-wage employment, often in positions that formerly had been unavailable—including welding and riveting in shipyards and aircraft and munitions factories.

Not all women worked in factories. Some women chose to enlist in the military. The military establishment frowned on deploying married women, and 90 percent of women soldiers were single. Half of these women had high school diplomas, and a quarter had been to college. This education level is in stark contrast to male recruits, of which only one-quarter had high school diplomas. Women enlisted in the female branches of the military: Women's Army Corps (WAC), Women Airforce

Service Pilots (WASP), Women Accepted for Volunteer Emergency Service (WAVES), and US Coast Guard Women's Reserve (SPARS). Often, these women took assignments that were considered acceptable women's work, such as typists or stenographers in office pools. Most women remained in these secretarial positions throughout the war. However, in 1943 the armed services began training a few in more nontraditional work—as parachute riggers and air tower controllers. Many women who took these jobs were subjected to hostilities, in contrast to the media attention and praise showered on women who performed the generally accepted work in factories. Women in uniform represented an assault on conventional roles.[11]

Others supported the war through work as a part of the Women's Land Army (WLA), a federally established organization that recruited and trained women to work on farms. The farm situation had become critical: by 1945, six million men left their fields and barns to join the war effort as soldiers or move to more lucrative war industry work. Although some states resisted female farmworkers, women worked to keep US farms

Figure 2.2. WASPs at Laredo Airforce Base, Texas, 1944. Source: Everett Collection/Alamy Stock Photo.

functioning. Farm experience was not necessary, and the WLA drew its recruits from a wide range of applicants: high-school and college students, secretaries, bank tellers, and women whose husbands were serving in Europe or the Pacific. Pay ranged from twenty-five to fifty cents an hour for seasonal work; year-round workers received twenty-five to forty dollars per month. Work included planting and harvesting, plowing, milking cows, and shearing sheep. Other women assisted female farmworkers with cooking, housework, childcare, and gardening.[12] The WLA did insist that all members "be physically fit and possess manual dexterity, patience, curiosity, and patriotism." Women's clubs and other voluntary organizations encouraged participation and implored, "War takes Food—Food for our fighting men. Food for our fighting allies. Food for workers at home. We need more Hands. Enroll now in the Women's Land Army."[13] In January 1943, President Roosevelt delivered a nationwide speech in which he emphasized the importance of agriculture in the war effort. "Food is the lifeline of the forces that fight for freedom."[14] An estimated two million women worked on US farms to keep the food supply moving. Once again, women rose to the occasion.

"But whatever else you do—you are, first and foremost homemakers—women with the welfare of your families deepest in your hearts."[15] The reality of World War II was that women's daily lives proved challenging. With husbands off to war and many in the workforce, women were still responsible for the day-to-day household duties, including cooking and childcare. Even though women were helping in the war effort through outside jobs, the bottom line read: without a woman in the kitchen—a woman who continued her domestic chores—the US would not win the war. Wartime propaganda carried a mixed message. Yes, women's work was needed outside the home to win the war. On the other hand, advertisements, cookbooks, and print media continued to stress the importance of women in the kitchen. "It is the sacred duty of every AMERICAN woman to see that her family is properly fed—to make Americans the strongest, healthiest people in the world."[16] Magazine articles, newspapers, and pamphlets reminded women of this "sacred duty." "This is where a wife should shine," proclaimed Mary MacFadyen, who helpfully provided a four-point plan for "your husband's keep-fit-for-defense program." This program included proper nutrition, sufficient exercise, adequate rest and recreation, and regular medical and dental checkups.[17] "Yes, American women are willing to scrub, work in defense plants, drive ambulances, and do hundreds of other things for victory. But with it all, not one of us will neglect the home."[18]

In 1942, Roosevelt declared that homecoming service members should be assured they could return to their prewar jobs. Despite many gains in wages and opportunities, the reemployment provisions in the Selective Service Act put women workers on notice that their husbands, fathers, and sons were returning from the battlefields to regain their places in the workforce. American women also were to remind themselves why soldiers were at war: to fulfill "the American dream," and those heroes needed to believe that dream could become a reality. Experts warned that two-and-a-half million men would be demobilized after the defeat of Germany, with more at the end of hostilities in the Pacific. As war industries reconverted to peacetime manufacturing for returning soldiers, women were expected to leave their jobs.

Unfortunately, a significant number of Americans agreed. Even Harry Truman noted in 1944 that though he thought women were entitled to have jobs, he believed it was time for women to return to the home. Others joined the growing chorus, including sociologists, such as William Waller, who felt that women with wartime jobs had "gotten out of hand" and claimed that the very survival of the home was in danger of collapse. "Women must bear and rear children; husbands must support them."[19] While praising the wartime work of women, Frederick Crawford, head of the National Association of Manufacturers, claimed, "From a humanitarian point of view, too many women should not stay in the labor force. The home is the basic American institution."[20] Florida Senator Charles O. Andres expressed an even more extreme point of view, and he tried to convince Congress that it was time to "force wives and mothers back to the kitchen."[21] Many women ignored this discourse, especially those whose circumstances required work. Others, however, took heed and headed to the suburbs.

The mood of Americans was jubilant at the end of the war. Years of turmoil included a decade of the Great Depression and nearly half a decade of war. "The postwar years became a period of testing, a time of transition, in which women themselves, and the society at large, sought to determine the proper boundaries of women's sphere."[22] Advertising campaigns promised a future that included a sparkly new kitchen with all the amenities to assure that women would return to their domestic duties after the war. Universal Appliances, Kelvinator, Westinghouse, and Magic

Chef rushed forward with advertisements that showcased consumer goods that the American housewife could expect in her new kitchen: ranges, refrigerators, toasters, coffee makers, electric carving knives, and electric can openers. Advertising drove its message home: now that women had satisfied their patriotic duties on behalf of the war (as well as maintaining domestic duties), American women were now ready for the next chapter in life: marriage, children, and a dream kitchen in a home in the suburbs with a yard. "The modern kitchen was transformed into a place of magic, where the housewife effortlessly flicked a switch and dinner was ready with no effort."[23]

Returning soldiers were dismayed to find that there was an acute housing shortage. "If this country can build an $80 billion war industry, make the atomic bomb and win the war, why can't it build enough houses?"[24] The federal government and real estate developers Levitt and Sons soon addressed the issue of housing. In his first community, Levittown, New York, developer William J. Levitt appealed to returning veterans and blue-collar workers in need of housing. He primarily targeted those who

Figure 2.3. Living the American way of life: a house in the suburbs, 1950s. Source: Pictures Now/Alamy Stock Photo.

did not want to return to cramped apartments of city life. The Servicemen's Readjustment Act of 1944 (the GI Bill) helped veterans of World War II by making low-interest mortgages available. Later, the developer offered the homes to anyone with cash in hand or credit with a bank. New suburban homes equipped with white picket fences, green lawns, backyards ready for barbecues, and modern appliances went on sale in March 1947. More than 1,400 houses sold in the first three hours. The flood of families to suburbia had commenced. However, Levitt refused to sell his homes to people of color and insisted on racial covenants in each deed. Thus, the new family unit—white, predominantly Protestant, and middle class—became the primary advertising target for more than a decade.

Throughout the early Cold War years, images of families in suburban households were displayed by print media, including women's magazines and television programs—all aided in great measure by the growing power of the advertising industry. The result was the creation of a stereotypical "ideal woman," and along with her husband and children, they formed the nuclear family defined as a working father, a stay-at-home mother, and children.

Women Are Encouraged to Leave Their Wartime Jobs for a New Life in the Suburbs

> America during the 1950s and 1960s was grounded in and centered on the conception of the nuclear family. The suburbanization of white, middle-class families after World War II yielded unique conditions for both media outlets and the U.S. government to push explicit messages on gender roles to preserve the sanctity of the nuclear family.
>
> —Elaine Tyler May (2008)[25]

At the end of the war, young adults married in unprecedented numbers, giving birth to more children at shorter intervals, sparking the baby boom. Millions of married women moved into the workforce during the war, but many quit or found themselves laid off at the end of hostilities. Some rejoined the workforce with lower-paying jobs such as teachers, salespeople, secretaries, waitresses, and clerical and service workers. The rest chose, or felt forced to choose, domesticity.

The economy of the United States in the late 1940s experienced a healthy upswing. For Americans who had experienced the Great Depression of the 1930s and suffered hardships during World War II, the new standard of living was now notable. The government had money for the military and investment in science, technology, and education. While the economic prosperity primarily benefited the middle-class white family, it was prosperity enjoyed by a more significant proportion of the US than at any other time in history.

Taking advantage of what they assumed were accepted images of women, advertising agencies depicted women as young, almost childlike, and always happy. Women in the 1950s were pictured in the kitchen, surrounded by appliances and gadgets, and neatly dressed (including a string of pearls), with perfect hair, a starched apron, high-heel shoes (so impractical in a kitchen), and a smile of anticipation—as if she were waiting for company or a lover. Advertising *did* sell kitchens as a setting for seduction.[26]

Foods that proved to have a longer shelf life and highly processed or precooked foods freed the housewife from the exhausting and supposedly tedious work of preparing meals. Prepackaged, canned, and frozen foods married to newly designed sleek kitchens offered the 1950s housewife choices and promised that she'd spend less time in the kitchen. Less time in the kitchen would allow time for herself or more time to spend with her family and on hobbies, as well as doing volunteer service for her community.

Madison Avenue advertising agencies and 1950s cookbooks targeted white, middle-class Americans beginning their married lives in the suburbs—men in the public sphere of the workplace and women in the domestic, private sphere of the home. In the form of small and large appliances, advancing kitchen technology may have suggested that working-class women could achieve middle-class status. For the most part, however, any new technology available for use in the modern kitchen fell far below the financial abilities of non-middle-class families. Also absent in this discourse are the men and women of color, and they remained invisible in these ad campaigns. For those who did not fit the stereotype, the ads were interpreted as aspirational.

It mattered little that women had full-time jobs and careers outside the home; the image of the contented housewife prevailed during the 1950s. She was to make her family happy by cooking, serving, and cleaning (using all the recommended consumer goods), and her pleasure was to witness her family's happiness. Referencing George Kennan's theory of containing the spread of communism,[27] historian Elaine Tyler May eloquently argues that the United States endorsed a policy of sexual and social "containment" of women during the early years of the Cold War. "In the domestic version of containment, the 'sphere of influence' was the home. Within its walls, potentially dangerous social forces of the new age might be tamed, so they could contribute to the secure and fulfilling life to which postwar women and men aspired. More than merely a metaphor for the cold war on the home front, containment aptly describes how public policy, personal behavior, and even political values were focused on the home."[28]

Figure 2.4. A mother proudly presents a dish to her appreciative husband and children, 1950s. Source: Pictorial Press Ltd/Alamy Stock Photo.

Elizabeth Virginia "Bess" Truman, first lady of the United States, 1945–1953, once noted, "A woman's place in public is to sit beside her husband, be silent, and be sure her hat is on straight."[29] Bess also enjoyed cooking.

BESS TRUMAN'S COCOANUT COOKIES

National Park Service, Harry S. Truman National Historic Site[30]

Cream ½ cup butter & 1 c. sugar. Add 1 egg ¼ c. milk

½ c. Drom [Dromedary brand] cocoanut [sic]. Roll thin & bake in quick oven [375 degrees].

Unlike her predecessor Eleanor Roosevelt, Bess Truman (1885–1982) preferred to stay in the background of political life and considered a woman's role to be a conventional housewife. She chose, instead, to be active in her favorite charities, including the Girl Scouts, the Red Cross, and the Washington Animal Rescue League. Her quiet support of these values helped make her a popular first lady.

During World War II, American women performed essential jobs at home, in war-related work, and in uniform (some 350,000 women served in the military). Government and industry propaganda strengthened the idea that women had a duty to aid in the war effort. While magazines, newsreels, and Madison Avenue glamorized war work, women—especially those working in factories—were to maintain their femininity. For example, Boeing airplane factories offered charm courses; another factory advised women to "be feminine and ladylike even though you are filling a man's shoes."[31] This notion of femininity was the foundation of a movement to encourage women to return to their kitchens as fully domesticated housewives. At the end of the war, many desired to keep their jobs, but others quit to make way for returning soldiers. While some left well-paying factories for lower-paying jobs, others stayed in the workforce in jobs considered appropriate for their gender—secretarial and clerical work, nursing, and teaching. Domesticity became an essential component in the American way of life in the postwar transition. Women were under "immense pressure from their country to protect and defend steadfastly the very idea of traditional home and family, and their central place in it."[32]

Chapter 3

Little Girls Make Fluffy Jell-O Desserts
Little Boys and Their Fathers Grill Steaks

> Juvenile cookbooks accomplished more than affirming that girls, not boys, should be responsible for cooking domestic meals. The books were a small cog in the much larger machine that instructed children about the complex world of food and cooking and the "correct" gendered relationship they should adopt.
>
> —Sherrie A. Inness (2001)[1]

How do young girls and boys learn about gender-appropriate behavior apropos of food and cooking? The numerous cookbooks explicitly published for young people proved one of the most effective approaches in the 1950s (and earlier). Since women have overseen cooking for eons, it is not surprising that most of these gender-specific works center on young girls. Fewer publications focus on young boys, but they too emphasize the importance of masculine boundaries regarding food and cooking. Some cookbooks are written for an audience of both girls and boys; others are not gender-neutral but focus their attention on girls, often in subtle ways. For example, it is not uncommon to see girls cooking or cleaning up; the boys are eating or standing in the background. The message is clear: girls cook and clean while boys eat. Teenage girls also learned lessons from the era's cookbooks: they needed to have cooking skills to get a boyfriend and, when older, to "catch" a husband. The books also emphasized that once women were married, good cooking skills were necessary for keeping that husband happy.

Miss B.'s First Cookbook (1950) demonstrates the importance of a mother's input, providing advice to help the youngest little girls, thus reinforcing the bond between mothers and daughters in passing down gendered ideas. "Help her where you can. At first, she will think she is cooking if she does nothing but stir while you measure and add the ingredients." "A message to your mother from Miss B.'s mother" continues by supporting the awareness that well-cooked and beautifully presented food will result in praise, a goal often noted in adult cookbooks. "Give her the rewards of praise that mean so much. Let her pass the cookies or candy to guests with the remark that she made them."[2] Praise will also come when the little cooks show ingenuity or creativity in their presentations, again a trend also stressed in adult cookbooks. Mother is present in many of the cookbooks. For example, *Betty Crocker's Junior Baking Book* prefaces each recipe with "Have Mother turn on the stove." Julia Kiene instructs her young readers to start with an easy recipe. "Perhaps you better talk this over with your mother and ask her advice."[3]

Figure 3.1. Wearing an apron identical to her mother, a young girl learns about baking cakes. Source: ClassicStock/Alamy Stock Photo.

On the other hand, cookbooks for young boys do not encourage help from their mothers, except in asking *how* to use the stove. Unlike cookbooks for young girls that encourage becoming their mother's little helper, boys looked at cooking with suspicion. Boys were advised not to use their mothers' aprons. Instead, he was urged to take a clean dish towel and tuck it into his belt if he could not find an appropriately masculine apron. In a rare nod to cleaning up, one book warned, "If you don't leave [the kitchen] as clean as it was when you started, the kitchen may be ruled Off Limits."[4]

Girls probably noticed that their mothers did all the cleaning in the kitchen, and most of the books assumed that little girls would clean up just like their mother. *Little Mother's Cook Book* even suggested that it was possible to have as much fun cleaning up as cooking. Little girls' memories of "fun" while cooking (or cleaning up) are essential lessons that would carry into adulthood, preparing them for their roles as women responsible for family meals—day in, day out.

Figure 3.2. Wearing a chef's hat, a young boy cooks while his sisters and the family dog watch. Photograph by H. Armstrong Roberts. Source: ClassicStock/Alamy Stock Photo.

Cookbooks for girls stressed that the aesthetics of food presentation were more important than taste; taste for boys was more important. Aesthetics included creativity both in choices of ingredients and in finishing garnishes—elements also noted in cookbooks for adult women. In a section on sandwiches titled "Be an Explorer," *Fun to Cook Book* encourages the young cook to display some creativity. The author notes, "Try combining thinly sliced ham, chicken or beef with cheese. When there's cream cheese in the refrigerator, mix it with chopped nuts or sliced olives. Try using sliced hard-cooked eggs and crisp left-over bacon."[5] *The Betty Betz Teen-Age Cookbook* notes, "Amateur culinary artists are those who are able to add this or that to the regular formulas." Setting the table also was an essential part of food presentation. Girls were reminded that tablecloths, freshly laundered napkins, spotless glasses, and attractive centerpieces would make "even a quick snack taste like a banquet."[6]

Women are assumed to prefer sweet foods and foods with lots of whipped cream or cream sauces. Even the youngest girl had the opportunity to make a sweet, creamy dish. This simple dessert called Franny Frog's Lily Dessert consisted of a box of lime Jell-O, lettuce for the gelatin to sit on, and whipped cream.[7] Also based on a package of lime Jell-O, *Miss B.'s First Cookbook* presents a recipe for Fluff-Duff. This recipe, created for older girls, fulfills the feminine preference for sweet and creamy, utilizing a can of whipped milk. Other ingredients include sugar, a can of crushed pineapple, a banana, shredded coconut, maraschino cherries, and a package of chocolate or vanilla wafers. A cookbook for teenage girls, *Date Bait*, recommends Monkey Pudding, a concoction of instant coconut pudding topped with whipped cream and garnished with maraschino cherries. A recipe for Strawberry Bavarian Cream from *The Betty Betz Teen-Age Cookbook* (1953) demonstrates the sweet and fluffy side of cooking that was assumed to be preferred by women. The recipe begins by dissolving a package of strawberry-flavored gelatin in one cup of hot water and one-half cup of cold water to the dissolved mixture. The directions call for folding three-fourths cup of whipped cream and one-half cup of thawed, frozen strawberries into the gelatin mixture, then spooning it into a mold or sherbet glasses. After chilling, one serves the Bavarian Cream with the remaining strawberries.[8]

While girls were presumed to prefer sweet and creamy, boys learned that their food choice was different and that their selections needed to be masculine. "Girls may like to excel in pastries, and so forth, but boys want food that sticks to the ribs."[9] This language found in 1950s barbecue cookbooks written for adult men echoes in little boys' cookbooks that emphasize the most masculine of foods: meat. "You can't really call yourself a cook unless you can prepare the main dish of most meals, and that is, as if you didn't know, *meat*." To emphasize meat's wild and manly nature, the authors Helen Evans Brown and Philip S. Brown provide instructions for Cannibal Steak. "Feel like eating raw meat? You aren't alone if you do. Raw beef, [is] known in fancy restaurants as *Steak Tartare*."[10] Other masculine-approved recipes in *The Boys' Cook Book* that might remind little boys (or their fathers) about hunting in the wild, wild West included fried rabbit, duck stew, roast leg of venison, and simpler meals of hamburgers and chili cheeseburgers. The book emphasizes the pleasures of the outdoors, and the book includes recipes for many types of freshly caught fish: catfish, codfish, halibut, salmon, and swordfish, as well as shellfish such as clams, scallops, lobster, and shrimp. "Clean the [fish] at once—we don't have to tell you how to do that."[11]

As in cookbooks for adult men, boys are also encouraged to prefer cooking outdoors. "Outdoors is where a man can really shine and cook! When you cook inside, you have usually borrowed the use of the kitchen from your mother. But with outside cooking, boys or men take over completely. The world around you is your kitchen."[12] In line with men's barbecue cookbooks that provide instructions for building simple to complex outdoor grills, *The First Book of Boys' Cooking* offers directions for creating various types of campfires: hunter's fire, a trench fire, fire in a hole, a tepee fire, a crisscross fire, and a reflector fire. Illustrations in these books often show boys in cowboy outfits, reinforcing the basic theme of going back to nature while also attempting to create nostalgia for the long-ago days of pioneering. Television programming in the 1950s romanticized images of the wild West and the cowboys that roamed the prairies, including *The Lone Ranger, The Roy Rogers Show, The Life and Legend of Wyatt Earp, Wagon Train, Maverick, Rawhide*, and *Bonanza*.

In addition to cooking meat, salads were another acceptable food for boys to prepare. "In many families, the man is considered the expert when it comes to mixing a salad." The book provides two recipes: potato salad and coleslaw—hearty salads appropriate for men and boys.[13] The chapter on outdoor cooking suggests that boys might attempt a Wild Salad. "Many plants that grow wild are good to eat. The young leaves of dandelions, clover, deer grass, oxeye daisies, thistle, sorrel, and pepper grass are some of them." Underscoring the inherent risks of the dangers of untamed nature, the author adds, "It is important to learn what edible wild plants grow in the part of the country where you live."[14] Danger also lurked for grown men, who were encouraged to wear asbestos gloves to avoid burns while using the barbecue.

Occasionally a cookbook for boys will offer a salad that could be mistaken as a feminine dish. In these cases, the authors always explain, often improbably. For example, *The Boys' Cook Book* presents an Avocado Mousse and a Tomato Aspic. The Avocado Mouse is described as a party dish, but the authors assure readers that it is also "he-man stuff—and there's nothing like a he-man at a party." The book's Tomato Aspic is portrayed as a jellied salad that meets the approval of males because it isn't a "sissypants sweet one. And, of course, it isn't really a salad."[15]

Date Bait (1952) by Robert H. Loeb Jr. summed up his philosophy in the title for chapter one: "Cook the Bait to Bait the Hook to Hook the Date."[16] For teenage girls, cookbooks provided lessons in snagging a date, a boyfriend, or, eventually, a husband. *The Betty Betz Teen-Age Cookbook* noted, "Let's face it if a girl is reasonably attractive and a good cook as well, she has better odds for marriage."[17] Cooking to attract boys went mainstream at the 1953 Pillsbury Bake-Off with a second prize awarded for a junior category dessert called Blueberry Boy-Bait. During the 1950s, teenagers often pushed boundaries of acceptable behavior in dealing with authority figures, and Loeb goes so far as to suggest that cooking for one's parents might lead to lesser punishments for being out late or as a bribe to use the family car or borrowing Mom's clothes. However, the central theme remained: cooking to catch a boyfriend.

With a novel approach to cooking, *Let's Cook Without Cooking* by Esther Rudomin suggests that boys and girls who are too young to use a stove still like to cook, and those old enough to manage a stove do not want to cook in a hot kitchen. "Mothers and fathers need not fear burned fingers, leaking gas, or scorched pots and pans as a result of youthful culinary enterprises."[18] This book offers recipes that require absolutely no cooking, ranging from Chicken-Apple Salad to Swiss Cheese and Deviled Ham on Rye Bread and Chocolate Banana Pudding to Salted Crackers and Potato Chips with Special Dip. Every possible processed food is utilized, such as canned chicken, tuna, deviled ham, canned juices, bottled French dressing, instant vanilla and chocolate pudding, instant coffee, and processed cheese.

Another popular dish in children's cookbook literature is the Candlestick Salad (sometimes called Candle Salad). Photographs of this concoction often result in gasps from adults due to the phallic look of the finished product. The ingredients are canned sliced pineapple, bananas, almonds, and lettuce. "Wash a lettuce leaf well and shake off the water. Then lay it on a plate. Place a slice of pineapple on the lettuce leaf. This will be the base of the candlestick." For the candle itself, "Cut a banana in half crosswise and stand it in the pineapple hole. For the candle flame, stick an almond in the top of the banana."[19] Some recipes call for a maraschino cherry instead of the almond, and others recommend red-dyed mayonnaise to suggest dripping candle wax. Some sources even suggest lighting the almond.

In the 1960s, a version of *Betty Crocker's New Boys and Girls Cookbook* includes the same recipe but identifies the dish as "Rocket Salad," in an obvious nod to the US space program. Although not found in mainstream adult cookbooks, the Candlestick Salad moved into the grown-up world in 1957. The Columbia Federal Savings and Loan Association in Washington, DC, published a pamphlet including a recipe for "Christmas Candle Salad." The only change is raspberry gelatin in star molds that replace the pineapple as a base. In 2008, the Candlestick Salad reappears in a "healthy" version. Alfalfa sprouts replace the lettuce base, fresh strawberries substitute for maraschino cherries, and strawberry yogurt for the wax "drip."[20]

Author Sherrie A. Inness notes, "Juvenile cookbooks and cooking articles sent different messages to girls and boys. Boys—if they learned to cook at all—learned they should become knowledgeable about only a few limited items."[21] These restricted items were identified as "masculine," such as meat, and the cookbooks emphasize that boys should not consider taking over or assisting with their mothers' daily cooking chores, and instead they were encouraged to cook with their fathers. On the other hand, girls learned that cooking was one of the most joyous tasks they would perform in their households; it was something that they should perceive as a pleasure—a joy and a responsibility "to more than the individual girl or her family; it was a responsibility to all humanity."[22]

The following description is an early example of a recipe for pigs in a blanket, an appetizer that continues to be popular, even with adults. *Betty Crocker's Cook Book for Boys and Girls* (1957) begins by making biscuits according to a Betty Crocker Bisquick package and cutting them into twelve four-by-three-inch forms. Wieners are wrapped within the biscuits, "Letting the ends of wiener peep out." The pigs are baked in a 450°F oven for about fifteen minutes. The recipe also notes, "There are two kinds of hot dogs. *The wiener*—short and skinny [and] *the frankfurter*—long and plump."[23]

Boys were encouraged to cook with meat, and the following recipe utilizes processed soup as its base. (Unlike similar recipes for adults, which call for browning the chopped beef, this one asks the young cook to add it directly to the soup, uncooked.)

> **JIFFY STEW**
>
> *The First Book of Boys' Cooking* (1957)[24]
>
> Line up:
>
> 1 can of condensed vegetable soup
> ½ pound of chopped beef
> Water
> Saucepan, Can opener, Spoon
>
> 1. Open the can and empty the vegetable soup into a sauce pan. Fill the empty can with water and stir into the soup. Place over the heat and when the liquid is just about to boil, lower the light.
>
> 2. Break the meat up loosely with your fingers. Add small amounts at a time to the soup. Stir constantly and cook for 15 minutes. Serve.

Beverages were essential components in meals, and the emphasis seemed to be on fun. *The See and Do Book of Cooking* suggests cutting off the top of a lemon and inserting a hollow hard candy stick into the lemon, "Squeeze the lemon slightly and sip."[25] A recipe for a Purple Cow probably would please children as the resulting color is "a pleasing purple, or a violent violet, or a livid lavender." One was to place a scoop of vanilla ice cream in a glass and add grape juice to cover, then fill the glass to the top with carbonated water or milk.[26]

The Backyard Barbecue—A "Man's World"

[Steak] is the heart of meat, it is meat in its pure state; and whoever partakes of it assimilates a bull-like strength.

—Roland Barthes (1957)[27]

Cooking is intensely gendered and evident in the fundamental division of kitchen labor. In feeding a family, women are responsible for menu planning, shopping, cooking, and serving food (and, of course, the cleanup—except for taking out the heavy garbage). Cooking expectations for men are profoundly different. Men would assume a cook's role *if* the food was defined as "manly." For example, meat must be a part of the menu, and in cooking meat, especially steak, this meat should be cooked outdoors.

During the 1950s, a man's "kitchen" and his only acceptable cooking locale was the outdoor barbecue. Barbecue also represented a place of safety, given unstable international and domestic politics. "Red meat's protein and iron nourished and strengthened the individual body, so too could its consumption fortify the body politic," writes Kristin L. Matthews in "One Nation Over Coals."[28] The barbecue served as a Cold War political statement: strong men would protect their families from all danger, including the threat of communism. It also signified masculinity and the rugged outdoors, with grilling cookbooks often referencing the "wild West" or "pioneering spirit." (These traits also are evident in cookbooks for young boys.) As food author James Beard noted, "Eating outdoors is one of life's finest pleasures. It is not just a trick of the imagination that makes food smell and taste better under blue skies or under the stars. The fire in your grill and the freshness of the air add savor to every dish."[29] The language may have indicated the rugged outdoors, but these white, middle-class men were grilling in a suburban backyard, and that is what the era's images illuminate.

Meat, commonly steak, was the primary food for a barbecue and represented the aspirations of a true American while "conjuring cowboys, expansionism, and the western frontier."[30] As depicted in men's cookbooks, young boys wear cowboy outfits with toy guns, and 1950s television strongly reinforced the idealized West and pioneering spirit with no fewer than twenty programs. About cooking meats, *Better Homes and Gardens Barbecue Book* echoed other publications. It advised, "This is Dad's domain," "Sit back, Mom; admire Chef. He has the fascinating how-to on big steaks other juicy meats that take to charcoal. There's rotisserie roasting, cooking on skewers, grilling whole meals in foil; plus how-to-talk-knowingly with the meatman."[31] Another passage reads, "Steak is the favorite food of Americans of all ages, both male and female, and has been ever since the first prime steer came off the mid-west ranches." Reinforcing the necessity of cooking beef in the outdoors as the pioneers would have done, the book notes, "And charcoal broiling is certainly the preferred way to prepare steaks."[32]

Suburban life could be isolating, and the backyard barbecue served as a method of gathering and unifying neighbors. "You can laugh at bumper-to-bumper traffic on steaming highways as you play host in your own backyard. Be the Barbecue Leader in your neighborhood. Your friends will call you the best host in town. Then they'll invite you to their backyards,"[33] advised one cookbook. *The Complete Barbecue Book* (1951) claimed that when a man cooked barbecue, he "will take on a somewhat godlike stature. Your every performance before pit or grill will both please the eyes and tickle the palates."[34] Women, however, needed to know their place: "The main role is masculine. No woman looks her best leaning over a bed of glowing charcoal, and she knows it.[35]

As with other cookbooks for men, *Big Boy Barbecue Book* made note of the specific role of women: "Husbands become the experts and do the barbecuing. Wives take it easy. All they have to do is make the salad and dessert. The kitchen stays clean. The house remains neat. There is almost no wash-up afterwards."[36] "Whenever the menu calls for a delicate dish or fancy pie, most men are more than happy to let their wives take care of the cooking. When it's a matter of steak, the tolerant attitude is replaced by an unassailable belief in masculine know-how. Steak is a man's job."[37] Clearly, women did not understand the art of cooking meat. In the men's world of barbecue, the literature rarely shows women in the act of cooking on an outdoor grill.

In the early 1950s, George Stephen created a kettle-shaped covered grill, later sold under Weber Kettle. The Kingsford Chemical Company took over Ford's charcoal briquettes manufacturing, making charcoal briquettes for barbecues mass-marketed and easy to acquire. Appliance companies, such as Kenmore and Sears and Roebuck, offered backyard grills. Barbecue equipment (long-handled knives and forks) was advertised to women as gifts for their husbands. These accessories represent a completely different set of cooking implements. Besides fireproof gloves, the man at the grill needed tongs, forks, and knives much larger than the more "feminine" and petite implements typically found in a kitchen. Even his apron was large, unlike the dainty apron favored by women. In a chapter devoted to outdoor barbecuing, the *Good Housekeeping Cook Book* (1955) provides a barbecue equipment checklist, including asbestos gloves and monosodium glutamate. Perhaps to underscore the cowboy influence in barbecuing, *The Master Chef's Outdoor Grill Cookbook* (1954) recommends a water pistol to control flare-ups. *Sunset Barbecue Cook Book* suggests the following as a minimum: "Large bib apron, asbestos gloves or half flour sacks for pot holders; long-handled spoon, fork, spatula; poker and ash shovel; clothes sprinkler; large skillet; Dutch oven; and a giant coffee pot."[38] James Beard offers suggestions (and also noted the importance of "size"): a spatula, skewers, wooden spoons, good "French or German" knives, a carving board, a big peppermill, a giant salt cellar, big bowls. In an innovative twist, cookbook author Mary Meade suggests that men use an ice pick to check for tenderness.[39] In case one's asbestos gloves failed, Beard recommends men "keep a jar of Vaseline and some gauze handy."[40] The *Good Housekeeping Cook Book* issued sound guidance for the cook: never heat canned foods on a grill in an unopened can. Manly men should be prepared for the worst.

"Home is home no longer sans a barbecue,"[41] and America's suburban families concurred. While community unity was a positive aspect of the backyard barbecue, in an era where the threat of communism was on the minds of many, this unity was not to be confused with the doctrine of socialist solidarity. This difference is demonstrated in the various instructions on building a barbecue, ranging from simple examples to elaborate models. The point stressed in the literature is do-it-yourself projects, where individuality and creativity were encouraged, principles opposed in communist doctrine. James Beard wrote about a friend who ingeniously constructed an outdoor grill out of an oil can and cooked on grills salvaged from an old bank teller's window. Other resourceful ideas included barbecues constructed out of old refrigerators. Of course, if one did not wish to build a barbecue from scratch, there were always commercial models to purchase and assemble, such as the Weber grill, or if the backyard space would not accommodate a large grill, one might acquire a hibachi—a small grill of Japanese origin that utilized charcoal.

Women provided side dishes to accompany grilled steaks. Three bean salad and Boston baked beans were both standard and made, of course, with available canned products. After the government lifted the prohibition against aluminum foil (unavailable during the Korean War), foil-wrapped baked potatoes and crusty bread, placed directly on the grill, became popular side dishes. Women were also responsible for the "less glamorous chores, like paring vegetables, setting tables, etc."[42] "When a man works all day to support his family, it seems only proper that his home should be as much of a castle as his wife can make it. . . . I do whatever advance preparation is required."[43] Hence, accepted gender roles are clearly outlined: the husband is the cook, usually called a "chef" in the literature, and the wife preps the meal, makes side dishes, and cleans up. This division of labor is suggested at a young age and is accompanied by appropriate clothing. The cover of *The See and Do Book of Cooking* (1959) pictures a young boy in a chef's hat (licking his fingers) while a young girl, decorating cookies, is wearing a frilly apron. Sure enough, the cookbook provides instructions for creating both a chef's hat and a frilly apron.

Boston baked beans was considered an appropriate side dish to accompany barbecued meat. If one had little time, Poppy Cannon suggested opening two cans of baked beans (with pork and molasses) and adding a bit of dry mustard, molasses, an onion, and bacon or salt pork. Her Boston Baked Beans Gone to Heaven would be ready to take from the oven in thirty to forty minutes.[44] On the other hand, if one had time and wanted to impress the guests, Freda De Knight offered four recipes for Boston Baked Beans, all made from scratch. De Knight credits the following recipe to Nadine Wright Goodman of Cambridge, Massachusetts.

NADINE'S BOSTON BAKED BEANS

A Date with a Dish: A Cook Book of American Negro Recipes (1948)[45]

1 cup navy beans
¼ lb. salt pork (or fat from ham or bacon ends)
2 tbsps. sugar
½ tsp. dry mustard
1 large onion
2 cups boiling water
2 tbsps. Molasses

Soak beans overnight, well-covered with water. Drain and add fresh water. Boil until tender, but not until skins pop off. Drain and place in an earthen pot. Cut salt pork into small cubes. Brown in skillet. Add sliced onion to fat and brown. Add onions and fat and pork cubes to 2 cups of water. Add sugar, molasses, salt and mustard. Pour over beans, cover until tender, thoroughly flavored, and dry. If needed, add boiling water during baking. Serves 6. [Note: De Knight does not provide an exact cooking time.]

De Knight also counsels the cook: "The measurements of sugar, molasses, onions, dry mustard are approximate rather than absolute. Flavor beans to suit your individual taste."

Illustrated print advertisements strongly reinforced these gender roles within the family unit. For example, some publications portray the nuclear family members as three or four, including a barbecue father, a side-dish mother, and one or two hungry children (and often, a family dog). Others paint a picture of suburban community spirit by representing groups of pleased men with their sons, who presumably are learning their

Figure 3.3. Little boys and their fathers grill steaks and the women present side dishes, 1950s. 7 Up magazine advertisement. Source: Retro AdArchives/Alamy Stock Photo.

future place in the barbecue world. The jovial women are assembled in the background.

Another development that aided in the growing popularity of the backyard barbecue was the introduction of Tupperware in 1951. During the 1950s, Tupperware home parties were the only way to obtain the line of plastic storage containers created by Earl Tupper that enabled women to store leftovers and easily carry food to community potluck dinners, picnics, or barbecues.

Figure 3.4. A woman displays her impressive collection of Tupperware, c. 1955. Source: Pictorial Press Ltd/Alamy Stock Photo.

The product offered women an opportunity to participate in a flourishing enterprise, and many suburban women started their home businesses selling Tupperware. Those who became top sellers were rewarded with extravagant gifts, such as diamond rings and designer wardrobes.

Often, some cookbooks colorfully and nostalgically describe the barbecue as a pastime of prehistoric man or solely as a pioneer and Western frontier experience. Generally, however, the roots of American barbecue are ignored. In suggesting a tongue-in-cheek history, *General Foods Kitchens Cookbook* (1959) states, "One day, a couple of million years ago, one of our ancestors was having a snack of saber-tooth tiger steak, when it accidentally fell into the fire. Before he could get it out, it was ruined—all horrible brown, instead of nice and bloody. Nevertheless, since the cave was running low on saber-tooth tiger that week, he decided to

Figure 3.5. Cooking meat over a fire on a raised platform was a traditional method employed by Native Americans. In this illustration, the Timucuan from central and northeastern Florida grill alligators. From *Brevis narration eorum quae in Florida Americae provi[n]cial Gallis acciderunt*, published in Frankfurt, Germany, 1591. Source: Science History Images/Alamy Stock Photo.

eat it anyway. And he liked it!"[46] Along similar lines, the *Big Boy Barbecue Book* (1956) proclaims, "Back in the days of cave men and wandering tribes—when cooking first began—men used to roast or broil their food in the open air. There was no other way to do it. Pioneers, cowboys, and hunters also barbecued, not as a hobby or diversion, but just to eat."[47] No matter the origins, author Kristin A. Matthews adds that barbecuing promoted "individualism, determination, adventurousness, hope, and true grit—reinforcing America's uniqueness and exceptionalism while simultaneously asserting that its pioneering spirit lives on."[48]

The earliest barbecuing in the Americas involved cooking meat over a framework of sticks often built on a raised platform placed over a shallow pit—a traditional cooking method among indigenous peoples. This slow-cooking practice was called "barbacoa" by the Taino people of the Caribbean, described as early as the sixteenth century by Spanish explorers. While the accepted narrative has been that barbecue's origins are Native American and European, a similar practice has been observed with the Hausa of West Africa. Eventually, enslaved Africans in the Caribbean combined their inspiration and methods with indigenous Caribbean peoples. As the Spanish traveled from the Caribbean to the Americas, they brought barbecue to the British colonists. In the title of a 2015 article, author Michael W. Twitty sums up its origins, "Barbecue is an American Tradition—of Enslaved Africans and Native Americans."[49]

BARBECUED FISH

Cherokee Cooklore: To Make My Bread (1951)[50]

Cut fish into strips or chunks, string on pieces of sharpened sticks and hang over or before a fire. Turn often and keep before the fire until fish does not drip any more. Hang up for later by stringing on thongs, bear grass, etc. Use by making stew or soup.

Except for barbecue, men were considered inept cooks. To simplify cooking for men, Robert H. Loeb Jr. wrote a book, *Wolf in Chef's Clothing* (1950), that consists entirely of step-by-step illustrations. Other cookbooks informed men that they could cook and still be manly, effectively distancing themselves from their wives' mundane daily cooking. With tongue in cheek, Loeb declared that his book would "enfranchise the male, to unshackle him from being a parasitic gourmet forced to feed on the leftovers of female cookery. Instead, he can become a gustatory eagle, king of the kitchen, and baron of the bar."[51] Some employed masculine titles to separate gendered cookbooks: *What's Cookin' Men? A Handy Cookbook for Men Who Enjoy Outdoor Cooking* (1957) and Paul K. Tibbens's *Cookin' for the Helluvit* (1950). The latter featured recipes for He-Man Salad and Bullyboy Soup. Often, men's cookbooks took on a distinctly macho or sexualized tone, presenting recipes for such boastful dishes as Wieners Royale (hot dogs stuffed with cheese and wrapped in bacon), "But let's start with husky, meat-filled Franks—none of the puny, anemic, cereal-stuffed dogs will do."[52] Brick Gordon's *The Groom Boils and Stews: A Man's Cook Book for Men* (1947) provides a recipe for Sweater Girl Salad, calling for canned peaches, cottage cheese, mayonnaise, and maraschino cherries—all arranged to look like a female breast. *Cookin' for the Helluvit* offered a "hot dish" and "luscious tomato." Sherri Inness suggests, "By sexualizing cooking, men's cooking literature took it out of the kitchen and into the bedroom, a sphere where men have traditionally demonstrated and affirmed their masculinity."[53]

Cooking with alcohol was a hallmark of many cookbooks for men (as was a more copious use of seasonings, such as chili peppers and liberal amounts of garlic). Robert H. Loeb's *Wolf in Chef's Clothing* discusses before-, during-, and after-dinner drinks as well as alcoholic beverages that have "nothing to do with meals." James Beard's recipes use whiskey, red and white wine, sweet sherry, and port—up to one cup of alcohol per recipe for his barbecue meat marinades. As in Loeb's book, Beard also includes a section he calls "cocktails & long drinks." "Now for the heartier drinks—the cocktails that sharpen appetites, the long thirst-quenchers for lazy summer days."[54] These cocktails included Bloody Mary, Planter's Punch, martini, and mint julep.

BULLSHOT

"The Bullshot is the Bloody Mary's Salty Cousin from Detroit," *Esquire* (2019)[55]

1 serving
1½ oz. Tito's vodka
4 oz. Campbell's beef broth
1 dash Worcestershire sauce
Lemon juice
Hot sauce (optional)

> 1. Mix a shot of Tito's vodka with 4 oz of Campbell's beef broth, a dash of Worcestershire, a squeeze of lemon juice, and if you like things spicy, a few dashes of your favorite hot sauce. Stir.
>
> 2. Pour into a highball glass over ice, drink, and tell the following story to anyone who will listen.

The *Esquire* article notes that Detroit's Caucus Club created the drink in the 1950s. "The Club's owner struck up a conversation with John Hurley, an employee of the Madison Avenue agency, BBDO. Hurley was on the Campbell Soup account, and he was having trouble finding a way to market its canned beef broth. Broth and vodka: the perfect mix, and the Bullshot was born."

Most cookbooks for men centered on recipes that contained ingredients available in a typical suburban supermarket. The more exotic fare might include partridge, quail, or venison. If a backyard cook wished to experience the "pioneers of the Far West in the early days," one could utilize James Beard's recipe for "Pheasant, pioneer style" or his recipe for grilled bear steak. First published in the early 1940s, Frank Shay's *The Best Men Are Cooks* presents hare, rabbit, squirrel, and possum recipes. "Have a kettle of boiling water big enough for you to immerse the whole 'possum. Grab the animal by the tail and lower it head-down into the water for a minute."[56] The recipe continues with instructions on how to remove the entrails and brain and how to cut off the feet. While this is a manly recipe, it is doubtful that any suburban, middle-class man would dare attempt such a meal.

The ritual of the 1950s backyard barbecue was a symbol of healthy suburban living, and it fulfilled a sense of community and glorified homeownership. In promoting consumerism (considered a patriotic duty) and the American way of life, the illustrations and photographs accompanying cookbooks and magazine articles always emphasized the abundance of food available in the United States, often to excess. Charles and Ray Eames's film *Glimpses of the USA*, created for the American National Exhibition held in Moscow in 1959, describes the backyard barbecue as one of the significant rituals performed by the typical American family. It remains so today.

Big Boy Barbecue Book (1956) provides a typical recipe for grilling meat. For example, to make Beef Roly Poly, one should allow two cube steaks per person. "Pound the steaks with a wooden mallet to flatten them.

Spread them with prepared mustard and sprinkle with a little drained sweet pickle relish." The cook is instructed to roll up the steaks, fasten them with metal skewers, and brush each with melted butter. Charcoal briquettes are spaced one-half to three-quarters of an inch apart and the grill is rubbed with cooking oil. "Lay the beef rolls on the grill about 2 inches above the briquettes and grill about 10 minutes, turning once."[57]

Barbecue Sauce [For chicken]

Paynie's Parties (1955)[58]

½ c. vinegar juice
1 lemon
2 tsp. Worcestershire Sauce
1 tsp. black pepper
1 tsp. salt
1 tsp. sugar
¼ lb. butter
1 T. prepared mustard
pinch cayenne pepper

Heat all together until butter is melted. Salt chicken (slightly). Place in roaster with ½ c. water in pan. Let steam about 15 minutes in oven at 350°. Mix sauce and pour over chicken. (Be sure no water is in pan.) Baste often and continue to cook slowly until tender.

How do adults arrive at their ideas and beliefs about cooking and food preferences? One way is through the gender-specific literature that targets young boys and girls and the cookbooks written about appropriate cooking for men. Illustrations show young girls cooking and cleaning, wearing aprons (often like their mothers). Young boys often wear chef's hats and are seen eating. Adult men (who also wear chef's hats) are charged with cooking meat, preferably outdoors. Men also oversee cocktails, a task considered to be inventive and thus better understood by men. Young boys learned that these activities helped define masculinity. The adult women hover over their daughters, turn on the oven for sons, and provide side dishes for barbecue events.

Meanwhile, the author of *Date Bait* clearly expresses the importance of young women learning to cook. He hammers the message that a young girl must cook to get a boyfriend or snag a husband. A wife must be able to cook to please her husband, and, once married, the cookbook world offered titles such as Blanche C. Firmin's *Peggy Put the Kettle On: Recipes and Entertainment Ideas for Young Wives* (1951) or Poppy Cannon's *The Bride's Cookbook* (1954). As with all cookbooks of any era, it is not certain just who read and used them. However, what is clear is that the gender-specific cookbooks of the 1950s were elemental forces in shaping notions about the place of men, women, and children and their relationships to cooking and eating. Even today, these gender-specific concepts are still very much a part of how we look at cooking and food choices.

Part 2
Sitting Down and Unfolding Our Napkins

Chapter 4

"If I Knew You Were Comin', I'd Have Baked a Cake"

Cookbooks, Cooks, and Cooking

> The personality of a cookbook is as apparent as it is important. It is composed of known and stable ingredients with unknown and elusive ones to make a mixture as familiar, friendly and exhilarating as a pine woods early on a summer morn. The elusive charm of this personality stems from clear overtones: a light touch—a sense of humor—a flair for the clever idea in cooking and serving that results in something called style, but above all a feeling for the kind of beauty that women want about them in their work-a-day world.
>
> —Culinary Arts Institute Encyclopedic Cookbook (1950)[1]

Cookbooks can be a valuable source of information, chronicling the various changes in cooking and kitchen culture throughout the years. In the 1950s, suburban women experienced a revolution in the advancement of kitchen design and the introduction of new, modern appliances and processed foods. There was a keen interest in cooking, and publishers returned this enthusiasm with a literal landslide of new books. As Americans began to take vacations throughout the country, a renewed interest in regional foods created a new generation of cookbooks, focusing on the many cuisines found in the United States. Other cookbooks focused on quick meals and provided suggestions on how to effectively use the seemingly endless parade of new processed foods. Cookbooks also emphasized the era's growing trend in entertaining—dinner parties, outdoor barbecues, and theme parties. Cooks were introduced to up-to-date technologies, such as freezing, and appliance manufacturers informed how to cook with the modern electric ranges and refrigerators and newly available electric gadgets—skillets, deep fryers, blenders, and mixers.

Culinary literature in the 1950s also tells us much about gender roles and how these publications pushed appropriate images of gender, particularly in the kitchen. Illustrations reveal well-dressed women in aprons, usually wearing high heels and jewelry, with never a hair out of place. Cookbooks also reinforced gender norms that targeted children and men, outlining appropriate foods to cook and to consume, ideals set forth by industry and advertising agencies. On the other hand, as Jessamyn Neuhaus has noted, "They tell us less about the real, lived experience of women in the kitchen than about how cookbook producers imagined the ideal, 'normal' American home and the roles that men and women would play within it."[2] Many of the mainstream and specialty books do tell us about the types of cuisine and cooking methods. However, there were pockets of resistance. Many specialty cookbooks promoted originality in menu planning and creativity in meals and advocated fresh ingredients and cooking from scratch. The suburban woman did have choices.[3]

Mainstream Cookbooks

These popular cookbooks include *The Boston Cooking-School Cook Book* (1896, with a new edition in 1951), which set the standard and format for future cookbooks, and two other popular 1950s mainstream cookbooks, *The Joy of Cooking* (1931, with many editions, including a 1951 revision) and *Betty Crocker's Picture Cook Book* (1950). These cookbooks have been enormously popular, have gone through numerous editions and modifications, and represent longevity within the cooking canon.[4] Other comparable cookbooks were also updated or revised during the 1950s, such as Lizzie Black Kander's *The Settlement Cook Book: The Way to a Man's Heart*, first published in 1901. By 1965 the volume had gone through thirty-three editions, with an updated edition called *The New Settlement Cookbook: The First Classic Collection of Ethnic Recipes* (1991/1997), released in 1991.

Referring to Fannie Merritt Farmer (1857–1915) as the "dour spinster," authors John and Karen Hess waste no time taking her cooking methods to task. "Beginning with her the home economists, nutritionists, and instant chefs pushed aside the cooks, and cookbooks became sets of idiot directions

Figure 4.1. Four women and two cookbooks collaborate to bake a cake. Source: RetroAd Archives/Alamy Stock Photo.

for other noncooks. No longer were taste, texture, freshness of produce lovingly discussed. Nor would technique be sensual and individual. From now on, things would be measured by the one-eighth teaspoon and the milligram of riboflavin. Welcome to the twentieth century."[5]

In all fairness, Farmer was but one of the progressive era's cookbook authors attempting to change approaches to food. Now, the emphasis was on science, hygiene, and health. Others took Farmer's ideas further: immigrants were discouraged from cooking traditional foods, and New England regional foods became the standard. The Hesses noted that enjoyment of food and a disregard for sensuality and texture is evident in Farmer's book.

Farmer's book *The Boston Cooking-School Cook Book*, published in 1896, was followed by many editions.[6] (The ninth edition, retitled *The New Fannie Farmer Boston Cooking-School*, was published in 1951 and the tenth edition, in 1959.) Cooks in the 1950s would have had easy access to any number of Farmer's cookbooks. Farmer's 1896 edition contained thirty-nine chapters that range from recipes for beverages, bread, and cereals to eggs, soups, fish, vegetables, salads, and various meats and poultry. Following earlier cookbook traditions, Farmer includes hints for young housekeepers, menus, recipes for the sick, and information on preserving and canning. Emphasizing the interest in sweets that continued throughout the 1950s, Farmer offers three chapters on cakes and cake fillings.

"The mixing and baking of cake requires more care and judgment than any other branch of cookery; notwithstanding, it seems the one most frequently attempted by the inexperienced."[7]

> **POUND CAKE**
>
> *The Boston Cooking-School* (1896)[8]
>
> 1 lb. butter.
> Whites 10 eggs.
> 1 lb. sugar.
> 1 lb. flour.
> Yolks 10 eggs.
> ½ teaspoon mace.
> 2 tablespoons brandy.
>
> Cream the butter, add sugar gradually, and continue beating; then add yolks of eggs beaten until thick and lemon colored, whites of eggs beaten until stiff and dry, flour, mace, and brandy. Beat vigorously five minutes. Bake in a deep pan one and one fourth hours in a slow oven; or if to be used for fancy ornamented cakes, bake thirty to thirty-five minutes in a dripping-pan.

The book lists the ingredients and the required amounts for short, simple recipes before describing the directions. Farmer provides the entire recipe in narrative form for longer recipes, including the ingredients and quantities. Both formats are popular in cookbooks published throughout the twentieth century.

The book's thirteenth and final edition in 1990 is credited to Marion Cunningham. Farmer's *The Boston Cooking-School Cook Book* thus became the standard go-to cookbook for generations of cooks.

Irma R. Rombauer and *The Joy Of Cooking*[9]

Keep calm even if your hair str[u]ggles and you drip unattractively. Brush up before serving. Your appearance and the appearance of the food are important, but eating in a quiet atmosphere is even more important to the family's morale and digestion.

—Irma R. Rombauer (1951)[10]

Irma R. Rombauer's *The Joy of Cooking* seems to be a statement against Fannie Farmer's formal, strict, and humorless approach (that took the joy out of cooking). "Indeed, it is said she wrote the book in protest against the antiseptic, loveless approach of Fannie Farmer."[11] The book's friendly, casual, and very personal approach stands in stark contrast to Fannie Farmer. Rombauer's connection with her audience is unique and is a factor in the book's universal popularity. In the cookbook, Rombauer tells stories, shows her wit, and displays her "excruciatingly corny puns, making sure everybody knows that cooking is not an occult science or esoteric art."[12]

In 1930, after the death of her husband, Rombauer was encouraged by her children to take on a meaningful project, and they suggested writing a cookbook. Subsequently, after gathering recipes, she and her daughter Marion embarked on testing them. Rombauer had no literary agent or lawyer; she simply called a local printer: A. C. Clayton, who had no book publishing experience. After Rombauer invested $3,000 in 1931, A. C. Clayton issued three thousand copies of the 396-page volume, titled *The Joy of Cooking: A Compilation of Reliable Recipes with a Casual Culinary Chat*. The book begins with some general rules, a table of weights and measures, and an index (located at the front of the work). Then, Rombauer launches into her recipes. The first recipe in the book is for a Gin Cocktail. "Most cocktails containing liquor are made today with gin and ingenuity. In brief, take an ample supply of the former and use your imagination."[13] Thus, it set the tone for Rombauer's first edition.

The book's success invigorated Rombauer, and she began to look for an established book publisher. In 1936, the Bobbs-Merrill Company published a trade edition, representing the first revision of Rombauer's 1931 edition. Page numbers expanded from just under 400 to 640, and by 1941 this edition had five printings. In 1936, the recipe format changed to a chronological listing of ingredients, which preceded instructions for preparation.

In the late 1940s, Rombauer brought her daughter, Marion Rombauer Becker, to work on future editions. Paper quotas stymied the 1943 edition, but the page count increased again to 884; the next edition in 1946 included World War II rationing information. In the 1951 edition, Marion Becker became more closely involved as Rombauer's health declined. Aided by Becker's emphasis on health and nutrition, the 1951 edition does not focus as much on shortcuts and processed foods. Instead, the book included new "material as meats 'roasted' in foil, aspic base made 'from scratch,' and whole-grain bread (with expanded information on flours), and sought to bolster coverage of weak areas, such as fish."[14] The book devotes sections to new, modern freezing techniques and information on electric blenders and pressure cookers. The 1951 edition also expanded to over one thousand pages. (The 1953 edition is a reprint of the 1951 version with a new index.) Subsequently, five more editions were released between 1962 and 1997. In 2006 the seventy-fifth-anniversary edition was published by Scribner. Except for Irma Rombauer and Marion Rombauer Becker's names (and three other family members), it bears little resemblance to older editions.

Irma Rombauer notes that she associates the following recipe with luxury, but "today it is within the reach of anyone with a few extra cents and a glass bowl that fits closely over a baking dish."[15]

Mushrooms Under Glass

The Joy of Cooking (1951)[16]

4 servings

Trim the stems from 1 lb mushrooms

Beat Until creamy: ¼ cup butter

Stir in very slowly: 2 teaspoons lemon juice

Add:

1 tablespoon chopped parsley
⅓ teaspoon salt
¼ teaspoon paprika.

Cut with a biscuit cutter and toast:

4 rounds bread ½ inch thick

When cold spread them on both sides with ½ the butter mixture. Spread the rest on the tops of the mushroom caps. Place the toast in the bottom of a small baking dish and heap the mushrooms upon them. Pour over them:

½ cup cream

Cover them closely with a glass bowl. Bake them in a moderate oven of 375° for 25 minutes. Add more cream if they become dry. Just before serving add: 2 tablespoons sherry

Serve the mushrooms garnished with: Parsley.

It is important to note that in contrast to *Betty Crocker's Picture Cook Book*, backed by an empire of flour and processed foods, Rombauer had neither product advertisements nor endorsements. After completing the 1951 edition, Rombauer told her daughter that she was "finished"—reluctantly but for good. "She had planted the acorn and performed a stupendous and winning job of cultivation. The sapling she nurtured had grown to a tree of broad caliper, and she was at last ready to rest in its grateful shade."[17]

For its centennial celebration in 1995, the New York Public Library included *The Joy of Cooking* as one of the 150 most influential books of the twentieth century. "Since it was first published in 1931 it has provided encouragement, information, and remedies for kitchen emergencies to countless uncertain brides, college students, experienced cooks, innocents, and snobs [and] it has been the reference book of choice for those interested in traditional American food."[18]

Betty Crocker's Picture Cook Book[19]

In 1945 Fortune magazine declared Betty Crocker the second most popular woman in America. Former First Lady Eleanor Roosevelt placed first.

—Faces of AAUW[20]

Published in 1950, *Betty Crocker's Picture Cook Book*, known as "Big Red" because of its vivid red and white cover, quickly became a best seller. Betty Crocker was not a real person but a creation born in the board room of Washburn-Crosby Company (later General Mills) in 1921; thus, unlike *The Joy of Cooking*, it was challenging to instill much personal narrative in the work. The recipes resulted from concentrated collecting and testing over the years by General Mills and its staff of home economists. The cookbook noted that the production of this work required ten years of planning and another three years of development. This cookbook is one of many to come in the following decades that assures its readers that home economists tested and approved the recipes.

Betty Crocker was a household name long before the publication of her cookbook. Soon after the Washburn Crosby Company launched a contest that resulted in her "birth," the company's staff hired personnel to respond to letters (over 250,000 in 1940), answer telephone calls, and send out recipes. The Betty Crocker radio show premiered in 1924 as a "casual womanly talk program," and by 1925, a Crocker impersonator hosted two radio shows. The voice familiar to many Americans via the radio was Marjorie Child Husted, the woman behind Betty Crocker for twenty years.

During the Depression, Betty Crocker advised her radio listeners how to select ingredients and cook good, nutritious food on a minimal budget. As World War II loomed, Betty Crocker became an essential wartime resource. "Betty was everywhere—on the radio, in women's magazines, in newspaper columns, in the mail, and in recipe booklets available in grocery stores—sending messages of empowerment and civic pride."[21] In 1945, she became the daily host of the Office of War Information's radio program *Our Nation's Rations*.

The book's official launch came in early September 1950 on *The Betty Crocker Magazine of the Air*. The success was overwhelming, and it was a national bestseller within a year. Recipes were traditionally all-American, such as Oatmeal Raisin Cookies, Chicken à la King, Spaghetti and Meatballs, and Tuna-Potato Chip Casserole. *The New York Times* enthusiastically reported, "The new Betty Crocker cookbook is going through the stores at the rate of 18,000 per week. Not bad when you consider that Hemingway, at the top of the best-seller list, is doing about 3,500."[22]

While periodicals such as *The New York Times*, *Saturday Review*, and *Chicago Sunday Tribune* favorably reviewed the book, there also was criticism, and writer Helmut Ripperger noted in 1951, "Many of the receipts are capricious, unoriginal or, contrariwise, so original as to make the classic cook shudder." Ripperger continues with critical comments on Crocker's recipe for Potage St. Germaine and the book's suggestion to garnish the soup with slices of bologna. He concludes by complaining that the book represents nothing "but a glorified piece of advertising."[23] In this, he somewhat might have been correct. The book's photographs, text, and illustrations highlight Gold Medal Enriched Flour, Softasilk (sifted cake flour), Wheaties, Cheerios, Kix cereals, Bisquick, and Betty Crocker boxed cake mixes. However, only Gold Medal Enriched Flour and Softasilk actually appear in the recipes.

POTAGE ST. GERMAINE

Betty Crocker's Picture Cookbook (1950)[24]

"Wonderful soup, so rich and green"

[The cookbook asks the cook to follow the basic recipe for Split Pea Soup, to garnish with thin slices of Bologna sausage, and serve with rye bread.]

Place together in kettle: 2 cups dried split peas [soaked overnight], 3 qt. cold water, 1 ham bone or small shank end of ham, 1 large onion, minced.

Then add: 3 stalks celery (with tops), chopped fine, 1 sprig of parsley.

Bring slowly to boiling point. Cover and simmer 4 to 5 hr. until peas are tender and the liquid partially cooked down. For smooth soup, rub through a coarse sieve. Skim off excess fat. Thicken, if desired with 3 tbsp. butter, 3 tbsp. flour. Dilute as desired with additional milk or water. Season to taste with salt and pepper. Serve hot. Amount: 8 servings.

Ripperger also decried the imbalance of desserts compared to meat and fish recipes, but he failed to note that this was the case with all mainstream cookbooks of the era. New industrial techniques made the milling of white wheat flour and refined sugar easier, more accessible, and less expensive. Thus, one notes the massive increase and popularity of sweet desserts throughout the twentieth century. Ripperger also failed to recognize that *Betty Crocker's Picture Cookbook* also advocated baking from scratch, especially cakes. Indeed, one of the most compelling sections of the cookbook is on desserts, especially made-from-scratch cakes, fillings, and frostings. As critical as it seemed, this review certainly did not curtail sales: by 1951, more than two million copies had sold.

In a departure from *The Joy of Cooking*, the book's format consists of drawings and photographs. It utilizes various typefaces, making the book attractive, inviting, and user-friendly. Color photographs, within the first pages, show the "home of Betty Crocker service," the "kitchen of tomorrow," and the "kamera kitchen," which, according to the text, contained "three complete working units, where foods that are to have their pictures taken are 'made up.'" Other pages—full- or two-page color spreads—display cooked foods, all attractively staged. The book also contains black-and-white photographs that provide a bird's-eye view of the cooking process—reminiscent of the camera techniques used by televised cooking shows that would become popular in the 1950s.

Tips on nutrition, meal planning, setting the table, hints, quick tricks, and "dos and don'ts" round out the advice. The book interweaves bits of food history, including notes on tea, coffee, chocolate, hoecake, and corn pone. (Some of this information is historically dubious.) In a section called "short cuts, make every motion count," Crocker devotes two pages to quick household and personal tips for the cook, ranging from "Keep all cleaning supplies and equipment in a basket and carry from room to room while cleaning" to "Eat proper food for health and vitality. Every morning before breakfast, comb hair, apply makeup, a dash of cologne, and perhaps some simple earrings. Does wonders for your morale." She includes advice for the busy housewife, such as "'Recreation' means 're-create' . . . for enthusiasm and courage. Garden, painting pictures, pursue any hobby, look through a magazine for home planning ideas, read a good book, or attend club meetings."[25]

The 1950s provided Betty Crocker with new challenges; she encouraged her readers to become dedicated consumers of General Mills products, including boxed cake mixes. However, she made sure that her supporters knew that she was still on their side, urging women to take pride in their homemaking skills. Ernest Dichter, a pioneer in motivational research, noted that the self-doubting housewife would find in Betty Crocker "a vindication of the value, dignity, and importance of the role of the homemaker and cook."[26]

"If I Knew You Were Comin', I'd Have Baked a Cake" | 77

Figure 4.2. Magazine advertisement in 1959 for Betty Crocker's Yellow Cake Mix. Source: Neil Baylis/Alamy Stock Photo.

Even though all mainstream, commercial cookbooks went through new editions and revisions during the late 1940s and the 1950s, the popularity of these books was waning. The market for cookbooks became more prominent, and publishers struggled to make their offerings bigger, showier, and more colorful. Women's magazines also provided significant competition by offering recipes with full-color layouts. These recipes were easy to read, simple to cut out, and less expensive than purchasing a cookbook. Indeed, one will often find recipes clipped from magazines taped or glued to front or back covers of used cookbooks or simply stuck in between random pages.[27]

The cookbook market had grown substantially. While publishers reissued updated versions of the classic cookbooks, eventually they published glitzier books with more color photographs and eye-catching covers. This trend culminated at the end of the decade with Time's *Picture Cook Book* (1958), one of the most visually spectacular cookbooks of the 1950s. Enveloped in bright orange and red cover with gold embossed lettering, nearly every page of the book has a color photograph. Measuring an astonishing ten-and-a-half by fourteen inches, this is not a practical book for use in a kitchen, and it elevates cookbooks to coffee-table status. The editor notes that while the book is for practicing cooks, it "is designed in part for armchair gourmets, who, far from the kitchen, may want to tempt themselves with culinary delights."[28] Often, cookbooks published in the 1950s provide a gustatory armchair thrill by printing recipes that describe what people *wished* they could consume. Given its showy appearance and inclusion of six hundred recipes such as Classic Bouillabaisse, Oysters Poulette, and *Tripe à la Mode de Caen*, one might think this book represented fine gourmet cooking, and indeed it sometimes does. However, the book's editors bring the armchair enthusiasts down to earth, and the era's processed foods creep in with recipes calling for frozen vegetables, canned foods, and packaged pudding mixes.

Charity Cookbooks

Often referred to as fundraising, charity, or community cookbooks, this genre of specialty cookbook harkens back to the Civil War, when women organized to raise money for medical supplies, orphans, and war widows. Over the decades, fundraising cookbooks have been compiled by communities of women, gathering around a common cause such as volunteer organizations, schools, churches, synagogues, hospitals, preservation of heritage, fraternal organizations, and immigrant groups. Examples of titles, representing a sample of the range of causes, included *Secrets from Bergen Kitchens*, Teaneck New Jersey Jewish Community Center Sisterhood, 1947; *Loyalty Cookbook*, Native Daughters of the Golden West, Sebastopol,

"If I Knew You Were Comin', I'd Have Baked a Cake" | 79

California, 1953; and *Angel Food: From the Recipe Files of Our Lady of Mercy School Mothers Club Members and Friends*, East Greenwich, Rhode Island, 1959.

Often privately printed (sometimes even hand-typed) for a limited audience, many fundraising cookbooks do not appear in standard catalogs. An example is the following recipe, contributed by Mrs. Elmer Johnson from Wisconsin's Tippecanoe Presbyterian Church.

CINNAMON MUFFINS

Favorite Recipes of the Women of Tippecanoe Presbyterian Church (1949)[29]

1½ c. sifted flour
⅓ c. sugar
2¼ t. baking powder
½ t. nutmeg
¼ t. salt
1 egg
¼ c. melted shortening
½ c. milk
⅓ c. melted butter
⅓ c. sugar
1 t. cinnamon

Sift flour, baking powder, salt, sugar, and nutmeg. Combine well beaten egg, milk, and melted shortening; add to sifted dry ingredients and blend lightly (about 25 strokes). Half fill greased muffin pans. Bake 12 minutes in 425° oven. Remove muffins from pans immediately and roll them in melted butter, then in mixture of sugar and cinnamon. Yield about 16 muffins.

One of the most intriguing of this cookbook genre is *Who Says We Can't Cook!* written by members of the Women's National Press Club. The foreword notes, "This Women's National Press Club Cook Book is not so much a defense of the culinary talents of newspaper women as it is a profit-making venture. We want a clubhouse of our own. With the help of this book, we expect to have a clubhouse, sooner."[30] The book of recipes from 140 journalists has a story to accompany each recipe. For example, Alice Frein Johnson, Washington correspondent for the *Seattle Times*, provides a recipe for Chicken Curry given to her mother by Queen Liliuokalani of Hawaii. On assignment in Shanghai after the war, Jessie Stearns of *Business International* contributes a recipe for Sukiyaki, "dished up" by uniformed Harvard men awaiting assignment in Tokyo. Stearns explains, "I never expected to eat Sukiyaki in the heart of Shanghai. The air was thick with foreign intrigue as we rendezvoused at a secret place, with Geisha girls present and the American officers cooking the Sukiyaki."[31]

SUKIYAKI

(To fry over low fire)

Who Says We Can't Cook! (1955)[32]

1½ pounds lean round beef suet
¼ cup soy sauce
1 bunch green onions
1 tablespoon sugar
2 cups celery
2 cups shredded spinach (frozen kind is good)
1½ cups bamboo sprouts
1 cup sliced ripe olives
2 cups mushrooms
1 tablespoon cornstarch
1 bouillon cube
¼ cup water
½ cup water
1 egg
Hot, cooked rice

Cut the beef paper thin. If you freeze it first, it will slice easily. Render suet and remove cracklings. Add beef slices to suet and cook until three-fourths done. Remove beef. Add to suet the onions, celery, sprouts, all cut in 2-inch lengths, and the mushrooms, sliced. Saute until partly done. Drain on a paper towel.

Dissolve bouillon cube in ½ cup water, add soy sauce and sugar. Place the partly cooked mixture in another skillet or a chafing dish and pour the liquids over it. Cover and steam 10 minutes, or longer. Add shredded spinach, olives, cook 3 minutes longer. Mix cornstarch with ¼ cup water and stir in to thicken liquid. Bring to boil, add egg. Serve at once over hot, cooked rice.

Six servings.

Southern Regional Cooking

Cookbooks that focused on geographical regions of the US first appeared in the nineteenth century. These books remained popular during the early Cold War years when ideals of democracy were wrapped up in a blanket of patriotism and nationalism. The books were published or reissued in two primary formats—first, cookbooks that include recipes from the entire US but are divided up into specific regions, and second, those that focus on one area or state. As characterized in the 1950s, regional cooking rarely acknowledged or recognized foods or traditions originating in Africa, the Caribbean, or throughout the Americas and assumed that all cooking practices derived from the early European, specifically British, colonists. Years later, this assumption is alive and well. "Americans manifested a remarkable degree of resistance to the culinary influence of other cultures. Even before independence, waves of immigrants from Europe and Africa washed onto America's shores, but left few traces of their cuisines on the American table."[33]

The American South is considered one of the unique regional cuisines, and according to author John Egerton, this is not an accident. "Throughout 350 years of slavery, segregation and legally enforced white primacy, the vast majority of women of African ancestry in the South—and many of the women of European lineage who oversaw their work—lived lives tightly circumscribed within hailing distance of the region's domestic kitchens. To them fell the overarching responsibility for the feeding of the South."[34] But these women are seldom, if ever, mentioned in Southern cookbooks. African American contributions to cookery are generally undocumented or unrecognized, as are the one-hundred-plus species of plants introduced through the slave trade: okra, taro, pearl millet, sorghum, watermelon, black-eyed peas, kola nut, sesame, melegueta pepper, ackee, various squashes, yams, castor beans, and more. Author William C. Whit adds to that list spinach, oranges, avocados, eggplant, cassava, sweet potatoes, chilis, and coconuts. Some are indigenous to Africa, and others were introduced into Africa and the United States via the Caribbean, Europe, Asia, and the Americas.[35]

Green rice, red beans and rice, southern rice, rice dumplings, crab or okra gumbo served with rice, jollof rice, and shrimp or crab jambalaya—rice is everywhere in Southern cooking. Author Judith Ann Carney notes that enslaved Africans "saw their traditional agriculture emerge as the first food commodity traded across the ocean on a large scale by capitalists who would later take complete credit for the innovation."[36] European colonists in the US tried to grow rice and failed. It did not flourish until the arrival of enslaved peoples from Africa, who brought their knowledge about growing, harvesting, and cooking rice to the plantation system, which defines much of Southern agriculture, especially the low country and sea islands of South Carolina and Georgia. Enslavers often sought to purchase men and women from specific rice-growing parts of West Africa to ensure the success of the crops.[37]

Of the approximately two hundred cookbooks written by African Americans through the end of the twentieth century, only a handful were published from the late 1940s to the end of the 1950s. That few were published is not a surprise. Much about cooking is an oral tradition, passed from mother to daughter. "Slaves used smell and taste, touch, sight, and sound in order to cook."[38] Publishing was expensive, and without a patron it was beyond the reach of most domestic cooks—African American or white. For Southern cookbooks, a white patron or sponsor was necessary. During the 1950s, Southern cooking is often described throughout regional cookbooks but written by whites for a white audience. Author Karen Hess notes the "near mythic quality of Southern Cooking," which is "attributed to the presence of African American women cooks [who] did the cooking; it's as simple as that." She emphatically states, "I should note that most of the recipes in *all* Southern cookbooks are, in fact, largely recipes gleaned by the writers from African American cooks."[39] Laura Schenone, in *A Thousand Years Over a Hot Stove*, observes that despite vast challenges, food and cooking provided African American women a platform to take a small measure of control over their lives.[40]

Except in condescending caricatures, African Americans are rarely mentioned in white cookbooks. *Charleston Receipts* (1950), a compilation of recipes collected by the Junior League, begins each section with a quote in a dialect the reader would assume was African American. For example, to introduce a section on soup and a recipe for She-Crab Soup, "Crab got tuh walk een duh pot demself or dey ain' wut." The narrative in the rest of the section is English (although South Carolina whites also have a dialect, which is often difficult for outsiders to understand). This choice of language is a not-so-subtle suggestion that black people are illiterate and speak a dialect that is not considered English—further identifying them as the "other."

Another example appears in an illustration accompanying the section "Southern Cook Book from Away Down South in Dixie," in *The United States Regional Cook Book*. A "mammy" figure frames the title, and the following page repeats this derisive image.[41] These mammy images emerge in the era's food advertising and cooking literature. Known as Aunt Jemima, the stereotypical image of the African American cook "sprang to life: a jolly fat black woman in a do-rag, cooking up a storm."[42]

African American voices have been missing from what we have assumed is American cuisine. As Barbara Haber observed, African Americans are invisible or described as passive cooks who perform strictly by instinct.[43] The following four cookbooks will challenge this perception and demonstrate that these cooks were creative, skilled, and thoughtful.

Jesse's Book of Creole and Deep South Recipes, with recipes compiled by Edith Ballard Watts and her husband, John Watts, is one of the 1950s-era cookbooks devoted to Southern food, specifically food from New Orleans, with a few recipes from the Florida Keys. Jesse Willis Lewis was born in Mississippi and joined the kitchen staff of Marshall Ballard, editor of the *New Orleans Item*, working for the Ballards and their five children for forty years.

Ballard Watts notes, "Mother took him in hand and taught him how to prepare and serve properly and smoothly the famous Creole dishes of New Orleans to adapt the exotic and flavorsome meat, game, and fowl concoctions of the Deep South to the fastidious taste of Father and his gourmet friends." Despite Mrs. Watts's paternalist tone, which was not uncommon for the era, the recipes are accompanied by Jesse's cooking tips, guidelines, and history "through stories that recall wonderful wisdom and hospitality, sometimes all in one recipe."[44] Jesse is referred to just by his first name; only the back cover jacket provides his surname. Jesse had many opinions, and many of his recipes are long—Creole Gumbo, Boiled

Sheepshead [a Southern fish] with Cucumber Sauce, and Buttered Broiled Chicken with Sherry run a full two pages. A recipe for Vol-au-Vent of Chicken takes over five pages. Jesse also had opinions on his ingredients. Oysters, crabs, and fish must always be fresh—never canned or frozen, and while fresh shrimp was preferable, Jesse allowed that frozen shrimp would do. Likewise, okra had to be fresh or frozen, never from a can.

SHRIMP JAMBALAYA

Jesse's Book of Creole & Deep South Recipes (1954)[45]

An old standby in Creole cookery. Fresh oysters may be substituted for the shrimp.

3 tablespoons lard
2 bay leaves
2 onions, chopped fine
1 sprig thyme
2 cloves garlic, chopped fine
1 tablespoon chopped fresh parsley
1 slice (about ½ lb.) cured ham, diced
½ tablespoon chopped celery
1 No. 2 can tomatoes
salt and pepper to taste
2½ cups raw rice
dash of cayenne pepper
1 lb. fresh or frozen cleaned, uncooked shrimp (or 1 pt. oysters)
1 teaspoon sugar [Note: the recipe specifically does not indicate when to add the sugar]

Melt the lard in a pot—preferably of heavy iron or aluminum—brown the onions and garlic, then add the ham. Let the ham sauté with the onions and garlic for 5 minutes, then add the tomatoes and let cook for 3 minutes. Wash the rice thoroughly and place in the pot. Add the shrimp or oysters and the bay leaves, thyme, parsley, celery, and seasonings, and let cook slowly about 45 minutes. Salt and pepper to taste. Serves 6 or 7.

Paynie's Parties: A Collection of Party Recipes from Mrs. Jessie Hargrave of Lexington, North Carolina (1955) was also compiled by others, in this case Mrs. J. F. Spruill and Mrs. Stokes Adderton of Lexington, North Carolina. The foreword, written by Adderton, describes how "a tiny little Negro girl" learned to cook from her mother and provides some personal information on Jessie Payne (known as Paynie), listing the many people for whom she worked as a cook. "Visitors to Lexington invariably are impressed at the beautiful and wondrous food when Paynie is presiding in the kitchen. She is known and beloved by hundreds today, both white and Negro."[46] The compilers warn the reader that the recipes are not short nor easy but elaborate, painstaking, and "worth all the trouble." Indeed, some of the recipes are complicated, and others are witty. For example, a recipe for a very ornate Bunny Salad (a dish often found in children's cookbooks) not only has a "carrot" carved from soft pimiento cheese with parsley as the stem and leaves, but the "bunny" sits on "grass" made by forcing lime Jell-O through a ricer.

Paynie also paid close attention to the details of garnishes. For example, she provides instructions for creating cucumber tulips, green or red pepper rings (to hold stalks of asparagus or whole string beans), jellied ginger ale cubes, radish roses, and a fancy watermelon bowl. Many of the recipes are explicit in their ingredient amounts and cooking times; other recipes are vague and assume the reader has some cooking knowledge. The following recipe for Quail on Toast would require such a cook.

Quail on Toast

Paynie's Parties (1955)[47]

Wash carefully after quail have been cleaned and picked and salted well. Add 1 pt. good rich chicken stock and 1 pt. water. Place birds in double roaster. Break up quarter pound butter and place over birds. Sprinkle bl. pepper. Steam on top of stove, medium heat until tender. Place in oven to brown, basting every 15 minutes. Be sure to have broth enough for gravy, by adding water as needed. Toast bread, place quail on toast, and pour gravy over birds.

Garnish with parsley.

The Historical Cookbook of the American Negro (1958) is a history book masquerading as a cookbook. It is not organized as a traditional cookbook but is based on a monthly calendar that emphasizes history as much as food. As the year progresses, each page notes facts about influential African Americans (and a few whites such as Abraham Lincoln, George Washington, and Harriet Beecher Stowe), a celebration, or an organization. For example, the book begins with January 1, "New Years, and Emancipation Proclamation Day (1863)." Recipes for this day include Southern Hopping John, Minced Clam Stuffing, and New England Plum Pudding. A few of the celebrated African Americans found throughout the book include George Washington Carver (accompanied, of course, by numerous peanut recipes), Frederick Douglass, Dred Scott, Harriet Tubman, and Dr. A. Clayton Powell.

The book's compiler, Sue Bailey Thurman, noted in the foreword to the 1958 edition that the work represented "a new, unique and 'palatable' approach to history."[48] In the 2000 reprint, scholar Anne L. Bower provides an introduction, a user's guide for the recipes, and an index.

Southern Hopping John

The Historical Cookbook of the American Negro (1958; 2000)[49]

1 lb. (2 to 2¼) cups dried blackeye peas
2½ quarts water
8 slices bacon, cut in small strips, or 4 ounces salt pork
1½ cups chopped onion
2 buds garlic minced
1 teaspoon hot pepper sauce
1 tablespoon mixed herbs
2 cups uncooked rice
chopped parsley

Wash beans and soak in water overnight. Fry bacon over moderate heat until brown. Add onion and continue cooking until onion is tender. Add garlic, salt, pepper, hot sauce, herbs In large pan combine soaked peas, water, bacon and onion mixture. Cover pan, bring to boil. Simmer until beans are tender, about an hour. Stir in rice and cook under low heat 30 to 40 minutes or until rice is tender and fluffy. Spoon into large serving dish, garnish with chopped parsley.

A Date with a Dish: A Cook Book of American Negro Recipes by Freda De Knight (1909–1963) is also a cookbook that showcases African

American history and culture. The book, published in 1948, is a collection of recipes, hints, and menus from ordinary housewives, chefs, celebrities, and caterers. Woven throughout the book is De Knight's lively, witty, and friendly narrative. De Knight was a food columnist for *Ebony* magazine, and thus her book was nationally advertised and distributed. Unlike the era's preoccupation with processed foods, De Knight offers recipes for real food.

De Knight emphatically declares, "It is a fallacy, long disproved, that Negro cooks, chefs, caterers, and homemakers can adapt themselves only to the standard southern dishes, such as fried chicken, greens corn pone and hot breads. Like other Americans living in various sections of the country [African Americans] have naturally shown a desire to branch out in all directions and become versatile in the preparation of any dish."[50] Although she branches out from traditional Southern cooking, De Knight does offer recipes such as Crab Gumbo, Okra Creole, Shrimp Jambalaya, and Louisiana Oyster Loaf. However, De Knight's range of recipes is enormous and more sophisticated than most mainstream 1950s cookbooks, offering Filet Mignon with Chicken Livers, Lobster Newburg and Lobster Farcie, Salmon or Lobster Mousse, Crab Flake Cutlets, Asparagus on Toast, Creole Baked Red Snapper, and a myriad of oyster recipes. Many of the of dishes also would have been comfortable in any middle-class white household, such as pumpkin pie, baked pork chops, waffles, welch rarebit, and old-fashioned split-pea soup.

To help with selecting recipes for her cookbook, De Knight created an assistant that she calls the Little Brown Chef. The Little Brown Chef helped De Knight search the country for recipes. If the Little Brown Chef liked a dish, he "dated the dish" and the recipe would be a part of De Knight's collection. (A "dish" is a term for an enthralling woman.) Janet Theophano has noted that De Knight's provocative use of her assistant, "playfully allude[s] to the relationship between food and sex."[51]

Gertrude Blair, who wrote the introduction to the book, remarked, "Freda De Knight is a cultivated Negro woman, writing the first book of its kind, a cook book of American Negro cooking." Blair adds, "It is equally important that the book can stand on its own merit in competition with any other cook book."[52] Indeed, it does. Considering the politics of the late-1940s and 1950s, it is entirely possible that had the author been white, De Knight's cookbook could have been (and should have been) a mainstream cookbook, such as *The Joy of Cooking* or *Betty Crocker's Picture Cookbook*.

Red Snapper

(Creole Baked)

A Date with a Dish: Cook Book of American Negro Recipes (1948)[53]

1 Red snapper (3–4 lbs.)
1 pod garlic
1 lb. boiled shrimp
1 doz. Oysters
1½ cups bread crumbs
several crawfish or ½ cup crabmeat
2 large tomatoes, or 1 cup canned tomatoes
4 tbsps. Butter
1 can mushrooms
½ cup celery, chopped
2–3 bay leaves sprig parsley
½ doz. whole allspice
sprig thyme
2 cups white wine
several cloves
1 tsp. paprika
salt and pepper to taste

Clean fish and remove head. Make 3 diagonal cuts on the skin of fish. Rub fish inside and out with a paste made of mashed garlic, salt, pepper, paprika, and thyme.

Make stuffing as follows: wet bread crumbs and squeeze out water. Saute onion and celery in butter. Add 2 tablespoons crumbs with salt and pepper. Add 6 oysters cut in pieces and stuff fish. Sew up well. Grease outside of fish. Just before placing fish in oven, pour wine over it. Bake in moderate oven 30 to 40 minutes.

While fish is baking, prepare sauce as follows: Brown onion, parsley, and bay leaf in remaining fat. Stir constantly. Add tomatoes and rest of herbs and remaining oysters and juice. Simmer. Heat shrimp and mushrooms with ½ cup chopped parsley in a bit of butter. Do not brown. Remove fish from oven, place on a platter. Arrange shrimp around and on top of fish artistically. Pour sauce over fish and serve garnished with parsley. Serves 6.

Crawfish may also be used to decorate dish and are most colorful. Sauce may be poured over crawfish and dish may then be run into oven just before serving.

In writing about African American cookbooks, author Hodding Carter ponders, "Why don't we celebrate their contributions to American culture the way we venerate that of the imaginary Betty Crocker?" Well, according to Carter, "The jury is still out."[54] Following in the footsteps of Malinda Russell (1812–c. 1866), Edna Lewis (1937–2016), and others, a new generation of cooks and historians is setting the record straight, including Jessica B. Harris, Michael W. Twitty, B. J. Dennis, Marcus Samuelsson, and Toni Tipton-Martin.[55]

Chapter 5

"Honey, I'm Home. What's for Dinner?"

The 1950s American Diet, Part I

In a scathing critique of the sprawling, new suburban communities built throughout the United States during the 1950s, John C. Keats's *Crack in the Picture Window* traces the day-to-day activities of fictional characters John and Mary Drone.

> Mary took down a prepared spaghetti dinner from her shelves, a can of peas, and, casting around for dessert, decided on mixed fruit. She emptied the spaghetti and the peas into saucepans, put the saucepans on the stove; emptied the canned fruit into a bowl and put the bowl in the refrigerator."[1]

Throughout the 1950s, the food and advertising industries encouraged American women to utilize convenience foods—canned, boxed, dehydrated, frozen, even aerosol. The message was simple: convenience foods will build a healthy and happy American family. So prevalent was the opinion that such foods were best for the American family that magazines provided recipes for taking full advantage of the riches of processed foods. *Good Housekeeping* featured an entire menu of nutritious dishes created out of canned or frozen foods in its July 1956 issue. The dinner included SPAM®, instant mashed potatoes, frozen peas, a dessert made from fruit cocktail, store-bought sponge cake, and a packet of instant pudding. Marketed to women as time-saving convenience foods, some argued that there was little evidence of meaningful time saving and that advertising campaigns designed promotions to boost sales—however, these processed foods, advertised as "modern," resonated with many women.

Most packaged, processed foods remained popular throughout the 1950s, reshaping the definition of a home-cooked meal. To reinforce this modern characterization of a home-cooked meal, cookbook author Poppy Cannon reassured new cooks that anyone could produce masterpieces with processed foods. She noted in *The Bride's Cookbook*, "This is a very different book because it is based on a new theory: that some of the best meals of our time are whizzed together in a matter of minutes, often with the sketchiest of equipment and by the most blissfully untutored impresario. In this book, the can opener, the mix, and frozen food take their place among the immemorial little gods of hearth and household."[2]

Print advertisements and cookbooks often implied that cooking was work and that using convenience foods would take the struggle out of the process. It was said, for example, that canned, condensed soups would miraculously turn another can of something else into a magnificent meal. (One was supposed to ignore the fact that canned soups of the time were overly salty and had a metallic aftertaste.) For example, the main ingredients in a recipe for Chicken Noodle Casserole included a can of condensed chicken broth, canned boned chicken, and a can of button mushrooms. Likewise, a recipe for Tomato-Crab Bake called for a can of condensed tomato soup, a can of evaporated milk, and a can of king crab meat.

The food industry wanted to convince women that cooking could be fun and an enjoyable, creative experience. The logic followed that processed foods were fast; thus, the cook would have more time to be inventive in the food's presentation at the dinner table. Cooks were encouraged to exercise their imaginations and turn ordinary meals into memorable occasions, paying attention to garnishes and proper table settings. Dishes such as Jell-O salads and all sorts of casseroles were supposed to taste good, but they also had to be visually attractive. *Carnation Cook Book*, written by the fictional Mary Blake, devoted an entire section to garnishes. Garnishes for fish included lemon dipped into minced capers or parsley and crossed by strips of pimiento, lemon halves filled with chopped pickle, and beet relish. Suggestions also included mayonnaise or tartare sauce, lemons cut into any fanciful shape, curled celery, tiny whole tomatoes marinated in French dressing, dressed cucumber, and shoestring potatoes.[3] Poppy Cannon urged brides to be creative in presenting their meals to their new husbands, and each of her recipes followed with a series of suggestions that she called "At serving time." For example, Cannon's simple recipe for Curried Cream of Chicken Soup called for a can of chicken soup, milk, a little curry powder, and a bit of lemon juice. "At serving time" suggested garnishes that often likely took much more preparation than the actual soup. "Pass a variety of curry accompaniments, such as coarsely chopped, thinly sliced green or sweet red peppers, chutney, very thinly sliced, unpeeled tart red apple, scallions cut into ½-inch pieces, peanuts, or pistachio nuts, and a small amount of flaky rice."[4] Meals are described as visual events, assuming women had the instincts to turn a monotonous meal into a spectacular creation. The idea that eating is a multisensory experience became widespread, backing up the ancient Roman saying that "We eat first with the eyes, then with the nose, and then with the mouth." Or, as fictional author Mary Blake summarized, "Just remember that a little 'dressing up' will do wonders for the plainest of food."[5]

Canned Foods

Canned foods, which had been difficult for consumers to purchase during the war because of their extensive use by the military, became a standard 1950s food commodity. Easily acquired, convenient, and relatively cheap, cans were among the few food products to be purchased by all classes

Figure 5.1. A billboard in Los Angeles, advertising Libby's Canned Peaches, c. 1955. Source: RLFE Pix/Alamy Stock Photo.

of people. Unlike fresh vegetables and fruits, which were available only seasonally, canned foods meant that the cook had many choices—year-round. Cans represented speed and up-to-date cooking, defined as "the perfect symbol for the modern 1950s kitchen."[6] The canned food industry boldly reminded women, "Nothing is added to canned fruits except a sugar syrup; and nothing to canned vegetables except water and sometimes a little salt or sugar for seasoning." The industry also noted, "The use of commercially canned foods saves many hours of preparation of raw fruits, vegetables, fish and meats, and also assures no waste."[7]

Poppy Cannon, author and noble supporter of canned foods, suggested, "The can opener should be regarded as permanent equipment—not as a kitchen gadget, especially in the hands of those brave, young women, nine million of them (give or take a few thousand here and there), who are engaged in frying as well as bringing home the bacon."[8] Cannon smugly declared, "Armed with a can opener, I become the artist-cook, the master, the creative chef."[9] The American Can Company created full-color print advertisements during the 1950s and published recipes that required only a can opener to make a complete meal, including items for a Texas barbecue supper called Texas Kabobs. This meal required one can of button mushrooms, two cans of Vienna sausage, one can of luncheon meat, one can of whole white onions, and one can of whole pimentos.

Canned fruit, specifically canned fruit cocktail, proved to be a popular choice for a fast and easy dessert. For example, *Choice Recipes and Menus using Canned Foods* presents a quick and straightforward recipe for Fruit Cocktail Ambrosia, which uses canned fruit cocktail, two bananas, lemon juice, and canned shredded coconut. Numerous canned products, including pineapple, citrus fruits, cherries, and apricots, are often found in the era's recipe books and used to make ice cream; added to pudding mixes or Jell-O, cakes, meat dishes, bread; or eaten straight out of the can. In 1957, the magazine *American Home* noted that it was no longer necessary to purchase, wash, and prepare a myriad of fruits when all one had to do was buy a can of fruit cocktail—all the work was done for you.

Campbell's canned condensed soups were not new in the 1950s, and they had been on grocery store shelves since the turn of the century. Advertising agencies reinforced the idea that canned soup was indispensable in cooking, and soon condensed soups became a mealtime staple. *Cooking with Condensed Soups* (1952) devotes a section to "New Soups to Try." One can of vegetable soup added to one can of bacon soup will yield "Vegetable Soup Peasant Style." One of Campbell's most versatile soups, cream of mushroom soup, might be mixed with one can of chicken noodle soup, generating a new dish, "Old-Fashioned Velvet."[10] While these might have been simple recipes, cookbooks advised not to overlook appearance in serving soups. *Better Homes and Gardens New Cook Book* recommended garnishes of salted whipped cream, shredded toasted almonds, minced chives, and cheese popcorn for cream soups, as well as chowders and meat soups served with thin slices of frankfurters or chopped crisp bacon. Other suggestions included lemon slices, minced parsley, crispy dry cereal, croutons (including peanut butter-flavored croutons), radish wheels, and carrot rounds.[11]

In his book *50 Chowders: One Pot Meals—Clam, Corn & Beyond*, Jasper White notes that in the history of American chowders, the 1950s is considered the dark ages. "Chowder making in many homes begins with a can opener, and in the hands of professional cooks of questionable ability, chowder is quickly being degraded to a soup-like paste, with pathetic bits of rubber-like clams and tasteless potatoes."[12] Poppy Cannon's New England Clam Chowder was, indeed, a can opener's dream. The ingredients comprised a can of condensed clam chowder, milk, sauterne, Rhine wine, or hock, paprika, chives, or parsley. The instructions say to add one can of milk (or one-half can of sauterne, Rhine wine, or hock) and heat but not boil. When serving: "Place a pilot cracker in the bottom of a heated bowl or soup plate, ladle the chowder over the cracker and sprinkle with paprika, chopped chives, or parsley."[13]

Casseroles

> Tuna-noodle casserole is the emblematic dish of the postwar kitchen. It's bland enough to offend no one, not even fussy children; it's cheap and it's filling.
>
> —Mary Drake Mcfeely (2000)[14]

Canned soups, advertised as an excellent way to start a simple meal, also became the standard ingredient as the foundation for casseroles. "Casserole meals have long been favorites at our house, but I really hit my stride the day I discovered canned soup as a casserole ingredient."[15] The casserole served directly from the oven to the table is most often identified with the 1950s. Print advertisements distributed by food companies and writers who contributed recipes to magazines and cookbooks praised casseroles as versatile time savers. Their principal virtue was that they were quick and easy to make, even for the most inexperienced cook.

Usually, casseroles included canned fish or meat, cooked pasta or noodles, and maybe some peas, all mixed with a can of condensed cream of mushroom, cream of chicken, or cream of celery soup. The contents are put in a shallow casserole dish, topped off with some sort of pastry crust, canned fried onion rings, crushed potato chips, or shredded American processed cheese and baked in a moderate oven for half an hour or so. Indexes in mainstream cookbooks often had a casserole section, providing easy access to a quick dinner. For example, the Culinary Arts Institute's 1950 *Encyclopedic Cookbook* lists nearly fifty recipes for various casseroles. *Betty Crocker's Picture Cook Book* (1950), *Better Homes and Gardens New Cook Book* (1953), and *The General Foods Kitchens Cookbook* (1959) all have separate entries for casserole recipes. Irma S. Rombauer's 1951 edition of *The Joy of Cooking* does not contain a particular index category for casseroles; nevertheless, casserole recipes lurk within its pages. For example, the recipe for Tuna, Noodle and Mushroom Soup Casserole is located under "tuna." (Other publications also list casseroles under their main protein ingredient.) Some cookbooks do not always call their recipes "casseroles," but they are, nevertheless, casseroles. *Chiquita Banana's Recipe Book*'s recipe for Ham Banana Rolls with Cheese Sauce requires baking in a typical casserole vessel: a greased shallow baking dish.[16]

The casserole exemplifies several characteristics of the 1950s ideal, flexible cooking. It could be a simple, one-dish meal, created in a matter of minutes with just a few canned products, or it might also be more elaborate, a dish that would display the imaginative talents of the cook. Cooking literature describes three types of casseroles: First, the simplest, using inexpensive canned goods, such as the *Good Housekeeping's Casserole Book* Quick Bacon-Noodle Casserole or Turnip Fluff. Second, casseroles created for company or special occasions might utilize more expensive canned ingredients, such as canned shrimp, crab, or lobster. Third, a casserole made from scratch, using few or no canned products. These "gourmet" casseroles were considered party or company food and required more preparation.

Often a casserole is served as a connection to unfamiliar, possibly exotic locations. Nedda Anders's cookbook *Casserole Specialties* (1955) and *Good Housekeeping's Casserole Book* (1958) offer casseroles that claim to be international. Anders asserts, "Here in these pages are recipes for casserole *specialties*—interesting and different meal-in-one combinations that are a culinary heritage from the Greeks, Germans, Scandinavians, the Russians, Armenians, Italians, the Spaniards, Jews, and Chinese."[17] However, rarely do these recipes reflect an international or authentic foreign influence. They seldom use any spices and rely on easily obtained ingredients. Other recipe titles that suggest faraway places included Normandy Casserole, Danish Pork Chops and Fruit, Belgian Meatballs, and Turkey Monte Carlo. The 1950s family might consume dishes named for mysterious and exotic locales, but nobody wanted to be *too* adventurous. Salt and pepper were the most common, sometimes the only, seasonings. Recipes seldom called for anything more, except maybe a pinch of chili powder and a few grains of cayenne pepper.

Although casseroles were promoted as a simple meal, according to cookbook authors women were encouraged to think creatively about the ingredients. Adding a personal touch of creativity would provide enjoyment for the cook, but it also served as a vehicle for the cook to display her domestic talents. Authors were quick to encourage experimentation, noting that not only might the cook impress her husband's boss at a dinner party, but her family would also be pleased, showering accolades on her. "If you can take a familiar dish, add a little of this and that to change the flavor a bit, the family takes complimentary notice and your job as cook is infinitely more fun."[18]

Cookware manufacturers were quick to recognize the growing popularity of casseroles. A line of colorful new products developed by the Corning Glass Works included oven-to-table casserole dishes in various sizes. Although clear Pyrex cookware had been available since 1915, the 1947 introduction of bright and versatile kitchenware helped make Pyrex significantly more popular. Many casseroles images from the 1950s feature Pyrex kitchenware.

A simple casserole might be chicken à la king or Poppy Cannon's Casserole à la King. Cannon's recipe calls for one can of chicken à la king, one can of macaroni in cream sauce with cheese, packaged breadcrumbs, and butter, parsley, or watercress. Cannon's instructions are to heat the contents of each can separately. "Arrange in layers in shallow casserole. Top layer should be macaroni. Sprinkle with 4 tablespoons grated cheese mixed with 4 tablespoons packaged bread crumbs. Dot with butter." This was set under a broiler to "become bubbly and brown," and when it is time for serving, Cannon suggests a garnish of parsley or watercress.[19]

The following recipe is a more expensive casserole, using a few processed foods, and suitable for special occasions.

Tomato-Crab Bake

"A wonderful company quickie."

Good Housekeeping's Casserole Book (1958)[20]

1 tablesp. butter or margarine
½ cup fresh bread crumbs
2½ cups thin spaghetti, broken into halves
1 can condensed tomato soup, undiluted
1 tall can evaporated milk, undiluted
1 6½ oz. can king crab meat, flaked (1 cup)
1 cup grated process Cheddar cheese (¼ lb.)
¼ cup minced green peppers
1 tablesp. Minced onions
½ teasp. Salt
Dash dried thyme

Start heating oven to 350° F. In small saucepan, melt butter; toss with bread crumbs; set aside. Cook spaghetti as package directs; drain. In 2-qt. casserole, combine spaghetti with soup, milk, crab meat, cheese, green peppers, onions, salt, and thyme. Top with crumbs. Bake 45 min. Makes 8 servings.

Cooking literature noted that a casserole made from scratch was always an excellent choice to impress your husband, his boss, or special guests.

Casserole of Savory Spanish Rice

Casserole Specialties (1955)[21]

Oven Time: 35 minutes at 350°

8 small sausages
1 clove garlic, mashed
3 tablespoons olive oil
1 large sweet onion, chopped
1 green pepper, chopped
2 large tomatoes, chopped

1 cup uncooked rice
2 tablespoons chopped parsley
1 cup beef stock, or bouillon cube dissolved in hot water
Salt and pepper to taste
Pinch of saffron.

Brown the sausages and garlic in hot oil for 2 minutes. Add onion, green pepper and tomatoes, and sauté 3 more minutes. Add rice and parsley and sauté until rice is golden brown. Pour in beef stock. Sprinkle with salt, pepper and saffron. Transfer to casserole and bake until done. If you have left-over cooked chopped giblets, they can be added to this casserole. Sauté them with the sausages.

Frozen Foods

Frozen vegetables are God's own gift to the busy housewife.

—Blanche C. Furman (1951)[22]

Because many industries turned their operations to wartime production, fabrication of home refrigerators and freezers virtually ceased during World War II. However, production restarted at the war's end, and food industry spokespersons assumed that by the mid-1950s, as much as 25 percent of US food outlays would be for frozen foods. The frozen food industry convinced consumers that utilizing their products would significantly free up time for women. Alongside the advertising industry, it worked hard to persuade American families to purchase new refrigerators with built-in freezers. The industry argued that freezers and frozen food "offered more individuals more freedom of choice [and] consumers envisioned frozen foods as meshing comfortably with a wide range of lifestyles, from the traditional husband and wife to the modern, unmarried female executive."[23]

The first popular frozen food was orange juice, which by 1953 represented 20 percent of all sales of frozen products. The Florida citrus industry gushingly referred to the new food product as a marvel of modern food know-how. The American Can Company went so far as to declare that during 1951–1952 "frozen orange juice had saved housewives the equivalent of 14,000 years of drudgery."[24]

100 | Casseroles, Can Openers, and Jell-O

Figure 5.2. A 1950s magazine advertisement for Birds Eye frozen vegetables. Source: Hector/Alamy Stock Photo.

Although Clarence Birdseye began experiments in freezing seafood in the 1920s, the frozen food industry did not become a robust business until Carl A. Swanson's company furthered Birdseye's innovations, including moisture-proof cellophane packaging and a three-compartment tray made of aluminum. In 1952 Swanson's began to sell frozen turkey dinners. By 1953 more than 50 percent of American families owned a television, and, in a stroke of marketing genius, the Swanson Company branded their frozen meals as "TV dinners." A 1955 commercial noted that the ordinary housewife could prepare a dinner consisting of "hearty slices of moist, tender Swanson turkey, with whipped sweet potatoes and golden Swanson butter." The third compartment held "garden fresh" peas. Tucked under the turkey slices and covered with gravy is a cornbread dressing.[25] The six-color, laminated parchment box "was the wonder of the industry because it reproduced the contents with such stunning, lip-smacking fidelity."[26]

Frozen foods had become so popular that by the end of the 1950s Americans spent 2.7 billion dollars on frozen food—an astonishing 2,700 percent more than in 1949. Consumers spent most of this capital on frozen foods that were heat-and-serve foods, such as Swanson's frozen dinners, and by 1956 Swanson was selling thirteen million dinners annually. TV dinners also provided a less expensive and faster alternative to a home-cooked meal, priced initially below one dollar.

Boxed Cake Mixes

All cooks know that baking is the most exacting of the culinary arts, and many are fearful of trying and failing. However, 1950s advertisers of products such as Pillsbury's Brown 'n Serve Dinner Rolls, General Mill's Bisquick, and Betty Crocker cake mixes tried to convince American women that baking was easy. The first cake mix appeared in 1933, introduced by P. Duff and Sons. It was a mix of dehydrated molasses, flour, sugar, and eggs. The mix only required water to create gingerbread. After some years of development, General Mills offered its Betty Crocker Ginger Cake Mix in 1947, a box with premixed dry ingredients. One had only to add water and stir. Devil's Food and Party Cake mixes followed in 1949, yellow cake and white cake in 1952, honey spice and angel food in 1953, marble cake in 1954, and chocolate cake in 1955.

At first, women balked at purchasing mixes that required nothing but water. While processed foods often met with skepticism, dried cake mixes were the most difficult sell. A 1953 Gallup poll showed that cakes were, indeed, a test of a woman's ability to cook. General Mills hired Ernest Dichter, a known psychologist who worked with the advertising industry, to conduct interviews with cake mix users. He concluded that the mixes were too simple. The food industry soon realized that if they omitted the mix's dried eggs and allowed women to add fresh eggs, their products would be much easier to promote.

Figure 5.3. A woman proudly shows off her Pillsbury Cake Mix creation. Source: Retro AdArchives/Alamy Stock Photo.

General Mills also pulled in women shoppers by colorful packaging and navigated them away from the simplistic preparation method by relying on one of the central themes of women's cooking: creativity. As with all aspects of 1950s cooking, creativity was encouraged by crafting extravagant cakes, even when using boxed cake mixes. An advertisement for Betty Crocker cake mixes provided recipes for seven decorated cakes, one for every night of the week. Intended to be original and creative, cake mix companies went to great lengths to encourage women to use their products, suggesting adding their personal touches. Myrna Johnson's 1953 article in *Better Homes and Gardens* enthusiastically supported this idea. "You can put your own effort into glorifying your cake with frosting, dreaming up an exciting trim that puts your own label on it."[27] A notable example of a "creative" cake is the Christmas Candle Cake made from a recipe in *The Holiday Cook Book: Special Foods for All Special Occasions* (1959). The recipe for this "special food" represented all the glories of processed foods and included packaged cherry cake mix, canned pineapple, one package of lime Jell-O, red food coloring, and candied cherries. The result must have been exceptional indeed. Cakes represented in advertisements utilized bold frosting colors and myriad different toppings: marshmallows, colorful sprinkles, shredded coconut, and candied fruits. Wilton Enterprises produced catalogs that offered cake decorating tools, such as pastry bags, and tips for the more adventurous. Cakes were now decorated with roses and leaves and surrounded by elaborate piping.

Cakes were traditionally a celebratory food, perceived to be acts of love because of the time involved in their creation—and women had always baked cakes from scratch. Advertising encouraged the idea that baking cakes is an expression of love, and a cake made from a packaged mix is still a cake, thus making it is still an act of love.

Canned, boxed, and frozen processed foods proved popular during the 1950s. Still, often their origins and development can be traced back to the mid-nineteenth century or earlier—repackaged, perhaps reformulated, and aggressively marketed for a mid-twentieth-century consumer. After World War II manufacturers produced aerosol-propelled and dehydrated (later freeze-dried) foods, usually based on military development. These new foods were touted by the advertising industry as products for the modern woman, even if these products were often short-lived.

Aerosols

> Imagine. Elegant canapés crowned with gobbets of liverwurst and cheese-spread, sprayed from a can [and] the main course: a cloud of fluffy mashed potatoes alongside a slurry of barbecued meat, finished off with a misting of hickory flavor. Push-button cuisine is one of the great, unrealized dreams of postwar food technology.
>
> —Nadia Berenstein (2016)[28]

Although the history of aerosols is traced back to German and French technology from World War I, the US Department of Agriculture researchers developed the first portable aerosol spray can for use by the military in World War II. Filled with an insecticide and pressured by a liquid fluorocarbon gas, the invention proved critical in protecting US troops against malaria-carrying mosquitos.[29] After the war, agricultural spraying utilized aerosol technology to deliver such pesticides as DDT (dichloro-diphenyl-trichloroethane), and aerosol containers continued to dispense insecticides for the domestic market. The first mass-produced aerosol valve for food, patented in 1949 by Robert Abplanalp and issued in 1953, led the way for various food products such as Whisp, a vermouth spray for martinis. Other products included Sizzl-Spray, a barbecue sauce marketed for backyard grilling, and Tasti-Cup, an aerosol coffee concentrate that was even faster to make than instant coffee. The short-lived Betty Lou Cheese shot ribbons of a cheese product that, with a bit of practice, might land on your cracker.

Two 1950s aerosol products are still popular today: Reddi-wip whipped cream (a 1948 advertisement claimed, "It's the same pure cream—but Reddi-wip whips it for you!") and PAM nonstick cooking spray. During World War II, Reddi-wip was called "Sta-Whip" and was made not from cream but from vegetable oil. In 1948, Sta-Whip's creator Aaron S. "Bunny" Lapin and his collaborator Aaron Block developed a new aerosol valve better suited to dispensing cream. Reddi-wip received national distribution in 1954. In 1957, Leon Rubin and Arthur Meyerhoff Jr. received a patent for a nonstick cooking spray, and PAM hit the market in 1959. (PAM is an acronym for **Product of Arthur Meyerhoff**.)

Most aerosol-propelled food products faced significant challenges: the sensory qualities of foods often were compromised to work with a specialized nozzle, a propellant, and added stabilizers, all of which hindered color and taste. In the end, very few of these aerosol-propelled foods survived the 1950s. As well as food, manufacturers introduced myriad aerosol commodities, including spray paint, deodorants, hairspray, and shaving cream, which continued to be popular.

A mid-1950s survey commissioned by Dupont, one of the principal producers of chemical propellants, claimed that 91 percent of American families utilized aerosol products. The postwar industry had high hopes for aerosol foods. (Madison Avenue proclaimed, "Nobody can resist a push button.") Aerosol food products promised big rewards for many industries: chemical and container companies and food processing companies all stood to increase their profits. Aerosol foods did not require

"Honey, I'm Home. What's for Dinner?" | 105

Figure 5.4. 1950s Reddi-Wip magazine advertisement Source: Retro AdArchives/Alamy Stock Photo.

refrigeration and had a longer shelf life, adding to their promise as an essential consumer product. But it was a dream that never came to pass. Technical issues included appropriate dispensing valves that would permit foods of varying textures and viscosities to be delivered and the corrosion of the canisters. Early aerosol food items used compressed gases such as nitrous oxide, carbon dioxide, and nitrogen. These gases required large containers that often lost pressure, rendering the product useless. Non-food aerosol products employed chlorofluorocarbons (CFCs), but the Food and Drug Administration disapproved of CFCs for food propellent until the early 1960s.[30] Unfortunately, CFCs are an ozone-depleting substance, which also raises environmental concerns. (Today's aerosol products use a more earth-friendly propellant.)

Author Nadia Berenstein has noted that aerosol foods proved to be too expensive to produce, and consumers were not impressed by the convenience of spray foods. Many consumers harbored misgivings about a product associated with dangerous, non-food aerosol items, such as insect repellants and spray paints.

Dehydrated Foods

> The day is coming when a woman can buy a boiled dinner and carry it home in her purse . . . when a well-stocked pantry will be reduced to a few boxes . . . when you'll serve the girls a bridge luncheon of dehydrated meat and potatoes with powdered potatoes and powdered onions, a dehydrated cabbage salad, and custard made with powdered eggs and powdered milk for dessert.
>
> —Eleanor Early (1942)[31]

As with aerosol-propelled foods, dehydrated foods also promised a bright future. Their popularity grew during wartime because they were relatively inexpensive to produce and lightweight, thus more accessible for soldiers to carry. Powdered milk, coffee, eggs, and other dehydrated foods became a part of a soldier's rations, and flavorings included dry onion powder and an orange cheese powder. However, the domestic market proved to be more difficult. Many dehydrated products often require a rehydration process, usually completed by soaking the food in water. Since convenience was a selling point for most processed foods, dehydrated foods were not as popular as canned, frozen, or boxed.

One of the first commercially available but short-lived dehydrated foods came in 1947 from General Mills: Betty Crocker's Pyequick, a box mix that included dehydrated apples. Pyequick did not catch on, but a Betty Crocker dehydrated soup proved to be quite popular. First introduced in the 1930s, by the 1940s three other companies offered a variety of dehydrated soup choices: Lipton sold onion soup, noodle soup, and black bean and pea soups and Skinner and Eddy sold a vegetable soup and a chicken-flavor noodle soup. Finally, Dainty Food Manufacturers (a Kraft Cheese affiliate) presented a noodle soup. The soups were inexpensive: less than ten cents per serving. They were also popular because the soups were fast to make and provided the cook with flexibility. The dehydrated product could be consumed as soup or sauces for casseroles or poured over meat and poultry dishes.

In 1907, a potato dehydrating process received a patent, but further development came from military requirements during World War II. The first commercial product originated from the R. T. French Company, which launched its commercial version of dehydrated potatoes in 1946. The product was not popular with the public, but in the early 1950s General Foods introduced a product that proved to be better tasting. At the same time, R. T. French began to use a package that extended shelf life and permitted the availability of dehydrated potatoes in hot and humid locations. By the mid-1950s, the US Department of Agriculture developed a flaked version, which, when reconstituted, had a noticeable improvement in taste and texture over the granular product previously used.[32] (The Department was also working to create a dehydrated potato chip that could be stacked. The outcome, Pringles potato chips, mounded neatly in a single row in a can, was introduced in the late 1960s.)

Freeze drying, a new dehydration process, had been employed during the war for pharmaceuticals—especially penicillin and blood plasma, both of which needed refrigeration. Freeze drying provided a chemically stable and viable product without refrigeration. The dehydration process removes 80 percent of the food's water; freeze drying removes 98 percent. Thus, freeze-dried foods became more popular with the general population as the process not only rehydrates more quickly but also retains its texture, shape, and color.

More Processed Foods: Some Fun, Others Not So Fun

Packaged-food cuisine was widely understood to be women's cuisine. Canned and frozen products, food that had been stripped, sanitized, and rendered lifeless, was perfectly suited to the kind of women shown in the ads for refrigerators and ranges, all smiles in their aprons and high heels.

—Laura Shapiro (2004)[33]

In the 1950s, processed cheese came in many forms: slices, blocks, and spreads as well as in dehydrated and aerosol versions. Often referred to as "cheese food," the product was made from regular cheese (cheddar, gouda, Swiss, and others) with added emulsifiers (sodium and potassium phosphates), food colorings, and whey. A popular staple in grocery stores, processed cheese was advantageous because it did not spoil and was less expensive to produce. When melted, the product did not separate, run, or change texture, making it a popular ingredient for baked casseroles. One of the era's most famous processed cheese foods is Kraft's Cheez Whiz, a spreadable cheese product (containing very little actual cheese) popular as a snack, debuting in 1952. James L. Kraft, who holds the first patent for processed cheese, created what would become known as American cheese. His technique required the grinding of a variety of cheeses into quickly made, low-grade, cheese-like paste, adding salt and other ingredients and pasteurizing the resulting glop, resulting in a cheese with a long shelf life and an even, low-temperature melting point.[34]

Velveeta is the most famous brand of cheese food products. Writers have proclaimed Velveeta to be proof of the wondrous power of American food processing, noting it can be mixed into a casserole, melted, and even baked into fudge.[35] Velveeta was the product of New York's Monroe Cheese Company. Broken Swiss cheese wheels that came from the factory were unusable. In 1918 company officials sent the cheese to its in-house cheese maker, a Swiss immigrant named Emil Frey. (Yes, one might say it is ironic that a gentleman from Switzerland—a country known for its excellent artisan cheeses—was responsible for a cheese food product.) Frey discovered that he could create a stable, smooth, and silky effect by adding numerous products to the discarded cheese. Frey named it "Velveeta" because of its velvety consistency. Five years later, Kraft Foods purchased the Velveeta Cheese Company.

Unarguably, macaroni and cheese is one of the all-time most popular comfort foods. It is also a simple dish: a mixture of elbow macaroni—boiled to a very soft consistency—combined with a cheese sauce and baked. In 1937, an employee of Kraft recommended that Velveeta be added to a box of macaroni. A new product emerged, called Kraft Dinner. The dinner cost nineteen cents, cooked in nine minutes, and a box provided a hardy meal for a family of four. One cooked the packaged dried macaroni with the packet of processed cheese powder (Velveeta), leaving the cook to add butter, margarine, or milk and perhaps a topping of bread crumbs, if desired (or available). Made without dairy products or meat, only requiring water, with a shelf life estimated to be ten months, it was a popular item during World War II on the battlefield and domestically. (For only one food ration stamp, consumers received two boxes.)

For those who wished to make macaroni and cheese from scratch, many 1950s cookbooks provided recipes—most calling for boiled macaroni, American cheese (cooks knew that Velveeta was the best for melting), and perhaps the addition of a bit of milk or cream. Some called for a can of cream of mushroom soup, and others added minced onion, chopped green pepper, or a little paprika. Cookbook author Poppy Cannon (1951) advised making the dish based on canned macaroni and cheese. Likewise, Irma S. Rombauer, in the 1951 edition of *The Joy of Cooking*, suggests that canned macaroni in cream sauce with cheese is "a fine base to serve with other ingredients. Heat the macaroni, make a mound of it, surround it with a buttered vegetable and serve it with a meat or fish dish in place of potatoes."[36]

The following recipe from Michael Reise expands on the box macaroni and cheese dinner.

Packaged Macaroni Dinner

The 20 Minute Cookbook (1953)[37]

Put water for macaroni on to boil. Start broiler pre-heating to medium hot.

To prepare the macaroni: Boil as directed on package, adding a small onion to the water.

Drain, discarding onion.

Add:

1 tablespoon butter
1 teaspoon chopped parsley
¼ cup light cream or sour cream
salt and pepper

Mix macaroni with all ingredients, seasoning lightly with salt and pepper.

> *To season the cheese:* Taste cheese, If salt is needed, add up to ¼ teaspoon. If cheese seems to be too sharp for your taste, dilute it with very fine bread crumbs.
>
> *To serve:* Reserve 2 tablespoons cheese. Combine remainder of cheese with macaroni mixture and turn into a heatproof casserole. Mix 1 tablespoon bread crumbs with reserved cheese, sprinkle over macaroni, dot generously with butter, and brown under the broiler.
>
> 1 package serves 3 or 4

Reise, who was keen on the use of packaged foods, also provides a recipe for canned macaroni and cheese, noting, "If this product is available in your grocery, sharpen the flavor by turning into a casserole, heating in a moderate oven, and spreading liberally with grated or diced sharp Cheddar. Place under medium broiler heat for a few minutes, or until cheese bubbles slightly."[38]

Wonder Bread first appeared in the market in 1921, and in 1930 it was one of the first presliced loaves of bread. This technology was a noteworthy innovation for the time, leading to the famous phrase "the greatest thing since sliced bread." Unfortunately, during World War II, a shortage of steel used for the slicing machines required the manufacturer to revert to whole loaves and institute a new advertising campaign, "Lady! Sharpen Your Bread Knife." By 1945, the slicing machines were back in action. During the 1940s, Wonder Bread also added vitamins and minerals as part of a government-sponsored program for white bread for soldiers. In the 1950s, the company was advertising these enrichments via the popular television personalities Howdy Doody and host Buffalo Bob Smith, who informed audiences that "Wonder Bread builds bodies eight ways." (By the 1960s, this had expanded to twelve ways.) In the late 1950s, Wonder Bread unveiled an innovation by wrapping its bread in cellophane, intended to keep it soft and moist.[39]

Marshmallows are one of America's favorite foods, and they are sweet, sticky, and comforting. Marshmallows of the 1950s, and as we know them today, are not a natural product but a mixture of water, vanilla, sugar, and gelatin (or egg whites), all whipped together into a firm but pliable consistency. "Whoever would dream that marshmallows would be so good cooked up in a peanut-butter sandwich? Then there's chicken—it blends well with marshmallows, and they're in the recipe and atop it. And—most irresistible of all—make a delectable cake and decorate it with our marshmallow posies."[40]

An extrusion process developed in the 1950s meant that production was easier. A machine churned out the marshmallow into long strips, then cut them into the familiar marshmallow shape. The modern marshmallow was now available for mass consumption. The recipe has not changed very much: sugar, water, and a whipping agent (egg whites or gelatin). Although marshmallows are available in every grocery store, some cooks prefer to make their own using a mixture of corn syrup, sugar, and gelatin—all whipped together.

During the 1950s, desserts with marshmallows became a popular treat. Marshmallow is a sweet confection, and because the literature assumed young girls preferred sweet foods, one finds numerous recipes for marshmallows in cookbooks targeted at young girls. *The Betty Betz Teen-Age Cookbook* includes marshmallows for the ever-popular chocolate fudge bar. A dessert in *Miss B.'s First Cookbook* offers "Gypsies," a baked confection containing graham crackers, peanut butter, marshmallows, and Red Hots (cinnamon candies).

Cookbooks for adults also praised the marshmallow. For example, Lessie Bowers contributed a recipe for Marshmallow Chocolate Pudding, calling for three pounds of marshmallows to serve twenty-five people.[41] *Betty Crocker's Picture Cook Book* (1950) suggested Orange Marshmallow Cream and Pineapple Marshmallow Cream (store-bought marshmallows). *The General Foods Kitchens Cookbook* (1959) gave us Marshmallow Chocolate Drops, Marshmallow Fudge, and Cinnamon Marshmallows (also using store-bought marshmallows).

Perhaps the most popular method of eating marshmallows is roasting them over an outdoor campfire: the outside turns brown and crispy, and the inside becomes soft and gooey. In 1927 the Girl Scouts published a recipe for "Some More," known soon after as S'mores. This recipe is found in many cookbooks for boys and girls.

"Some More"

Tramping and Trailing with the Girl Scouts (1927)[42]

8 Sticks 16 graham crackers
8 bars plain chocolate (any of the good plain brands broken in two)
16 marshmallows

Toast two marshmallows over coals to a crisp gooey state and then put them inside a graham cracker and chocolate bar sandwich. The heat of the marshmallow between the halves of chocolate will melt the chocolate a bit. Though it tastes like "some more" one is really enough.

Baked sweet potatoes with marshmallows is a holiday favorite, often found on Thanksgiving tables.

BAKED SWEET POTATOES MARSHMALLOW

Jesse's Book of Creole and Deep South Recipes (1954)[43]

4 large or 8 small sweet potatoes
1½ tablespoons sugar
1½ cups sweet milk
2 teaspoons cinnamon
¼ lb. butter
2 eggs, well beaten
Pinch of salt
1 package marshmallows

Boil the potatoes until soft, let them cool, peel them, and mash them in a bowl. Add milk, butter, salt, and sugar, stirring until fluffy. Add cinnamon and eggs. Mix well, place in a large Pyrex dish, and bake in a 350° oven until brown. Take out, cover with marshmallows, and brown quickly in the broiler. If you haven't a very large baking dish, you may have to use two smaller ones. Serves 7 to 8.

Author Mimi Graney has noted that Marshmallow Fluff has been around for one hundred years, "Everyone can associate it with their own childhood. The packaging hasn't changed very much, people feel that sense of familiarity. It's got that patriotic red, white, and blue label so it feels very American."[44] Never Fail Fudge, which has appeared continuously on the Fluff label since 1956, is another classic Marshmallow Fluff delicacy. Mamie Eisenhower (1896–1979), first lady of the United States, is said to have created the original recipe. (Other Fluff products, such as Kraft's

Jet-Puffed Marshmallow Creme and Kroger's Marshmallow Crème, also offer similar versions of Eisenhower's recipe.) The following is Mamie's original recipe.

Mamie's Million Dollar Fudge

Eisenhower Presidential Library[45]

4½ cups sugar
Pinch of salt
2 tablespoons butter
1 tall can evaporated milk
12 ounces semi-sweet chocolate bits
12 ounces German-sweet chocolate
1 pint marshmallow cream
2 cups nutmeats

Boil the sugar, salt, butter, evaporated milk together for six minutes

Put chocolate bits and German chocolate, marshmallow cream and nutmeats in a bowl. Pour the boiling syrup over the ingredients. Beat until chocolate is all melted, then pour in pan. Let stand a few hours before cutting. Remember it is better the second day. Store in tin box.

The last words for this chapter on processed foods belong to noted food writer M. F. K. Fisher, in her foreword to Jane and Michael Stern's *Square Meals* (1985). "Once I went to a potluck supper for the 4-H club my children belonged to, and seventeen of the twenty women on the Food Committee brought quivering green and pink molded 'salads' striped with marshmallows and store-bought mayonnaise. Their hardworking rancher husbands circled the three tuna-noodle casseroles like hungry coyotes until the desserts of packaged cake mixes heaped with aerosol Fudge Whippo were served forth."[46]

Chapter 6

SPAM® and Jell-O Tell Their Stories While We Sit Back and Enjoy a Cola

The 1950s American Diet, Part II

The production of processed foods to feed troops during World War II and later to provide sustenance to nations rebuilding after the war proved to be an economic boom to many US industries. At war's end, these companies were in no mood or rush to discontinue production that had been so profitable, so they brought war-inspired food processing techniques to the consumer. From the beginning of the twentieth century, when the industry first offered processed foods to the public, the products had several drawbacks: the foods themselves were unfamiliar to most families, they didn't always taste delicious, and perhaps most importantly they required that women change their cooking habits, which previously involved cooking a meal from scratch. Therefore, it was necessary for advertising campaigns to promote and explain the benefits of the new modern foods.

While the availability of processed foods made it possible for more people to purchase a wider variety of foods that didn't spoil as quickly, these newly created foods lacked taste and visual appeal. The industry made up for this by adding salt, sweeteners, food coloring, and other preservatives to make the foods uniform in flavor and presentation. By the end of World War II and after nearly fifty years of consuming industrialized foods, a food historian notes that "there wasn't much the food industry could do to repel a nation that was already stirring chopped tomatoes and pickles into strawberry Jell-O for a Red Crest Salad."[1]

SPAM®, Jell-O, and Carbonated Drinks Demonstrate Their Versatility

Two of the most versatile and popular processed foods during the 1950s were SPAM® and Jell-O. SPAM® could be eaten on its own—hot or cold—and as part of breakfast, lunch, and dinner recipes. SPAM® was a popular casserole staple and a common ingredient for outdoor barbecued shish kabobs, and during World War II SPAM® was associated with the military, feeding hungry men. Jell-O graced many a 1950s table, appearing as a salad that might include chopped vegetables or as a dessert mixed with canned fruit and whipped cream. Sometimes it was used to make frosting for cakes or eaten just plain. Consumers considered Jell-O a feminine dish, and it usually was eschewed by men ("many men scorn a dish made with gelatin").[2]

Like SPAM® and Jell-O, carbonated beverages of the era were highly adaptable yet ungendered, appreciated by both men and women. Enjoyed right out of the bottle or at the local soda fountain, these beverages were also used as ingredients in cakes or as a glaze or marinade for meat. Often the beverages replaced some or all the liquid required to make Jell-O. Carbonated beverages were used to top off alcoholic drinks, such as a Tom Collins, or poured over scoops of ice cream, such as root beer over vanilla, creating a popular delight called Brown (or Black) Cow. These carbonated beverages became customary as mixers in alcoholic cocktails, such as a Cuba Libre (rum, lime, cola); Horse's Neck (lemon, gin or whiskey, ginger ale), and one of the 1950s favorite mixed drinks, the Whiskey Sour (powdered sugar, lemon and lime juice, rye whiskey, and club soda).

More about Canned Food: SPAM®

Ode to Spam

We've had it tucked in salads,
With cabbage for corned beef.
We've had it for an entrée
And also aperitif.
We've had it with spaghetti,
With chili and with rice.

(We all remember one bright day
We had it only twice.)³

In 1937, the Hormel company marketed precooked, processed luncheon meat known as SPAM®. Jay Hormel created the product out of pork shoulder, an undesired and unprofitable cut of meat during the 1930s. Throughout World War II, US and Allied troops relied heavily on this canned meat. After the war, the US continued to export it to a rebuilding and hungry Europe as part of its postwar initiatives such as the Marshall Plan. SPAM® continues to be popular in many countries today, despite the observation from *The New York Times* columnist that this "gelatinous 12-oz rectangle of spiced ham and pork may be among the world's most maligned foods."⁴ The origins of its name are vague and often sarcastic, for example, **s**cientifically **p**rocessed **a**nimal **m**atter or **s**omething **p**osing **a**s **m**eat. (In the UK, SPAM® was known as **s**pecial **p**rocessed **A**merican **m**eat; in Russia, it was known as Roosevelt sausage.)

After its initial introduction in 1937, sales for SPAM® were slow because people did not believe canned meat was safe. However, within a brief time, dozens of different brands of canned luncheon meat hit the market. To counteract the competition, Jay Hormel began to sell SPAM® in the now highly recognizable shape and with a name that could be trademarked. But he needed a name, so Hormel hosted a party and offered a reward for the best name. Kenneth Daigneau, brother of a Hormel vice president, won one hundred dollars for coining the term "SPAM," meaning spiced ham or shoulder of pork and ham. (Although this story has been circulating for decades, author Carolyn Wyman claims the Hormel company disagrees with this interpretation.) Many competitors quickly went out of business, and SPAM® persevered because of its quality and price point: it was economical and within reach for families of all income levels. Hormel heavily advertised SPAM®, reaching as many potential buyers as possible. For example, the company hired one of the most famous acts in the country, the comedy team of George Burns and Gracie Allen, and composer and bandleader Artie Shaw and his orchestra. In one advertisement, George asks Gracie, "If all your relatives dropped in for dinner, what would you say?" Gracie replies, "SPAM!"⁵

Magazines published recipes for using SPAM® for breakfast, luncheon, and dinner. For example, in June 1954, a Del Monte ad in the magazine *Women's Home Companion* provided a luncheon or dinner recipe for a SPAM® Loaf that included unflavored gelatin, Del Monte fruit cocktail, two (12-oz)

Figure 6.1. Canned luncheon meat is elevated to a fancy meal in "Crown Roast Dinner." The center of the roast is potatoes rolled in parsley. The roast is flanked with asparagus, covered in a quick hollandaise sauce. Slices of pineapple topped with strawberries are tucked between the asparagus. *Better Homes and Gardens New Cook Book*, 1953. Used by permission of Meredith Corporation. Source: Author's collection.

cans of SPAM®, green olives, celery, and Miracle Whip. The July 1956 issue of *Good Housekeeping* suggested a quick dinner menu of sautéed SPAM® to highlight the era's emphasis on quick meals using processed foods. The meal also included instant mashed potatoes, frozen vegetables, and a fruit trifle created from a can of fruit cocktail, sponge cake, and instant vanilla pudding. Often, SPAM® and Jell-O were combined to make a single dish.

At the beginning of the US entry into World War II, the Hormel company shipped four million SPAM® cans to the US government. This volume increased to over fifteen million cans per week at the height of the war. Soldiers and the general population in England, Russia, and Italy also regularly received cartons of SPAM®. One of its main benefits is that SPAM® can be heated or eaten cold right out of the can. One cannot overstate the importance of this product to feed both military and civilian personnel during World War II. Nikita Khrushchev noted in his biography, "We had lost our most fertile food-bearing lands—the Ukraine and the Northern Caucasus. Without Spam we wouldn't have been able to feed our army."[6] Another SPAM® recipient, Mrs. Amelia A. Garret of London, enthusiastically endorsed the product as "the best tinned food that I've tasted in two wars. It's 100 percent nourishment—and tasty."[7] By the end of the war, Hormel had shipped one hundred million cans overseas.

By 1944, Allied forces received 90 percent of Hormel's canned meat. Soldiers consumed all things SPAM®, including soups, salads, meatballs, and fritters, as well as combinations mixed with dehydrated potatoes or dehydrated eggs. There was so much SPAM® that soldiers referred to Uncle Sam as "Uncle Spam," and the European invasion fleet was known as the "Spam fleet." SPAM® was considered "ham that did not pass its physical," "meatloaf without basic training," and "special Army meat."[8] Metal SPAM® cans turned into cooking pots or even makeshift stills for alcohol production. Leftover SPAM® grease was utilized as a lubricant for artillery and as a sort of skin conditioner. Other companies also provided their versions of canned meat to the military, often made with inferior and questionable animal parts. However, SPAM® had the most recognized name; therefore, all canned meat was known as SPAM®. By the end of the war, some viewed SPAM® as everything that is wrong with American processed food, and on first inspection, it is not so appetizing, seemingly just a pinkish lump of salted, oily pork product. Its nutritional value is suspect, and it is high in calories, fat, and sodium. Still, to many, and when prepared properly, it is a treat.

The Hormel Girls, aka the "Spamettes"

When GIs returned home after the war, they were unenthusiastic about eating more SPAM®. Sales plummeted, and the Hormel company began looking for ways to counteract this trend. During the summer of 1946, Jay Hormel established the all-female American Legion SPAM® Post 570 in Austin, Minnesota, headquarters of George A. Hormel and Company, and he began recruiting former servicewomen who displayed some musical ability and a knack for sales. By July 1947, Hormel had recruited fifty-six white females for an act that would become the Hormel Girls Drum and Bugle Corps (known informally as the Spamettes). The troupe entered the all-male twenty-ninth American Legion National Drum and Bugle Corps championship competition one month later. The Hormel Girls placed a respectable thirteenth out of forty-nine groups.

The Hormel company decided to start a radio show and recruited more women the following year. Authors Jill M. Sullivan and Danielle D. Keck note that the musical ensemble consisted of brass instruments, woodwinds, a set of drums, and an accordion.[9] The radio show was first broadcast on March 20, 1948, from station KHF in Los Angeles and quickly caught public attention. Two months later, twenty stations carried the Sunday evening show. During the week, the Hormel Girls formed a convoy that went from town to town to sell Hormel products.

By the 1950s, the Hormel company abolished the requirement for a Hormel Girl to be a veteran of World War II and expanded the radio program. After recording the radio show, some Spamettes would change into costumes for a stage show. This musical act, performed for the in-house radio audience, usually began with the song "George Hormel Had a Farm" with the Hormel Girls wearing barn animal masks ("ee-i-ee-i-oh"). In 1951, the show presented a glossy program for its radio audience, depicting Hormel products in full color and featuring the performers wearing more revealing costumes. While the radio show enjoyed great success, it did not translate well into America's new medium of television. In 1953, the Hormel Girls disbanded, and Hormel moved to more traditional avenues for advertising, including magazine ads that featured SPAM® recipes.

SPAM® was always available, even for breakfast. And just like SPAM® and Jell-O, it was common for two different products to join forces so companies could market their merchandise, in this case, Hormel's SPAM® and Betty Crocker's Bisquick.

NEW WITH SPAM! NEW WITH BISQUICK!

"SPAM CAKES"![10]

Bisquick's going to help you more than any other package in the grocery store . . .

[signed] Betty Crocker.

SPAM bakes right in the middle: This is fun! Both in the making and the eating. The folks'll love these tender golden Bisquick pancakes . . . each one centered with a sizzling slice of SPAM.

Here's how you do it:

Make Bisquick pancake batter (directions on box)

Brown SPAM slices on griddle . . . 2 to 3 inches apart.

Turn SPAM slices . . . pour batter over each slice. Turn again . . . And there you are, with big hungry-size pancakes . . . a savory SPAM slice baked right in the middle.

In 1959 Hormel announced that it had sold its one billionth can of SPAM®. As part of a four-color print ad celebrating the milestone, Hormel provided a new recipe as well as instructions and a form to fill out for a vacation sweepstakes promotion. The advertisement noted, "1,000,000,000 cans of SPAM! Enough to reach around the world 2½ times! That's how many cans of this internationally popular meat have been produced to date. SPAM is sold, loved, used in famous native dishes in dozens of foreign countries. It's the world's most famous meat." Perhaps it is fitting that Hormel's "around the world" meal is a casserole—the most beloved and traditional of 1950s American dishes. As with many of the era's other recipes, this one is also anchored with a can of Campbell's Cream of Mushroom soup, making the dish an authentic American meal.

SPAM "Around the World" Dinner Casserole (1959)

Four-color print ad published in major magazines[11]

Exciting one-dish meal especially developed for SPAM "Billion Can Festival"!

Try it for a dinner that's quick, easy, and *good*.

COOK and drain 1-8 oz pkg egg noodles

SPREAD in broad, shallow 2-qt casserole.

TOP with 1-lb can French-style green beans, drained, 1 can SPAM sliced and cut in ½" strips.

Pour over all 1 can Cream of Mushroom soup, mixed with ½ can ¾ cup milk and 3 tbsp. Worcestershire sauce

TOP with crisp cracker crumbs. BAKE at 350° 30 minutes.

Egg and SPAM® Et Cetera Abroad

In London during World War II, Edward R. Murrow, a famed American correspondent, reported that Christmas dinner "will not be lavish, but there will be SPAM for everyone."[12] During the postwar rebuilding of Europe, the US sent large quantities of SPAM® and other canned meat products to the UK. To reminisce about this dark era of British food, the BBC television program *Monty Python's Flying Circus* ran a short comedy sketch in 1970 about the prevalence of SPAM® during the war years. The sketch is situated in a café where almost every item on the menu includes SPAM® (egg and SPAM®; egg, bacon, and SPAM®; egg, bacon, sausage, and SPAM®, etc.). A chorus of Vikings occasionally drowns out the dialogue throughout the sketch with a boisterous song, "SPAM, SPAM, SPAM, SPAM . . . Lovely SPAM! Wonderful SPAM!" The skit has become a classic, which can be viewed on the Internet, eventually giving birth to the term *spam*, meaning unwanted and unsolicited junk email. Thus, spam lives on—still annoying even if one does not have to eat it.[13]

SPAM® Appropriates the Foreign Enemy

During the Cold War and despite the ongoing fear of the communist USSR, suburban-cooked meals such as beef stroganoff—or any dish that utilized Russian words or names such as "stroganoff" or "Romanoff"—were considered by many residents of suburbia to be gourmet foods.

SPAM 'N NOODLES ROMANOFF

Four-color SPAM advertisement from *Good Housekeeping*, May 1959[14]

SPAM-dandy oven dinner. Gourmet Flavor . . . on a budget!

Mix together: 1 cup cottage cheese, 1 cup sour cream, 2 cups drained hot boiled noodles (cook 5 to 6 oz.). Add 1 can SPAM sliced, cut in 1" squares. Season with: minced onion, garlic, Worcestershire sauce, dash of Tabasco and ½ tsp. salt. Place in greased 2 qt casserole (8"). Sprinkle with grated cheese. Bake at 350° for 40 minutes. Serve Hot.

Dwight D. Eisenhower has the last word on SPAM®. As the supreme commander of the Allied Expeditionary Force in Europe during World War II, Eisenhower certainly knew a thing or two about SPAM®. In 1966, Eisenhower wrote a letter to a retired Hormel executive, noting, "During World War II, of course, I ate my share of Spam along with millions of other soldiers. I'll even confess to a few unkind remarks about it—uttered during the strain of battle, you understand. But as former Commander-in-Chief, I believe I can still officially forgive you your only sin: sending us so much of it."[15]

Following the war, SPAM® became extremely popular in parts of the world where US troops had been stationed, especially Guam, the Philippines, Hawaii, and Okinawa. For example, in the twenty-first century, restaurants in Hawaii offer SPAM® in ramen noodle soup and, most commonly, in sushi known as *musubi*. The McDonald's in Saipan offers SPAM® burgers. In 2007, Hormel sold the seventh billion can of SPAM®.

Jell-O Tells Its Story

What makes the Jell-O salad such an icon if its time? Shaped by the rise of home economics, the industrialization of the food system, World War II, and changing expectations about women's labor, few foods can tell us more about life in 20th-century America than the wobbling jewel of domestic achievement: the Jell-O salad.

—Sarah Grey (2018)[16]

Gelatin salads and desserts were not new in the 1950s, as gelatin had been popular before the eighteenth century. Through the decades, recipes often detail the painstaking effort required to produce gelatin. Mrs. Child's *The American Frugal Housewife*, published in Boston in 1833, describes the technique as first boiling four calf's feet, letting the substance cool, and skimming off the fat. Then one adds wine, sugar, egg whites, some spices, and lemon juice. These ingredients are all boiled and strained into glasses or jars. Some recipes note that this process might take more than twenty-four hours.

After watching his wife struggle with making gelatin from scratch, Charles B. Knox developed a granulated form of gelatin in 1894. He packaged the product and sent out door-to-door salespeople charged with explaining how to use it. Knox promoted the product at the Louisiana Purchase Exposition 1904 (known as the St. Louis World's Fair), and he sponsored a Knox cooking contest the following year. Mrs. John Cooke of New Castle, Pennsylvania, placed third with a gelatin salad called "Perfection Salad." This winning salad turned out to be an aspic made with Knox unflavored gelatin with finely chopped cabbage, celery, and red pepper. The success of this simple recipe began a chain reaction of popularity for serving molded gelatin salads and desserts. Noted chef and author James Beard caustically remarked that Mrs. Cooke's triumph "unleashed a demand for congealed salads that has grown alarmingly, particularly in the suburbs." He sarcastically listed "outlandish" 1950s salads, including "Butterfly Salad, Candlelight Salad, and Santa Claus Salad. They prevailed at luncheons and dinner parties and were served up covered with appalling sweet dressings and decorated with maraschino cherries."[17]

In 1895, Pearle Wait, a carpenter from Leroy, New York, whose side business was the formulation and patenting of medicines, was credited as the first to add color and flavor to granular gelatin. As with Charles Knox, Wait sold his raspberry, lemon, orange, and strawberry flavored

Jell-O door-to-door for about two years. (Jell-O was the name given to the product by his wife, May.) After two years, lacking in business acumen and marketing skills, Wait sold his interest and the Jell-O name to Orator Frank Woodward, owner of the Genesee Pure Food Company in upstate New York. By 1902, Woodward was aggressively promoting Jell-O, and annual sales jumped. Woodward's company began to circulate pamphlets with recipes in 1904, and in 1923 the Genesee Pure Food Company changed its name to the Jell-O Company, celebrating the company's signature product. In 1925 Jell-O was acquired by the Postum Cereal Company (later to become General Foods Corporation, which, in turn, merged with Kraft Foods in the late 1980s). John L. and Karen Hess noted the steady decline of taste that began during the latter part of the nineteenth century and harshly judged the growing affection for Jell-O as the "sugary, gummy messes, chock full of synthetic flavors and colors, [that have] blanked the country."[18]

Sugar rationing during World War II constrained the manufacture of Jell-O. One of the benefits of Jell-O was that it already contained sugar and did not require anything except water. Thus, when it was available, Jell-O did not require using valuable ration points for sugar during the war. Production and purchases resumed with vigor once sugar became available to industries in June 1947. The postwar production of refrigerators also helped generate sales. With refrigeration, gelatin salads and desserts could be held at a consistently cool temperature.

Tomato aspic (as well as shrimp, chicken, and even canned clam aspics) made with unflavored gelatin was a popular luncheon dish during the 1950s. Most mainstream cookbooks published during the late 1940s and 1950s offer recipes for creating dishes out of both unflavored and flavored gelatins. The creator of *River Road Recipes* (1959) provided a recipe for an aspic-based salad, the Tomato Soup Salad. The recipe's title noted, "Men like it." From their earliest days, gelatin salads and desserts were considered feminine, and men often had to be reassured that everybody understood that it was not a masculine food.

Canned cherries played a prominent role in Jell-O salads, and *Better Homes and Gardens New Cook Book* (1953) has a recipe that consists of canned cherries, orange-flavored gelatin, pecans, and a bottle of stuffed olives. Stuffed olives added to canned cherries is a bit unnerving, but this combination often appears, including a recipe for Bing Cherry Salad in *Peggy Put the Kettle On* (1951). A Texas twist on a black cherry Jell-O salad has no olives but calls for one cup of port to replace one of two cups of liquid.

Cherry Coke Salad

Gourmet of the Delta (1958)[19]

2 pkg. Cherry Jello
2 bottles Coca Cola
1 No. 2 can crushed pineapple
1 c. pecans, chopped
1 No. 303 can black cherries
2 c. juice

Dissolve Jello in hot juice drained from pineapple and cherries; then add Coca Cola. When Jello starts to jell, stir in pineapple, quartered cherries and pecans. Chill in refrigerator. Serves 16.

Some recipes suggest the addition of a tablespoon of brandy or sherry to selected Jell-O salads or desserts. Sometimes the addition of alcohol would not seem to improve the dish's taste. For example, *Peggy Put the Kettle On* provides a recipe for a Burgundy Salad Ring of canned pineapple, lime-flavored gelatin, and one cup of burgundy wine. Another somewhat horrifying combination in Poppy Cannon's *The Bride's Cookbook* (1954) called for lime gelatin, green crème de menthe, peppermint, or spearmint flavoring, served with canned plums. Serving instructions for this peculiar dessert note, "Pass the liqueur bottle for those who would add."[20] (It is hard to imagine that extra crème de menthe would improve this dessert.) A more palatable use of alcohol might be the addition of a tiny bit of sherry to a Gelatin Cream Charlotte: orange-flavor gelatin, ladyfingers, and whipped cream topped with pecans or a maraschino cherry. This recipe can be found in Gwen French's *Anybody Can Cook* (1954), a volume that provides more than twenty pages of instructions for every sort of imaginable gelatin salad or dessert (well, some unimaginable, too).

The era's popular appliances also were touted as aids in making gelatin dishes. *Mary Meade's Magic Recipes for the Electric Blender* (1952) devotes a chapter to "salads, blender-made" with seventeen molded salads or desserts, ranging from Chicken Salad in Sherry Aspic to Ham and Potato Salad Loaf—gelatin salads created with an electric blender.

Other popular flavored gelatins included lime or lemon, usually mixed with cream cheese or cottage cheese and enhanced with shredded carrots and crushed pineapple. However, if these recipes did not suit your creativity, one might try lemon-flavored gelatin and red kidney beans or lemon-flavored gelatin and cooked peas, sliced raw mushrooms, sliced cooked sweetbreads, and two or three sliced smoked oysters. This rather odd concoction was served with mayonnaise mixed with cocktail sauce.[21]

During the 1950s, Jell-O executives took note of the growing popularity of dinner and luncheon salads. They added savory flavors such as celery, Italian seasoning, and tomato, alongside the regulars: strawberry, raspberry, orange, lemon, and lime. The savory flavors were not popular and soon disappeared. Other flavors that vanished in the 1950s include apple, grape, orange-banana, and pineapple-grapefruit. However, during the 1950s, the Jell-O family grew to include Jell-O tapioca pudding in vanilla, orange coconut, and chocolate, as well as instant puddings and pie filling, which included lemon, coconut cream, vanilla, chocolate, and butterscotch. One simply added liquid and cooked it on the stovetop for pudding and pie fillings. Michael Reise's *The 20 Minute Cookbook* (1953), which has no recipes using gelatin because it requires more than twenty minutes, devotes a section to "cooked-pudding desserts," all of which, of course, take twenty minutes or less to create. To keep to his twenty-minute maximum and if the pudding needed cooling, he suggested placing it in the refrigerator or freezer, thus cutting time. The following recipe is Reise's adaptation of packaged butterscotch pudding, which he claims requires a mere ten minutes to prepare.

BUTTERSCOTCH PUDDING

The 20 Minute Cookbook (1953)[22]

1 package butterscotch pudding mix
2 teaspoons butter
Milk for liquid ¼ teaspoon
maple flavoring
Few grains of salt
2 drops brandy extract

Measure liquid into a saucepan (see package for quantity), add pudding mix and salt; beat lightly to mix. Cook as directed on package. After removing from heat add butter and flavoring, beat briskly with a rotary beater. Pudding is ready when slightly cooled. Serves 4 to 6.

Jell-O: A Quivering Mound of Flavored Gelatin or an Accomplice to Treason?

One of the critical pieces of evidence used against Julius and Ethel Rosenberg, who were tried for treason against the United States of America in 1951, turned out to be a label torn from a box of Jell-O.

The alleged scene has been described as follows: "Julius took a Jell-O box from the kitchen cabinet, removed the contents, and cut the side panel of the box into two irregularly shaped pieces. One he kept, the other he gave to Ruth, who took it into the living room to show her husband. David [David Greenglass, Ethel's brother] would later testify that he remarked on what a clever idea the Jell-O box was and Julius, obviously pleased, replied, 'The simplest things are the cleverest.'"[23] Julius allegedly gave half to Greenglass and half to a courier to identify each other. Roy Cohn, who later served as chief counsel to Senator Joseph McCarthy's House Un-American Activities Committee (HUAC), went to a grocery store to purchase a box of Jell-O as a prop to show to the jury. Cohn asked Greenglass to demonstrate how Julius utilized the Jell-O package. Greenglass cut the flap of the carton, and the box entered into evidence. (Greenglass had, at that point, turned state's witness, but in 2001 he admitted to having perjured himself to protect his wife and to save himself.) Assistant US Attorney and Chief Prosecutor Irving Saypol argued that the box of Jell-O "forged the necessary link in the chain that points indisputably to the guilt of the Rosenbergs."[24]

In the end, the Rosenbergs were convicted of passing top-secret information to the Soviet Union and, after a failed appeal to the US Supreme Court, were executed on June 20, 1953. Roy Cohn's Jell-O box prop is housed in the National Archives and Records Administration in Washington, DC. A box prop also is displayed in Washington DC's International Spy Museum.

In *Jell-O: A Biography*, author Carolyn Wyman suggests that beyond serving as a popular food, Jell-O plays an important position in America's history and culture.[25] This history and culture include the dark days of Julius and Ethel Rosenberg's trial and subsequent execution for treason, as well as the light-hearted jokes about Jell-O, which continue to this day. To celebrate Jell-O, the Smithsonian National Museum of American History hosted a pseudo-academic and humorous conference in 1991 that focused on Jell-O in American history. The Jell-O Museum opened in Leroy, New York, in 1997, and in 2001 Jell-O was named the official snack food of the state of Utah. During the 1950s, Jell-O salads and desserts were universal. Today they often are viewed as a relic, akin to Mrs. Cooke's 1905 Perfection Salad: "a once-loved dish safely congealed in the decorative mold of history."[26]

After a Meal of SPAM® and Jell-O, Now I Am Really Thirsty

The 1950s may be known as the Decade of Conformity and the Nifty Fifties, but the era is also known as the golden age of Coca-Cola.[27] Originally intended as a patent medicine in the late nineteenth century, Coca-Cola, a sweet, carbonated drink, was shrewdly and widely marketed. By the mid-twentieth century, Coca-Cola had become the beverage of choice for the entire family to drink, especially while watching television. Author Sidra Sitch wrote that this beverage "affirmed the glories of capitalism in the face of communism."[28] In an unprecedented cover photo that displayed a consumer product, *Time* magazine, which had previously always celebrated people on its covers, proclaimed in its May 15, 1950 issue that Coca-Cola "is simpler, sharper evidence than the Marshall Plan or a Voice of America broadcast that the U.S. has gone out into the world to stay."[29]

Flavored soft drinks often were the result of pharmaceutical experimentations. During the 1880s, an Atlanta druggist, John Stith Pemberton, began looking for a beverage that might be used for medicinal purposes. In 1884, he started distributing a medicinal drink known as Pemberton's French Wine Coca, but new temperance legislation prevented the use of alcohol, so he was forced to cease production. By 1886 he created a new medicine, claiming it worked as a nerve stimulant for high-strung women and for headaches, indigestion, impotence, and morphine addiction. (As a Civil War veteran, Pemberton himself was addicted to morphine.)[30] The medicine consisted of sugar and coca leaves and kola nut extract—sources of cocaine and caffeine.[31]

A year later, Pemberton mixed his syrup with soda water. Willis Venable bought the company after Pemberton's health declined and boastfully claimed his mixture was a "brain tonic and intellectual soda fountain beverage." After Pemberton died in 1888, another druggist, Asa Candler, obtained the rights to the formula. Within the year, Coca-Cola was a soda fountain drink. Candler was not interested in bottling the product, so he gave Benjamin Thomas and Joseph Whitehead the bottling rights. However, the Women's Christian Temperance Union and other similar organizations

Figure 6.2. Teens ordering food from a drive-through restaurant, magazine advertisement for Coca Cola, c. 1959. Source: f8 archive/Alamy Stock Photo.

protested the use of cocaine in the product. While the company limited the amount of cocaine, it was unable to remove it until 1913, when it changed the ingredient to "spent coca leaves"—which are still used today. However, the product continued to contain caffeine, and in proclaiming it to be unhealthy for both children and adults, "food faddists and temperance women fought against Coca-Cola."[32] World War II disrupted the success of the soft drink industry. Sugar rationing threatened to shut down nonessential businesses. Still, Coca-Cola received government contracts for the military and was thus able to continue production throughout the war. Coca-Cola executives advertised their product as "a symbol of our way of living."[33] A soldier enthusiastically noted, "It's things such as this that all of us are fighting for."[34]

Challengers to Coca-Cola: Other Popular Carbonated Drinks

While Coca-Cola may have been the most popular soda at mid-century, 7 Up was in the early stages of a massive advertising campaign by the late 1940s. The advertising focus was selling 7 Up as the "all family drink." This campaign is one of the best examples of Cold War advertising that supported and echoed the storybook ideal of the nuclear family in suburban life. 7 Up not only advertised the excellence and purity of its product, but its ads always pictured a romanticized family, and like the beverage itself, the family was wholesome and pure.

In 1929, Charles Leiper Grigg of St. Louis created and marketed a soft drink with the clumsy name "Bib-Label Lithiated Lemon-Lime Soda." (The product did include lithium citrate, a trace element found in rocks and natural spring water. Often used to treat mental illness, it is a controlled drug.) Grigg soon dispensed with the long name and called his soft drink 7 Up and advertised it as "seven natural flavors blended into a savory, flavory drink with a real wallop."[35] 7 Up's arrival just after Prohibition ended was fortuitous and it was marketed as a mixer for alcoholic drinks. Sales soared, and by the mid-1940s it was the third-bestselling soft drink in the world.[36] A 1953 print advertisement that appeared in numerous magazines noted, "Cake mixes taste better made with 7-Up." One was instructed to simply "follow the directions on the package of prepared cake mix. Use 7-Up instead of the liquid in the recipe." The advertisement suggested that this would work with any kind of packaged cake mix: white, yellow, spice, and chocolate. The ad also suggested that cooks should "keep a bottle of 7-Up handy to sip while you're cooking!"

Pepsi-Cola

The Pepsi-Cola origin story is another example of a druggist creating a beverage for local soda fountains. In 1893, Caleb Bradham of New Bern, North Carolina, produced a popular beverage known as "Brad's drink." In

Figure 6.3. Nikita Khrushchev enjoys a Pepsi Cola, poured by the Pepsi-Cola Company chairman Donald M. Kendall. Vice President Richard Nixon intently looks on. American National Exhibition, Moscow, 1959. Source: Heritage Image Partnership Ltd/Alamy Stock Photo.

1898 he changed the name to Pepsi-Cola. By 1893, his mixture of sugar, water, caramel, lemon oil, kola nuts, nutmeg, and pepsin—an enzyme that aids in digestion—was selling to drug stores and other locations throughout North Carolina. Fifteen years later, Bradham's soda was sold in twenty-four states. Due to sugar procurement and missteps made by Bradham during World War I, Pepsi-Cola went bankrupt in 1922.

Charles Cuth, president of the Loft Candy Company, procured Pepsi-Cola in the early 1930s. The formula for Pepsi changed, eliminating pepsin, and Cuth began to organize bottling operations. By the late 1930s, Pepsi's net earnings had risen to more than $5.5 million.[37] Cuth wrongly believed he held the rights to Pepsi, and upon leaving Loft Candy Company, he took the product with him. After a lawsuit, financier Walter Mack took control from Cuth.

World War II significantly shook the soft drink industry, including Pepsi-Cola, whose worldwide operations were interrupted in countries invaded by Germany and Japan. Learning from mistakes made about sugar rationing during World War I, Pepsi-Cola set up a plant in Mexico that allowed it to fulfill its contracts with the US military. After the war and the end of sugar rations, Pepsi-Cola expanded its sales throughout Europe and Latin America.

In 1959 Nikita Khrushchev, leader of the USSR, and Vice President Richard Nixon were photographed drinking Pepsi-Cola at the American National Exhibition in Moscow's Sokolniki Park. They were standing in the kitchen of a model home, where the two leaders discussed the merits of democracy versus communism in an event later called the Kitchen Debate, a debate that is considered a turning point in the Cold War.

Ginger Ale

Initially, this carbonated beverage came in two forms: a golden style credited to Thomas Joseph Cantrell, an Irish doctor, and a pale style with a much milder ginger flavor, credited to Canadian citizen John McLaughlin. Commercial ginger ale is made of carbonated water, sugar, artificial or natural ginger, lemon, and lime flavorings.

Author Ruth Tobias points out that US pharmacists invented the soda fountain, which initially sold soda water for health benefits. Soda fountains soon became a meeting place for patrons who drank for pleasure rather than for health.[38] Ginger ale's acceptance was such that it was one of the most popular carbonated beverages until the 1940s—not only for drinking at the soda fountain but also as a popular cocktail mixer. By the 1950s, Coca-Cola and Pepsi-Cola dominated the market through ads that touted colas as a drink for youth—ginger ale was considered quaint and old world. However, ginger ale was an ideal mixer for hard liquor cocktails, nonalcoholic beverages, and popular Jell-O salads.

Figure 6.4. Canada Dry Ginger Ale and Club Soda are advertised to adults as mixers for alcoholic beverages, c. 1950s. Source: Neil Baylis/Alamy Stock Photo.

Arctic Cooler

a guide to pink elephants (1952)[39]

1½ oz. Rye or Bourbon
1 orange
Ginger ale

Cut off skin of orange into shaker. Add the juice of the orange; 1½ oz of Rye or Bourbon whiskey. Shake with ice and strain into a tall glass. Fill up with ginger ale.

Gingerale Salad

Loyalty Cook Book: Native Daughters of the Golden West (1953)[40]

Ingredients:

1 small can grated pineapple (drained)
8 diced marshmallows
1 cup finely chopped cabbage
1 package lemon jello
½ cup pineapple juice
1½ cups ginger ale

Method: Heat pineapple juice and pour over jello. Cool. Add pineapple, cabbage, and marshmallows. Add ginger ale last and mix well. Pour in flat dish or molds. Set in icebox to thicken.

Root Beer

A popular beverage since the eighteenth century, root beer can be made from many different plants and spices, including roots and bark, such as from the birch tree. Other ingredients include flower buds and leaves from wintergreen or sassafras, sarsaparilla vines, and flavorings such as vanilla, wild cherry, ginger, nutmeg, and cinnamon. Andrew F. Smith notes that the earliest known commercial version of root beer was available in 1850 in a syrup mixed with soda water, although it was (and often still is) made at home. One of the original brands was Hires Root Beer created by Charles E. Hires. Hires Root Beer Household Extract was exhibited at the Centennial Exposition in Philadelphia in 1876 and advertised as "the national temperance drink" and "the greatest health-giving beverage in the world." Other noted brands included Barq's, available at the end of the nineteenth century, and A&W (1919). Roy Allen and Frank Write opened A&W stands throughout California, Utah, and Texas. Eventually, A&W was franchised and became one of the earliest fast-food chains in the US. Some A&W stands were fashioned as drive-ins, featuring carhops, who brought orders directly to customers in their cars.[41] *The Boys' Cook Book* (1959) notes, "Nothing tastes better on a hot day than a long cold one." The straightforward instructions for a root beer float are to place two scoops of vanilla ice cream in a tall glass and fill it up with cold root beer. "Stir and sip."[42]

Seltzer

Often referred to as soda water or charged water, seltzer is an artificially carbonated beverage and is the only carbonated beverage that contains no added flavor extracts. The name originates from Niederselters, a German location known for naturally carbonated mineral water springs. It was exported to the US as early as the eighteenth century, but the cost of importing the water became prohibitive. "Seltzer," utilizing artificially carbonated domestic water, containing chemicals and salt, replaced the imported water. By the end of the nineteenth century, seltzer morphed into a simple, carbonated beverage of filtered tap water. It is also known as club soda.

WHISKY SOUR

Cooking by the Clock (1948)[43]

1 teaspoon powdered sugar
1 jigger rye
Juice of ½ lemon
slice of orange
Juice of ½ lime
Club soda

Shake with cracked ice, strain, decorate with ½ slice orange, and add enough club soda to fill a 4 ounce glass.

The Last Word on Processed Foods

Known for her "take no prisoners" and humorous descriptions of 1950s life, American author Betty MacDonald often wrote about the less-than-desirable meals she confronted—meals that represented some of the worst uses of processed foods:

> It was at another baby shower that I first encountered a ring mold of mushroom soup, hard-boiled eggs, canned shrimps (that special brand that tastes like Lysol) and lime Jello, the center heaped with chopped sweet pickles, the whole topped with a mustardy, sweet salad dressing. At another shower we were served *tuna fish* chow mein with rancid noodles. A garden club meeting, creamed tuna fish and peanuts over canned asparagus. A hospital group dredged up a salad of elbow macaroni, pineapple chunks, Spanish peanuts, chopped cabbage, chopped marshmallows, ripe olives and salad dressing. I don't know what is happening to the women of America but it ought to be stopped.[44]

Criticism of processed foods echoed throughout the 1950s culinary world. Sales of these products continued to expand, so whatever was happening to the women of America, it was clear that they were *not* going to stop.

Chapter 7

Fancy Appetizers, Beef Stroganoff, and an Atomic Cocktail

Fun and Elegant Entertaining in the Suburbs, Part I

> Poise is more difficult to attain and sustain when a woman must emulate the mental quickness of Groucho Marx and the physical agility of a flea. Sometimes it takes a superhuman effort to fling aside her kitchen apron as the door bell rings announcing the arrival of the first guests, and to assume a manner devoid of exhaustion or concern when greeting them.
>
> —Irma S. Rombauer (1951)[1]

President Eisenhower's 1956 Federal-Aid Highway Act promised suburban dwellers more convenient access to entertainment centers and restaurants—but the project would take at least thirteen years to complete. Meanwhile, suburban families were skilled in the art of entertaining right in their homes—parties of all sorts, from intimate dinner parties for a few choice friends to cocktail parties for larger groups, from unique patio or barbecue gatherings to themed parties, such as a Hawaiian luau. Author Elaine Tyler May notes, "Young postwar Americans were homeward bound," creating a family-centric culture. "The legendary white middle-class family of the 1950s, located in the suburbs, complete with appliances, station wagons, backyard barbecues, and tricycles scattered on the sidewalks, represented something new."[2] Although homeward bound, it was still essential to get to know one's neighbors and community in an era when isolation in the suburbs could be a new and unsettling experience. This knowledge was critical during the early years of the Cold War, when citizens were instructed to be alert, suspicious, and on guard for undesirables, such as communists, who might be posing as neighbors.

Cookbooks provided recipes for a variety of party foods. They also offered helpful hints on a range of related subjects, such as issuing invitations, placement of ashtrays, seating arrangements, decorations, appropriate menus, and entertainment. Hostesses were encouraged to please their guests by considering comfort. "When you plan your table arrangement, remember the number one rule: plan everything—from the way you place the salad fork to the way you serve dessert—with one thought in mind: your guests' convenience." Cookbook author Freda De Knight warned her readers, "Do not overcrowd your table with a conglomeration of food. The idea is to please the eye as to appease the stomach, not to crowd it with a weird assortment of dishes."[3] *Better Homes and Gardens Cook Book* contains a wealth of practical information on selecting linens, china, and glassware; choosing a centerpiece; setting the table; and serving food. Cookbooks often went together with industry pamphlets, which offered instructions and recipes for using the newly available electric appliances that every modern family desired. These appliances included electric casseroles, blenders, coffee pots, and electric chafing dishes essential in the arsenal of cooks and party hosts. According to 1950s cooking sources, suburban party planning had become a science.

In 1955, journalist Hal Boyle noted, "The cocktail party isn't a feature of modern living. It is a factor in modern dying. Anyone who has ever stood upright at a cocktail party (and who ever gets to sit down at one?) can never forget the sinking feeling in his arches, the popping out of new varicose veins, the slow numbness as of death creeping over him."[4] Other writers complained that the hostess did not consider the contents of the entire menu and, often, the appetizers clashed with the main course or were so heavy they numbed one's appetite for dinner. "We settle for a tidbit or two in the living room—pâté, or shrimps, or simply nuts and olives. We frown on hot hors d'oeuvres for two reasons: the hostess must shuttle back and forth between the kitchen and the living room; and the rich, appetite-dulling gadgets rarely tie in with the meal to follow."[5] Along these lines, *The Joy of Cooking* provided a helpful tip: for example, if you prepared an appetizer of hollowed canned or fresh beets filled with caviar, it would be best to forget the very existence of beets as a dinner vegetable.

While cocktail parties were an essential part of suburban life, disapproval was evident. Author Sylvia Lovegren suggests that the "chicest thing to do about cocktail parties was to detest them—or to spoof them."[6] Richard Williams writing for *House Beautiful* in 1951 commented,

> I presume that the way to shorten the duration of a cocktail party is to starve your guests. Hunger might make them go. However, your pride as a hostess does not permit you to be ungenerous. I don't know which is worse. I've attended cocktail parties where the food consisted of potato chips, mucilaginous olives, and peanuts. I have been to others where hors d'oeuvres rich enough for Chateaubriand or Honoré Balzac were served: smoked turkey, Nova Scotia salmon, caviar (though mostly red caviar), water chestnuts wrapped in bacon, meatballs, shrimps Orleans, piroshki, and petit saucissons (hot dogs).[7]

Canapés and Hors D'oeuvres

> The tidbits usually served at cocktail parties simply slay me. I've reached the conclusion that someone must have offered an annual Pulitzer Prize for the most deadly hors d'oeuvre. The competition for the ickiest appetizer seems to be pretty keen. Some of the stuff sensible women are dreaming up would make L. Borgia pack up her little black bag and go home. Tell me, do the people who make these damned things ever eat them themselves, or do they have a special tray with the good ones on it hidden in the kitchen? The average American hostess needs a swift kick in her culinary pants.[8]

Complaining about cocktail appetizers became a national pastime. Cookbooks vary in descriptions of appetizers. Often canapés and hors d'oeuvres are listed separately, while other cookbooks contain all cocktail foods under one heading: appetizers, which include canapés and hors d'oeuvres. Most cookbook authors agree that a canapé is a small bite on a cracker, piece of bread, or chip. Betty Crocker notes that a canapé is "to be eaten gracefully from the fingers." *A Taste of Texas* defines the canapé as one that "has a little smidgeon of some sort of fish—the hors d'oeuvre can be any sort of appetizer." The author continues with a caustic comment that seems to have reflected the thinking of many. "Most canapes can be divided into two categories: those that merely get you in the mood for dinner and those that nearly get you out of it. Canapes should whet the appetite—sharpen it up, and if you serve relishes, sandwiches, nuts, olives, practically picnic basket style, you don't whet it—you douse it."[9] Others complained that predinner appetizers were simply too much food. "Some hostesses of great imagination never seem to be able to leave well enough alone and their guests get such good things before dinner that dinner is no longer a necessity."[10]

An assortment of cheese dishes was a cocktail party favorite appetizer and cheese balls were always popular. Betty Crocker provides the following recipe for a Green Cheese Ball.

GREEN CHEESE BALL

Betty Crocker's Picture Cook Book (1950)[11]

Soften equal amounts of sharp American, white cream [cheese], and Roquefort type cheese. Season well. Mix in chopped pecans and minced parsley. Form into a large ball. Roll in minced parsley and chopped nuts.

While Betty Crocker's recipe for Green Cheese Balls requires some manual labor on the part of the cook, *Mary Meade's Magic Recipes for the Electric Blender* reminds her readers that in creating cheese appetizers, "The blender is your servant: it will swallow up the garlic and the parsley, making them one with the cheese."[12] In a recipe similar to Crocker's, the Blue Cheese Dip with Sauterne calls for Roquefort or Gorgonzola blue cheese, cream cheese, a bit of sauterne, a dash of Worcestershire, some garlic, and a few sprigs of parsley. All ingredients are placed in the blender's jar and mixed until smooth.[13]

On the other hand, an hors d'oeuvre is described as a more complex, sometimes hot offering, which might require plates and forks or toothpicks for spearing the morsels. "For hot appetizers firm enough to be impaled on toothpicks, there are many attractive and amusing gadgets." The author suggests that grapefruit, eggplant, an apple, or a small cabbage might be employed "on which the toothpicks carrying their savory burdens may be studded."[14]

While some cookbook authors discouraged hot hors d'oeuvres, *Silver Jubilee Super Market Cook Book* felt differently. "Everyone likes hot savories with cocktails, but they must deserve the adjective 'hot.'" Freda De Knight pleaded, "Don't try to fix too many hot dishes. Don't work yourself to death! Create a picture in your mind, and arrange your spreads and tidbits so that they will look attractive, be less trouble, and taste better."[15] Logistics for serving hot hors d'oeuvres were critical: not only should they look appealing, but they must also be kept hot throughout the evening.

While canapés might have been considered lighter fare, examples of heavy, usually hot appetizers abound in cookbooks. For example, *Gourmet of the Delta* provides appetizer recipes ranging from Apple Fritters to Shrimp and Curry Mold and Vienna Sausage Pick-Ups. This last hot hors d'oeuvre called for just two ingredients: three cans of Vienna sausages and one 10-oz bottle of Lee & Perrins Worcestershire sauce. The instructions are to pour the entire contents of the bottle of Worcestershire sauce over Vienna sausages, put this on the stove, and boil. The following recipe for Cocktail Meat Balls in Wine Sauce—as delicious as it might be—would seem to be a heavy appetizer and might lessen your appetite for dinner.

COCKTAIL MEAT BALLS IN WINE SAUCE

Gourmet of the Delta (1958)[16]

Recipe provided by Lola Fort Ricketts

1½ lb. ground beef
2 t. paprika
5 slices bread soaked in milk
1 t. dried herbs
1 onion, grated
1 t. dry mustard
2½ t. salt
½ t. black pepper
2 t. mace
3 eggs

Squeeze bread dry, discard milk, add bread to other ingredients, mix thoroughly. Chill. Make into bite size balls. Brown in Wesson oil and drain on brown paper until cold. Simmer in the following sauce for 20 minutes.

MEAT BALL SAUCE

1 c. catsup
1 T. Lee & Perrin Worcestershire sauce
1 c. Burgundy or Sherry
½ t. oregano
salt and pepper to taste

On the other hand, if a hostess was determined to show off her most prized appetizers, there was the option of a cocktail party that also was dinner. Guests grazed on numerous appetizers (and drank) from cocktail hour through the dinner hour. In this case, the hostess would provide a substantial selection of both cold canapés and hot hors d'oeuvres. While more informal than a full-fledged dinner party or buffet, it created much work for the hostess, who needed to refresh, refill, and reheat the offerings. (The man of the house would be busy making drinks all evening.) The following is an adult version of the well-loved pigs in a blanket, always a popular hors d'oeuvre at cocktail parties.

TINY WIENER APPETIZERS

A Date with a Dish: A Cook Book of American Negro Recipes (1948)[17]

Recipe credited to Hattie McDaniel (Best Supporting Actress Oscar winner for her role in *Gone with the Wind*)

To your favorite biscuit dough add:

3 doz. Tiny frankfurters
2 tbsps. prepared mustard
1 cup sauerkraut, chopped

Roll dough thin. Cut in circles about three inches in diameter. Spread each circle sparingly with mustard. Place 1 tablespoonful sauerkraut and one frankfurter in center. Roll tightly, place on a greased baking sheet and bake 20 minutes. Serve hot. Yield: approximately 36 biscuits.

To Cilantro or Not to Cilantro? That Is the Question (a Word about Avocado Spreads or Dips, aka Guacamole)

In the Southwest, the avocado pear is a common fruit that grows in the Rio Grande Valley. Texans use it in and out of salads and as an hors d'oeuvre. To the unconverted, regardless of what is done to the avocado it still tastes like green toothpaste—to the enthusiast it's No. 1 on the dish parade. Often whole pulp is mixed with such things as Worcestershire sauce, lemon juice, tabasco, horseradish and garlic—to make a wonderful dip for fritos or toasted tortillas.

—*A Taste of Texas* (1949)[18]

A Taste of Texas includes four different recipes for an avocado dip, as well as one that is called "guacamole." As described in this cookbook (and others), guacamole differs from avocado dips and spreads because it contains chopped tomatoes—however, the one thing all four recipes have in common: no cilantro. Fresh cilantro is not used—except in sporadic cases—in 1950s recipes and never as a component of guacamole or avocado spreads.

Ground coriander is the seed of the herb cilantro and its green leaves and stems are prevalent in foods throughout Asia and the Middle East. The cilantro plant was brought to Mexico in the 1500s but did not often appear in its cuisine—at least that which was available in the US in the 1950s. Cilantro is often described as Chinese or Mexican parsley or *culantro*, which is in the same family as coriander but a different genus. Many people dislike the taste of fresh cilantro because of the natural aldehyde chemical contained in the plant, and a certain percentage of the population is allergic to it. (Thoughtful contemporary recipes will acknowledge this and suggest cilantro to be an optional ingredient.)[19]

The chapter on Mexican and Latin dishes from *A Taste of Texas* provides the following recipe for a guacamole, which contains tomatoes. Frequently, cookbooks will include recipes for both avocado dip and guacamole, which contain chopped tomatoes, making it Mexican in the eyes of some authors.

Guacamole

A Taste of Texas (1949)[20]

Recipe attributed to Mrs. D. A. Lawshae of Maracaibo, Venezuela.

6 avocados
1½ teaspoons salt
2 teaspoons vinegar
2 tablespoons mayonnaise
1 teaspoon salad oil
6 drops tabasco
½ small hot pepper, minced
½ cup finely chopped raw tomato
¾ cup finely chopped onion

Remove skin and seeds. Place halves in bowl. Add remaining ingredients. With stainless-steel knife, chop avocados until pieces are fine and seasoning well-mixed. Do not stir more than necessary or mash while mixing. Taste, add more salt and tabasco, if needed.

This cookbook provides an additional two recipes for "Avocado Canapes," and another called "Alligator or Avocado Hors d'Oeuvre," which calls for mayonnaise and curry powder. The following recipe contains neither tomatoes nor mayonnaise but adds horseradish and pimientos.

Avocado Canapes, II

A Taste of Texas (1949)[21]

Recipe attributed to Mrs. Charles Williams, New York, NY

1 cup avocado pulp
2 tablespoons prepared horse radish
4 teaspoons lemon juice
2 pimientos, finely chopped
1 teaspoon Worcestershire sauce
½ teaspoon salt 8 drops tabasco

Combine ingredients lightly without beating. Serve on crackers, toasted rounds or triangles of bread.

Poppy Cannon's *The Can-Opener Cook Book* adds parsley or chives, chili sauce, and French dressing to a recipe titled Mexican Guacamole. Indeed, it is possible to find 1950s recipes for avocado dips that contain many untraditional (and often unsettling) ingredients. Examples include curry powder, canned tuna, horseradish, cottage cheese, salad dressings, pimiento, green pepper, celery, scallions, mayonnaise, brandy, sour or sweet cream, bacon, stuffed olives, hard-boiled eggs, cream cheese, chili powder, green food coloring, or liverwurst. Yes, liverwurst. *Cooking by the Clock* (1948) instructs the cook to "mash equal amounts of liverwurst and avocado. Sprinkle avocado with lemon juice to prevent darkening; add liverwurst, season with onion juice, salt, and a dash of paprika. Spread on crackers and serve."[22] *How to Eat Better for Less Money* offers a recipe for an avocado dessert that calls for mashing two avocados with lime juice, a pinch of salt, and two-thirds cup of sugar—whipping the concoction until light and chilling it for an hour. "This is delightful and different."[23]

Most cookbooks instruct the cook to mash the avocado or combine the ingredients lightly without beating, as suggested in the previous recipe for Avocado Canapes II. *Modern Magic in Food Preparation with the Waring Blendor* and *Mary Meade's Magic Recipes for the Electric Blender* instructs the cook to place all ingredients (tomato, avocado, green onion, lemon juice, hot peppers, or Tabasco) into the blender's glass container and blend until smooth. (*Mary Meade's Magic Recipes* also provides a pronunciation guide. "Pronounce it hwoc-a-MO-lay.")

However, most recipes for avocado dips, spreads, and canapés in the 1950s remain simple, with a few chosen ingredients—mashed avocado, lemon or lime juice, perhaps a small amount of minced onion, salt, and pepper—allowing the subtle taste of the avocado to be the star.

Three Mexican cookbooks that include recipes for guacamole or avocado spreads without cilantro are Myrtle Richardson's *Genuine Mexican and Spanish Cookery Recipes for American Homes* (1934), Erna Fergusson's *Mexican Cookbook* (1934), and Natalie Scott's *Mexican Cook-Book: Mexican Dishes for American Kitchens* (1953). Elena Zelayeta's *Elena's Secrets of Mexican Cooking* (1958) does utilize cilantro in three recipes, but none involve an avocado. Zelayeta was born in Mexico but moved to San Francisco when she was young, basing her recipes on family cooking. She provides a recipe for a sauce for tostadas and tacos, *Salsa Para Tostadas y Tacos*, recognizable as the salsa (often called *pico de gallo*) found in Mexican and Tex-Mex restaurants. Included in this recipe are two tablespoons of chopped fresh cilantro or one teaspoon coriander seeds mashed.

A glance at recipes for avocado spread (now generally called guacamole) in the twenty-first century demonstrates how taste has changed over the decades. In contemporary recipes, the avocado is no longer the subtle star. Recipes are laden with onion, cilantro (ranging from a few tablespoons to an entire bunch), jalapeño peppers, lime juice, tomatoes, and ground coriander. Virtually all online recipes declare the authenticity of their guacamole, with some invoking the recipes of their *abuelas* (grandmothers) or insisting on the use of the traditional Mexican *molcajete* for mashing the avocado. The recipes are introduced as "authentic," "traditional Mexican style," "perfect," "the best authentic Mexican guacamole," or "the best ever." Others tout the dip's health benefits: "fresh, healthy, ingredients," or "naturally gluten-free and vegan." However, all the examined online recipes call for cilantro; very few note that it might be necessary to cut back or eliminate the cilantro for those who dislike or are allergic to the herb.[24]

Nevertheless, cilantro is not always part of contemporary guacamole. Two cookbooks published in New Mexico—with a rich heritage of Native American and Mexican foodways—do not include cilantro in guacamole recipes. *Southwest Indian Cookbook* (2010) presents two recipes; one contains onion, garlic, tomatoes, hot peppers, lemon, or lime juice. The ingredients for the second recipe include tomatoes, garlic, and one-quarter teaspoon of coriander. (In an unusual twist, this recipe adds chopped piñon nuts as a garnish.) *Tasting New Mexico: Recipes Celebrating One Hundred Years of Distinctive Home Cooking* (2011) notes, "We think it succeeds best as an exercise in simplicity, so we avoid extra ingredients that entice many cooks, such as garlic, tomatoes, and new Mexican chile."[25] Let the subtle flavor of the avocado be the star.

Drinks

The fate of the postwar cocktail can be read as a cold war allegory. The sanitized version of middle-class life that defined the 1950s, or served as its official myth, influenced the nation's drinking habits. Social and political circumstances deeply hostile to eccentricity tamed its wayward creativity, and the appetite for novelty that had launched a thousand cocktails of the golden age and the Roaring Twenties disappeared. The man in the gray flannel suit drank a dry martini, a gin and tonic, a Scotch and soda—safe choices that put you in solidly with the right people.

—William Grimes (2001)[26]

With the repeal of Prohibition and the aftermath of World War II, a pro-alcohol culture appeared. The 1950s witnessed the publication of many specialty cookbooks that instructed its readers on using both wine and spirits, and mainstream cookbooks jumped on the cocktail bandwagon. Author Irma S. Rombauer quipped with her usual, straightforward humor in her 1951 edition of *The Joy of Cooking*, "To give this book the impression of sobriety and stability it deserves, the alcoholic cocktails have been relegated to the chapter on Beverages. There they may blush unseen by those who disapprove of them," adding that cocktails will "loosen tongues and unbutton the reserves of the socially diffident."[27]

Martini—Medium Dry

a guide to pink elephants (1952)[28]

1 oz. dry Gin
¼ oz. dry Vermouth
¼ oz. Italian Vermouth

Stir well with cracked ice. Rub rim of glass with lemon peel. Strain drink into prepared glass and serve with small olive or pearl onion.

Americans continued to express uneasiness about the global spread of communism, and author William Grimes posits that the cocktail "faithfully mirrored the political anguish." As the US continued its domestic and international war against communism, previous favored American cocktails were "being infiltrated—and falling, one by one, like so many dominoes—by vodka."[29]

Russian Cocktail

a guide to pink elephants (1952)[30]

½ oz. Vodka
½ oz. Gin
½ oz. Creme de Cacao

Shake with cracked ice. Strain into a chilled cocktail glass.

Not all mainstream cookbooks of the era provide recipes for alcoholic drinks. *Betty Crocker's Picture Cook Book* (1950), *Better Homes and Gardens Cook Book* (1953), and *The General Foods Kitchens Cookbook* (1959) confine their beverage selections to coffee and nonalcoholic punches. Others, such as *The Joy of Cooking*, and some specialty books, such as *The Frozen Food Cook Book*, often provide recipes for both alcoholic and nonalcoholic drinks. As expected, this cookbook utilizes several frozen fruit products.

Strawberry Punch

The Frozen Food Cook Book (1948)[31]

(Yield: 36 punch cup servings)

Barely defrost: 2 pkg. Frozen Strawberries

Crush strawberries from one package.

Add to crushed strawberries and let stand for about ½ hr. : ½ c. sugar (or less if desired)

Add: 1½ c. defrosted lemon juice*, 2 c. defrosted orange juice*, 1½ qts. ice water

Just before serving, stir in package of uncrushed strawberries. Serve while still very cold.

*If concentrated, dilute before using.

Fancy Appetizers, Beef Stroganoff, and an Atomic Cocktail | 151

Mary Meade's Magic Recipes for the Electric Blender claims suburbanites who own a blender have the ability to make thousands of different kinds of drinks. ("Drinks are what blenders were invented for.")[32] This cookbook also provides valuable lists of bottled spirits and bar utensils and accessories that the well-equipped household should have on hand. The book provides thirty-one pages of alcoholic drinks to be made with an electric blender, including a Frozen Peach Daiquiri, a choice of pink ladies, Hawaiian Punch, a gin-based mint cocktail, a Frozen Scotch, and a Grasshopper. A popular 1950s cocktail, the Grasshopper requires four ounces each of white crème de cacao, green crème de menthe, and whipping cream. These ingredients along with one cup of crushed ice are placed in the blender. "Switch on motor for a few seconds; then off, and strain."[33]

Figure 7.1. Downtown Las Vegas, Nevada, 1950s. A cloud from a recent atomic test can be seen in the background. The Nevada Test Site was a mere sixty miles north of Las Vegas. Courtesy of Nevada National Security Site, Nuclear Testing Archive, Las Vegas, Nevada. Source: Author's collection.

Atomic Cocktail

In 1945, musician Slim Gaillard recorded his song "Atomic Cocktail." "It's the drink you don't pour, now when you take one sip you won't need anymore. Boom! Atomic Cocktail."[34] During the 1950s, Las Vegas, Nevada, was known as the Atomic City, as it was a mere sixty-five miles north of the Nevada Test Site. The Sky Room Cocktail Lounge of the Desert Inn served as the proving ground for numerous cocktails that referenced atomic bombs, rockets, and other suggestions of the nuclear age. At the time, the Desert Inn was the tallest building in Las Vegas and the Sky Room became a favorite viewing spot to observe atomic test explosions.

> **ATOMIC COCKTAIL**
>
> *Foodviva.com*[35]
>
> 1½ oz (45 ml) Premium Vodka
> 1½ oz (45 ml) Brandy or Cognac
> ½ oz (15 ml) Dry Sherry

Figure 7.2. "Wilbur Clark's Desert Inn, Las Vegas, Nevada," 1951 postcard. The glass enclosed Sky Room Cocktail Lounge was located just under the "Desert Inn" sign. In 1951 the hotel was the tallest structure in Las Vegas and a popular gathering spot to watch the nuclear bomb tests from the Nevada Test Site. Source: Heritage Image Partnership Ltd/Alamy Stock Photo.

1½ oz (45 ml) Brut Champagne
1 Small Orange Wedge
Ice Cubes

1. Combine first three ingredients in the cocktail shaker and add ice cubes. Put the mouth cap on shaker and shake well for approx. 15 seconds.

2. Remove the cap and strain drink into chilled martini glass and then pour champagne.

3. Place orange wedge on the rim of glass as garnish and serve.

J. Robert Oppenheimer was director of the Los Alamos Laboratory (New Mexico) during the Manhattan Project. He is often called the "father of the atomic bomb."

Oppenheimer Martini

"Oppenheimer, Martinis, and the Atom Bomb" (2015)[36]

"The Oppenheimer Martini is Dr. Oppenheimer's recipe for the cocktail, making do with the limited supplies available at Los Alamos. You may not be splitting the atom, but that doesn't mean you can't drink like Oppenheimer!"

4 oz. Gin
Smidgen of Dry Vermouth
Lime Juice
Honey

Stir the gin and vermouth with ice until chilled. Then strain into a chilled martini glass whose rim has been dipped in equal parts lime and honey.

The Formal Dinner Party and Buffet Dinners

Dinner for "company" ought to be something a little bit special. The service is likely to be a bit more formal, the table a bit more festive looking than usual.

—*The General Foods Kitchens Cookbook* (1959)[37]

One of the issues with 1950s suburban dinner parties was that most new houses in suburbia did not have a formal dining room. It was a room that builders felt was not compatible with modern living. Suburbanites had few options: only invite the number of people who would comfortably fit around the kitchen or dining table or place the food, cutlery, and dishes on the kitchen counter. After filling their plates, the guests would sit down at a table. Tables were to be uncluttered, stainless steel was preferred over sterling silver, and centerpieces were to be modest. (It is with some irony that cookbooks, such as *The General Foods Kitchens Cookbook*, provided precise instructions for placement of silverware and glasses that would never be used, such as special forks for consuming oysters.)

Since formal, sit-down dinner parties often presented logistic problems, *The Silver Jubilee Super Market Cook Book* noted, "Buffet meals solve

Figure 7.3. An elegant buffet dinner consisting of Veal with Wine and Mushrooms over rice, broccoli, and a Chocolate Sponge Mold with Eggnog Sauce. *General Foods Kitchen Cookbook*, 1959. Used by permission Kraft Heinz Foods Company. Source: Author's collection.

the problem of entertaining large groups."[38] Food might be served from the kitchen or placed on a table pushed against a back wall. If the dining table was used to serve food, cocktail tables, end tables, television trays, and other temporary small tables, such as card tables, were enlisted to provide a surface to place one's plate.

The General Foods Kitchens Cookbook (1959) observes that a good buffet must include a hot and a cold dish, a variety of breads, and relishes. The book suggests a buffet menu of beef stroganoff, French fried onions, radishes and celery, rolls, salad, and Miracle Cherry Pie for dessert.

MIRACLE CHERRY PIE

The General Foods Kitchens Cookbook (1959)[39]

2 cans water-packed pitted red sour cherries, drained—about 3 cups
2½ cups cherry juice and water
2 packages vanilla pudding and pie filling mix
½ teaspoon salt
½ cup sugar
4 teaspoons lemon juice
2 tablespoons butter
Few drops red food coloring
2 baked 8-inch pie shells, cooled

Combine cherries and 1 cup of the water ad cherry juice in a saucepan. Bring to a boil. Meanwhile, combine pudding mix, salt, sugar, lemon juice, and remaining 1½ cups liquid. Stir to form a smooth paste. Add to boiling fruit, stirring to blend. Then cook and stir until mixture comes to a *full* boil. Remove from heat. Add butter and food coloring. Cool 5 minutes. Pour into pie shells. Let pies stand about 3 hours, or until firm.

The Holy Trinity of Suburban Fancy Dishes: Beef Stroganoff, Chicken Divan, and Lobster Thermidor

Rich and velvety main course presentations were popular dishes for formal dining and buffets. Beef stroganoff was one of the favorite dinner party entrees, used for sit-down and buffet dinners because of its easy preparation and eye-catching appearance. "There is something intrinsically Soviet about Beef Stroganoff, but it's not easy to pinpoint what has made it so popular. One factor could be the relative simplicity of the recipe: a short list of ingredients combined using straightforward techniques."[40] Beef stroganoff *was* exotic for suburban Americans, making its appearance at the table seem that more mysterious and sophisticated.

Although extremely popular during the 1950s, beef stroganoff recipes appear in cookbooks dating from the mid to late 1930s, such as the recipe in the 1943 edition of Rombauer's *The Joy of Cooking*. As with other recipes published during the war when meat was rationed, it is unlikely to have been seen in many US dining rooms until after the war.

At the beginning of the Cold War, Alexandra Kropotkin published *How to Cook and Eat in Russian* (1947). "Nowadays any mention of Russia brings on a red-hot argument." Kropotkin maintains that the Russian people are forgotten with all the noisy conversations and, further, Russians can be good neighbors.[41] Soviet writer Elizavetta Dmitrovna contributed the following recipe in her cookbook, published in Richmond, Virginia.

BEEF STROGANOFF

Samovar: A Russian Cook Book (1946)[42]

1½ lbs. veal fillet or round steak
4 or 5 tbsp. sour cream
Salt and pepper
1 tbsp. tomato sauce
1 tbsp. flour
1 chopped onion
2 tbsp. butter
1 medium-sized can mushrooms
1 tsp. dry mustard

Cut into thin strips veal or fillet (the length of your little finger and half the width). Season with salt and pepper and let stand for 1½ hours in cold place. Fry flour with butter. Mix well and add gradually one cup stock, the dry mustard, sour cream and tomato sauce. Bring this to a boil. Fry separately chopped onion until soft and brown. Add meat and fry briskly for five minutes. Add mushrooms sliced in half and fry again for three minutes. Turn this all into the first mixture and simmer slowly for ten minutes. Stir several times.

While all beef stroganoff recipes called for sour cream, some Americanized recipes included garlic, Tabasco sauce, or Worcestershire sauce. Numerous 1950s American recipes incorporated tomato purée or tomato paste and mushrooms. Kropotkin acknowledges that the classic Russian recipe changed by adding tomato purée and mushrooms, which cooks in the south of Russia often include. However, she adds, "The result is tasty. But it isn't Beef Stroganoff." The following recipe recommends serving the dish with boiled rice, and other serving suggestions include kasha or noodles. The recipe utilizes both mushrooms and tomato paste and a combination of sour cream and heavy cream.

BEEF STROGANOFF

Jersey Shore Cooks and Artists (1958)[43]

½ cup minced onion
½ pound mushrooms-cleaned and sliced
3 or 4 tbsp. butter
1½ lbs chuck, cut in ¾ inch cubes
2 tbsp. flour
1 cup bouillon
½ tsp salt
2 tbsp. tomato paste
¾ tsp. Worcestershire sauce
½ cup thick sour cream
¼ cup heavy cream

Saute onion and mushrooms in butter for five minutes, and set aside. In another pan put 3 or 4 tbsp. shortening and brown meat which has been mixed with flour. Add bouillon, onion, mushrooms and remaining ingredients. Stir to blend, reduce heat and simmer about 1½ hours or until the meat is tender.

In describing her recipe for Quick Beef Stroganoff, Poppy Cannon makes the following observations, "Paper thin slices of beef that are known as chip steaks and are generally available in most meat markets are ideal for the making of this delicious entrée. It is a fine concoction for your chafing dish, though of course you could cook it behind scenes and amaze your guests with your speed and prowess."[44] While more traditional recipes often require cooking times of one-and-a-half to two hours, Cannon's meal comes together in just over 5 minutes, using chip steaks, onion, sour cream, tomato juice, and canned beef gravy. She suggests that the dish be served with canned noodles.

Chicken divan first appeared on the menu of Divan Parisien Restaurant in New York City sometime in the 1940s or 1950s (although it was a popular dish as early as the 1930s). It is a staple recipe in many fundraising cookbooks, such as *Jersey Shore Cooks and Artists* and *River Road Recipes*.

In her 1950 book *New York Travel*, Eleanor Early describes the original recipe. "Most people go to the Divan [Parisien] because of a specialty called Chicken Divan. Which is a wonderful dish that you can make at home. You start with a good big fowl, which you have boiled until it is delectably tender. Then you make a rich sauce." Early adds two cups of the chicken stock and a cup of cream but notes that the restaurant uses plain white sauce with a bit of added whipped cream and hollandaise sauce. "Add to the sauce a few tablespoons of sherry, a pinch of nutmeg and a teaspoon of Worcester sauce. Cook a package of frozen broccoli, drain and arrange in a casserole or deep serving platter." Parmesan cheese is spread over the broccoli, the slices of chicken are placed over the broccoli, and the sauce is poured over the casserole along with more Parmesan cheese. (Early estimates that she uses about one cup of Parmesan in total.) The dish is set under a broiler and cooked until brown and bubbly.[45]

Cooking with lobster was a special occasion and helped middle-class suburbanites to reimagine themselves as sophisticated urbanites. Author Megan J. Elias notes that cooking with lobster "marked this cuisine as one of worldliness and lavishness, but also under girded by the modern technology that made possible inland transportation of lobster."[46] Lobster thermidor was, perhaps, the most expensive and elegant of all luxury party main courses served in the 1950s.

LOBSTER THERMIDOR

Jesse's Book of Creole and Deep South Recipes (1954)[47]

This is one of the regal dishes of the South. Either Maine or Florida lobsters may be used.

6 large live lobsters
1½ cups fresh light cream
2 cloves garlic, chopped
9 canned mushrooms, cut up
1 onion, chopped
3/8 teaspoon French mustard
½ cup salt
3 tablespoons chopped fresh parsley
2 teaspoons pepper
¾ cup butter, plus 3 level tablespoons butter
1 cup sherry
3 dashes paprika
½ cup flour
Parmesan cheese

Put the lobsters to boil for 30 minutes in a pot of water seasoned with the garlic, onion, salt, and pepper. Let cool, remove from the pot, and cut in half. Remove the meat from tails and claws or "feelers." Dice and set aside. Save the shells.

Melt ¾ cup butter in a pot, add the flour, and stir until smooth. Add the cream and stir until the sauce is thick. Take off the heat and set aside. Sauté the lobster meat and mushrooms in 3 tablespoons butter for 5 minutes. Add the lobster meat and mushrooms, mustard, and parsley to the cream sauce, stir for 5 minutes, then add the sherry and stir in well. Add paprika, then place the mixture in lobster shells, sprinkle with Parmesan cheese, put in a 450° oven, and bake for 15 minutes. Serves 6.

The next version uses cream, a cream sauce, and adds hollandaise, another very rich sauce. The recipe also calls for tarragon vinegar, which would help to balance the creaminess.

LOBSTER THERMIDOR

The Perfect Hostess Cook Book (1955)[48]

[Pre-heat oven to 450°]

2 freshly cooked lobsters (2 pounds each)
3 ounces butter

⅔ cup Cream Sauce
1½ cups Hollandaise Sauce
1 pint cream
1 overflowing teaspoon tarragon vinegar
1 teaspoon chopped parsley
1 tablespoon dry mustard
1 tablespoon butter
2 lemons, quartered Grated Parmesan cheese (optional)

FIRST Remove the meat of 2 two pound lobsters and cut into cubes. Render 3 ounces butter in a good-sized skillet. Toss the lobster meat into the butter and simmer for a few minutes.

SECOND Make ⅔ cup Cream Sauce [a mixture of mushrooms, milk, onion, butter, flour, eggs]. Stir in 1 pint cream and add to lobster a little at a time.

THIRD Cream 1 tablespoon dry mustard with 1 tablespoon butter and add to sauce. Blend well, shaking skillet back and forth. Remove from flame and cool a little.

FOURTH Make 1½ cups Hollandaise Sauce I [note: the author provides a recipe elsewhere] and stir in 1 overflowing teaspoon tarragon vinegar and 1 teaspoon chopped parsley. Stir into lobster until the whole is well blended. Pack the 4 lobster shells with the meat of the lobster. Distribute any left-over sauce evenly over the lobster meat. Set the filled shells in a 450° oven for 5 to 10 minutes. Serve hot and bubbling with quartered lemons on the side.

NOTE If desired, the filled lobsters may be sprinkled with Parmesan cheese before setting them in the oven.

All recipes for lobster thermidor in 1950s cookbooks are detailed, time-consuming, and somewhat complicated. However, if one did not want to go to so much trouble, there was always Poppy Cannon, who managed to turn the dish into a casserole, using cooked lobster meat, a can of condensed cream of mushroom soup, and a little Parmesan cheese for a topping.

A glance at the many types of published 1950s cookbooks reveals that beef stroganoff and lobster thermidor recipes are often found, and chicken divan appears less frequently. This is not surprising. When serving a party dish, one would want to present something unique, and beef stroganoff and lobster thermidor fit the requirements—sumptuous, velvety, and sophisticated. On the other hand, chicken divan is a simple casserole, sometimes making it difficult to identify in cookbooks as it was often called Chicken and Broccoli or Chicken and Vegetables. In the eyes of many cookbooks, it is just an ordinary casserole and not a dish to serve to the company.

The last words on dinner parties and cocktails are left to Irma S. Rombauer, who, along with her daughter Marion Rombauer Becker, published the 1951 edition of *The Joy of Cooking*. Rombauer always managed a light-hearted spin on life. "No matter whom you are entertaining, try not to be unduly impressed with the fact that something unusual is expected of you as a hostess. It isn't. Distinguished persons are usually simple. They dislike ostentation, and nothing is more disconcerting to a guest than the impression that his coming is causing a household commotion."[49] In other words, just as in the best avocado dip recipes: keep it simple.

Chapter 8

More Parties, the Cult of the Chafing Dish, and the Suburban Luau

Fun and Elegant Entertaining in the Suburbs, Part II

In a chapter titled "Drama at the Table," author Poppy Cannon notes, "If your food is basically good and if you have contrast in texture, color, and flavor, that's more than half the battle. Add drama and you're sure to make yourself a reputation."[1]

With or without drama, cookbooks were generous with advice for producing successful brunches, luncheons, teas, and theme dinners. Other special gatherings included patio parties, dessert parties, bridge parties, television and theater parties, open houses, and potluck dinners. Even the ordinary backyard barbecue could be more elegant with nontraditional barbecue foods. For example, in a section titled "Big Party Dishes," *Jim Beard's complete book of barbecue & rotisserie cooking* (1954) provides nontraditional party barbecue recipes for serving twenty-four or more people, including Brunswick Stew, Clam Chowder, Spaghetti and Meat Sauce, and Chicken with Green Molé Sauce. One might begin the festivities with Beard's suggestion for champagne cassis. ("For a festive occasion, serve ice-cold champagne and add a dash of Cassis to each glass.")[2] According to cookbooks of the era, there was never an inappropriate time for a special gathering of friends and neighbors. In addition to recipes, cookbooks often included menus and provided helpful hints on how to serve meals that hosts hoped would be memorable.

The Hawaiian-themed party (luau) was the most popular of all the era's suburban backyard, themed events. Hosts had a wealth of publications to consult, including specialty cookbooks, such as *A Hawaiian Luau*, published by the Dole Company, and those that detailed instructions for decorations, menus, beverages, music, and entertainment. Suggestions included Westernized interpretations of hula dancing, a hula girl fortune teller, or even guessing how many eyes are in a fresh pineapple. "Entertaining the Hawaiian way means putting the emphasis on informality, friendliness, and fun with sweet Hawaiian music playing softly; and with simple but oh-so-good things to eat, you have the makings of a Hawaiian-style party wherever you live and whatever the occasion."[3]

Brunch and Luncheon

The daytime gatherings of brunch and luncheon were considered feminine events, usually hosted by women for women. " 'Brunch' is one of the finest innovations in eating. It's fun to plan the breakfast-luncheon combination, using the best parts of each meal."[4]

Picture Cook Book (1958) suggests that some sort of fruit would be appropriate as a first course, followed by a main dish based on a traditional breakfast meal—eggs, sausage, or pancakes.

HAM AND EGGS

Carnation Cook Book (1948)[5]

8 eggs
6 tablespoons Carnation Milk, undiluted
½ teaspoon salt
Dash of pepper
3 tablespoons butter
6 thin slices boiled ham

Beat eggs thoroughly with milk and seasonings. Pour into medium hot frying pan in which butter has been melted. Cook eggs slowly, stirring occasionally. Place spoonful of cooked eggs on ham slices and roll. Place on baking dish in moderate oven of 350°F. for 10 minutes, or until ham is thoroughly heated. Serve hot with white sauce. Garnish with parsley. Serve with bran muffins. Serves 6

While most cookbooks emphasize the simplicity of brunch, other sources provide elaborate and more adventurous menus, complete with entrée, side dishes, salad, and dessert. For example, *Gourmet of the Delta* suggests one of the era's most popular brunch (and luncheon) dishes, Chicken à la King. In this case, served with toast or patty shells from a chafing dish.

CHICKEN A LA KING

Gourmet of the Delta (1958)[6]

Recipe credited to Mrs. Shields Hood

½ c. butter
2 c. hot chicken stock
½ c. flour
½ c. heavy cream
2 c. chicken, cut in strips [note: previously cooked]
¼ c. milk, scalded
½ c. pimientos, chopped
1 t. salt
1 c. sliced mushrooms
Few grains paprika
Toast or patty shells

Melt butter, add flour and paprika, blend well. Add chicken stock, milk and cream, bring to a boil and cook until thick. Add chicken, pimiento, and mushrooms, serve on hot buttered toast or in patty shells.

The General Foods Kitchens Cookbook (1959) includes a section titled "She's Just Moved In, and I Think You'll Like Her." One of the essential functions of 1950s entertaining, from formal dinner parties to informal gatherings, was that these events provided opportunities to get to know neighbors, especially new neighbors. Most 1950s suburban entertaining was community-oriented and meant to instill trust among members of the community. Luncheons could be buffet-style or family-style sit-down affairs. "Most luncheons are purely feminine affairs, although a Saturday before a football game in the fall, or a summer Saturday or Sunday may be chosen for informal buffet luncheons which are so deservedly popular with the men."[7]

In her plea to add drama to the table, Poppy Cannon insisted that the choice of dishes, silverware, napkins, tablecloth, and centerpieces were vital in hosting a successful luncheon. Of course, in presenting luncheons, it was essential to the hostess's reputation that the food be extra special, even elegant. Authors suggested that the hostess pick dishes with which she is thoroughly comfortable and avoid anything too strange or she might face criticism from the other women. One was never, ever to experiment with a new dish. Cookbook authors often emphasize the importance of serving a luncheon dish that, according to the *Silver Jubilee Super Market Cook Book* (1955), is one "which you know by experience is certain to be a success."

Hostesses were encouraged not to serve more than one main dish and limit the courses to three. Light beverages before the meal, such as juices, should always be available. Pre-luncheon tidbits should be confined to raw vegetables and a simple dip. "There are few women today who enjoy over-eating even at a luncheon party."[8] The era's advertising always depicted thin women with tiny waists, and traditionally women of the 1950s were (or were supposed to be) delicate eaters.

Most cookbooks provided luncheon menus that were lighter fare than dinner, often with suggestions such as *The Joy of Cooking*'s menu of molded pineapple ring filled with chicken salad on lettuce, served with rolls and chocolate spice cake for dessert. On the other hand, *Gourmet of the Delta* presents a luncheon menu that rivals any formal dinner party. The menu includes a breast of chicken with wine and mushroom sauce, deviled egg and shrimp casserole, tomato aspic ring with hearts of artichokes, green asparagus served with mayonnaise, and hot rolls, finished with plum ice cream and butter nut squares for dessert.

DEVILED EGG AND SHRIMP CASSEROLE

Gourmet of the Delta (1958)[9]

Recipe credited to Mrs. Charles Clower

10 hard boiled eggs
2 T. flour
1 can shrimp

2 T. butter
1 stalk celery, very finely chopped
1 c. evaporated milk
Onion juice
1½ c. sharp Cheddar cheese
Prepared mustard
1 c. sweet milk Mayonnaise
Buttered bread crumbs

Cut hard boiled eggs lengthwise. Remove yolks and mash well. Add mustard, mayonnaise, onion juice, red pepper, salt and celery. Have mixture slightly stiff. Stuff egg whites. Make cream sauce with flour, butter and milk. Add salt, Tabasco and Worcestershire sauce to taste. Melt cheese in sauce. In a greased casserole place a layer of deviled egg halves, then half the shrimp. Cover with half of sauce. Repeat. Top with butter bread crumbs and bake at 350° for 35 minutes. Serves 8–10. [NOTE: this recipe calls for ingredients that are not listed: red pepper, Tabasco, and Worcestershire sauces.]

Teas

Teas were special events hosted by women, usually given for other women, held in the late afternoon, between 3 p.m. and 6 p.m. *Betty Crocker's Good and Easy Cook Book* (1954) provides information on informal afternoon teas and formal teas. "A small informal tea has the charm of easy hospitality. Set the tea table in the living room with the tea or coffee service near your chair, as hostess. Guests sit informally around the room." Crocker admonishes the hostess to be sure that the food is simple but appealingly arranged. Food suggestions included small biscuits, rolls, muffins, cakes, or cookies that should be warm from the oven.[10]

On the other hand, formal teas were served from the dining room table "and arranged with simple elegance." "The tea service is at one end, the coffee at the other." And, in a distinct difference from the informal tea, two friends of the hostess would be responsible for pouring the beverages. Food suggestions are more elaborate: floating island punch, party sandwiches, little cakes, fancy cookies, salted nuts, fondant mints. *Betty Crocker's Good and Easy Cook Book* (1954) provides a simple recipe

168 | Casseroles, Can Openers, and Jell-O

Figure 8.1. "Come for tea," *General Foods Kitchen Cookbooks*, 1959. The teapot and matching cup and saucer, along with an assortment of toast, jam, desserts, and sandwiches, are set on an elegant tray, with a warm, inviting fireplace as background. Used by permission Kraft Heinz Foods Company. Source: Author's collection.

for Frosted Tea Cakes. The cook is instructed to make an oblong cake, using Betty Crocker white, yellow, chocolate devil's food, angel food, or honey spice cake mix. After cooling, the cake is to be cut into one-inch squares. Then, an icing of one's choice (Crocker recommends butter icing) is poured over the cake squares.[11]

Good Neighbor Gatherings

House-to-house dinner parties, where guests would travel from one home to another for each course of the meal, as well as potluck dinners that required everybody's contribution of a dish, proved to be popular at 1950s community gatherings.

Potluck originally meant that a last-minute invitation was issued and the get-together was an informal family dinner. The guest simply ate what the family had planned to eat that evening. In the 1950s, potluck came to mean a gathering where the guests each brought food, "the 'luck' now lies in the uncertainty about what everyone will bring. The host can suggest what might be needed but cannot control the quality of the offering."[12] In this case, the balance of power has reversed: the host is no longer in charge, for the guests are dictating the offerings. Margaret Visser notes that "pot luck" dinners "usually celebrate the intimacy of the guests or at least the hope that they have a great deal in common." In giving up some authority, the host still regains responsibility to pay for a party "even if the guests help and [the host] must accept the blame for the food provided, [thus] shouldering the burden and the risk of inviting people for 'pot luck.'"[13]

Entertaining and the Cult of the Chafing Dish[14]

> You couldn't ask for a more charming way to entertain than with a chafing-dish supper. The flame that does the cooking or keeps the food warm adds to its friendly flow to the candlelight. You serve casually in the living room. And if you wish, you can cook before guests with all the fanfare of a magician."
>
> —*Better Homes and Gardens New Cook Book* (1953)[15]

In the late nineteenth century, chafing dishes were trendy in middle-class homes and were among the first electric home appliances available.[16] The chafing dish was a popular wedding gift during the 1950s, either one of the new electric models or an old-fashioned version, heated by a small can of Sterno. *Good Housekeeping* (March 1952) suggested that a chafing dish is "perfect for the girl who is cook, hostess, and waitress, too."[17] It was considered a perfect vehicle for the hostess wishing to infuse drama as well as charisma, glamour, and stylishness into at-home parties. The main benefit of the chafing dish was that the hostess could be at the party while cooking in front of the guests and not hidden out-of-sight in the kitchen. However, there were specific steps necessary in this type of cooking. The ingredients needed assembly ahead of time. Other advice included holding a dress rehearsal to ensure the cook was confident. Chafing dish cookery was a departure from the usual as the hostess was the cook and an actress, performing for her audience (the guests). Cookbooks also suggested that the hostess provide a first course for the guests while she assembled ingredients in the kitchen. Lastly, and in front of the guests to add mystery and drama, the cook should noiselessly stir the dish using a long-handled wooden spoon. Many chafing dish meals were served with rice, noodles, or boiled potatoes, so it was imperative that they also be prepared ahead of time and kept hot while the hostess performed her magic with the chafing dish.

Chafing dish cookery encompassed a range of foods, from the ridiculous to the sublime. For example, Kraft Foods Company's dip, Crabmeat Delight, consisted of one pound of Velveeta, milk, and a six-and-a-half ounce can of boned and flaked crabmeat, melted and served on toast triangles. On the opposite side of the spectrum, more elaborate chafing dish presentations included the following recipe for Lobster Newburg.

LOBSTER NEWBURG

Wick and Lick (1954)[18]

1 lb lobster, cooked
⅛ t cayenne pepper
3 T butter
1 t chopped onion
1 T flour
¼ c cognac
½ c mushrooms, sliced
¼ c sherry
½ t salt
3 egg yolks
Dash paprika
1 c cream

Cube lobster. Melt butter in pan of chafing dish over hot water and blend in flour. Add salt, pepper, onion, mushrooms. Add cream to egg yolks and beat well. Add lobster, cognac and sherry to onion mushroom mixture. Stir well. Add cream and egg yolks and stir gently over fire until well thickened and hot. Can substitute shrimp or crabmeat for lobster or use in combination.

Welch rabbit (rarebit) was the dish most often associated with chafing dish cuisine in the 1950s, and it appears in specialty, mainstream, and gourmet cookbooks.

Welch Rabbit

Wick and Lick (1954)[19]

1 T butter
1 T Worcestershire sauce
¾ lb sharp cheddar cheese
⅛ t mustard
¼ c milk
¼ t salt
1 egg
Dash cayenne pepper

Cube cheese and add to melted butter in chafing dish pan over hot water pan. Add seasonings. When blended add egg beaten with milk and cook 1 minute. Serve on crackers or toast triangles.

Setting Your Food on Fire

Flaming Cherries Jubilee . . . Royale Peaches Aflame—these are names to stir the blood. Make them! Strangers will whisper your name with awe, and monarchs vie for your attention."

—*The Chafing Dish Cookbook* (1958)[20]

Cookbooks suggested lighting a bit of warm brandy or other liquor to finish off a dish to add spectacle to a dinner. Recipes range from flaming brandy or maple sauce for a steamed pudding to flaming apricots or peaches. One source even suggested setting your fruit cake on fire—sprinkle a half cup rum over the fruit cake and let it soak—place in a chafing dish and heat two tablespoons of rum. Pour rum into the center of the cake and ignite. Serve flaming.[21] (Or, perhaps fruitcake haters might just let it burn up.) Flaming desserts, especially cherries jubilee, usually served in a chafing dish, proved to be very popular at 1950s fancy buffets and dinner parties.

172 | Casseroles, Can Openers, and Jell-O

Figure 8.2. "The prettiest party of the season is the one you give." The centerpiece is a baked ham, glazed with a mixture of herbs, vinegar, and lemon Jell-O. It is decorated with scallion tops, stuffed olives, and cucumber rounds. The ham sits on a base of Jell-O cubes, surrounded by sweet potato rosettes. A chafing dish (*top left*) holds the dessert of cherries jubilee. *General Foods Kitchen Cookbooks*, 1959. Used by permission Kraft Heinz Foods Company. Source: Author's collection.

Cherry Jubilee

Wick and Lick (1954)[22]

¾ c. currant jelly
½ c. Cognac
1 large can pitted Bing cherries
1½ qt. vanilla ice cream
½ c. blanched almonds

Put jelly in chafing dish pan over direct flame and stir until melted. Drain cherries and stuff with almonds. Add cherries to jelly and simmer slowly. Place ice cream in individual dishes. Pour cognac into cherries and let it heat. Ignite with match and spoon flaming cherries over ice cream. Makes 8 servings.

While many flaming recipes call for a chafing dish, any durable casserole dish or pan would work. If you desire just a little bit of Sterno flavor with your sausage, here is a recipe for you!

Betty Crocker's appetizer centerpiece, Flaming Cabbage, begins with cleaning a large cabbage, curling the outer leaves back from the top, and hollowing out about six inches of the center. "Place a Sterno lamp in the cavity (lamp hidden, but flame should come almost to top of cabbage)." The cabbage was then placed on a serving plate and surrounded with parsley. "Thrust wooden picks through cocktail sausages and stick into the cabbage. Stick an olive onto end of each (to protect fingers from flame)." Guests are instructed to "broil their own sausages."[23]

John and Marie Roberson's *The Chafing Dish Cookbook* (1953) summed up the chafing dish's appeal. "The chafing dish is a symbol of some of the best things our civilization has produced—good fellowship, good living, good conversation, and, above all, good food."[24]

Theme Parties

Not only did theme parties often dominate the type of food served at special suburban parties, but guests regularly were encouraged to dress in appropriate costumes. The host and hostess provided decorations and, often, music and entertainment (in the form of party games, such as charades).

Theme parties increased in popularity during the 1950s and even extended to the outdoor barbecue. *Better Homes and Gardens Barbecue Book* (1956) declared that barbecued shish kebabs provided an excellent vehicle for presenting theme-party foods. A Middle Eastern theme would include skewers of eggplant and zucchini; a British Isles theme would utilize kidneys, mushrooms, and bacon; a tropical theme would see shish kebob skewers threaded with pineapple, bananas, and SPAM®; and a California-themed barbecue might include shish kebabs of hot dogs, bacon, and ripe olives.

The 1950s witnessed a surge of recipes with foods broadly considered Polynesian. Recipes abound utilizing pineapple, mango, papaya, banana, and coconut. Often, the foods had names vaguely reminiscent of far-off island locales or tropical paradises. One encounters recipes such as Bali Beef Casserole (*Meat Recipes 'Round-the-World*, 1955–1956); Salmon Salad Tropical (*Chiquita Banana's Recipe Book*, 1956); Hawaiian Barbecued Crown of Pork (*Cooking with the Experts*, 1955); Luau Spinach (*The General Foods Kitchens Cookbook*, 1959); and Honolulu Tuna (*Martha Deane's Cooking for Compliments*, 1954). Other exotically named dishes include the mysterious *Poulet Paul Gauguin Retour de Tahiti* (*Paris Cuisine*, 1952) and a slightly suggestive appetizer called Island Beach Boy Morsels found in *A Hawaiian Luau*, a pamphlet published in the 1950s by the Hawaiian Pineapple Company (later called the Dole Company).

The Backyard Hawaiian Luau

Heading the list of popular theme parties would be the Hawaiian luau that combined a mishmash of foods, drinks, music, and decorations drawn from the cultures of New Zealand, Hawaii, and other South Pacific Islands, as well as Rapa Nui (Easter Island).[25] Authenticity was never the goal, and cultural appropriation was not part of the era's discourse.

In the islands, a *luau* is a communal event of grand celebration involving music, dance, stories, and feasting. In America—and California specifically—the backyard luau was still very much a festive event, with any number of island-themed food and drinks. Still, it was much more of a statement. On the one hand, the food, music, and decor flew in the face of the still-prevailing conservative values of the time. On the other, nothing said success like a backyard luau—it was the perfect subversion.[26]

Tiki: The Beginning of a Movement

Until Hawaii became the fiftieth state in 1959, California was considered the closest thing to exotica. With the Pacific Ocean as its western frontier and real or imagined lush scenery, it is not surprising that California became the birthplace of the tiki movement. The suburban Hawaiian luau is just one small part of a movement established in 1933 with the opening of Donn Beach's (aka Ernest Raymond Beaumont Gantt) popular California restaurant Don's Beachcomber (later changed to Don the Beachcomber). Later, Victor Jules Bergeron Jr., better known as Trader Vic, opened Hinky Dinks in Oakland, California (later renamed Trader

Vic's), thus beginning his international empire of Polynesian-themed bars and restaurants. Joseph Stephen Crane, an actor who appeared in several B movies (and was married to actress Lana Turner—twice), opened The Luau on Rodeo Drive in Beverly Hills in 1953. This Polynesian-themed restaurant had a menu and decor like Don the Beachcomber and Trader Vic's. In 1958 Crane opened a Kon-Tiki chain of restaurants in the Sheraton Hotels that competed directly against Trader Vic's restaurants in the Hilton Hotels. The 1950s tiki craze had launched.

Don the Beachcomber and Trader Vic's served exotic drinks, created chiefly from rum, a liquor that originated in the Caribbean. However, the cocktails had names that might suggest the Pacific Islands or other ambiguous, mysterious, or dangerous locations: Scorpion's Bowl, Islander's Pearl, Sumatra Kula, Cobra's Fang, Shark's Tooth, and Zombie. The names often suggested exoticism and peril, two essential elements of the tiki movement. These theme-inspired restaurants and bars served Americanized Cantonese (Chinese) food (usually with a bit of pineapple added for island flavor) and decor that suggested tropical islands: fiery torches, fishing nets and driftwood, volcanoes, flower leis, garish fabrics, artificial waterfalls, and large wooden-carved images of "gods." Guests consumed cocktails in coconut shells, hollowed-out pineapples, or ceramic mugs that boldly displayed tiki gods or partially nude women. Of course, one sipped while experiencing the lush greenery of plastic palm trees (perhaps live plants in California).

Interest in island life grew during the 1950s due to the increasing affordability of visiting the Hawaiian Islands. Airlines aggressively marketed such journeys, which were now within the financial reach of many Americans. (Absent from this advertising push to get tourists to the Pacific Islands was any acknowledgment of the struggles of colonialism these islands endured.)

After Captain James Cook's disastrous arrival in Hawaii in 1776, where he was beaten to death by the island's inhabitants, the Hawaiian Islands became vulnerable to the dangers of European and US domination. US Christian missionaries first arrived in March 1820. Funded by the American Board of Commissioners for Foreign Missions, the first fourteen missionaries were Presbyterians, Congregationalists, and Dutch Reformists from New England. Their focus included converting the Hawaiians to the Christian faith, but they also suppressed much of the native culture and introduced Western ideas and customs. While the missionaries developed a written form of the indigenous language, they insisted on making English

Hawaii's official language.²⁷ In the 1830s, American growers established the sugar industry, which resulted in significant changes in the political, cultural, and economic lives of the native Hawaiians. Over the following decades, numerous treaties were signed, and as part of a new Hawaiian constitution, the US established a naval base in 1887 at Pearl Harbor. In 1890 the McKinley Tariff law raised import rates on foreign sugar, enraging the American sugar planters working in Hawaii. However, they realized that if Hawaii were to be annexed by the US, the tariff problem would disappear. In January 1893, under the urging of plantation owner Samuel Dole, US troops invaded the Hawaiian Kingdom, leading to surrender by Her Majesty Queen Liliuokalani. When the Spanish-American war broke out in 1898, the US realized the importance of naval bases in the Pacific to reach the Spanish Philippines. The US was also concerned that Hawaii might become part of a European empire. Congress approved formal annexation, and Hawaii became a territory in 1900. In 1959 Hawaii entered the United States as its fiftieth state.²⁸

Pre–World War II tiki bars and restaurants were considered exotic places for drinks and dinner, and the movement gained traction at the return of the thousands of American servicemembers who fought in the Pacific. Recognized as one of the most brutal war conflicts, the Pacific Theater was a battleground for the ultimate and most dreadful new weaponry, ending with the dropping of atomic bombs on Nagasaki and Hiroshima, Japan. These Polynesian-styled bars and restaurants now took on a new significance: reminding weary soldiers of the beauty and naturalness of the Islands. In other words, it was possible to create a unique, romanticized memory of the horrors of war: warm breezes, calm blue-green water, miles of white and sandy beaches, and beautiful (and scantily clad) island women. Trader Vic's and Don the Beachcomber offered a fantasy alternative to the years of the Great Depression, war, and the eventual blandness of suburban life and, perhaps, even 1950s processed foods. In any case, these experiences condensed into a popular suburban ritual: the Hawaiian luau.

Hollywood Movies, Forbidden Sex, and the Sultry Landscapes of the Tropics

Americans mainly experienced the tropics through the lens of Hollywood in films that emphasized lush jungle-like scenery, pristine beaches, endless blue skies, warm trade winds, and gorgeous women. The two elements of an imagined Polynesian life that appealed to the fantasies of ordinary people included forbidden love and the danger of the unknown.

Hollywood films inspired by island fantasies proved popular, beginning in the 1920s. One of the first films in this genre was *White Shadows in the South Seas* (1928), MGM's first sound picture). Other early films include *The Love Trader* (1930), distributed by Tiffany Productions and preserved as part of the National Film Registry at the Library of Congress, and *Bird of Paradise* (1932). This pre-code, sexually explicit movie starred Dolores del Río and was the film debut of Lon Chaney (appearing under his real name Creighton Chaney). It was directed by King Vidor and produced by David O. Selznick, distributed by RKO Radio Pictures. *Ships Ahoy* (1942) starred Eleanor Powell, Red Skelton, and the Tommy Dorsey Band. The era produced many popular, tropical-themed B movies, including *She Gods of Shark Reef*, directed by Roger Corman. The *Los Angeles Times* noted it had only two redeeming characteristics, "It is in color and it is only 63 minutes long."[29]

More Polynesian-inspired films were issued in the 1950s. Although filmed on the MGM studio lot and in Florida, *On an Island with You* (1948) is a musical comedy that featured a blockbuster cast of Esther Williams, Cyd Charisse, Peter Lawford, Ricardo Montalban, Jimmy Durante, and Xavier Cugat. The film contains all the requirements of an excellent island-based film: tropical setting, romance, and cannibals. Another was *Pagan Love Song* (1950), featuring Esther Williams, Howard Keel, and Rita Moreno; directed by Robert Alton; and distributed by MGM. (Films with Esther Williams are known as "song-and-swim musicals" because their star, Williams, had been a competitive swimmer.) *The Bird of Paradise* (remade in 1951) was based on a 1912 play by Richard Walton Tully and starred Debra Paget and Louis Jourdan. Distributed by 20th Century Fox, the film centers on one of the favorite themes for this genre: a white man falling in love with an island maiden. In 1952, Warner Bros. released *Big Jim McLain*. Starring John Wayne and James Arness, this political thriller touched on two 1950s themes: its plot centers on two investigators from the House Un-American Activities Committee who are looking for communists, and the film is set in postwar Hawaii. Situated in the waning years of World War II, *Mister Roberts* (1955) stars Henry Fonda, James Cagney, William Powell, and Jack Lemon (who won an Academy Award for Best Supporting Actor). In 1959 the film *Gidget*, starring Sandra Dee and 1950s heartthrob singer James Darren and featuring the music of the Four Preps, started a surfing-movie craze.

Figure 8.3. Movie poster for *She Gods of Shark Reef* (1958). Directed by Roger Corman, the movie centers on two brothers (one wanted for murder), who find themselves shipwrecked on an island inhabited by attractive young women. Source: Everett Collection/Alamy Stock Photo.

More Parties, the Cult of the Chafing Dish, and the Suburban Luau | 179

Perhaps the two most influential films of the 1950s that highlight island life are the documentary *Kon-Tiki* (1951) and the Richard Rodgers and Oscar Hammerstein II musical *South Pacific* (1958). *Kon-Tiki* is a Norwegian-Swedish documentary based on an exploration led by Thor Heyerdahl, and the film was released in the US in 1951 (and received an Academy Award for Best Documentary Feature). Heyerdahl's book, *Kon-Tiki: Across the Pacific in a Raft* (published in Norwegian in 1948 and English in 1950), is based on Heyerdahl's theory that ancient cultures might have made long ocean journeys during the pre-Columbian era. In a raft built from the technology and materials available during the pre-Columbian period, Heyerdahl and a crew floated for 101 days across the Pacific Ocean from Peru to the Polynesian Islands. Although today's experts reject Heyerdahl's thesis, the book and film continued the fascination of all things Polynesian during the 1950s.

South Pacific began as a musical that opened on Broadway in 1949. The music was composed by Richard Rodgers, with lyrics by Oscar Hammerstein II, and based on James A. Michener's Pulitzer Prize-winning 1947 book *Tales of the South Pacific*.[30] Starring Enzo Pinza and Mary Martin, the musical won ten Tony Awards. Unusual for the era, the play's direct message about and confrontation with racism provoked some controversy,

Figure 8.4. Thor Heyerdahl's raft, Kon Tiki, 1947. Source: Everett Collection Historical/Alamy Stock Photo.

180 | Casseroles, Can Openers, and Jell-O

Figure 8.5. Mitzi Gaynor as Ensign Nellie Forbush in the 1958 film adaptation of Rodgers and Hammerstein's Broadway hit musical *South Pacific*. Source: Album/Alamy Stock Photo.

especially in the southern US. It was made into a film in 1958 and nominated for three Academy Awards. Rodgers and Hammerstein had hoped to use the Broadway leads, Enzo Pinza and Mary Martin, in the movie, but Pinza died suddenly in 1957 and they sought to recast both roles. Doris Day was offered Martin's role of Nellie but she refused, and Elizabeth Taylor auditioned but was rejected by Rodgers. Eventually, the part went to Mitzi Gaynor. The role of Emile was turned down by Charles Boyer, Vittorio De Sica, and Fernando Lamas. Rossano Brazzi ended up with the role (dubbed with the voice of Metropolitan Opera star Giorgio Tozzi).

Island Cocktails

These aren't really drinks. They're trade winds across cool lagoons. They're the Southern Cross above coral reefs. They're a lovely maiden bathing at the foot of a waterfall.

—From the Warner Bros. film *The Blue Gardenia* (1953)[31]

Many wax sentimental about the cocktails served at Polynesian-themed bars, at restaurants, or in one's backyard. The truth is, like the rest of the romanticized tiki life, the drinks represented a jumble of cultures. Bartenders forgot that rum-based beverages are not from the Pacific Islands, even when mixed with tropical juices, but originate in the Caribbean. The ever-present pineapple originated in Brazil and grew in other South American countries, eventually cultivated throughout Central America and Mexico. Pineapples appeared in the United States in the eighteenth century, and soon the Spanish brought the pineapple to Hawaii. Perhaps the most successful pineapple grower was James Dole, who moved to Hawaii at the very end of the nineteenth century and, within a few years, was growing pineapples, which became a major export commodity for the islands. Dole established the Hawaiian Pineapple Company, later named Dole Food Company. (James Dole was a cousin of Samuel Dole, who served as governor of the Republic of Hawaii after the 1893 overthrow of the monarchy and strongly advocated for the annexation of Hawaii.)

Almost all the recipes for drinks served in Trader Vic's bars and restaurants were Polynesian in name but often Caribbean in flavor. For example, in his cookbook, Trader Vic acknowledges the contribution of bartender "Constantino, of La Florida Bar in Havana" and provides recipes for four "La Florida Daiquiris." While Constantino (Ribalaigua Vert) was a bartender, the Cuban bar was called El Floridita and is the bar made famous by writer Ernest Hemingway. Known in Cuba as the "king of cocktails," Ribalaigua's special version of the El Floridita daiquiri was well-loved by Hemingway. Hemingway's version (known as the Papa Doble), called for twice the amount of rum, a bit of lime juice, and no sugar. Later, Riblaigua added maraschino liqueur as a sweetener.[32] The following recipe differs from traditional daiquiris by using grapefruit juice.

La Florida Daiquiri No. 3.

Trader Vic's Book of Food & Drink (1946)[33]

2 ounces Bacardi [rum]
1 teaspoon of sugar
1 teaspoon grapefruit juice
1 teaspoon maraschino
Juice of ½ lemon
Shaved ice.

Shake well; serve frappé [not strained].

Figure 8.6. A 1950s magazine advertisement for Dole canned Hawaiian pineapple juice. Source: f8 archive/Alamy Stock Photo.

Decor, Food, and Entertainment for the Suburban Luau

Author Kaori O'Connor notes that the luau is one of the few indigenous feasts that became a part of mainstream American culture. In 1819 the strict eating taboos of native Hawaiians were canceled, and men and women of all social classes could eat together. The first luaus included pig, fish, and chicken accompanied by sweet potatoes and poi, a starchy substance originating from the tuber taro, boiled and then pounded into a paste. During the 1820s, American missionaries attempted to eradicate indigenous foods and festivals centering on food. With the overthrow of the monarchy and Hawaii subsequently annexed by the United States, luaus and traditional hula dancing disappeared as US officials attempted to Westernize Hawaiian culture. "However, the efforts to promote the islands as a typically American tourist resort were a resounding failure because the attraction of Hawaii was, and is, the exotic and strange, albeit in a safe setting." Thus, the luau was reinstated and reinvented for the tourist trade.[34]

How You Can Give Hawaiian Parties (1959) provides information on how to give Hawaiian theme dinners, luncheons, teas, receptions, housewarmings, buffet suppers, fundraisers, and beach parties. This book is written by the Hawaiian Pineapple Company home economics expert, Patricia Collier. (Collier, like Betty Crocker, did not exist.) For decorating, Collier suggests iris and gladiolus from the garden, Queen Anne's lace from the side of the road, or potted philodendrons. Potted palm trees are a nice touch, but if they are unavailable, Collier provides instructions for constructing larger versions from paper or tiny palms out of pipe cleaners. Directions also are provided to turn pineapple cans into flower or candle holders.

A flower lei helps your guests get in the mood, and according to Collier, you can make one with lots of flowers, needles, and thread. She suggests carnations, noting that one will need approximately six dozen carnations for each lei. If one has eight guests, that is 48 dozen carnations, which would require a significant investment of money. Perhaps that is why she also suggests, "Use your own ingenuity!" For a Hawaiian party around Christmas when fresh flowers are harder to find, one can always string popcorn or cranberries (a string of peanuts will do at any time of the year). Collier also provides information on the "graceful way to give a lei": the traditional way to give a lei is to place it gently around the neck of the recipient, accompanying it with a kiss of greeting. The host presents a lei to each woman guest, and the hostess, to each man. (Collier assures her readers that, indeed, men wear them, too.) If one does not know how to pronounce lei, Collier is there to help: "Pronounced lay."[35]

As well as providing floral arrangements, it was necessary to decorate the table and arrange a centerpiece. "For the tablecloth use coarse or fine mesh curtain net. Under it lay paper cut-outs of tropical fish, starfish, and sea moss." Bamboo-designed wallpaper might cover tables. Centerpieces can be created by laying "a sea of blue paper and in it set an island of green modeling clay covered with sand. In the clay anchor small palm trees, tiny figures, and perhaps a little grass shack made by thatching a small box with grass."[36] "An amusing edible decoration for a large open-house gathering: a 'pineapple'—any size—made of liverwurst shaped around an inverted jelly glass, with sliced stuffed olives for 'eyes,' and iris leaves for top."[37]

Hawaiian food takes two forms: the traditional food of native Hawaiians and the diverse foods introduced by later arrivals that blended into the cuisine. First, the New England missionaries arrived with salted meat and fish. Later, immigrants from Japan, China, Korea, Okinawa, the Philippines, Puerto Rico, and Portugal came to seek work, followed by immigrants from Samoa, Tonga, Vietnam, and Thailand. "As each ethnicity adapted their cuisine to the readily available ingredients and as dishes were borrowed and exchanged among groups, local food was born."[38]

ISLAND BEACH BOY MORSELS
(BACON WRAPPED CHUNKS)

A Hawaiian Luau (c. 1950)[39]

[The recipe directions provide hors d'oeuvres for 25, 50, and 100 pieces. The following is for 25 pieces.]

25 Pineapple Chunks
13 slices of Bacon, cut in half

Wrap ½ bacon slice around each chunk and secure with toothpick

Broil on each side until lightly browned or fry in deep fat fryer until bacon is crisp.

Pork Hawaiian

Wiki Wiki Kau Kau (1954)

6 Pork Chops
3 medium-sized sweet potatoes
4 bananas
4 fresh pineapple sticks
Shoyu [soy sauce]

Soak chops in shoyu for 5 minutes. Brown on top of stove and then place in roasting pan. Cut potatoes in half inch slices crosswise and put into oven with chops (350 degrees) and cook for 15 minutes. Add bananas and pineapple. Sprinkle with brown sugar and pineapple juice if desired and bake 15 minutes longer. Serves 4.

Pineapple Sticks

Wiki Wiki Kau Kau (1954)[40]

Fresh Pineapple Sticks
½ cup rum

Pour rum over pineapple and set in refrigerator to chill. Turn sticks occasionally. This makes a light and refreshing dessert.

"An enchanting, teeming, intoxicatory and festering easy-listening sub-genre that vexed many an unsuspecting ear."[41] This music is exotica, a *tropical ersatz* of an inauthentic experience consisting of a mixture of music from the Pacific Islands, Japan, China, the Caribbean, Africa, and Latin America. Or, as another writer proclaimed, exotica's geographic location might be summed up as "places with palm trees."[42] Author Joseph Lanza further notes, "Just as we annexed Hawaii as a full-fledged state of the union, thousands of Americans and European tourists never before exposed to the Pacific side of paradise, heard the best symphonies of conch shells, wind chimes, ukuleles, koto, bamboo sticks, and tropical bird calls." Anyone could experience this music in their own homes as a staggering number of recordings were available.

Popular music of the 1950s, criticized for its perceived uncivilized rhythms and often referred to as "jungle" or "savage," was condemned by clergymen, educators, and parents. This "adults only" genre of music was best known for these very same inspirations. Although Xavier Cugat employed jungle sounds in the 1940s, one of the first musicians to explore exotica music was Les Baxter, known for his television and movie scores. His 1950 *Le Sacre du Sauvage* (Ritual of the Savage) is considered one of the most important contributions to the exotica genre. Other contributors include Martin Denny, who infused jazz and Latin American rhythms, birdcalls, and even croaking frogs into his music. Denny's album *Exotica* reached the top of *Billboard*'s charts in 1959. Arthur Lyman, the "king of lounge music," also created popular ersatz Polynesian music during the 1950s and 1960s. Discovered by Les Baxter, Peruvian soprano Yma Sumac, with a famous vocal range of more than four and a half octaves, was one of the most famous exponents of this music. As an example of the range of influences in this genre music, Sumac made a series of best-selling recordings featuring arrangements of Incan and South American folk songs.

To sell processed pineapple products both canned and frozen, several of the booklets published by the Hawaiian Pineapple Company assisted suburbanites in recreating Hawaiian home entertainments. However, popcorn-strung leis and pipe cleaner palm trees would be a far cry from the exotic offerings of a Trader Vic's or other Polynesian-themed restaurants—and many imitators of Trader Vic and Don Beachcomber were springing up all over the US. Perhaps the guests tried guessing the number of eyes on fresh pineapple, attempted hula dancing or ukulele playing, or strained their backs attempting the limbo (a dance that originated on the Caribbean Island of Trinidad). Still, there was nothing of the imagined island danger, excitement, romance, sexuality, or atmosphere in these suburban luaus. For their island experiences, people turned to the glamour of Hollywood films, read James Michener's books, viewed Paul Gauguin's paintings, and listened to the music of Les Baxter, Arthur Lyman, or Jacques Brel. Perhaps they prepared one of the innumerable recipes for imagined island feasts suggested by the era's cookbook authors. For most suburbanites, these were the only passports to the mythical and exotic tropical lands that lived only in imaginations.

Chapter 9

Foreign Foods?
Chop Suey, Tamale Pie, Chef Boy-Ar-Dee, and Some Curry

> Fifty years ago, "foreign foods" were viewed with suspicion and horror. Our forebearers were solidly behind the opinion that all foods with foreign names were simultaneously too greasy and too hot. This is ridiculous, we realize now.
>
> —*Simple Cooking for the Epicure* (1949)[1]

Food trends in the 1950s are full of paradoxes. The era is known for SPAM® sandwiches, Velveeta, colorful Jell-O creations, and casseroles based on cans of soup. However, the period also marked a growing interest in international and gourmet foods. America's "kitchen bibles,"[2] issued by large corporations at the beginning of the 1950s, soon gave way to specialty books. These books provided recipes based on regional cooking, chafing dish cooking, casseroles, cookbooks focused on pies or cakes, gourmet cooking, and international cuisines. The market flooded with cookbooks on Chinese, Mexican, Russian, French, Italian, Jewish, Indian, German, Scandinavian, and other cuisines, all for the suburban American housewife. Authors assured readers that the home economics professionals vigilantly tested each recipe and adapted it to the American palate. *The Time Reader's Book of Recipes* (1951) guaranteed that the recipes "are exotic enough to intrigue your guests, not *too* exotic to alarm their palates."[3] Food writer Clementine Paddleford (1898–1967) observed, "Even with the increasingly popular trend toward foreign foods, the dishes come to the table with an American accent."[4]

Middle-class acceptance of ethnic cuisines, meaning non-Anglo food, increased in postwar America. For those who preferred to avoid the trouble of cooking, experiencing foreign foods meant going to a restaurant. Here one might find Americanized versions of pasta or pizza at an Italian restaurant, chop suey in a Chinese establishment, Tex-Mex tacos from a fast-food restaurant, or a pastrami on rye sandwich at a Jewish deli.

> If I consult a cookbook at all, it is likely to be by one of these sensible, flat-heeled authors like the famous Mrs. Kander.
>
> —James A. Beard, American chef, author, and television star[5]

As an example of one of the most financially successful fundraising or charity cookbooks ever published in the US, *The Settlement Cook Book: The Way to a Man's Heart* was initially created as a simple pamphlet for young immigrant women and was published in 1901. It was compiled by Lizzie Black Kander (1858–1940) and grew out of cooking classes she conducted for new immigrants at Milwaukee's Settlement House. Kander was "tasked with teaching a recent wave of Jewish immigrants—many from Russia—how to, essentially, keep good, clean, middle-class homes, [and] she thought a book might be a good way to do it."[6] Kander's philosophy of assimilation was in sync with the prevailing progressive-era goals.

Although the book's early editions contained few Jewish recipes, over the next forty years Kander revised the text to include more Jewish dishes (especially for the holidays) and foods from other cultures. While some of the recipes were kosher, others were not. The 1954 edition included bacon, pork, ham, and pork sausage recipes. This edition also contains recipes for Chow Mein, Egg Foo Yung, Chili Con Carne, Risotto, and several curries.[7] She oversaw the book through twenty-three editions before she died in 1940. The book's last edition appeared in 1991 (reprinted in 1997), called *The New Settlement Cookbook: The First Classic Collection of Ethnic Recipes*, credited to author and compiler Charles Pierce.

Mainstream and Specialty Cookbooks Tackle Foreign Foods

During the 1950s, cookbook approaches to ethnic cuisines were guarded. *Betty Crocker's Picture Cook Book* (1950) represents typical American cooking, embracing selected international recipes such as Araby Spice Cake,

Hungarian Goulash, and Mexican Liver. However, most internationally inspired dishes focused on the German-Scandinavian immigrants that settled in the upper Midwest, where the book was published.

The Joy of Cooking (1951) also offers assorted international recipes, including representatives from the German heritage of authors Irma S. Rombauer and her daughter Marion Rombauer Becker, such as Blitzkuchen, Blitztorte, Braunschweiger Pie, Koenigsberger Klops, and Hasenpfeffer. Not just limited to German foods, *The Joy of Cooking* also includes recipes for other international (or internationally inspired) dishes, including Blini, Beef Chop Suey, American-style Koumiss (a fermented drink), and Japanese Sukiyaki.

As mainstream cookbooks included more and more German recipes, eventually these recipes were not considered unusual or even ethnic, and much of the cuisine gradually subsumed into the American food repertory. Thus, dishes such as kuchen, streusel, or braunschweiger were often as familiar as chop suey. However, the one German food that most influenced American taste was the sausage, specifically the frankfurter (better known as the hot dog), which became an all-American food and reigned supreme at barbecues, providing unlimited possibilities for casseroles and even making its way into Jell-O salads.

Specialty cookbooks often sacrificed authenticity for ease and familiarity of ingredients. *Carnation Cook Book* (1942), written by Carnation's imaginary spokeswoman Mary Blake, offers several "international dishes." Recipes include Chinese Eggs, Scotch Shortbread, Swedish Meatballs, Polish Salad, and Spanish Fried Rice. Most require Carnation Condensed Milk. *The Melting Pot: A Cookbook of All Nations* (1958) presents its version of dishes from Italy, Vienna, Scandinavia, and various recipes called "Oriental." The recipes are easy to follow, contain no unusual ingredients, and rely on the availability of processed foods. For example, a recipe for Finnish Herring Salad includes cans of peas, carrots, and red beets mixed with a jar of herring fillets.

International Dishes Turn into Suburban Casseroles

International recipes often utilized the era's popular processed foods, specifically canned cream soups, canned fish, and canned vegetables and regularly reduced them into the familiar 1950s casserole. *The ABC of Casseroles* (1954) offers a worldwide hodgepodge of casseroles that emphasizes the names of geographic locations such as Armenian Casserole, Austrian Stuffed Cabbage, Belgian Meatballs, Beef Parisienne, and London

Fish Soufflé. *Good Housekeeping's Casserole Book* (1958) also offered its casserole versions of foreign cuisine with contributions including Swedish Meatballs, Arroz con Pollo ("A dandy dish from South America"), Coq au Vin, Betty's Armenian Casserole, Mexican-Border Casserole, and Ham Ling Lo (anchored by two cans of luncheon meat, probably SPAM®).

Casserole Specialties (1955) noted, "Here is a love of a cookbook, filled with a wide variety of recipes from other countries. You will find many specialty party casseroles, the kind that prompt other husbands to say 'Get the recipe dear.'"[8] Dishes include Eggs Bombay, Kasha Casserole, Riso Neapolitan, and Sole en Papillotes. Interestingly, the names of some recipes would have meant nothing to many suburbanites, such as Ghivetch Bucaresti (a Romanian vegetable stew); Kibbi (a Middle Eastern dish of spiced, chopped meat, and bulgur), and Lahmajoon (thin dough topped with meat, vegetables, and herbs, like a pizza).

Americans Take On French Cuisine

With travel newly affordable in the 1950s, a taste for new cuisines in the United States accelerated, especially for French foods. Considered a refined, high-status food in the growing gourmet arena, cookbook authors tried to convince the average housewife that French cooking was not difficult and that fancy, complicated recipes did not always mean a good French-inspired meal. Instead, housewives might ignore "the fancied-up type of cooking that so frequently passes for traditional French cooking—dishes which are far too complicated for every day use."[9] *Pardon My Foie Gras* (1956) suggests that although French cooking is challenging, much of it is very simple if done with care. Another publication written for ordinary cooks is *The Melting Pot: A Cookbook of All Nations* (1958). Here the author presents a variety of French dishes all greatly simplified for the home cook. Recipes include Vichyssoise (a soup created in New York City), Fish en Gelée, Crêpes Suzette, and Duck à L'Orange.[10]

In *Pardon My Foie Gras*, Ruth Chier Rosen observed that in mastering the sauces she has provided, "you have accomplished half the battle." Rosen provides recipes for fourteen sauces, ranging from Marchand de Vin to Sauce Chasseur and Bearnaise Sauce.[11] Peggy Harvey's *When the Cook's Away* (1952) also stresses the importance of sauces in French cuisine. Her "orthodox sauces" include Hollandaise Sauce, Curry Sauce, Barbecue Sauce, and Spaghetti Sauce—all staples of 1950s suburban cooking; "unorthodox sauces" include Velouté and Béchamel.

In January of 1941, Condé Nast published its inaugural issue of *Gourmet* magazine, the first US monthly periodical dedicated to fine food and wine. *Gourmet* was to food what Vogue was to fashion.[12] *The New York Times* declared that the magazine represented "the end of domestic science and food economy and the beginning of the era of the gourmet." Many of the era's most celebrated writers and food experts contributed to *Gourmet*, including M. F. K. Fisher, James A. Beard, Louis Diat, Lucius Beebe, Clementine Paddleford, and Trader Vic.[13]

Famous Champions of Gourmet Cooking in America

Three of the primary advocates for gourmet cooking included Louis Diat, Dione Lucas, and James A. Beard. French American Louis Diat (1885–1957) was world-famous for his more than forty-year tenure as chef at Manhattan's Ritz-Carlton and six cookbooks published between 1941 and 1961. He is often attributed as the creator of the soup *Crème Vichyssoise Glacée* or Vichyssoise—even if that credit is disputed in the culinary world. Diat was popular despite his harsh words for American housewives, claiming that "they are always in too much of a hurry, and they won't learn to make sauces. They skimp on butter, in a mistaken sense of frugality, and often ruin good food trying to save a few cents or a few minutes."[14] (His book offers forty-five recipes for a variety of sauces.) Diat's French recipes are often complicated, requiring a wide range of ingredients. For example, recipes such as Ragoû d'Agneau ou Mouton and Duckling Chipolata Menagere both call for more than fifteen ingredients. A recipe for a "simple" tomato soup (Crème de Tomate) requires fourteen ingredients.

> **DUCKLING WITH PEAS (CANARD AUX PETITS POIS BONNE FEMME)**
>
> *Louis Diat's French Cooking for Americans* (1946)[15]
>
> 1 duckling, 5–6 lbs.
> 6–8 small onions
> 2 cups shelled peas
> ½ cup water
> ½ cup diced fat salt pork, sautéed until crisp

1 faggot
2 to 4 leaves green lettuce
1 tablespoon butter
1 teaspoon flour

Clean and singe duckling and truss legs and wings close to body. Season with salt, put in a casserole in a moderately hot oven of 425 degrees and roast ½ hour. Remove duck from casserole and pour off all the fat from the casserole. Mix together peas, pork dice, lettuce leaves and onions and put in casserole. Add water and faggot, bring to a boil and lay duck on top. Cover casserole, return to oven, and continue cooking 45 minutes to 1 hour or until duckling is done. Remove duck to service dish, correct seasoning of cooking liquid and thicken it with Manié Butter, made by creaming together butter and flour. Carve duck and serve surrounded with vegetables and sauce. Services 4 to 5.

[On page 294 Diat explains that a faggot consists of sprigs parsley, celery stalks, ½ a bay leaf, and a pinch of dry (or fresh) thyme tied together in a small bundle and cooked in a stew or sauce.]

Englishwoman Dione Lucas (1909–1971) was one of the earliest chefs to host televised cooking shows. Born in Italy and raised in France, Lucas was the first female graduate of the famed Paris cooking school Le Cordon Bleu. Upon immigrating to the US, she opened her own Cordon Bleu cooking school and restaurant in New York City and then became a television celebrity hosting *To the Queen's Taste* (1947–1953), *The Dione Lucas Cooking Show* (1953–1956), and *Dione Lucas's Gourmet Club* (1958–1960). She published eight books, and in the introduction to the *Cordon Bleu Cook Book* (1947), Lucas mirrored Diat's perception of American homemakers. "In the United States, with an abundance of food never known in Europe, and with all the native talent and ability available, it is unfortunate that more emphasis is not placed on the importance of cooking as an art. There is a tendency to whisk in and out of the kitchen, to be lured by dishes that can be made most quickly." She notes that cooking is not the same as making beds or washing dishes.

It requires "time, skill and patience." Her books were tailored to assist those "who love good food, to inspire them to the level of the creative artist, so that they too will know the real satisfaction that comes from dishes well prepared."[16]

Coquilles St. Jacques en Escalopes (Baked Scallops)

The Cordon Bleu Cookbook (1947)[17]

2 scallops per person
2 tablespoons melted butter
½ cup good dry white wine
1 cup cream per 4 scallops
Salt and pepper
handful bread crumbs
Small lump butter

Open scallops by putting them in the oven for a few minutes. Remove the black frill. Put the wine in a pan, adding to it salt, pepper and a little water before adding the scallop meat. Drain and cut the scallops in thin slices. Put them in a pan with the melted butter. Cook very gently for about 4 minutes. Season well and add the cream. Mix well. Fill the deep shells, which have been well scrubbed out. Sprinkle thickly with fine bread crumbs. Put a lump of butter on top of each and brown quickly under the grill.

American chef, author, and television star James A. Beard (1903–1985) is considered the dean of American cuisine and is recognized as "one of the most influential exponents of good cooking in the twentieth century."[18] Beard wrote more than thirty books on cooking, seven written in the 1950s, including *Jim Beard's complete book of barbecue & rotisserie cooking* (1954) and *Casserole Cookbook* (1955). *I Love to Eat* (1946–1947) was America's first live television cooking show, where Beard became well-known to suburban housewives. Often criticized for his merchandise endorsements, Beard used income from the sale of French's Mustard, Green Giant's Corn Niblets, DuPont chemicals, and other products to establish the James Beard Cooking School in New York City.

Paris Cuisine (1952), cowritten by Beard and British journalist Alexander Watt, is described as a "spectacular book of cooking in the great French tradition." The front cover jacket notes, "Mr. Beard and Mr. Watt admit that some of the recipes in their book may be something of a challenge to the beginner; obviously, some are both expensive and elaborate. But they guarantee that every recipe can be prepared in the average American kitchen, with the use of a little ingenuity and substitutions where indicated." Based on recipes from some of the most famous Paris restaurants of the 1950s, the authors declare that the cookbook is "an exotic cook book and an exclusively one in the sense that we have striven to set down for you in black and white the best of the best."[19] Similar to Diat's cookbook, the recipes in *Paris Cuisine* are more complex than those found in 1950s mainstream cookbooks. Although the authors note that "fresh truffles are not available as a general rule in this country," they provide instructions for Truffes en Serviette as served at the famous 1950s Paris restaurant L'Escargot, located at 38 Rue Montorgueil. The recipe, which serves one, calls for a large fresh truffle, a couple of tablespoons of butter and madeira, a tablespoon of cognac, and reduced veal stock. Additions include salt, pepper, and paprika. After brushing and pricking a fresh truffle, it is seasoned with salt, pepper, and paprika. "Place it in a small saucepan with the melted butter, Madeira and Cognac." The veal stock is added after cooking the truffle for seven to eight minutes. "The truffle is served in a small silver or copper cocotte (casserole) in a napkin folded so that the cocotte is practically surrounded by the linen napkin."[20]

In discussing the definition of gourmet foods, *The Gourmet Foods Cookbook* (1955) suggests a more practical approach. Gourmet food is "food with a flair. It is sometimes a familiar food in a striking new dress with a retinue of unusual flavors. Or a beloved favorite cast in a new role in the drama of the dinner menu."[21] French-inspired recipes range from Bordelaise Sauce, various brioches and croissants, *Pâtés de Bison Bourgeoise* (Bison or Buffalo Pies), *Escargots Bourguignonne* (Snails Burgundy), and *Caneton à l'Orange* (Duckling with Orange). The cookbook includes Lamb Chops Hawaiian, Almond Schnecken, Fresh Shrimp Curry, Cherry Soup, and Luscious Chocolate Rum Cake.

Ruth Chier Rosen's *Pardon My Foie Gras* offers recipes "in the French manner." Rosen also reminds the cook that, with care, French cuisine is not complex. Organized by region, the cookbook offers the following from

Brittany. (Fresh truffles were almost impossible to obtain and cooks relied on a canned product. Nevertheless, Rosen's recipe requires four truffles.)

Fillet of Sole en Papillote

Pardon My Foie Gras (1956)[22]

6 sole fillets
1 T chopped chives
2 c. crabmeat
¼ lb. butter
1 clove garlic, minced
2 oz. white wine
1 c. mushrooms, chopped
1 T chopped olives
4 truffles, chopped
2 T sour cream
Salt and pepper

Mix crabmeat, garlic, mushrooms, truffles, chives, and sour cream. Place spoonful of mixture on each fillet and fold over. Brush with melted butter and pour on olives and wine. Wrap in parchment and bake in hot oven 30 minutes. Serve in papers.

Italian Food in America

> The conception that most Americans have of Italian cookery has been built largely upon the traditional Italo-American restaurant, specializing in antipasto, minestrone, spaghetti, veal scaloppine and spumoni—a combination that you would have some difficulty in obtaining on Italian soil.
>
> —*The Talisman Italian Cook Book* (1950)[23]

By the 1950s, distinctions among Italian regional cuisines had disappeared. To Americans, the food was simply known as Italian, with cookbooks offering an array of "traditional" as well as Americanized dishes. A popular dish many Americans assumed originated in Italy is spaghetti and meatballs. However, in Italian cuisine, meatballs are served as a standalone dish, called *polpette*. Although these small meatballs were often served without sauce, Italian immigrants found that meat was abundant and relatively affordable in the US. Thus, meatballs soon appeared in homes, accompanied by a sauce made from canned tomatoes and served on cooked, inexpensive dried pasta.

Betty Crocker's Picture Cook Book lists six dishes under the term "Italian," including stuffed artichokes and a recipe for Italian eggplant (a casserole consisting of noodles, tomatoes, and eggplant, topped with Wheaties cereal or cracker crumbs). Crocker provides a recipe for Spaghetti with Meatballs but not listed in the Italian section; thus, by 1950 and in the eyes of many cookbooks, the dish was already established as American fare.

Better Homes and Gardens New Cook Book (1953) offers two unusual dishes, Irish-Italian Spaghetti and Mexitalian Spaghetti. In a similar, transnational vein, *Simple Cooking for the Epicure* (1949) provides a recipe for Chinese enchiladas. (While the names seem odd for the era, perhaps, they can be considered models for the future of fusion foods.) The only recipe in the book's index identified as "Italian" is a twenty-minute spaghetti sauce cooked in a pressure cooker. *The Joy of Cooking* (1951) suggests that for an authentic presentation in Italy, "the spaghetti is served in one dish, the sauce in another and grated cheese in a third."[24] *Joy* provides nine spaghetti "sauce" recipes, including meat sauce, anchovy sauce, tuna fish sauce (with canned tuna), liver sauce, and a seafood sauce. (*Joy* also suggests putting all the ingredients in an electric blender, creating a liquified spaghetti sauce.)

The tomato-based seafood stew known as cioppino originated in late nineteenth-century San Francisco by Italian fishermen. In *How America Eats*, Clementine Paddleford vividly describes eating cioppino at Tarantino's Restaurant on Fisherman's Wharf. "I poked into the dish with an exploring fork, a strange gathering of seafare—oysters, lobsters, crab, clams. Then the first rapturous taste of the sauce-steeped garlic bread—delectable sauce. The dish is made over charcoal braziers, made of whatever the day's catch supplies. It may be shellfish entirely, or seafood and shellfish, the various kinds washed, cleaned, layered in the pot; then a rich garlicky tomato sauce added and the collection cooked."[25]

Veal Parmigiana originated in the US from the Italian diaspora and is based on a breaded eggplant dish called *melanzane alla parmigiana*. Cooks could find Parmigiana recipes throughout 1950s cookbooks.

Veal Parmigiana

The General Foods Kitchens Cookbook (1959)[26]

2 pounds veal cutlets, ¼ inch thick
1 egg beaten
¼ teaspoon salt
Dash of pepper
¾ cup bread crumbs
5 tablespoons grated Parmesan cheese
⅛ teaspoon oregano (optional)
Olive oil or shortening
1 can (8 oz.) tomato sauce
½ pound mozzarella cheese, sliced thin

Pound cutlets and dip into egg, which has been seasoned with salt and pepper. Then dip into a combination of bread crumbs, 3 tablespoons of the Parmesan cheese, and the oregano. Sauté cutlets in oil or shortening until well browned. Place in a shallow baking dish. Pour tomato sauce over cutlets; then top with slices of mozzarella cheese. Sprinkle with remaining Parmesan cheese. Bake in moderate oven (375° F.) about 20 minutes. Makes 6 servings.

As early as 1950, pizza restaurants were offering refrigerated pizzas to be cooked by their customers at home, and within a few years commercially produced frozen pizzas were widely available in supermarkets. Canned Italian foods also proved to be extremely popular throughout the 1950s. At the end of the nineteenth century, Alphonse Biardot founded the Franco American Company, featuring canned soups and pasta. The company was acquired by the Campbell Soup Company in 1915, selling its line of canned spaghetti until the brand was discontinued in 2004.

Unlike Betty Crocker and other fictional cooks, Chef-Boy-Ar-Dee foods are based on the real thing. Born in Piacenza, Ettore Boiardi arrived in the US in 1914 and opened his first restaurant in 1926 in Cleveland, Ohio. He found that his customers often asked for recipes or samples of his spaghetti sauce, and with the assistance of two patrons, Boiardi began to can his sauce in 1927, forming the Chef Boiardi Food Company in 1928. Fearing that non-Italians would have difficulty pronouncing his name, he sold his products under Chef-Boy-Ar-Dee.[27] Boiardi's products still line the shelves of most grocery stores.

Chinese Food in America

> [Chinese food] was engendered by a politically disfranchised, culturally despised, economically marginalized, and numerically insignificant group of people: individual Chinese immigrants.
>
> —Yong Chen (2014)[28]

Chinese cuisine became popular via restaurants that primarily catered to Chinese patrons, and the first restaurant opened in San Francisco in 1849. To encourage American customers, restaurants often offered familiar foods, such as steak, fried chicken, pork chops, hot dogs, and apple pie. Located in the Chinatowns of urban centers, these restaurants were vital for Chinese immigrants and other marginalized people. The low cost and ability to take the food home appealed to neighboring communities of African Americans and Hispanics. Although pork was the main ingredient in many Chinese dishes, many scholars have written about the Jewish fascination with and consumption of Chinese food.[29]

A backlash against Chinese workers in the 1870s resulted in the Chinese Exclusion Act, which disallowed Chinese immigration.[30] The act was in effect until 1943 and, according to the US Department of State, abolishing the act was necessary to aid "the morale of a wartime ally during World War II."[31] Just as Chinese Americans and their cuisine became more accepted, the image was again attacked. In October 1949, the Chinese Revolution's leader Communist Mao Zedong established the People's Republic of China,[32] and in 1950 China intervened against the US (and United Nations) in the Korean War. Senator Joseph McCarthy's anti-communist crusade created one more anti-Chinese component that made the 1950s dangerous for Chinese Americans.

Unlike Italian immigrants, who fused available foods into their cuisine, Chinese immigrants remained dedicated to their native foods, and they were adept in producing their vegetables and herbs. By the 1950s, imports of Chinese food goods were available to Chinese immigrants, but many items, such as soy sauce, could already be found on the shelves of suburban supermarkets. As with Italian cuisine, Chinese cooking encompassed many styles, ingredients, and regions, but by the 1950s it was simply considered "Chinese food."

Chinese cuisine requires much precise chopping, slicing, and mincing fresh vegetables and small amounts of meat, all of which are cooked quickly over a high fire. Referred to as "stir-frying," this cooking method was in opposition to the Anglo-American principle that vegetables and meat should cook for a long time. As well as unfamiliar cooking techniques, Chinese cuisine had no history of dairy products and used sugar sparingly—again, contrary to 1950s American tastes. Herbs, spices, and seasonings often were difficult to obtain and strange to American palates. To further separate them from mainstream America, the Chinese ate with chopsticks rather than the Western tradition of knives and forks, except for soup eaten with porcelain spoons.

By the end of the nineteenth century, recipes for modified Chinese dishes could be found in many American cookbooks. Most American mainstream cookbooks of the 1950s that offered Chinese recipes stuck to a predictable selection of bland submissions with a heavy reliance on white sauces, as observed in the following recipe. Crocker notes that this is a "main dish of a prize-winning party menu."

Chow Mein Loaf

Betty Crocker's Picture Cook Book (1950)[33]

First make 3 cups of Medium white Sauce [elsewhere Crocker provides the following for one cup of medium white sauce: 2–3 tbsp. butter; 2–3 tbsp. flour; ¼ tsp. salt; ⅛ tsp. pepper; 1 cup milk]

Combine gently . . .

1¼ cups of the hot Medium White Sauce
2 egg yolks, well beaten
1 cup tuna (7-oz. can), flaked
½ cup toasted split blanched almonds
2 cups chow mein noodles (4 oz)

Fold in . . .

2 egg whites, stiffly beaten

> Pour into well greased 9 × 5 × 3" loaf pan. Bake. Unmold on hot platter and serve with remaining 1¾ cups Medium White Sauce to which 2 tbsp. capers or chopped crisp pickles have been added. Temperature: 350° (mod. Oven). Time: Bake 30 minutes Amount: 8 servings.

"Translation" of Chinese Culture and Cuisine for American Cooks

> If ethnic foodways are used to draw boundaries, to separate "us" from "them" (in either a hostile or a supportive manner), they may also be used to bridge the gap between nationalities. Selectively sharing ethnic food . . . is a rudimentary way of giving strangers and friends a glimpse of one's culture while projecting a positive image of one's self and one's group.
>
> —*The Taste of American Place* (1998)[34]

Indeed, many of the 1950s Chinese cookbooks, written for an American audience, acted as bridges to explain cultural differences. Of course these cookbooks provided recipes, but more importantly they often articulated information about China's civilization, culinary traditions, and history. By sharing this information, the perceived exoticness of Chinese food was somewhat muted.[35] For example, Doreen Yen Hung Feng noted that every facet of Chinese food "is analyzed, from its palatableness to its texture, from its value to its effectiveness, and from its fragrance to its colorfulness; until, as in other works of art, proportion and balance are instilled in every dish."[36] Another cookbook author, Isabelle Chang, said, "China, a land laden with tradition had many dining customs just to foster gracious living. Thus, the variety of foods used, and methods of preparation were and are, almost limitless."[37] Cookbooks were one of the only means for 1950s Americans to learn about Chinese cooking and Chinese culture.

The most eminent of the era's Chinese cookbook authors is Buwei Yang Chao.[38] A medical doctor by training, Chao's *How to Cook and Eat in Chinese* was first published in 1945, with revised editions in 1949 and 1963. With the assistance of her linguist husband Yuen Ren Chao and her daughter Rulan, Chao's book focuses on educating American housewives about Chinese culture through food and cooking techniques. Author Janet

Theophano argues that Chao's book is an act of interpretation by unraveling the mysteries of Chinese home cooking and translating it for the American kitchen. Of particular interest is the preface, written by Pearl Buck, winner of the Nobel Prize for Literature in 1938. Buck begins not by identifying herself as a renowned author and an authority on Chinese culture but as an American housewife—one who is responsible for her family's daily meals and establishing herself as an American housewife to Chao's readers. Buck goes so far as to suggest that Mrs. Chao should be nominated for the Nobel Peace Prize. "For what better road to universal peace is there than to gather around the table where new and delicious dishes are set forth. What better road to friendship, upon which alone the peace can stand? I consider this cookbook a contribution to international understanding."[39]

RED-COOKED MEAT PROPER: PLAIN

How to Cook and Eat in Chinese (1949)[40]

For this type of Red-Cooked Meat, the order of preference of cuts should be: fresh bacon, fresh shoulder, fresh ham, pork chop.

3–4 lbs. pork
1 tsp. Salt
1 cup water
4 slices ginger (if you can get it)
2 tbsp. Sherry
½ cup soy sauce
½ tbsp. Sugar

Wash meat, cut into 1- or 1½-inch cubes. Put meat and 1 cup water in a heavy pot and use big fire. When it boils, add sherry, soy sauce, salt, and ginger. Cover pot tight and cook over very low fire for 1½ hours. (In case of pork chop, use only 1 hour here.) Then add sugar. Again, over low fire, cook for ½ to 1 hour. Test meat same way as for whole shoulder. [To test your cooking, stick a fork or chopstick through the meat. It is done when the stick goes through very easily. If not, cook over low fire, a little longer. Make allowances of course that that prongs of a fork are sharper than most chopsticks.]

As might be expected, most of these cookbooks assured American housewives that they would have no problem assembling a Chinese meal. Author Mei-Mei Ling suggested that the purpose of her book was "to introduce a new method of cooking to the American housewife."[41] Myrtle Lum Young, author of *Fun with Chinese Recipes*, assures readers that the recipes "have been simplified and condensed to make them easy to follow. Each recipe has been carefully tested to the taste of the Western world."[42] As a whole, 1950s Chinese cookbooks for Americans steer clear of exotic delicacies such as bird's nests, shark fins, bear paws, and sea cucumber. (Myrtle Lum Young and Buwei Yang Chao are exceptions, providing recipes for both Shark's Fin and Bird's Nest soups.) Isabelle Chang further subverts Chinese preferences by incorporating milk products and conventional American baking practices into her recipes. American standards about Chinese cooking are further disrupted in the opening to her section on "hints." Here Chang most likely alarmed the most adventurous American cooks: "In this book all ingredients except rhinoceros are available in the U.S.A." (Later in the volume, Chang references the Asian belief that the rhinoceros has medicinal values, especially for restoring lost vitality. There are no recipes for cooking the creature.)[43]

Chop Suey: Chinese or American?

The ABC of Casseroles (1954)[44]

In far-away China
With guests on the way,
They cook a chop suey
And call it a day!

"Chop Suey is known to us Chinese only as an agreeable foreign dish."[45] Ironically, by the end of the nineteenth century, this non-Chinese dish became an American Chinese favorite. It consisted of a "mess of veal, mushrooms, parsley, and a kind of macaroni, with a peculiar pungent sauce."[46] An early twentieth-century cookbook called for a cooking time of an hour and a half for chop suey—a length of time that suggests how far removed the dish was from traditional Chinese cooking techniques.[47] Soon, the familiar components of Chop Suey were established—pork, beef, chicken, celery, onions, and other vegetables with a sauce or gravy of water, soy sauce, and cornstarch.[48]

CHOP SUEY

Chop Suey: A Collection of Simplified Chinese Recipes Adapted for the American Home (1953)[49]

INGREDIENTS:

4 c. raw vegetables, stripped [cut in thin slices]; may be all or combination of the following: carrots, celery, string beans, cauliflower, round cabbage, Chinese peas, Chinese potato, broccoli

¼ lb. pork or beef, stripped
½ m. round onion stripped

SAUCE

½ tsp. salt
½ tsp. sugar
1 tsp. soy sauce
½ tsp. cooked oil
¼ tsp. liquor

GRAVY

½ tsp. salt
½ tsp. sugar
1 tsp. cornstarch
2 tsp. soy sauce
¼ tsp. liquor
¼ c. water

METHOD:

Marinate pork in sauce 5–10 minutes. Pan fry onion, add pork and fry until done. Add vegetables, mix well and fry 1 minute; add gravy and cook 2–3 minutes. Serve.

Chun King's founder, Jeno Paulucci, offered canned bean sprouts and crispy chow mein noodles in the 1940s. One of Chun King's most popular offerings was a canned chow mein, consisting of bean sprouts, celery, and a separate can of crisp noodles. Other Chun King canned

Figure 9.1. "For something to surprise." Magazine advertisement for Chun King's Canned Chicken Chow Mein, c. 1950s. Courtesy ConAgra. Source: Author's collection.

products included bamboo shoots, bean sprouts, and water chestnuts. In 1950, Percy Loy and his brother-in-law Robert Wong offered frozen chop suey under the brand name Kubla Khan. By the mid-1950s, canned and frozen Chinese foods were available in many suburban grocery stores, encouraging Chinese cooking in middle-class American homes.

Tex-Mex: The Rise of a New American Cuisine

Tex-Mex is the ugly duckling of American regional cuisines. Since it was called Mexican food for most of its history, nobody even thought of it as American until about thirty years ago. That was when the first authoritative Mexican cookbook in the United States, Diana Kennedy's *The Cuisines of Mexico*, was published [1972].

—Robb Walsh (2004)[50]

The roots of this often maligned and misunderstood cuisine coalesced in Texas by Tejanos (a mixture of Mexicans, Texans, and diverse groups of European immigrants). In 1972 British food writer Diana Kennedy (1923–2022) published *The Cuisines of Mexico*. Noting that although the US shares a two-thousand-mile border with Mexico, "far too many people know Mexican food as a 'mixed plate'; a crisp taco filled with ground meat heavily flavored with an all-purpose chili powder; a soggy *tamal* covered with a sauce that turns up on everything—too sweet and too overpoweringly onioned—a few fried beans and something else that looks and tastes like all the rest. Where is the wonderful play of texture, color, and flavor that makes up an authentic, well-cooked Mexican meal?"[51] In 1985, she further criticized Tex-Mex food as "over-seasoned, loaded with all those false spices like onion salt, garlic salt, MSG, and chili powder. They play havoc with your stomach, with your breath, everything."[52] Diana Kennedy declared Tex-Mex cuisine as blasphemy.[53] Ironically, Kennedy's objections led to accepting Tex-Mex food as separate and distinct from traditional Mexican cuisine.

Discussions about authentic Mexican food and the cuisine known as Tex-Mex (or its iterations of Cal-Mex, Sonoran-Mex, New-Mex-Mex, and others) have long consumed food writers and historians. Influenced by Anglo tastes, the cuisine known as Tex-Mex first originated in northern Mexico and Texas. The term "Tex-Mex" appeared in the late nineteenth century but was not used consistently until the 1960s, with little understanding of just what that meant. Some describe it as a combination of northern Mexican peasant food with what author John Mariani calls "Texas farm and cowboy fare." Food historian Waverly Root noted, "Tex-Mex food might be described as a native foreign food, contradictory though that term may seem. It is native, for it does not exist elsewhere; it was born on this soil."[54] A late nineteenth-century phenomenon considered by many to represent the definitive in comfort food, Tex-Mex has fought to become recognized as a regional cuisine and not a "lower-quality, corrupted version of traditional Mexican food."[55]

By the 1950s, with a surge of new Mexican immigrants, restaurants serving Tex-Mex cuisine (along with Chinese restaurants) began to move into suburban areas. In the 1950s, these restaurants were called Mexican or Spanish restaurants. (Even today, virtually all restaurants that serve Tex-Mex cuisine continue to call themselves "Mexican.") Like the red and gold pagodas and snow-capped mountain paintings found in Chinese restaurants of the 1950s, Mexican restaurants also provided a specific ambiance for their customers, such as hanging strings of dried red chilis, pottery, and paintings that depict imagined scenes of colonial Mexico.

Some Tex-Mex foods unique to its cuisine include chili con carne, which originated in Texas. Another popular dish is refried beans, a mistranslation of *frijoles refritos* (well-fried beans). The most common Tex-Mex menu item is the combination platter, which might include enchiladas, tacos, or tostadas, accompanied by refried beans, Spanish rice, and a mound of shredded lettuce and chopped tomatoes. The whole plate is slathered in melted yellow cheese. Fried tortilla chips originate from the mid-1940s, and soon chips and salsa appeared in Tex-Mex restaurants. (Nachos also come from the same era, made more popular using processed Velveeta cheese.)

According to the author, the following recipe for Chili con Carne requires only eighteen minutes to prepare.

Chili Con Carne

The 20 Minute Cookbook (1953)[56]

2 l-lb. cans chili con carne
1 teaspoon brown sugar
2 tablespoons butter
¼ cup chicken broth
1 fresh tomato, chopped
chili powder as desired (up to 2 teaspoons for *red* hot)
1 teaspoon onion juice
1 teaspoon sweet paprika

Turn chili con carne into saucepan and place over medium heat. Stir occasionally, until heated through. In another saucepan, melt butter, and add all remaining ingredients except chili powder;

simmer 5 minutes over low heat. Add to chili, combine, taste and correct seasoning, adding chili powder as desired. Simmer 3 or 4 minutes and serve with hot French bread. Serves 4 generously.

The taco is, perhaps, the most celebrated Tex-Mex food. As found in Mexico, a taco is a corn tortilla wrapped around a filling of meat, eggs, cheese, roasted peppers, beans, or other ingredients, meant to be eaten with the hands. American taco shells are deep-fried and bent into a U-shape, then stuffed with meat, lettuce, and tomatoes and topped with cheddar cheese.

Tamales were popular in the US by the late nineteenth century, and within a few years, canned tamales (along with canned chili con carne) became available. Cornmeal dough is wrapped in corn husks with meat and chili sauce for an authentic Mexican tamale, but the dish lent itself to the 1950s favorite: the casserole. Known as "tamale pie," Willow Borba's *Loyalty Cook Book* (1953) provides nineteen recipes for tamale pie or tamale loaf. The following recipe is typical of those found in 1950s mainstream American cookbooks.

Mexican Tamale Pie

Culinary Arts Institute Encyclopedic Cookbook (1950)[57]

1 cup cornmeal
4 cups water
1 teaspoon salt
1 medium onion
1 green or chili pepper
3 tablespoons cooking oil
2½ cups cooked tomatoes
2 cups ground cooked meat
1 teaspoon salt
Dash cayenne or chili powder

Cook cornmeal, water and salt in top of double boiler for 45 minutes. Chop onion and pepper and fry in hot oil. Add tomatoes, meat, salt and cayenne or chili and cook until thickened. Line greased baking dish with half the mush, pour in meat mixture, cover with remaining mush and bake in hot oven (375° F.) 30 minutes or until top is lightly browned. Serves 6 to 8.

Use 3 cups cooked rice instead of first three ingredients.

Another typical dish is the burrito, a large flour tortilla rolled around ingredients that include meat, beans, cheese, rice, salsa, or guacamole. Some claim the burrito is California-inspired; others believe it originates in the Southwest, somewhere between Tucson, Arizona, and Los Angeles.[58] Erna Fergusson's *Mexican Cookbook* (1934) offers an early recipe for a burrito

Figure 9.2. "For a fiesta of good eating." Magazine advertisement for Van Camp's canned Mexican-style foods, c. 1950s. Courtesy ConAgra. Source: Author's collection.

based on New Mexican cuisine. Her recipe consists of a corn tortilla filled with chicharrones (hog cracklings). Although claimed as a Tex-Mex dish, authors Diana Kennedy and Rick Bayless both provide recipes for burritos. Kennedy's burrito is a flour tortilla filled with shredded pork or beef, eggs scrambled with beef jerky, or beans. Bayless (1953–) provides a recipe for burritos with spicy shredded jerky and notes that burritos are filled with virtually any taco filling. (A chimichanga is a fried burrito.)[59]

Sometimes, mainstream cookbooks provided a few selected dishes, such as chili con carne and tamale pie, but the era's regional cookbooks contain many Mexican or Mexican-inspired dishes. For example, *Helen Brown's West Coast Cook Book* (1952) index lists more than forty entries under "Mexican." The Culinary Arts Institute of Chicago's *The United States Regional Cook Book* (1947) titles an entire section "Southwestern Cook Book of Spanish-American Recipes," and *Taste of Texas* (1949) provides a whole chapter, "Mexican and Latin Dishes." However, as with Chinese food, canned options were available, such as Van Camp's "delicious Mexican style foods."

By the end of the 1950s, tacos, chili con carne, tamales, and nachos were no longer considered ethnic. They had now achieved the status of authentic American food, alongside chop suey, spaghetti and meatballs, and hot dogs. Today, Tex-Mex restaurants are located on nearly every corner of the US.

Curry: Exotic South Asian Food or an All-American Delight?

> The word "curry" is as degrading to India's great cuisine as the term "chop suey" was to China's. "Curry" is just a vague, inaccurate word which the world has picked up from the British, who, in turn, got it mistakenly from us.
>
> —Madhur Jaffrey (1973)[60]

While South Asian cuisine might not have been a focal point for 1950s American cookbooks, practically every mainstream and specialty cookbook contained one or more recipes for Indian curry.

Curry was a staple of American cuisine as early as the 1820s and began with recipes found in Mary Randolph's *The Virginia House Wife* (1824). American curry dishes call for powdered curry powder, a ground blend of various spices first exported to Britain from India in the eighteenth century.[61]

A book focused on the American housewife, Florence Brobeck's *Cooking with Curry* (1952) explains, "Curries are simple, easy, delicious dishes that come from all over the world but most British, European, and Anglo-Indian cookbooks on the subject of curry frighten the wits out of a plain American cook."[62] Brobeck continues, "For curry beginners, these easily-followed recipes introduce a new taste delight. The curry powder is easily modified, less for a mild curry more for a hot one. Season and taste until you arrive at the right amount for *your* satisfaction." (She assumed, as did most American recipes, that one commercially available curry powder was appropriate for all types of curries.) However, Brobeck does offer several curry "sauces" that are enhanced with the addition of onions, carrot, celery, mace, dried thyme, bay leaf, parsley—all mixed with the curry powder and the 1950s go-to sauce: white sauce.[63] In her work on American regional cooking *How America Eats* (1960), Clementine Paddleford equated curry with Southwestern cuisine. In describing the cooking of Arizona (included with New Mexico and Texas as part of the narrative on the Southwest), Paddleford provides a recipe for Indian Chicken Curry. However, as delicious as this dish might be, curry cannot be said to be a traditional staple of Arizona cuisine.

Recipes for curry found in the American mainstream and specialty cookbooks of the 1950s frequently call for curry powder added to a white sauce (a mixture of flour, milk, or other liquid, and fat). The vegetables or protein (fish, shellfish, lamb, chicken, or beef) often are cooked separately with the curry powder added to a white sauce. The following recipe is typical of 1950s American-style curry, which contains a mere one-quarter teaspoon of curry powder and is served in a typical American white sauce.

DRIED-BEEF CURRY ON RICE

Culinary Arts Institute Encyclopedic Cookbook (1950)[64]

4 ounces dried beef
¼ cup fat
¼ cup flour
2½ cups milk
¼ teaspoon curry powder
2 cups hot cooked rice

Shred dried beef and brown lightly in fat in skillet. Add flour, stir in milk and cook until thickened. Add curry powder; blend well. Serve over rice. Serves 5.

Figure 9.3. A magazine advertisement for French's Currie Powder, 1950s. Source: f8 archive/Alamy Stock Photo.

Likewise, *The Joy of Cooking*'s recipe for curried lamb instructs the cook to place the cooked lamb on a platter and surround the lamb with the gravy that contains the curry powder. (Gravy, in this context, is a white sauce to which curry powder is added.)

An advertisement for a curry powder from a popular brand, French's, provides a recipe for Shrimp Rajah that is also based on a white sauce.

Dharam Jit Singh's *Classic Cooking from India* (1956) never uses prepared curry powders that one might purchase in a grocery store. Instead, each recipe utilizes a unique combination of spices ground in a mortar and pestle. Then, they are fried over low heat to intensify the flavors before adding the meat or vegetables, as is described in the following recipe.

Ek-Aur Chingra Korma

(*Korma Shrimp Curry*)

Classic Cooking from India (1956)[65]

2 pounds shrimps
5 tablespoons blanched almonds
6 tablespoons oil
salt
1 teaspoon black pepper
1 tablespoon pistachio nuts
6 cloves
4 cardamoms (seeds of)
½ to 1 cup yoghurt
1 tablespoon coriander

Clean, wash and dry the shrimps. Gash each with a sharp knife. Soak them in oil for ½ hour. Then remove from oil and reserve.

Heat 5 tablespoons of oil. Put in the black pepper, and after 15 seconds the shrimps and cardamon seeds. Fry till they are red on all sides. Mix the yoghurt with almonds, pounded, salt and pistachio nuts. Cook covered till done. In the remaining 1 tablespoon of oil, fry the cloves and coriander over low heat for 4 minutes. Then mix this with the shrimps. Cover tight. Place over high flame for a few seconds; then keep warm for 10 minutes before serving. For 4

Although highly influenced by British colonialist practices, Indian curry was the first international food to become a regular part of the American food canon, but most mainstream and specialty cookbooks never mention its origins. Like Chinese and Tex-Mex cuisines, Indian food is an expression of traditions but changed as required for a new circumstance—available foodstuffs, geography, and cultural practices. Joined by Chinese and Mexican-Anglo adaptations to traditional foods, curry now is as American as the proverbial Mom's apple pie.

"What kind of American consciousness can grow in the atmosphere of sauerkraut and limburger cheese or what can you expect of the Americanism of the man whose breath always reeks with garlic."[66] Thankfully, and for the most part, these earlier twentieth-century sentiments disappeared by the 1950s. And, with acknowledgments to immigrants from all over the world, "American" cuisine now welcomed German, Italian, French, Chinese, and Mexican (in the form of Tex-Mex) as well as other international foods. During the early Cold War years, the voyage of foreign foods from the uncommon, distasteful, and often undesirable to acceptance and eventually enjoyment became a familiar passage that inspired cooks to look beyond the sometimes bland and insipid offerings of the mainstream cookbooks to the possibilities of new spices, herbs, foodstuffs, and cooking methods found in the cuisines of America's ethnic communities.

Part 3
Indigestion

Chapter 10

Selling Plymouths to Men, Electric Can Openers to Women, and Televisions for All

> What is basic is that advertising, as such, with all its vast power to influence values and conduct, cannot ever lose sight of the fact that it ultimately regards man as a consumer and defines its own mission as one of stimulating him to consume or to desire to consume.
>
> —David M. Potter (1954)[1]

Postwar America posed challenging questions to its citizens. What does it mean to be a patriot? What are the appropriate roles for women in a postwar society? What about respecting family or civic authority? Am I doing enough to preserve our freedom by fighting communism? Madison Avenue advertising agencies and the US government also considered these questions, using them to shape their messages into a Cold War definition of the "American way of life." The American way of life became recognized as a "defining marker of our national character or, if you will, our brand."[2]

At the same time, the definition of "freedom" shifted from a more general idea, such as the freedom from tyranny, to freedom defined as the right to choose among the bounty of consumer foods and goods—brand, color, flavor, and price point. In his conversations with Soviet Premier Nikita Khrushchev during the famous Kitchen Debate at the American National Exhibition held in 1959 in Moscow, Vice President Richard Nixon spoke about freedom in consumer choices.

218 | Casseroles, Can Openers, and Jell-O

Figure 10.1. A late 1940s billboard in Dubuque, Iowa. Source: Shawshots/Alamy Stock Photo.

Dwight D. Eisenhower assumed the office of President of the United States in January 1953. In honor of this auspicious occasion, he composed a prayer to be used as part of his inaugural address. He was vocal about his belief in religious faith, considering it to be an essential foundation for democracy. Cabinet meetings always started with a moment of silent prayer. The phrase "under God" was added to the Pledge of Allegiance (1954) and Congress approved "In God We Trust" as the national motto (1956). Eisenhower frequently consulted with religious leaders, such as Rev. Edward Elson, Cardinal Francis Joseph Spellman, and Billy Graham. Following the president's lead, religion became an essential part of the American way of life.

Author Wendy Wall estimates that by 1950, less than 50,000 Americans, out of a population of 150 million, belonged to the communist party. Nevertheless, a fear that bordered on panic created an atmosphere of trepidation that the American Communist Party would somehow subvert the American way of life. Loyalty boards investigated federal employees, and more than forty states required all public employees, including teachers, to take loyalty oaths. In 1947, President Truman issued an executive order that created a Federal Loyalty-Security Program, giving the government the right to fire employees for any reason interpreted as treasonous or disloyal.[3]

Other events in the late 1940s and early 1950s that fed anti-communist reactions included the Soviet Union's successful nuclear weapon test in 1949; the Chinese Revolution of 1949, which established a communist government on mainland China; and, of course, the Korean War, which resulted in over 100,000 injuries and the deaths of 40,000 Americans.

In 1950, Wisconsin Senator Joseph McCarthy claimed he had proof of over two hundred communists in the US State Department, leading to a four-year witch hunt. McCarthy cared little for his tactics, which involved misinformation and false implications. When he began to investigate suspected communists within the Army, President Eisenhower and other influential politicians intervened, and in 1954, the Senate voted to censure McCarthy, thus dissolving his influence.

Figure 10.2. Crowds in Iowa protest the fall 1959 visit of Soviet Premier Nikita Khrushchev. Photograph by Thomas J. O'Halloran. Source: Glasshouse Images/Alamy Stock Photo.

Espionage cases involving the passing of secrets to the Soviets included the perjury trial of former State Department employee Alger Hiss and the trial and subsequent execution of Julius and Ethel Rosenberg. Ordinary American citizens were encouraged to watch their neighbors for any signs of disloyalty. (Assisted by widely available booklets published and disseminated with titles such as "How to Identify a Communist" and "How to talk to a Communist.")

Upholding traditional gender roles proved to be straightforward for advertising purposes. Madison Avenue supported efforts to lure women away from their wartime jobs to the gloriously described comforts of a home in the suburbs, surrounded by the latest gadgets. It displayed a contented, often childlike woman, always smiling and wearing signature kitchen attire including jewelry and high heels. After it became clear that many women never left their jobs or had reentered the workforce, advertising adapted quickly to focus on the working-woman market.

Racism Sells Pancake Mix

Aunt Jemima "began as a white man, in drag, wearing blackface, singing on the minstrel stage. She became a face on a bag of pancake flour, then a real-life ex-slave who worked in a Chicago kitchen but cobbled together enough reality and a fantasy of life under slavery to entertain the crowds of the 1893 World's Fair."[4]

In 1899, Chris Rutt and Charles Underwood of Missouri created a pancake batter composed of wheat and corn flours, lime phosphate, and salt that only required the addition of water. Their new product was called "Self-Rising Pancake Flour," sold in individual bags. Some months later, Rutt attended a minstrel show, where he heard the former slave song "Old Aunt Jemima" performed by white men in blackface. One of the singers was dressed as a mammy—a popular term and image for a slave woman associated with plantations of the South. Inspired, Rutt renamed his product Aunt Jemima. The product was the first ready-made pancake mix, pointing to the future and popularity of convenience foods, and was the first nationally sold product that featured a black person as its trademark.

After the company was sold to R. G. Davis of Chicago in 1890, Aunt Jemima became a national product with a new persona. Davis hired Chicago cook and ex-slave Nancy Green to impersonate Aunt Jemima. Green made her debut at the Chicago Exposition in 1893, where she cooked up pancakes while telling stories about life on a Southern plantation. Davis also created a mythical background for Aunt Jemima, which changed through the years but always emphasized her allegiance to an imaginary white enslaver, Colonel Higbee of Louisiana, whose "plantation was known across the South for its fine dining—especially its pancake breakfasts."[5]

Author Marilyn Kern-Foxworth notes that through the decades, Aunt Jemima became one of the best-recognized of the stereotypical African American advertising characters. She further comments that advertising through the 1960s continued to depict black people as subservient to white people, including Uncle Ben (rice products) and Rastus (Cream of Wheat). Trade cards, dolls, dishes, bottles, sugar bowls, cookie jars, and other paraphernalia "commonly portrayed blacks with thick lips, bulging eyes, and distorted grimaces."[6]

Nancy Green died in 1923 and was not replaced until the 1933 Chicago Century of Progress Exposition. The new Aunt Jemima, Anna Robinson, had a darker complexion and, at 350 pounds, was much heavier. Advertisers simply changed the image on the box to resemble Robinson. Quaker Oats acquired the Aunt Jemima brand, represented by the advertising agency Lord and Thomas. The agency designed a campaign centered around Hollywood and Broadway celebrities. Robinson was so successful that Quaker Oats commissioned a commercial artist to paint her portrait and incorporated her likeness into the brand. Anna Robinson died in 1951. Other women who followed in Green's and Robinson's footsteps included Edith Wilson, Ethel Ernestine Harper, Rosie Hall, and Aylene Lewis.[7]

During the 1950s, many different Aunt Jemimas appeared in tradeshows, supermarkets, and other public relations events that became a recognized model for sales promotion campaigns, generating a specific image. However, these racist images delivered a conspicuous message: when Aunt Jemima shared her cooking secrets "with the harried white housewife," it was a "message of subliminal enforcement of class. Even if a middle-class homemaker couldn't afford to hire a black servant, she could gain the advantage by using the products that shared the message of both superiority and Southern gentility."[8]

Although Aunt Jemima's appearance has changed over the decades—she traded the bandana for a more up-to-date hairstyle, started wearing pearl earrings, and appears slimmer—in fact, except for her skin color, she acquired the accepted look of a middle-class white woman. "The black woman on the box of Aunt Jemima pancake mix still smiles at us in much the same way she did in 1920 but she has not gone anywhere since the turn of the century. Maybe she keeps sticking around because she is more successful than ever, with her face on about forty products,

Figure 10.3. A 1950s magazine advertisement for Aunt Jemima Pancakes, featuring the face of spokesperson Anna Robinson. Source: Retro AdArchives/Alamy Stock Photo.

accounting for an overwhelming lead in market share in the ready-to-prepare breakfast category, with sales of more than $300 million annually."[9] Yes, racism sells pancake mix.

Segmented Advertising

Since the end of the nineteenth century, women have been the general focus of advertising. This demographic included white, married, middle-class women who lived in the suburbs in postwar America. (It would be decades before advertising seriously considered women of color.) Thus, the target audience were those who had the most available time to read magazines and watch television, absorbing the messages of Madison Avenue. Those women not directly a target audience for traditional advertising either because of race or class were still considered fair game. They were assumed to be desiring a better life.

Advertising worked to be sure that women were "consumers of images as well as goods." Cookbooks and magazine print ads provided images of the middle-class housewife "as scientist, artist, master chef, efficiency expert, perfecter of domestic bliss, earth protector, or patriot."[10] Created by the marketing men of Madison Avenue, these illustrations were intended to encourage women to stay at home by offering illusory ads intended to make housework—specifically cooking—seem as pleasing as paid work. Male advertising executives had no reason to question the prevailing view of traditional gender roles, and in 1950s ads women were always displayed performing housework surrounded by appliances while impeccably dressed.[11] Such portrayals made it abundantly clear that these housewives could not be hired servants. After all, they were attired nicely (if a bit overdressed for household chores), and thus they must be part of the suburban white middle class: advertising's primary target audience.

During the 1950s, numerous marketing studies determined which member of the typical suburban family decided what to buy. In general, the studies demonstrated that men had authority over the family finances as the "architect of the family's fiscal policy." The wife "serves as the purchasing agent with the limitation that her degree of authority over purchases is in an inverse ratio to the expensiveness of the item." While women still carried out most of the food shopping, a growing number of men began to play a significant role in purchasing groceries. Supermarket chains started to frame campaigns that focused on male shoppers.[12]

Men Purchase Cars and Women Purchase Electric Can Openers

Without the automobile, suburban life would not have been possible. A car was "the Conestoga wagon on the frontier of consumerism, a powerful instrument of change, a chariot of fiery desire."[13] Automobile ownership also created a car culture, which proved essential in generating demand for fast-food restaurants and suburban supermarkets.

Consumer car assembly, which had fallen victim to the production of military vehicles during World War II, soon moved into high gear. As the advertising industry began to see the potential in television, carmakers began to sponsor television shows. For example, Chevrolet sponsored the popular *Dinah Shore Show* from 1956 to 1963. She opened and closed her program with the Chevy "anthem," "See the USA in Your Chevrolet," declared to be one of the top ten jingles of the twentieth century. Television often relied on famous figures to sell cars. To influence a younger audience, Chevrolet sponsored singer Pat Boone in a half-hour variety program, *The Pat Boone Chevy Showroom*. Reinforcing the idea of glamour and sophistication of car ownership, Lincoln's spokesperson, Julia Meade, often appeared on the *Ed Sullivan Show*, always attired in an evening gown.

Figure 10.4. An elegantly attired couple prepare for a ride in their big-finned Plymouth, 1950s magazine advertisement. Source: Retro AdArchives/Alamy Stock Photo.

Car advertising during the early 1950s focused on men. Ads spotlighted the car's styling while showing beautiful models or elegantly dressed women to suggest sexual allure. With the establishment of suburban communities, most families owned a single automobile, which the breadwinner used to drive to work. This further isolated women, making it more difficult to visit friends and family. On the other hand, this lack of mobility helped create a stronger sense of community. Women needed to lean on each other for help in shopping and other tasks, building bonds as their husbands drove long distances to work and often returned home long after dinner. (The importance of these bonds is evident in the descriptions of buffets, luncheons, and tea parties that women organized for each other and can be found throughout 1950s cookbooks.)

As the middle class gained prosperity, a second car became a necessity. In evaluating the market, advertising saw two possibilities. First, car manufacturers attempted to design more feminine products to appeal to women—plush upholstery, subtle pastel colors, and even small nooks to hold cosmetics. Women and children were subtly included in the ads to make the advertisements more family friendly. Second, advertisers also helped promote obsolescence. Automobile design was now in the hands of "stylists," and Ford Motor Company's stylist George Walker explained, "We design a car to make a man unhappy with this 1957 Ford 'long about the end of 1958."[14] Harley Earl at General Motors concurred. "In 1934, the average car ownership span was 5 years; now it is 2 years. When it is 1 year, we will have a perfect score."[15] A profusion of television and print ads put a burden on families to "keep up with the Joneses." One consequence of these campaigns was that postwar personal indebtedness through the 1950s doubled because of the growing availability of credit cards and the "buy now, pay later" installment plans popular with many retailers, especially car dealerships.

America had a love affair with its automobiles—as brassy as they were—adorned with ornamented grills, wraparound windshields, push-button transmissions, retractable roofs, fins, and other decorations that often hinted at the era's obsession with all things rockets and space. In 1945 car manufacturers produced a mere seventy thousand cars; by 1950, this number had increased to over six million. Author Karal Ann Marling accurately sums up this preoccupation, "There's something wonderful, disquieting, and, in the end, embarrassing . . . the lunkers, the dreamboats, the befinned, bechromed behemoths that lurked in the driveways of several million new ranch houses in the suburbs (because they wouldn't fit in the garage!)."[16]

Electrical Servants

In the 1950s, few housewives were able to hire paid help, and thus they were assisted only by technology in such forms as washing machines and electric coffee pots. Author Ruth Schwartz Cowan in *More Work for Mother*, astutely noted that by committing to a life in the suburbs, somebody "(surely mother) would be at home to do the requisite work that made it possible for someone else (surely father) to leave early in the morning and return late at night." With this system, "father" would not have to worry about maintaining his home while he was away. Described in 1946 by Mary and George Catlin as "electrical servants,"[17] the house was stocked with labor and time-saving appliances designed to make the daily struggle of cooking and housework tasks seem more manageable. (Before the war, these tasks often were associated with hired, nonwhite

Figure 10.5. A woman cooks in her electric broiler. Source: ClassicStock/Alamy Stock Photo.

servants.) Without such help, suburban life would not be possible unless somebody ("mother") was home to operate all these machines.[18]

Thus, women purchased electric can openers; they also bought electric pressure cookers, blenders, ice cream makers, gadgets to melt butter, lemon squeezers, deep fat fryers, waffle irons, skillets, mixers, casseroles, popcorn makers, chafing dishes, coffee pots, and something called the Roto-Broil—the Cadillac of rotisseries. In addition to these tabletop or countertop electric appliances, women had a significant say in purchasing larger kitchen appliances, namely stoves and refrigerators, dishwashers, washing machines, and dryers. Manufacturers counted on this female influence and produced appliances in a wide range of colors that would appeal to the modern housewife, complete with instruction booklets that pictured a woman happy and content with her new machine.[19]

Food and appliance companies worked with advertising agencies to design campaigns for print and media. A popular method of advertising products was to create a small booklet, preferably one that included recipes, and the 1950s witnessed a wave of such publications. Because so many features of the new electric appliances often overlapped, each machine needed to demonstrate its unique and valuable abilities. For example, Marion Tracy's *Cooking Under Pressure* is very clear on what a pressure cooker does very well—boil and steam food in a shorter time than conventional cooking. Using a pressure cooker, according to Tracy, involves "no sniffing, no stirring, no tasing and adding seasonings with either deliberation or careless abandon. It is impersonal and scientific." Tracy notes that cooking with a pressure cooker is a bit like caring for an incubator baby, "There is no intimate contact, no easy affection."[20] *How to Get the Most out of Your New De Luxe Sunbeam Automatic Mixmaster Mixer*, produced by the Sunbeam Corporation in 1957, reminded users that the mixer would occupy only a tiny amount of space, an essential consideration because of the modest size of the kitchens in the new suburbs. Sunbeam emphasized that there was no end to its fantastic usefulness. It "will do all of your mixing, mashing, whipping, beating, stirring, blending, juicing, folding and creaming."[21] The forty-four-page booklet instructs the new owner on the machine's operation and provides recipes for cakes, frosting, cookies, candies, and pies, with a few pages devoted to salad dressings and vegetables.

One of the most popular electric appliances was the blender. *Modern Magic in Food Preparation with the Waring Blendor* (1953)[22] reminded its readers that its use was far greater than just a "splendid drink-mixer." It also made delicious salad dressing and had the ability to liquify garlic ("if you belong to that school"). The booklet claims that the machine would purée, grind, blend, and take the lumps out of gravy and that it would mix a prepared cake mix in thirty seconds or a cake made from scratch in a minute and a half. The booklet contains over fifty recipes, ranging from Meatless Spaghetti Sauce to Lemon Pudding Sauce. In a section described as "special tricks for men to try," recipes include Orange Sauce for Wild Duck and Bearnaise Sauce for steak.

The Roto-Broil Corporation of America also provided a book of recipes for its rotisserie. Still it emphasized that the machine would also barbecue, roast, broil, grill, toast, fry, boil, simmer, and bake. As well as published booklets by appliance manufacturers, full-length cookbooks were issued to describe the various uses of electric appliances. For example, Chicago's Culinary Arts Institute published *The Mixer, Hand Mixer, and Blender Cookbook* (1954), and John and Marie Roberson's 1953 *Complete Small Appliance Cookbook* contained an astonishing six hundred recipes for every conceivable small appliance available in the 1950s.

Changes in the Kitchen

As well as a bevy of electric appliances, the kitchen itself underwent changes that not only reflected the status of the housewife but in subtle ways also defined her class and race. Middle-class women who remained at home were mere workers (albeit without pay), while their husbands, who worked outside the home, were "professionals." Kitchen designers and builders suggested that a desk would instill a sense of professionalism in housewives. The idea of a desk, specifically designed for the kitchen, was not new. Dr. Lillian Gilbreth, an early twentieth-century industrial engineer and kitchen efficiency expert, suggested a "Gilbreth Management Desk," which contained a built-in radio, drawers for bills, a shelf for cookbooks, and a place for the telephone. Gilbreth declared that "the business of running a house demands a well-planned little 'office' just as surely as does any business run by a man."[23]

Better Homes and Gardens Decorating Book (1956) noted that the kitchen is where "the homemaker spends her 'office' hours." Others claimed that the kitchen was the nerve center of the house. "A good desk is an inducement to efficient household management. A good housewife, like a good executive, needs a good office, and the kitchen is the logical place for it."[24] Taken one step further, the command center, demonstrated by Whirlpool's 1958 Miracle Kitchen that was part of the US international trade show circuit, would allow a seated housewife to prepare a complete meal simply by pushing buttons. Along with improved storage for small appliances and groceries that kept clutter to a minimum, the 1950s kitchen would "give the appearance that women's housework was professional labor and that it was distinctly white labor."[25]

Architectural layouts of middle-class suburban kitchens changed. Traditional homes had closed kitchens designed for servants' work—out of sight. Now, the kitchen became a space open to the living areas of the house, serving as "a laboratory, a workshop, and an office, a site designed for a woman who might once have been a wage earner herself and for whom the kitchen's design became symbolic of her worth within the family's daily operations."[26] To further emphasize the difference between a mere servant and a middle-class housewife, publications such as Mary and Russel Wright's *Guide to Easier Living* highlighted the correct posture for housecleaning tasks that differentiate women from ordinary servants. For example, one should use a long handle-broom "so that you can sweep without stooping." Kitchen furniture, such as sink units, could be purchased to allow the housewife to sit while washing dishes or peeling vegetables. As well as the admonishment to avoid tasks that required stooping over, women were encouraged to stand upright and certainly never perform household jobs on their hands and knees.

Kitchen Appliances and Advertisements Find Beauty in Strong Colors

"Color was an index of status and fashion [and] a mark of futuristic technology at work, of miracle fabrics and plastics in a thousand unimaginable rainbow-tinted hues."[27] Not unlike the dazzling color hues of the era's Jell-O molds or frosted cakes, kitchen appliances and cabinetry appeared in intense blues, shocking pinks (First Lady Mamie Eisenhower's preferred color), and sunny lemon-yellow. Author Dianne Harris in *Little White Houses* (2013) observes that "the white-wall aesthetic of high architectural modernism seldom appeared in ordinary postwar houses." Instead, the bright, often garish colors found in both 1950s products and house interiors and touted by advertisers "conveyed a specific kind of middle-class modernity."[28]

Kitchens were a significant focus of color in the suburban house. In a section titled "How to Select a Kitchen Color Scheme," *Better Homes and Gardens Decorating Book* notes, "Kitchens today are alive with color. Both major and minor appliances feature colors—pink, turquoise, yellow, brown, bright red, and special finishes of copper, silver, gold, and brushed chrome are among the many choices now available." The book also stresses the importance of curtains, lighting, and accessories. ("A well-dressed kitchen wears its accessories wisely, just as does a well-dressed woman.")[29]

The "look" of food—precisely its color—was vital, be it frozen, canned, or dehydrated. To achieve maximum color effects, advertising agencies often hired color consultants and specialty photographers to construct the best images of foods. Decisions about the color of food were now in the hands of the advertising agencies. Author Ai Hisano in *Visualizing Taste* notes, "Colorful images disseminated by popular magazines, advertisements, and other print media served to represent, disseminate, and reiterate those ideas about the 'right' color of foods."[30] For example, labels for canned peas displayed the vegetable in vivid, intense greens (far from the actual contents that tended to be a grayish color). The six-color, laminated parchment box that housed Swanson's TV dinners "was the wonder of the industry because it reproduced the contents with such stunning, lip-smacking fidelity."[31] Summing up this trend in advertising, food writer M. F. K. Fisher complained about the "onslaughts of marshmallow-vegetable-gelatin salads and such which smile at me in Kodachrome from current magazine advertisements."[32]

The technology for creating color images in print materials is far better today than in the 1950s, where objects often appeared intense, with colors often bleeding into each other. On the other hand, Karal Ann Marling suggests these issues were repeatedly underscored by the "use of forced contrasts between one item and another, between object and background." In addition to color contrasts, the photographs also highlight textural contrasts. For example, in *Betty Crocker's Picture Cook Book*, a pink, yellow, and white baked Alaska is displayed on a silver tray, sitting on a dark table covering, showcasing a vase of pink camellias and shiny green leaves. Often, color illustrations in cookbooks such as *Better Homes and Gardens New Cook Book* (1953) and *The General Foods Kitchens Cookbook* (1959) showcase elaborately staged meals, for example a close-up of a bowl of peaches and strawberries set next to sugar-crusted grapes; casseroles displayed on patterned tablecloths; a picnic staged on a boat, framed by blue water; or a luncheon table set with plates of red tomatoes, pink shrimp, and green lettuce, flanked by fancy silverware, and a large centerpiece of pink roses featured in the center of the table.

Even the foods themselves often appeared in colors not seen in nature, such as Betty Crocker's Colorvision Cake, which required a white cake mix but turned the creation into a dazzling, multicolored masterpiece by adding brightly colored gelatin. Another colorful and showy cake, the Christmas Candle Cake, was made with cherry cake mix, canned pineapple, a package of lime Jell-O, red food coloring, and candied cherries. Another example was Tang, a popular dehydrated breakfast drink that was available in an unworldly, iridescent orange color.

In 1955, color invaded the cereal world. General Mills's Trix was a sugar-coated version of its Kix cereal. The orange, lemon-yellow, and raspberry-red cereal was best known for its animated rabbit and the 1959 introduction of the slogan "Silly rabbit! Trix are for kids," a campaign designed by Madison Avenue agency Dancer Fitzgerald Sample.

Color played an essential role in modern advertising, and multicolor magazine and newspaper ads often used recipes to catch the reader's eye and demonstrate the product's usefulness. Advertisements for SPAM®, cake mixes, Velveeta, cream cheese, Jell-O, and a host of other foods were presented alongside recipes with the finished products revealed in full, often garish color. These ads subtly reinforced the 1950s image of the average suburban woman and often depicted a highly idealized and stereotyped, apron-wearing housewife smiling as she presented her finished dish.[33]

Television, the Permanent Dinner Guest[34]

With US government–sponsored exhibitions abroad and print ads flooding the domestic market, all touting the latest kitchen appliances and gadgets, another item would soon catch the eye of the consumer: a television set. No other product in the 1950s influenced the lives of the American family more than did television. In 1946, television sets were found in only seven thousand homes in the United States. By 1950, this number grew to five million, and in 1960 45.7 million TVs were in American homes.[35] This new technology encouraged families to shift their leisure time away from activities in the public sphere—such as movies—to the private domain of the family living room. Television became the ultimate form of family entertainment. "It brought the world into the home [and] delivered hours of relaxing entertainment—all at the flip of a switch."

Figure 10.6. A happy couple welcomes a new Motorola television into their lives. Source: Shawshots/Alamy Stock Photo.

In a veiled nod to fears generated by the Cold War, *Better Homes and Gardens Decorating Book* reassured its readers, "Television is a friendly thing—your family gathers together for its entertainment, cozy against the outside world." Decorating guides frequently discussed appropriate placement within the living room, and some of these suggestions might seem obvious to today's readers. Still, it is essential to remember that this information focused on the first generation of television purchasers. "The set should be placed where the whole family can see it easily, where there is no glare on the screen. There should be seating units for everyone in the family, and they should be the soft, lounging kind." At least one light in the room should be on to prevent unnecessary eye strain, and seating should provide everybody an unobstructed view "without twisting and turning." In an era before remote controls, "Place a comfortable chair near the set, so that one viewer can work the controls without getting up."[36]

Daily life changed for suburban, middle-class families, and entertainment was now available in the family living room. It also transformed how people ate, with more families consuming snacks or full meals in front of the television set, such as popcorn and frozen TV dinners.

With the availability of such a convenient, tasty meal, which needed only heating in an oven, families were encouraged to move mealtimes into the living room. By 1956, Swanson was selling thirteen million TV dinners annually. Priced initially below one dollar apiece, these TV dinners often provided a less expensive and faster alternative to a home-cooked meal. As the result of the growing popularity of TV dinners, a significant cultural change occurred within families. Not only could family members each consume a different meal, but the use of "television trays" encouraged an easy transition from the dining room to the living room. Television trays—small, collapsible tables constructed from metal or wood—were introduced in 1952. As a result, the American family spent less and less time together at a formal dining table.

Snacking While Watching TV

With increasing hours of family time spent watching television in addition to dinner time, the question soon arose: What should one eat during this leisurely activity? Snacking, or eating between meals, traditionally had been condemned because it might ruin one's appetite for dinner. Once thought to be a habit of the lower classes, it became an accepted way to consume food and satisfy cravings during the postwar years. Snack foods "were conceived with television viewing in mind: they could be eaten with your hands, offered a variety of flavors and textures, and were easy to put together."[37]

All dips and sweet and salty snack foods instantly became popular, including peanuts, potato chips, and popcorn. In keeping with their theories of efficiency and simplicity, Mary and Russel Wright's *Guide to Easier Living* (1950) suggests one should just pour potato chips into a bowl—to save time. (These efficiency experts also encouraged the use of paper plates at dinner parties to save time washing dishes.) New snack foods were introduced, such as Fritos Corn Chips and Cheet-os (later Cheetos), a corn product that was artificially colored an intense orange by using dehydrated, powdered cheese and marketed by H. W. Lay and Company in 1948. Crackerjack, a perennial favorite whose popularity soared after the elimination of sugar rationing in 1947, had been around since the late nineteenth century. Kraft also introduced Cheez Whiz in 1952 via its sponsored television show, *KRAFT Television Theatre*. Andrew F. Smith calls Cheez Whiz one of America's iconic foods, in the same

234 | Casseroles, Can Openers, and Jell-O

Figure 10.7. A man stands next to a large billboard advertising Philadelphia Cream Cheese and a dip for potato chips (perhaps the popular, Kraft Clam Appetizer Dip). Source: RLFE Pix/Alamy Stock Photo.

class as SPAM® and Wonder Bread. The product, sometimes called "cheese food," is often criticized because it is highly processed and contains no nutritional value. Instead, it offers lots of fat and sodium.[38] Although crackers such as Cheez-Its, Triscuits, and Ritz Crackers were accepted vehicles for dipping or spreading toppings before the 1950s, the cracker industry made significant gains after World War II because of the cracker's versatility in shape and flavor and the growing popularity of spreadable appetizers.

"Clam Appetizer Dip" is one of the most well-known 1950s snacks. The recipe is found at the end of the nineteenth century, but its popularity skyrocketed after being advertised on *KRAFT Television Theatre* in 1951. Cans of minced clams and KRAFT cream cheese flew off grocery store shelves, making the dip one of the most popular snacks of the era. The following is from *Food Favorites from the KRAFT Television Theatre* (1951) but the recipe for clam appetizer dip is similar in other publications, including Freda De Knight's *A Date with a Dish* (1948), *Dishes Men Like* (1952), and *Loyalty Cook Book* (1953).

Clam Appetizer Dip

Food Favorites from the KRAFT Television Theatre[39]

1. Rub a mixing bowl with a garlic clove which has been cut in half, then place an 8-ounce package of Philadelphia Brand Cream Cheese in the bowl and cream it with a spoon until smooth.

2. Blend in 2 teaspoons of lemon juice, 1½ teaspoon of salt, a dash of freshly ground pepper and one 7 to 7½-ounce can of minced clams, well-drained. Gradually add 4 tablespoons of the clam broth.

3. Serve this Clam Appetizer Dip with potato chips, raw cauliflower buds or crackers. If a thinner dip is desired, add more clam broth.

Popcorn

In 1950, slightly more than 240 million pounds of popcorn were sold in the United States, and by the end of the decade more than 380 million pounds were consumed. Popcorn became the television watcher's nibble of choice. As widespread as it was, there was one significant drawback: somebody had to make it. Pouring potato chips, peanuts, or pretzels into a bowl is one thing, but popcorn took labor—put the oil in the pan, stand over the stove as it popped, clean up afterward. TV-Time Popcorn was the first company to address the issue by creating a hermetically sealed package that held oil on one side and the kernels on the other. Later, Jiffy Pop improved on this by providing an aluminum pan that contained all the ingredients. One needed only to put the aluminum package on the stove and wait. Served in its cooking pan, clean-up was simple: throw the aluminum package into the trash can.

"With this wonderfully work-free appliance, everyone can have the fun of watching the kernels go POP! Then . . . up jumps a mouth-watering taste treat of huge, fluffy popcorn."[40] For those who wished for something a little more trendy, West Bend and Dominion Imperial were among the manufacturers of electric popcorn makers. Using either Jiffy Pop or electric popcorn makers, nearly 64 percent of the nation was consuming popcorn in front of the television by the mid-1950s.[41]

Chocolate Popcorn Balls

Culinary Arts Institute Encyclopedic Cookbook[42]

2 cups sugar
½ cup water
Pinch cream of tartar
1 teaspoon vanilla extract
½ teaspoon almond extract
8 cups popcorn [previously popped]
Melted coating chocolate

Cook the sugar, water, and cream of tartar to 260°, or to the hard-ball stage; then add the flavors. Pour a portion of the sirup over the popcorn and let the remainder stand in a warm place. Form into small popcorn balls, then dip them into the remaining sirup, one at a time. Lay on waxed paper to become firm; then dip into melted chocolate.

Potato Chips

As a snack food, potato chips held a small portion of the market until the 1950s and the advent of television. Potato chips were bland at the beginning of the 1950s—even the salt was separate, contained in a sealed package located inside the chip bag. Lipton Dehydrated Onion Soup Mix, introduced in 1952, mixed with sour cream became an overnight sensation. "California Dip" led to a new snack-food phrase: "chips and dip." After earning the potato chip a permanent home in American snacking, other dips soon followed. By the end of the 1950s, potato chip companies produced thicker chips with ridges to accommodate the growing density and weight of popular dips.

Pretzels

Recognized by their distinctive looped form, pretzels were introduced to the US by German and Swiss immigrants during the eighteenth century.

Pretzels come in two forms, hard and crispy or soft and bread-like. Rolled by hand, one might find a soft pretzel at baseball games and roadside stands. New technology in the 1950s placed pretzels into the robotic hands of a machine, thus enabling them to be mass-produced. The hard form was preferred as a snack food because it would keep for a long time in an airtight container.

To distance the pretzel from its lowly roots, associated with beer or as a street food consumed by immigrants, a 1947 issue of *Kiplinger's* magazine announced the product release of the new "stick" pretzel. In promoting what the industry hoped would be the new upscale pretzel, the article declared, "The swankiest hotels in the country serve pretzels, and the most glamorous people enjoy munching them [and] while the pretzel is a highly nutritious food and easily digested by infants, it is also food for the gods. The ancient Greek gods chose ambrosia, but never got the chance to taste pretzels and ice cream."[43]

Hot Dogs

First Lady Eleanor Roosevelt and President Roosevelt entertained two extraordinary guests in June of 1939: Britain's King George VI and Queen Elizabeth, the first official visit of British royalty in 150 years. While the festivities included state dinners at the White House, Eleanor Roosevelt also organized a picnic at the Roosevelt family home in Hyde Park, New York. This picnic featured baked beans and the all-American favorite: hot dogs. Although she endured blistering criticism for offering this lowly food to royalty, the afternoon picnic helped cement a lasting relationship between the UK and the US—especially important during the era of economic disruption and impending war.[44]

The art of sausage-making arrived in colonial America with the early settlers, who used the process to preserve meat. Hot dogs ("defined as a sausage on a bun") usually were sold by vendors in amusement parks and roadside stands. Introduced to the American public as Frankfurter Würstchen, little sausages from Germany were available at the World's Columbia Exposition held in Chicago in 1893. (Hot dogs got their name because of a suspicion that they might contain dog meat; they were primarily made of pork.) One of these early twentieth-century vendors was Nathan Handwerker, who eventually became famous for the East Coast chain known as Nathan's Famous. Another vendor in Chicago, Oscar Mayer, opened a butcher shop and is credited with being the first to put

Figure 10.8. The Oscar Mayer Wienermobile appears in the Philadelphia Thanksgiving Day Parade, 1951. Source: M&N/Alamy Stock Photo.

his name on his meat products, including hot dogs. In 1936 the Oscar Mayer Wienermobile "began life as a traveling ambassador."[45] Even today, one can find the Wienermobile roaming throughout the streets of the US.

Snacks as Real Food

Advertisements often suggest that snack foods might be helpful as a main-meal ingredient. In the late 1940s, crushed potato chips and pretzels were used to bread meat or fish, extend ground beef, and stuff poultry. Throughout the 1950s, potato chips were the preferred topping for casseroles. In 1959, the Potato Chip Institute published *Recipes and Party Ideas Starring Potato Chips* that promoted its product as the main or supporting ingredient in various foods. Cooks used potato chips in dishes ranging from Welsh rarebit to apple pie, and a baking contest resulted in a potato chip cookie. Crushed or whole pretzels made their way into salads and Jell-O molds and onto the tops of casseroles. Pretzels were also used for making pie crusts.

Of all the snack foods that became popular main-dish ingredients, the hot dog most muddled the line between meals and snacking, finding its way onto the dinner table disguised in Jell-O molds, salads, and casseroles.

FRANKFURTERS IN CASSEROLE

The Perfect Hostess Cook Book (1955)[46]

[Pre-heat oven to 400°]

1 pound frankfurters
2 cups sour cream
1 quart sauerkraut
paprika

Serves 6

FIRST Peel and quarter 1 pound frankfurters. Mix with 1 quart sauerkraut. Heat in a 400° oven in a buttered casserole.

SECOND Add 2 cups sour cream and coat with paprika

[Pre-heat broiler]

THIRD Just before serving, place under the broiler to brown the top.

NOTE Be sure to serve crisp, hot, buttered French bread with this delectable supper dish.

Television, Food, and Cooking Shows

Throughout the 1950s, television advertising became increasingly sophisticated. Early on, processed-food companies partnered with appliance companies to pedal foods appropriate for television-watching enjoyment. Sponsorship by food companies provided the daytime viewer with cooking shows and provided an opportunity to introduce new products. In 1946, famed chef and cookbook author James Beard appeared on NBC in a cooking show called *I Love to Eat!*, the first nationally televised cooking show and sponsored by Borden Foods. (Borden manufactured pasta and pasta sauces, bakery products, snacks, processed cheese, jams and jellies, and ice cream.) Following Beard's appearance in 1947, noted chef Dione Lucas appeared on WPIX-11 New York and maintained a television presence until 1960.

From 1949 until the end of the 1950s, many cooking shows were available on local channels throughout the US. In 1954, Sibyl Johnson (WKKY-TV Oklahoma City, Oklahoma) was the first to participate in a regularly scheduled color television program in the US. In *Cooking with the Experts*, editor William I. Kaufman highlights forty-five of TV's best cooks, providing their favorite recipes and biographical information. Included in this number was one husband-and-wife team (Ken and Lu Calfee of WAAM-Baltimore, Maryland) and two men (Chef Jack Cardini of KGO-TV, San Francisco, and Scoop Kennedy of WDSU-TV, New Orleans). The rest of the television chefs were women. The recipes in Kaufman's book range from Oyster Stew and Chicken Pot Pie to the more adventurous Beef Fillet with Bordelaise Sauce and Pheasant en Casserole. (The latter required the cook to wrap a pheasant in a sherry-soaked towel overnight.) Some recipes are delightfully whimsical, such as Gelatin Easter Egg Salad from Dorothy Cook, WSPD-TV, Toledo, Ohio.

Gelatin Easter Egg Salad

Cooking with the Experts (1955)[47]

6 eggs
coconut
1 package flavored gelatin
sliced peaches (canned)

Make holes about size of lead pencil in small end of egg, using pencil or skewer. Stir yolk and white together so they can be emptied easily through the opening. Rinse shells in cold water. Prepare gelatin, following directions on package. Fill egg shells with gelatin. Place eggs on end in egg carton and chill until firm. To serve, remove shells and place gelatin eggs on nest of coconut; garnish with peaches. Serve with salad dressing. Yield: 6 servings

With a captive audience, advertising agencies initiated large-scale campaigns designed for television viewers. Food companies often sponsored popular television shows. For example, in 1954, Nabisco became a sponsor of ABC's popular program *The Adventures of Rin Tin*, promoting its saltine crackers, Ritz crackers, pretzels, and cookies. By 1957 Nabisco was a cosponsor of the series *Wagon Train* and the game show *Concentration*. KRAFT foods sponsored a live, hour-long series known as the *KRAFT Television Theatre*, which aired on NBC from 1947 to 1958. From 1953 through 1955, ABC also added its own *KRAFT Television Theatre* series, primarily created by KRAFT to promote its Cheez Whiz. TV-Time Popcorn sponsored *Annie Oakley*, and Kellogg's sponsored *The Adventures of Wild Bill Hickok*. By 1959, twelve network television shows were either sponsored or cosponsored by snack food companies, including *Howdy Doody*, which reached into the children's market, and *Rawhide*, striving to appeal to the man of the house.

The housewife provided the focus for most daytime television programming. As the "new iridescent screen began flickering to life during the day . . . a nascent industry searched for ways to entice women to their sets before dinnertime."[48] One example pitched to the female daytime viewer was *Queen for a Day*. This popular show originated in 1945 as a radio program, moving to NBC television in 1956. It was an unscripted show—what now might be recognized as a "reality show." Women contestants would relate their financial, family, and emotional difficulties in a format that often encouraged them to break down as they poignantly shared their troubles. Host Jack Bailey would ask, "Would *you* like to be queen for a day?" and a winner would be crowned based on an applause meter. Winners would receive many prizes: clothing, furniture, appliances, and, sometimes, a year's supply of groceries. Writer Mark Evanier has noted it was "one of the most ghastly shows ever produced . . . insulting and degrading to the human spirit."[49] Nevertheless, it proved so popular that the program was increased from thirty minutes to forty-five minutes to provide more time for commercials.

Although morning slots frequently were reserved for local programming, other national daytime programs included game shows and variety programs, such as *The Garry Moore Show*. Before moving to prime time, Moore's show was a daytime favorite among female viewers. He once mused that he hoped his show eased "the loneliness of women while their husbands and children are away."[50] Later in the 1950s and throughout the 1960s, soap operas would claim the top spots in popularity for daytime viewing. Evenings included theater programming such *Texaco Star Theatre*, Westerns such as *Gunsmoke* and *The Long Ranger*, game shows such as *The $64,000 Question*, and the ever-popular adult situation comedies that included *The Honeymooners* and *I Love Lucy*. With morning shows focused on the housewife and evening shows for the entire family, there was ample time for the food industry to make its mark through advertising.

High on the approval list were the family sitcoms, whose characters happily resided in suburbia, including *Leave It to Beaver*, *Make Room for Daddy*, *Father Knows Best*, *The Adventures of Ozzie and Harriet*, and *The Donna Reed Show*. These programs bolstered the stereotypical image of the ideal American woman. This stay-at-home wife cooked and cleaned while her professional husband left for work every morning and always returned to a home-cooked meal at night. Many episodes in these popular shows centered on the family and the dining room table. In this storybook world of idealized gender roles, wives were subordinate and children never got

Figure 10.9. Religion was an important component in the American way of life, often reflected in the era's popular sitcoms. Here, the Anderson family prays together before a meal: (*left to right*) Lauren Chapin, Billy Gray, Robert Young, Jane Wyatt, and Elinor Donahue in the television series *Father Knows Best*. Source: PictureLux/The Hollywood Archive/Alamy Stock Photo.

into serious trouble. Life seemed humdrum and unsurprising in a land devoid of racial tension or threats of communism.

No aspect of life in the 1950s was untouched by the advertising industry. After the difficulties of the Depression and World War II, Americans now had more disposable income and were eager to consume—cars, houses, appliances, and food. Advertising, especially on the growing medium of television, shaped lifestyles, changed how and where people ate, and defined the needs for living the American way of life.

Chapter 11

Step Away from the Donuts

The Importance of Staying Healthy
(in Case the Cold War Turns Hot)

> The truest patriot is the healthy one. Only healthy people can work hard, do their jobs better and help us win the war sooner!
>
> —"Keeping Your Family Fit in Wartime"[1]

The US declaration of war against the Axis powers, announced by President Roosevelt on December 7, 1941, had repercussions for every American family. Consumer goods quickly took a back seat to the production of military supplies, and nationwide rationing of certain goods started within a few months. In May 1942, the US Office of Price Administration froze prices for most everyday items, starting with sugar and coffee. War ration books containing coupons were issued to each American household, dictating just how much gasoline, meat, butter, silk, nylon, and other things in short supply any one person could buy. Eight thousand rationing boards were established across the country to administer these restrictions. A wartime edition of *The American Woman's Cook Book for Housewives*, containing revised recipes and advice on dealing with food shortages, was edited by Chicago Culinary Arts Institute's Ruth Berolzheimer and published by the organization in 1942. The following year, Irma S. Rombauer published a new edition of *The Joy of Cooking*, which also guided women coping with wartime rationing restrictions.

Despite rationing, health and vigor were vital. "A run-down civilian population is not able to do its best work and is a national liability at a time when we cannot afford liabilities,"[2] declared newspaper columnist Dr. Mary MacFadyen one year after the US entered World War II. During this time, unease regarding the health of Americans, especially American men, became an important issue and continued through the Cold War.

Industry-sponsored cookbooks, such as the 1942 Kerr Glass Works *Home Canning Book*, along with government pamphlets, also expressed concern about the state of America's poor health. Kerr Glass Works noted, "It is VITAL for the UNITED STATES to make IMMEDIATE USE of the newer knowledge of NUTRITION in the present NATIONAL EMERGENCY. To neglect this would be as hazardous as to neglect military preparedness."[3] World War II ration books also carried stern warnings. "It's our civic duty to keep ourselves and our families fit and well in wartime, thus the home front can support the nation's war effort. Good food and plenty of it is the first step toward health."[4] Not only was poor health

Figure 11.1. During World War II rationing in the US, many recipes circulated to encourage food conservation. This is a Baked Bean Loaf, described as a "healthy and nourishing meat substitute." Photograph by Ann Rosener for the Office of War Information, October 1942. Source: Glasshouse Images/Alamy Stock Photo.

threatening the front lines, but fear of inadequate nutrition would result in lost hours on the production lines and endanger the manufacture of goods necessary for the war. Conversations on nutrition during World War II emphasized the importance of keeping healthy to win the war. Soldiers needed nutritious foods to survive and beat the enemy; men and women who toiled in factories required good nutrition to keep the assembly lines moving. After a grueling day at the factory, tired women returned home to see that their children were well fed.

A Bulwark of White European Civilization

From the Progressive Era (1896–1920), the home economics movement pushed the New England diet as the best food plan for everybody, especially immigrants. This movement aimed to train women to be capable household managers and to educate them in numerous related subjects, such as nutrition, childcare, and their new roles as consumers. (Nutrition advice often was not in-line with today's health standards. For example, nutrition specialists preferred that Italian immigrants use less olive oil and more American butter in their diets.) Paul Freeman, author of *American Cuisine and How it Got this Way*, noted that from the 1890s to the 1930s, immigrants were thought a danger to "the moral as well as physical vigor of America. Dietary vigilance would help defend America as a bulwark of white European civilization."[5] Ellen Swallow Richards, the founder of the American Home Economics Association in 1909, preached that excessive eating would make the white race defenseless, remarking, "In all the discussion of the infertility of the higher branches of the human race, how little attention is paid to the weakening effect of the pampered appetite." Based on early writings on eugenics, Richards coined the term "euthenics," a movement that would forward the improvement of white people by innovations in cooking and housekeeping.[6]

Further Investigation of Calories

Wilbur Olin Atwater (1844–1907) was an American chemist who investigated the calorie and how it works. He had devoted his life to studying nutrition and human metabolism, and after working in German laboratories, in 1897 he devised a respiration calorimeter. This device "revealed precise measurements about human energy expenditure. [Additionally] the calorimeter determined the quantities of nutrients and energy that the human subject metabolized during different physical activities."[7] Later, Atwater's calorimeter proved an essential step in analyzing the caloric values of over eight thousand foods. During the 1950s, calorie counting and calorie charts became a serious business.

US Government Food Guidelines

In 1894, Atwater wrote the first official US Department of Agriculture (USDA) guidelines on food and nutrition, issued as a farmers' bulletin. In 1904, he published *Principles of Nutrition and Nutritive Value of Food*, advocating for variety and balance in food choices and stressing the importance of counting calories. In 1917, Atwater's daughter and USDA nutritionist Caroline Hunt published *How to Select Foods: What the Body Needs*. She categorized foods into five groups: (1) milk and meat, (2) cereals, (3) vegetables and fruits, (4) fats, and (5) sugars. The guidelines mirrored the era's emphasis on "standardization, order, and efficiency [that] were consistently present in the scientific approach to domestic space."[8]

With the onset of the Depression, Hazel Stiebeling, a respected chemist and head of food economics at the USDA Bureau of Home Economics, issued *Four Levels of Nutritive Content and Cost* in 1933. The USDA recognized that the Depression caused rampant unemployment, creating a sense of food insecurity. Thus, the guidelines called for acceptable nutrition levels based on economic status. At the same time, the guidelines stressed science by presenting readers with charts and graphs that detailed twelve food groups, but income now defined these food choices. Four levels of diets were created: (1) a restricted diet for emergencies, (2) an adequate diet at minimum cost, (3) an adequate diet at moderate cost, and (4) a liberal diet for those who did not need to consider income.[9]

As war loomed in 1941, the government issued its first Recommended Dietary Allowances (RDAs), which prescribed appropriate intakes of calories, calcium, phosphorus, riboflavin, thiamine, and various vitamins. The RDAs attempted to ensure that civilians and military personnel would receive adequate amounts of these nutrients. In 1943, government scientists, responding to continuing concerns about the nutrition of Americans, developed a new food guide bolstered by an aggressive advertising campaign directed by Roosevelt's Advertising Council of the Office of War Information. The *National Wartime Food Guide* revised the food groups and reduced the Depression era's twelve to seven: (1) green and yellow vegetables; (2) oranges, tomatoes, grapefruit; (3) potatoes, other vegetables, and fruits; (4) milk and milk products; (5) meat, poultry, fish, or eggs (substitutions included peanut butter, dried beans, peas, and nuts); (6) bread, flour, and cereals; and (7) butter and margarine fortified with added vitamin A. Sugar, rationed in May 1942, was not included. The advertising campaign also designed a circular presentation graphic of the seven food groups in place of the square blocks formerly used, and a different color represented each food group. To remind Americans that eating well continued to be a patriotic duty, the center of the graphic depicted a new symbol of a "healthy family group of four . . . thus shifting the emphasis from that of a nutrition program for the individual to one including the entire family." The new symbol contained the words "U.S. needs US strong—every day, eat this way."[10] However, the creators could not anticipate that by the end of 1943, rationing would include meat, cheese, fats, canned fish, milk, and other processed foods, rendering the guidelines useless until after the war.

Postwar USDA Food Guidelines

Thanks to the military's ability to provide copious amounts of food to its troops, those serving abroad during the war returned home as the "best-fed army in history." Author Jessica Mudry notes that World War II veterans had adapted to a super-sized diet based on the basic seven food groups and now anticipated the same sort of "salubrious meals" at home.[11] In the postwar era of bountiful food resources, the new 1956 food guidelines suggested that Americans could eat whatever they wanted after meeting the minimum daily requirements of essential nutrients. Rationing had ended and, thanks in part to agricultural practices, which emphasized pesticides, antibiotics, and hormones as well as advances in food processing, Americans had more food and more choices than ever before. However, processed foods often did not provide necessary nutrients. Instead, they offered synthetic chemicals, preservatives, and copious amounts of sodium and sugar. The USDA defined "good food"; however, it could not account for what people ate for enjoyment or taste. Thus, popular processed foods continued to be impervious to significant nutritional scrutiny by the government.

The 1956 USDA guidelines titled *Essentials of An Adequate Diet: Facts for Nutrition Programs* began by emphasizing America's food bounty. "Food supplies available in this country are sufficient in variety and amount to furnish every household with the nutrients recommended for good nutrition."[12] It simplified the primary food groups by reducing them from seven to four: (1) milk, (2) meat, (3) fruit and vegetables, and (4) bread and cereals. It also suggested daily caloric intake, noting that any remaining calories could be satisfied as one wished since only one-third to one-half of the daily caloric allowance would be guided by the pamphlet's numerous charts and tables. "To round out meals and to satisfy the appetite many people will use more of these foods and everyone will use foods not specified—butter, margarine, other fats, oils, sugars (to make meals flavorful and satisfying), and unenriched grain products."[13] In streamlining the new guidelines, foods in the four food groups were rated by a point system—each group required a daily minimum of twenty points. For example, foods in the milk group satisfied the daily requirement of calcium and calcium-rich foods in any other food group. The 1956 *Essentials of An Adequate Diet* remained the US standard for nutrition until 1992, when the USDA published its first food pyramid.

Sugary Cereals Add Pounds to the American Body

Sugar began to appear in cereals in the 1920s, starting with Kellogg's Rice Krispies in 1928. By the 1930s, marketers realized that children preferred sweeter cereals, and advertisers created cartoon mascots. Cereal boxes were displayed on supermarket shelves at a child's eye level, creating an instant interaction among the cereal box, the mascot, and the child. In 1928, Kellogg's Rice Krispies, which consisted of sugar and rice, introduced three elf mascots: Snap, Crackle, and Pop. In the 1930s, the Postum Cereal Company licensed the rights to Mighty Mouse, a Disney movie character. Other cereal box mascots have beckoned children throughout the years, including Captain Jolly, the mascot for C. W. Post's 1951 Corn-Fetti, the first sugar-coated corn flake. In 1958 Kellogg's Frosty O's, branded as "goodness in a sugar-charged oat cereal," presented Big Otis, a giant Scotsman who was later replaced by Yogi Bear. Perhaps the most famous cereal mascot is Tony the Tiger, who sprang from the boxes of Kellogg's Frosted Flakes in 1952. Mascots proved to be important not only for packaging but for television advertising, where animation gave the characters life.

High amounts of sugar continued to be introduced into cereals during the 1950s, and cereals maintained a high profile on children's television shows. It is somewhat ironic that the sugary cereals of the 1950s originated from a product meant to be health food. Dietary reformers such as John Harvey Kellogg, whose brother Will Keith Kellogg would establish the Kellogg Company, and Charles William Post touted their cereals as healthy alternatives to a diet that caused abdominal distress. These new products included Kellogg's Corn Flakes (1895) and All-Bran, "a natural laxative" cereal, introduced in 1916. Others included C. W. Post's Shredded Wheat (1893), Grape-Nuts (1898), and Washburn-Crosby Company's (now General Mills) Wheaties (1924).

In 1941, General Mills created a whole grain oat cereal called CheeriOats. Specifically designed as a breakfast food for the US military, in 1945 the name changed to Cheerios, and it remains one of the most popular cereals ever made. Another cereal that promoted health was Kellogg Company's Maizoy, which appeared in the early 1940s and was renamed Corn Soya Shreds in 1945. By 1950 the cereal was known as Corn Soya, which promised to keep men strong ("high-protein for manpower"). The box noted that one-half cup of cereal with four ounces of milk would equal one egg with three slices of bacon. Kellogg's Special K (1955) marketed its Concentrate as a low-fat cereal to appeal to the decade's growing concerns about obesity. Concentrate, a healthy cereal product, proclaimed that it might be used as a topping for ice cream and a filler for meat dishes (1959).

However, most of Kellogg's cereal introductions in the 1950s were known for their high sugar content. Corn Pops (1950), renamed Sugar Corn Pops in 1951, was the sponsor for the popular children's television program *The Adventures of Wild Bill Hickok*. Sugar Rice Krinkles arrived in 1952 and became known for its two unfortunate cartoon mascots, So-Hi, a Chinese child with slits as eyes, and later, a terrifying clown named Krinkles. The following year Kellogg's introduced Sugar Smacks, with a sugar content listed at a whopping 50 percent.

C. W. Post also introduced sugar-laden products, including Frosted Flakes (1952); Honey Smacks, also called Sugar Smacks (1953); and Heart of Oats (1959), a competitor of General Mills's popular Cheerios. Nabisco contributed Ranger Joe Popped Wheat Honnies in the late 1930s but simplified the name to Wheat Honeys in 1954. A companion cereal, Rice Honeys, entered the market in 1954. The product was made from honey, but the box read "sugar sweet" in case children feared that honey was not sweet enough.

Not wishing to be left out of the lucrative market for sugary cereals, in 1954 General Mills introduced Trix (a fruit-flavored cereal) and in

1956, Cocoa Puffs, a chocolate-flavored version of Trix. Sugar Jets arrived in 1953. The cereal's original name was Sugar Smiles. Still, it changed to reflect the growing interest in the space age (an ideal later capitalized on by Nabisco's 1958 Spoon Sized Shredded Wheat and its mascots, the Spoonmen).

One of the most successful cereal launches was Ralston Purina's Wheat Chex (1937) and Rice Chex (1952) (now owned by General Mills). Combining both kinds of cereal with added pretzels and nuts form "Chex Mix," a popular 1950s snack. When Corn Chex came onto the market in 1958, it too was added to Chex Mix.

Although cereals were easy to serve and enjoyed a long shelf life, by the end of the mid-1950s, instead of promoting good health it was clear that the evolution of cereals, many containing up to 50 percent sugar, resulted in a health issue.

Fast-Food Restaurants also Add Pounds to the American Body

The rise of fast-food restaurant chains and the ability of the family to experience these new "restaurants" was a source of pride for 1950s suburban Americans,[14] and the growing ownership of cars made it easier to consume a meal at a fast-food establishment. One of the messages that fast food delivered to both Americans at home and people abroad was that it was inexpensive and plentiful, thanks to the new assembly-line technologies (many adapted from World War II factory innovations). Fast-food restaurants were usually self-service, celebrating the American ideals of choice, independence, and individualism. These restaurants opened near the growing interstate highway system, finding ways to infiltrate the suburbs.

White Castle, generally acknowledged as the first fast-food chain in the United States and founded in 1921, served its signature small, square hamburgers, known as "sliders," at a meager price. It spread throughout the midwestern and mid-Atlantic states from the 1920s through the war years of the 1940s and beyond. The chain remains in operation to the present day. (In 2014, *Time* labeled White Castle sliders as "the most influential burger of all time.")

In 1940 brothers Richard and Maurice McDonald opened McDonald Brothers Burger Bar Drive-In, featuring hamburgers, barbecue, and hot dogs (along with twenty female carhops). Experiencing a labor shortage

Figure 11.2. The oldest McDonald's still in operation, located in Downey, California. Opening in 1953, it is an example of the 1950s architectural style used for McDonald's restaurants. Source: Robert Landau/Alamy Stock Photo.

after the war, the Drive-In radically shifted its operation. Concentrating on hamburgers and French fries, the brothers utilized an assembly line model used by car manufacturer Henry Ford. They aimed to create a self-service restaurant where unskilled workers were hired to perform simple tasks. The goal was to provide a full meal of a hamburger, French fries, and a drink in only twenty seconds. The brothers also dispensed with the use of plates and glasses, replacing them with disposable paper products. Orders were delivered in throwaway wrappers, and customers were required to walk up to the restaurant's window to place an order. As there was no indoor seating, the family car became the dining room. The restaurants were so successful that in 1952 they began to look at establishing franchises. The restaurants would have a new look, featuring a large letter M formed by golden arches that soon became the famous mark of the place to get a quick, tasty meal at a moderate price. Two years later, businessman Ray Kroc met with the brothers, who agreed that Kroc could sell McDonald's franchises nationwide. Kroc eventually bought out the brothers in 1961.[15]

In the 1950s, Bill Rosenberg opened his first Dunkin' Donuts in Quincy, Massachusetts, and Harmon Dobson and Paul Burton opened their first Whataburger in Corpus Christi, Texas. Later, following on the heels of the assembly-line model and success of McDonald's, other fast-food restaurants opened, including Kentucky Fried Chicken and Taco Tia (later Taco Bell) in 1952; Insta-Burger King (later Burger King) and Denny's (initially called Denny's Donuts) launched in 1953. In 1956 Carl Karcher opened Carl's Jr., an outgrowth of Carl's Drive-In Barbecue, and watched it spread throughout the western and southwestern states. Andrew F. Smith has noted that the appeal of these restaurants was (and continues to be) "consistency and predictability."[16] In addition to health concerns that slowly came to light in the 1950s, there was a downside to the growing popularity of fast food. "McDonalds and its imitators also undermined regional foodways, homogenized tastes, and often substituted less healthy industrially prepared food for locally sourced ingredients."[17]

Weight Gain Becomes an Obsession

Sporting a little extra weight during the Great Depression often indicated the wealth to procure food. However, by the end of World War II, America began to experience a preoccupation with fat. One of the most aggressive advertising campaigns was for the rye-based cracker, Ry-Krisp, first introduced by the Ralston Purina Company in 1899. As early as 1940, the company produced a series of advertising campaigns designed to shame women. In a campaign called "Eat and Grow Slim," the point was "Men don't love or marry fat girls." Even after the war, the focus remained on women's weight. Author Katherine J. Parkin describes one 1946 ad with the headline, "Too tubby for your hubby," which captioned a cartoon of a groom trying to carry his heavy bride across the threshold. "Better reduce the Ry-Krisp way!" Likewise, a 1947 ad featured a chubby bridesmaid wistfully watching a bride and groom. "Fated not to be mated? Alter your figure—it may be the first step to the altar!"[18]

The 1950s also witnessed a new tactic by the advertising world: targeting young girls. Ads frequently showed a mother on a scale, with her young daughter watching closely. Grape-Nuts featured a mother and a daughter—identically dressed, sporting measuring tapes around their wasp-like waists. Although Jell-O produced a sugar-free product in 1923, called D-Zerta, it continued to advertise its regular product as a reducing food.

Step Away from the Donuts | 255

Figure 11.3. Identically dressed mother and daughter show off their tiny waists in a 1950s Post Grape Nuts magazine advertisement. Source: Retro AdArchives/Alamy Stock Photo.

What Did the Cookbooks Say?

In an era that respected authority, it is possible to assume that cookbooks would encourage the nutritional guidelines presented by the US government. After all, most accepted that the government protected its citizens, including keeping everybody educated on the latest developments in health and nutrition. However, an examination of some of the popular

Figure 11.4. A young girl tries to exercise via television in a 1950s Jell-O magazine advertisement. Source: Retro AdArchives/Alamy Stock Photo.

cookbooks published during the early Cold War years demonstrates that writers insisted women were responsible for the welfare of their families by providing nutritious, tasty, and eye-appealing meals. Yet when it came to scientific nutritional evidence, the information did not appear to come from the myriad USDA publications. Cookbooks replaced the authority of the USDA by editing and watering down the official guidelines, and few of them went into the detail one finds in the official US publications.

Cookbooks written during the early years of the Cold War centered on a female audience and they included discussions on the importance of women in keeping their family well-fed, offering menus that emphasized sufficient vitamins and other nutrients. The protection, health, and future of the Cold War nuclear family centered on the food decisions made by women in the kitchen. Good health was necessary in case the Cold War turned hot.

Published in 1950, *Betty Crocker's Picture Cook Book* devotes five pages to nutrition in a section called "Good Nutrition Brings Double Happiness." Based on the 1943 wartime seven food groups, the cookbook also offers information on protein, carbohydrates, fats, vitamins, and minerals. After providing bare-bones suggestions for incorporating the seven food groups into meals, Crocker notes that adolescents (fourteen to twenty years) "need more food than at any time in their lives. A few pounds overweight at this period is an asset for health." The cookbook further notes that this will require double and triple servings. In conclusion, the book states that, above all, women should be confident that "meals are appetizing, attractive, and delicious to eat. For mealtime should help build happy home life."[19]

Irma S. Rombauer's first edition of *The Joy of Cooking*, published in 1931, arrived three years before the USDA released its Depression-era guidelines. In the preface to this edition, she notes in her singular, quirky manner, "In spite of the fact that the book is compiled with one eye on the family purse and the other on the bathroom scale, there are, of course, occasional lapses into indulgence."[20] That is all she had to say on the matter. Rombauer's 1939 book *Streamlined Cooking* devoted about three-quarters of a page to a "health chart." The 1933 USDA guidelines listed twelve food groups, but Rombauer mentions just six in describing "a daily diet list for balanced and protective meals." The groups consisted of milk (one quart for children and one pint for adults); vegetables (two, preferably three a day); fruit (two a day); eggs (one per day); meat, fish, and cheese (one serving per day); and starches. "These and other foods may be added to satisfy the family's appetite when the right amount of the protective foods has been eaten."[21] (The smaller portion of food reflects the Depression-era USDA guidelines.) The 1951 edition of *The Joy of Cooking* includes an expanded section titled "Nutrition and Calorie Chart." Rombauer asks, "Will our own intuitive desires lead us to a balanced diet, the same cravings that made our forebears gather greens each spring? Shall we follow scientists ceaselessly at work to uncover the secrets of human nutrition? Or shall we listen to the dicta of health faddists or the croaking of quacks?" She concludes that one should follow science even if "not all scientists are in agreement." The section concludes with four pages of foods and their calories and suggests that if counting calories, one should, "Let your contours be your guide."[22]

Initially published in 1901, *The Settlement Cook Book: The Way to a Man's Heart*, was compiled, edited, and published by Lizzie Black Kander. In the 1954 edition, the new "authors" (The Settlement Cook Book Company of Milwaukee, Wisconsin) completely revised and retitled the cookbook as *The New Settlement Cook Book*. The chapter "Feeding the Family" highlights the book's information on nutrition with additional sections covering infant feeding, invalid cookery, liquid diets, soft or semisolid diet, and wheat-free, egg-free, milk-free, low-starch, and low-sugar diets. The book recommends the 1943 wartime USDA guidelines, suggesting choosing foods from seven groups, and provides charts that detail the necessary daily requirements of vitamins (based on the 1941 RDA guidelines). Further, the book provides lists of foods as sources for vitamins and a table of food values. While much of the book's nutrition-related language is obtuse, there are recipes for each special diet, including a wheat-free soybean bread recipe that is flavored with spices such as caraway seed, anise, cinnamon, or nutmeg.

Of all the cookbooks published in the 1950s, *Better Homes and Gardens New Cook Book* (1953) provides the most comprehensive nutrition information—albeit a little heavy-handed. "You'll serve delicious, nutritious meals because the *Better Homes and Gardens New Cook Book* shows you the value of each vitamin, the foods in which it is found, the vitamin needs of each member of your family." The introduction to the cookbook also notes that one will learn how to prepare foods to save vitamins and provides a list of the vitamin and caloric ratings of many foods. It also endorses nutritious meal planning, offering several pages of suggested menus.[23] However, it is difficult to believe that any busy woman would wade through all the instructions, charts, and lists found in this publication.

The General Foods Kitchens Cookbook (1959) is easily the most user-friendly of popular 1950s cookbooks. The tone of other cookbooks often is "preachy," and the information (usually including lists and charts) appears in a separate chapter and is never mentioned again. In contrast, *The General Foods Kitchens Cookbook* weaves nutritional and diet information throughout the entire book. In the section titled "How to Tell if Your Family's Well Fed," the cookbook offers a very brief description of the four food groups and suggested number of servings—based on the 1956 USDA guidelines. In a significant departure from other cookbooks, and after acknowledging the importance of healthy eating, the narrative continues with "three tests for perfect meals." The book reminds the cook that nutrition is essential, but other things to consider in creating meals are flavor, texture, and color.

"When you know some or all of your guests are on a low-calorie diet, serve the kind of meal they can safely eat without overindulging. At the same time, you don't want to confront your non-dieting guests with starvation rations."[24] In a section called "Pamela's Dieting Again," *The General Foods Kitchens Cookbook* readers are provided with simple suggestions and sample menus that would satisfy both dieters and non-dieters. Ideas include letting guests serve themselves buffet-style. Salads and dressings, desserts, and sauces should be served separately to "let the guests do their own wrestling with their consciences."[25] First and foremost, the reader is admonished to speak only to a doctor about dieting—not a best friend, not one's mother, not magazines or the newspaper columnist "who writes so winningly about health problems." For further information, and in a first for mainstream 1950s cookbooks, *The General Foods Kitchens Cookbook* provides information on other diet and nutritional sources, such as the local health department, the American Dietetic Association, and the Visiting Nurse Association. The book contains comprehensive information on appropriate diets for people with diabetes; those with sodium restrictions or allergies (milk, eggs, or wheat); those on soft, bland, or low-residue diets; and those on low-calorie (weight control) diets. Again, readers are cautioned to consult their doctor before starting any weight-loss or food-restricted regime. In one of the era's few references to exercise, "Get some moderate exercise every day. And the easiest, cheapest, and most available exercise happens to be just about the best—walking!"[26]

Eggless-Butterless-Milkless Cake

The General Foods Kitchens Cookbook (1959)[27]

1 cup firmly packed light brown sugar
1 cup water

½ cup shortening
1 cup seeded raisins
1 teaspoon cinnamon
½ teaspoon nutmeg
½ teaspoon salt
2¼ cups sifted cake flour
1 teaspoon soda
1¼ teaspoons double-acting baking powder

Combine the sugar, water, shortening, raisins, spices and salt in a medium saucepan. Bring to a boil over medium heat and boil for 3 minutes, stirring constantly. Cool

Measure sifted flour, add soda and baking powder, and stir again. Gradually stir dry ingredients into raisin mixture. Then beat well. Pour into an 8x4x3-inch loaf pan, which has been greased generously on bottom and sides. Bake in a slow oven (325° F.) for about 1 hour.

[Note: shortening might have been a vegetable shortening such as Spry, Crisco, or margarine.]

A daily leaf of lettuce or vitamin tablet isn't going to make a heartbreaker out of you. But a wisely balanced diet will supply all the known and unknown physical ingredients of that alluring quality known as glamour, oomph, "it," sex appeal, or comehitherness.

—Donald G. Cooley[28]

Life insurance companies and public health officials noted in the early 1950s that Americans were getting fatter and fatter. In 1954, *Life* magazine suggested that obesity was the number one health problem in the US. Other mainstream publications followed suit, including an innumerable number of diet-related publications, many of which offered quick-fix diets often written by men and women with no nutritional training. These writers frequently emphasized calorie counting and the importance of vitamins, both in food and as supplements.

Extremely low-calorie diets were prevalent in many specialty books, periodicals, and pamphlets. One of these periodicals, the new 1954 edition *Eat and Get Slim*, includes "The New 10-Day Diet," submitted by Donald G. Cooley. This austere diet furnished about 750 calories a day for both men and women. The breakfast menu for day one of Cooley's diet demonstrates the bleakness of this regime (his lunch and dinner menus are equally as stark). Breakfast for the "first day—Monday" included tomato juice or unsweetened grapefruit juice, one poached egg, and black coffee.

According to Cooley, one might expect to lose about one-half pound per day on this regime. Further, he encourages plain water, tea, coffee, Postum ("in any reasonable amount"),[29] and skim milk. Cooley advocated using artificial substances such as saccharin or Sucaryl (cyclamate) to sweeten drinks or foods without discussing the possible side effects of the chemicals.[30]

In the same magazine, and written for women who wished for a less spartan diet, author Ann Williams-Heller provided a "Busy Woman's 7-Day Reducing Diet," which increased caloric intake to 1,100 calories per day. In a nod to 1950s housewives, Williams-Heller promises that not only will the dieter lose two pounds a week, but "to lighten your heavy schedule during the week, the lunches are so planned that you need not take time out from kitchen chores. The dinners are simple and ample to fit into family habits."[31] (Well, at least the housewife can complete her kitchen chores.) Salads play a significant role in Williams-Heller's diet plan, and she provides a Spicy Salad Dressing recipe that contains no oil and only two calories per tablespoon of dressing. The directions note to mix "1 cup bouillon or consommé with 1 tablespoon tomato catsup, 1 teaspoon onion juice, and salt and pepper to taste. Add 1 tablespoon wine vinegar if desired. Put in bottle; shake well."[32]

At the end of the same publication, Cooley returns to offer a similar recipe for a salad dressing consisting of salt, paprika, vinegar or lemon juice, and chili sauce or catsup. These are typical salad dressing ingredients for the era, but instead of vegetable oil, Cooley substitutes mineral oil. In a solid rebuttal to the use of mineral oil as a food substance, Carlton Fredericks, author of *Eat, Live and Be Merry* (1951), does not mince words. "Mineral oil is a motor oil in a sense. It is petroleum, specially refined to be free of odor, sulphur and other foreign matter—but essentially it is a substance utterly alien to the body, and undesirable in its effects."[33] Even exercise and nutrition guru Jack LaLanne provided an uninviting reason not to use mineral oil. "Never use 'mineral oil' internally as this is a coal-tar derivative, [it] tends to leak out from the bowels and [is] unsatisfactory in every respect."[34]

In her seminal book on healthy eating *Let's Cook it Right* (1947), Adelle Davis (1904–1974) wryly noted, "Surely the stoical eating of waterlogged, tasteless boiled vegetables is proof that Americans have character."[35] After spending three years studying home economics at Purdue University, she transferred to the University of California, Berkeley, graduating with a degree in dietetics. Davis worked in hospitals, traveled around Europe, and worked for the Alameda (California) Health Clinic during the interwar years. In 1938, she earned a master's degree in biochemistry. Davis advocated taking vitamin supplements and urged her readers to use whole grains and fresh ingredients to avoid processed foods. By 1947 she had produced four books on nutrition.

Davis's publication, *Let's Eat Right to Keep Fit* (1954), was intended as a straightforward book on nutrition while criticizing the basic American diet, which she felt contained too much salt, refined sugar, and preservatives. Flying in the face of chemical lobbies, she foreshadowed the publication of Rachael Carson's *Silent Spring* (1962) by condemning the use of growth hormones (including female hormones to fatten beef cattle) and pesticides. Her strong opinions brought her many enemies. Reviews of the book included comments such as "replete with misinformation." Another critic objected to its "inaccuracies and the over-dramatic manner in which the material is presented." *California Medicine* noted that Davis "indulges in amateur diagnosis . . . and her excursions into therapeutic programs are indeed naïve and, in some places, frankly misleading."[36] The criticism did not end with the 1950s reviews. In 1969 the White House Conference on Food, Nutrition, and Health's panel on deception and misinformation declared Davis to be "probably the most damaging source of false information in the nation."[37]

Quackery

In 1957, the US Food and Drug Administration (FDA) field offices held press conferences on nutritional quackery. Organizations joining the FDA included state and local health departments, the Better Business Bureau, and various medical associations, including the American Medical Association.[38] By the end of the 1950s and into the 1960s, the assault continued,

"It is clear that for nearly thirty years the Food and Drug Administration has been warning public health officials, the affected industries and the public of the insidious growth of this menace to the public health." Objections included misrepresented food supplement ingredients and the high potency of some supplements, which the government feared would be dangerous without medical supervision. The government also criticized "miracle foods," which promised cures such as ingesting carrot juice for leukemia, garlic pills for blood pressure, and powdered grapefruit for diabetes. Denunciation was harsh for products that supposedly helped one reduce. "There are no drugs which are effective in controlling appetite . . . what you pay for (if you expect any results) is the little circular with the dietary plan which tells you to eat less." In summary, the government took the position that the sundry diet and nutrition books were useless to most. "The average reader is not sufficiently informed to distinguish scientific fact from fiction."[39]

Carlton Fredericks (born Harold Frederick Caplan, 1910–1987) hosted a nationally syndicated nutrition radio program, *Design for Living*, and wrote fourteen books on nutrition. Although the title of Carlton Fredericks's first book, *Eat, Live and Be Merry* (1951), sounds upbeat, the text is full of graphic descriptions of post-nasal drip, bleeding gums, constipation, mucous colitis, flatulence, acne, and varicose veins. Fredericks takes issue with "fanatical leaders and charlatans who, glib of voice and promising Utopia, foist untruths upon a hopeful and gullible public."[40] In 1945 Fredericks pleaded guilty to practicing medicine without a license and paid a fine to avoid prison time. In 1961 the government charged that Fredericks's book *Eat, Live and Be Merry* "falsely represented and suggested that the ingredients of the products [Century Foods Company] were effective for preventing and treating cancer, diabetes, heart failure, and many other serious diseases." Additionally, the government stated Fredericks's declaration that he was "America's foremost nutritionist" to be false.[41] Other specialists also spoke out against Fredericks's claims and misinformation, including Fredrick John Stare, noted American nutritionist and founder of the department of nutrition at the Harvard School of Public Health.

The back cover of *Eat, Live and Be Merry* notes that Fredericks "practices personally the sage counsel he gives readers and listeners so that they may enjoy a fuller, longer, more healthful and merrier life." One might assume that would include warnings about the dangers of smoking tobacco. A life-long heavy smoker, Carlton Fredericks died of a heart attack.

But What about Exercise?

> While many are wondering and worrying about the possible effects of an H-bomb, far more people every year are killed by an imprudent diet. We dig our graves with our knives and forks.
>
> —Jack LaLanne (1954)[42]

Exercise is rarely mentioned in nutrition and diet books of the early Cold War years, and there was little official recognition of its importance until 1953. By then, processed foods laden with sugar and salt, and the rise of fast-food restaurants that encouraged consumption of hamburgers and French fries, led medical experts to agree that American children and their parents were grossly overweight and out of shape.

In December of 1953, the *Journal of the American Association for Health, Physical Education, and Recreation* published the article "Muscular Fitness and Health." Coauthored by Dr. Hans Kraus and Ruth P. Hirschland, the article noted that children needed some measure of muscular strength and flexibility. Kraus and Hirschland conducted studies among children ages six to nineteen, throughout urban and suburban areas of the northeastern United States. They discovered that more than half of the test subjects failed to meet "even a minimum standard required for health."[43]

In 1955 Kraus and Hirschland published another article in the *New York State Journal of Medicine*, which reported the results of a study of 4,400 students between the ages of six and sixteen in US public schools and 3,000 students in the same age range in Switzerland, Italy, and Austria. The report showed that 57.9 percent of American children failed one or more of the tests, while only 8.7 percent of European children failed the same tests. Further, 44.3 percent of American children failed one flexibility test. Still, only 7.8 percent of Europeans failed, and when given strength tests, 35.7 percent of American children failed one or more of the tests while only 1.9 percent of European children failed. These results led to a feature article in the August 15, 1955, issue of *Sports Illustrated* that reported, "The U.S. is rapidly becoming the softest nation in the world."[44]

As a former World War II general, Eisenhower, nearing the end of his first term as president, took notice of this report about "soft bodies." A high standard of physical fitness of the nation's youth was an asset needed during the Cold War. In the summer of 1956, following the President's

Conference on Fitness of American Youth, held at the US Naval Academy in Annapolis, Maryland, Eisenhower introduced Executive Order 10673, creating the President's Council on Youth Fitness, chaired by Vice President Richard M. Nixon. It stated, "Whereas recent studies, both private and public, have revealed disturbing deficiencies in the fitness of American youth; and whereas, since the youth of our Nation is one of the greatest of our assets, it is imperative that the fitness of our youth be improved and promoted to the greatest possible extent."[45] In early September 1957, the Conference on Fitness of American Youth met at the United States Military Academy at West Point, located on a western bluff overlooking the Hudson River in New York. It cannot have gone unnoticed that both meeting locations were full of healthy, physically fit young men ready to do service for their country.

In the private sector, Jack Lalanne took center stage. Considered the founder of the American physical fitness movement and author of books on nutrition, Jack LaLanne (1914–2011) believed that the country's well-being depended on the health of its population, noting that physical exercise and good eating habits would be "the salvation of America."[46] He has been described as a man "full of charisma and vitality and determined to make everybody look and feel better."[47] He was physically known to be massively strong; he undertook extraordinary physical challenges to prove that his nutrition and exercise program was not a fluke. For example, in 1954, at the age of forty, he swam the 1.7-mile length of the Golden Gate Bridge underwater and carried 140 pounds of air tanks. The following year he swam from Alcatraz to San Francisco's Fisherman's Wharf while wearing handcuffs, repeating the feat in 1974 when he was sixty-nine. This time he also towed a 1,000-pound boat. For his last stunt in 1984, when he was seventy, he towed seventy rowboats on a one-mile journey from Queen's Way Bridge in Long Beach Harbor to the docked Queen Mary.[48] He became a founding member of the President's Council on Physical Fitness in 1963 under President John F. Kennedy, and in 2002 he received a star on the Hollywood Boulevard Walk of Fame.

Unlike many other nutrition authors of the era, LaLanne had a good relationship with the American Medical Association. He even volunteered, if asked, to talk to anyone's doctor, although he had no time for "quacks." The tone of all three of his books is friendly, with much upbeat, positive reinforcement. *Your Health Cook Book* (1954) provides a list of principles, beginning with "Radiate love, joy and peace" and "Think positively, constructively." Other principles include "Drink more fresh juices, eat more fresh fruits, and eat more raw green salads." LaLanne felt everybody

Figure 11.5. Exercise and health guru Jack LaLanne poses in handcuffs for his 1955 swim from Alcatraz to San Francisco's Fisherman's Wharf. Source: Everett Collection Historical/Alamy Stock Photo.

should eat two salads a day: one vegetable (with the admonishment that one must wash them to remove chemical residue) and one fruit salad.

STUFFED BELL PEPPERS [VEGETABLE SALAD]

Your Health Cook Book (1954)

Green peppers, one for each serving
4 chopped tomatoes
1 bunch chopped green onions
2 teaspoons vegetable broth powder
2 teaspoons olive oil
1 cup cottage cheese

Hollow out as many green peppers as you have people to serve. For four servings, mix the tomatoes, green onions, cottage cheese, olive oil and broth powder. Stuff the pepper cases with this mixture and place in beds of endive. Garnish with ripe olives or grated carrots.

Combination Salad [Fruit Salad]

Your Health Cook Book (1954)[49]

Equal parts of: Bananas, celery, apples, pineapple
Lettuce leaves
chopped dates
fruit salad dressing

Line a salad bowl with lettuce leaves. Make a mixture of the above fruits and place on lettuce leaves. Garnish with chopped dates and serve with fruit salad dressing. [Lalanne's Fruit Salad Dressing consists of cream cheese, pineapple juice, honey, whipped cream, and lemon juice.]

Although LaLanne advocated eating fish and poultry, he also believed in eating meat—as long as it was fresh and lean. In the chapter "The Best of All Brain Foods Is Lean Beef," he condemns consumption of "cured, salted, spiced, pickled, preserved or embalmed" meat products. He also prefers roasting or broiling—never deep-fat frying. His list of other foods to avoid includes bakery goods, such as bread. He suggests avoiding all products made with white flour, white salt, white sugar, and white rice. (He also felt that vinegar was terrible for the body but good for cleaning windows.) His denunciation of white sugar is particularly harsh. "The use of white sugar acts as a 'leach' to eat up the food calcium in your system, causing teeth to crumble, rot and decay from the inside." He further notes that calcium provides "will power, mental dominance, leadership, rulership." When lacking calcium, the person becomes weak and inept.[50]

In *Foods for Glamor* (1961), LaLanne admits to being a vegetarian when he was younger. "I was wrong. It was too radical. I was a victim of the worst sort of health faddism—the self-directed kind."[51] By 1954 he was firmly against the practice (except for ethical or religious beliefs), describing vegetarians as those who "have no scientific knowledge of nutrition, they merely follow whim if avoiding meat, but over-eat on starches."[52] Nevertheless, his 1954 book includes recipes for several vegetarian dishes.

Although he did not believe in the use of white sugar, he wrote, "Desserts serve as a glad farewell to a nourishing meal. To make the completion of the meal a happy one the dessert must be appropriately chosen, and be in harmony with the meal eaten." He considered "elaborate pies and pastries and rich puddings and fancy cakes, and tarts" to be needless and criticized the efforts of women who made these desserts. Not out of character with the period, his condemnation of women for poorly feeding their families was a common leitmotif during the 1950s. "It is a culinary crime to waste otherwise good fruit in pies. Those soggy apple pies and fancy, iced pastries ruin health, [and] makes your husband irritable." LaLanne submits that eating these sugary foods is why a husband might be mean and crabby. Ultimately, a wife is responsible for his behavior because of the "stupid foods she feeds him daily."[53] His dessert suggestions tended to be simple, such as Banana Whip made from mashed bananas, honey, and whipped cream.

LaLanne is most well-known for his opinions on the importance of exercise. In 1936, at the age of twenty-one, he opened one of America's first health clubs in Oakland, California. In 1951 he began his early-morning television exercise program (KGO-TV San Francisco), which he geared toward women, using everyday household objects such as chairs and brooms as exercise equipment. In 1959 the program was nationally syndicated, running for thirty-four years. At the time, it was reasonably radical for women to exercise, some claiming that such activity would make women look masculine. To counter this criticism, LaLanne's wife appeared on the show to demonstrate the exercises and show that exercising would not ruin a woman's figure. LaLanne promoted diet and exercise to be vital for overall health, and he also promoted physical activity for senior citizens and disabled persons.

Jack LaLanne sharply criticized Madison Avenue; he was one of the loudest voices and provided a scathing commentary on the marketing of sugary cereals, fast food restaurants, and processed foods:

> Americans look to me as if they were turned out by an endless cookie cutter. I think it's because we're victims of Madison Avenue nutrition. Advertising hucksters, not nutritionists, have taken control of our eating habits. (Ironically, theirs is the profession known for ulcers, nerves, tranquilizers, pep-up pills and breakdowns.) They work from million-dollar budgets [and] brainwash us, through radio, television, the magazines,

every media of communication. They persuade us—if we're not wary—to eat junk almost any doctor and dentist would advise us to avoid. We look at the same TV shows and magazines, we of the mass market, and that's why Americans are coming to look all alike.[54]

From USDA publications to cookbooks and specialty publications, the 1950s reflected America's growing interest and concern about the ingredients in ordinary foods. Shortly before Thanksgiving 1959, the FDA discovered that much of America's cranberry crop was tainted with a carcinogen, and the cranberry industry came to a halt. The government issued warnings, and the "great cranberry scare" was covered in all media outlets. (On the presidential campaign trail, both Richard Nixon and John F. Kennedy [1917–1963] ate cranberries to support the industry. On the other hand, Mamie Eisenhower served applesauce at the White House Thanksgiving dinner.)[55]

Books and magazine articles on the dangers of obesity and how to lose weight offered solutions that were often misleading, and many publications and authors were labeled quacks. Exercise, promoted by the government as a critical component of good health, especially for adults, found little attraction in the early 1950s. Here, exercise guru Jack LaLanne stood alone, laying a foundation of interest that continues today.

Part 4

Watching History Unfold with an After-Dinner Drink

Chapter 12

The Kitchen Debate

Vice President Richard M. Nixon and Soviet Premier Nikita Khrushchev Meet in a Lemon-Yellow Kitchen, July 24, 1959

> The 1959 American National Exhibition in Moscow was the grandest, most complex, most ambitious cultural diplomacy project ever launched. The [Exhibition] was also the first big U.S. footprint on Soviet soil—and introduction to "everyday" America in brand new buildings totaling more than 400,000 square feet and filled with new, dazzling arrays of consumer goods and young, Russian-speaking American guides.
>
> —Efficacy and Evidence: Evaluating U.S. Goals at the American National Exhibition in Moscow, 1959.[1]

The American National Exhibition (ANE) held in Moscow was arguably the most well-known and elaborate of US-sponsored exhibitions and trade fairs of the 1950s. The exhibition was part of a 1958 agreement between the US and the USSR, both countries committing to a new, open exchange of ideas. The organizers proposed two events: a Soviet exhibition in New York City's Coliseum in June 1959 and a US exhibition scheduled for suburban Moscow the next month. The two powers agreed to focus on advances in science and technology and to steer clear of any political issues. Yet each side "envisioned the occasion for its own ends: the Soviets, to break out of their isolation and impress Americans with the progress the country had made [and] the Americans to confirm their belief that the more Soviet people knew about the United States, the friendlier they would be."[2]

Exhibitions and trade fairs had become a postwar tool of soft power but took on new urgency under President Eisenhower. From his leadership position as Supreme Allied Commander during World War II, Eisenhower understood the value of psychology or what he called the "P-factor." As President, he would make "psychological strategy a key element of his election campaign and a priority of his administration."[3] Upon taking office, Eisenhower had been dismayed that US foreign policy and its propaganda seemed ineffective. He was concerned that the portrayal of the US appeared to be unfavorable throughout much of the foreign media. He swiftly organized two committees to investigate the use of information overseas: the President's Committee on International Information Activities,[4] chaired by William H. Jackson, and the President's Advisory Committee on Government Organization, headed by Nelson Rockefeller.[5] In addition, the Subcommittee on Overseas Information Programs of the Committee on Foreign Relations also played an active role in the investigation of information and, after lengthy hearings, recommended in its final report of June 15, 1953, strengthening of an information program to bring about a more efficient and effective organization.[6]

From an advertising perspective, William Jackson and Rockefeller joined with C. D. Jackson, special assistant to the president and Eisenhower's adviser on propaganda. With input from Secretary of State John Foster Dulles, they deployed a plan that included forming the United States Information Agency (USIA) in August 1953.[7] The plan's goal was "to submit evidence to peoples of other nations by means of communication techniques that the objectives and policies of the United States are in harmony with and will advance their legitimate aspirations for freedom, progress and peace."[8] Thus, the new agency's primary mission was to foster public diplomacy through films, television, radio, and print media to establish the advantages of democracy and the American way of life versus communism or neutrality. Abbott Washburn, former head of General Mills, was named its first director.

Eisenhower had lofty goals for the ANE. In a mission that was to combine his two interests: psychological warfare and cultural diplomacy, he wanted to produce an impressive show that would recognize the American way of life and all its gadgets and technology. "He proposed an exchange of exhibitions that would give the United States an edge in the undeclared propaganda war [with] countless exhibits, and brand new buildings [that] would reach a larger segment of the Soviet population than anything tried before."[9] The expectation was that the Soviets would better understand America, and the massive displays of material wealth would cause the Soviets to wonder why their government could not produce the same, leading them to hunger for a better life.

The 1959 ANE in Moscow was not the first US-sponsored trade fair or exhibition to focus on a perception of the American way of life. The titles of the events often focused on the comforts of home and included We're Building a Better Life (West Berlin, 1952) and the America at Home exhibit (Frankfurt, Germany, 1955). While individually furnished rooms, such as kitchens or living rooms, were often a part of these exhibitions, the Berlin and Frankfurt exhibits also included completely furnished full-scale American modern homes. Technology in Daily Life (Valencia, Spain, 1955), a trade fair that underscored American technology and how it would change lives for the better, also included a full-scale residence.

As large corporate grocery store chains developed and spread throughout the US during the 1950s, supermarket-themed exhibits also played an important role in displaying America's food abundance and sophistication of its food processing technology, thus stressing the benefits of capitalism and freedom of choice. The American Way Supermarket (Rome, 1956) and Supermarket U.S.A. (Zagreb, 1957) exemplify such exhibitions.[10] Government and trade officials agreed that American supermarkets lowered prices, making the country's food bounty available to all, while honoring one of capitalism's favorite principles: freedom of choice. According to Max Mandell Zimmerman, founder of the Super Market Institute, supermarkets are "as powerful a weapon in the arsenal of western democracy as any to be found."[11]

Commenting on the model supermarkets constructed near the home sites, author Greg Castillo argues that the "model home clarified the relationship of the mechanized kitchen to its source of packaged industrially processed provisions."[12] (The ANE also contained a model supermarket.) The trade fairs and exhibitions that circled the globe in the 1950s focused on material abundance and prosperity, highlighting American exceptionalism. They became, in the words of art historian Robert H. Haddow, "pavilions of plenty." The Soviets retorted by accusing Americans of being "a gadget-loving people produced by an exclusively mechanical, technological and materialist civilization."[13]

276 | Casseroles, Can Openers, and Jell-O

The Soviet Exhibition, New York City

Figure 12.1. Cover, official USSR booklet for the 1959 exhibition in New York, 1959. Source: Author's collection.

> The USSR Exhibition of Achievements in Science, Technology and Culture gives the visitor an introduction to the tempestuous advance of the Soviet Union, its economy, engineering, culture, and other fields of the manifold life of the Soviet people. It will be seen that Russia, once backward in economy and culture, has become an advanced industrial power during Soviet years.
>
> —Official guide, USSR Exhibition, New York, 1959[14]

On October 4, 1957, two years before the exhibition, the Soviets launched Sputnik 1 into a low earth orbit, shocking the US in what became the opening salvo in the space race. The Soviets launched Sputnik 2 with a dog onboard one month later. Although the US successfully launched a satellite in January 1958, Sputnik 1 was a painful reminder that the Soviets were the first people in space. In June 1959, as visitors entered the Soviet exhibition that opened in New York City's Coliseum, they looked up to see a model of Sputnik 1 hanging from the ceiling. The replica hung "like the sword of Damocles."[15]

The emphasis of the Soviet exhibition was technology, and there were copious examples, including surgical supplies, machine tools, computers, a rocket engine, and a model of the TU-114 aircraft—at the time the world's longest and fastest passenger aircraft in the world, which carried the exhibition's personnel to New York. Other scale models included a Soviet factory, a ten-billion-volt atom smasher, the Stalingrad hydroelectric power plant, a nuclear reactor-powered ship, and a civilian airport, which American journalist Max Frankel claimed did not exist. He wrote that the exhibit showed the Soviet Union "not as it is, but as it wished to be."[16] Most reviewers found the displays impressive, including one from the *New Yorker*'s "Talk of the Town," which noted that the exhibition made "you stand and gawk." Frederick C. Barghoorn wrote the following year in the *Soviet Cultural Offensive* and observed, "It struck yet another salutary blow at what remained of American complacency regarding Soviet scientific-technological progress."[17]

The Soviets spent $12 million, while the American exhibition in Moscow only received $3.5 million in government support. Juxtaposing the Soviet emphasis on technology, the ANE exhibition centered on the American way of life. However, due partly to the meager funding provided by the US government, several of the exhibition's highlights were repurposed from other trade fairs, including Buckminster Fuller's geodesic dome, Disney's Circarama,[18] IBM's RAMAC computer, and Edward Steichen's *Family of Man* photographic exhibit. Whirlpool's Miracle Kitchen was borrowed from the 1958 Milan fair.

Even before the 1959 ANE, American kitchens already played an important part in demonstrating national ingenuity, providing concrete proof of the "superiority of the economic system that spewed forth labor-saving marvels."[19] On December 8, 1953, President Eisenhower made world headlines with his "Atoms for Peace" speech at the United Nations. In his remarks, Eisenhower proposed the creation of an international agency that would promote the peaceful uses of nuclear energy. In 1957, the US presented an exhibition in Amsterdam called The Atom. General Motors, an American car manufacturer, created a model of an atomic reactor alongside its Kitchen of Tomorrow, a precursor to Whirlpool's 1958 Miracle Kitchen. Greeted with "awe and disbelief as it promised to reduce the housewife's work to the simple act of pushing buttons," this futuristic (and quite fantastical) kitchen demonstrated that nuclear power would meet the expanded energy needs of an automated, push-button kitchen.[20]

The American National Exhibition

The ANE was a forty-two-day event held in suburban Moscow's Sokolniki Park. It opened on July 24, 1959. Vice President Richard M. Nixon hoped the exhibition would give the Soviets a positive portrait of life in the United States. One of the main goals was to emphasize the richness of American consumer goods that translated into the American way of life. The exhibition's organizers, the Department of Commerce, the State Department, the US Embassy, and the USIA joined over four hundred various private manufacturers, including Ford, Pepsi-Cola, McGraw-Hill publishers, American Express, General Electric, General Mills, General Motors, General Foods, IBM., Whirlpool, and Westinghouse. These corporations paraded an assortment of products, including twenty-two new car models shipped from Detroit and displayed alongside American-made farm equipment, plexiglass sailboats, voting machines, Polaroid cameras, large building cranes, televisions, and sports equipment. A small-scale model of a typical American supermarket appeared near a model home.

Figure 12.2. Russians view American television sets at the American National Exhibition, Moscow, 1959. Source: Everett Collection/Alamy Stock Photo.

In addition to the lemon-yellow kitchen in the model home and another in a model of an urban apartment (designed by Westinghouse), the exhibition contained two more kitchens. One was outfitted with the newest technology and stocked with processed convenience foods, courtesy of General Mills and General Foods. The fourth kitchen, known as the Miracle Kitchen, was sponsored by appliance manufacturer Whirlpool. This kitchen contained the latest futuristic technology, with dishwashers that traveled about on hidden tracks, a garbage disposal, a cordless vacuum cleaner, and a command center to run everything with the flick of a finger. The kitchen's electronic "brain" functioned "like a science fiction spaceship from a central control panel by a lab-coated home economist," who could cook an entire meal without even standing up. This display showed the Soviet visitors how technology took the work out of cooking.[21] With a strong emphasis on American kitchen technology, the exhibition moved the focus of the US-Soviet political conflict from military technology, specifically nuclear weapons, to a culture of mass consumption centered in domestic kitchens.

Considered the founder of American modernist design, George Nelson (1908–1986) designed the entire exhibition.[22] (Nelson also furnished the model five-room urban apartment with his signature modern furniture.) Within Fuller's geodesic dome (dubbed the "idea" building), the exhibition included a film entitled *Glimpses of the USA*. Designed by Charles and Ray Eames and shown on seven twenty-by-thirty-foot screens, the film was a thirteen-minute color documentary consisting of 2,200 still and moving images. Intended to demonstrate "a day in the life of the United States," the film included a backyard barbecue along with scenes of a wedding, a honeymoon, and a country-club dance.[23] (To reinforce "a day in the life of the United States," models in American clothing reenacted these rituals four times a day in an outdoor enclosure.)

Behind the dome stood the two-story, fifty-thousand-square-foot glass pavilion with a pleated, fan-shaped roof that was home to more than five thousand household items: small appliances, sewing machines, dishes, and pots and pans—all viewed from a special balcony that seemed to put the items just out of reach of the spectators. It was a not-so-subtle reminder to Soviet spectators that these items *were* out of reach. (Many of the items featured in the exhibit, especially those highlighted in the kitchens, were also out of reach for many Americans.) Additional articles on display included boxed cake mixes, other processed foods from General Mills and General Foods, vacuum cleaners, color televisions, dishwashers, and even wedding dresses and lipstick.[24] An advisor on the exhibition, Llewellyn Thompson, US ambassador to the USSR, suggested that the displays would make the Soviet people realize that the "slight improvements projected in their standard of living are only a drop in the bucket compared to what they could and should have."[25] Thus, seeing more "stuff" might help the Soviet visitors realize that capitalism would be a better alternative.

On the other hand, Thompson told Washington officials that he was concerned about emphasizing propaganda and argued for highlighting the quality of goods. For example, a display of unfinished furniture and plastic dishes was considered a disappointment to Soviet visitors. Thompson also advocated for more focus on culture and history. Still, the USIA insisted that the exhibition's goal was to show the importance of technology in achieving a high standard of living.

The ANE demonstrated America's technology through advanced household products, showcased to impress the Russians and, ultimately, to establish America's superiority in providing quality of life for its citizens. One of the attractions at the Moscow exhibition was a full-scale, three-bedroom suburban ranch home decorated by Macy's department store, with $5,000 worth of furnishings (nearly $50,000 in 2022 dollars), blue carpeting, and built-in appliances. It had been constructed much like a dollhouse, split so that visitors could better view the rooms. The model home, dubbed "Splitnik," was advertised as within reach for America's working-class (Nixon bragged that it only cost $14,000). Telegraph Agency of the Soviet Union (TASS) doubted that this home was attainable for the average American family: "There is no more truth in showing this as the typical home of the American worker than say, in showing the Taj Mahal as the typical home of a Bombay textile worker."[26]

The American Kitchen

The design of the kitchen in the model home had been of particular concern to US officials. Abraham M. Sirkin, a USIA policy officer, explained the problem, "The question was, do we show the most up-to-date kitchen [that] only a few people will have, to show the best we could possibly do? Or do we show an average class, good kitchen, not with all the latest frills, so we can say this is the kitchen [that] is in so many million homes and not just the best of the best?[27] The exhibition planners decided to go with the most elaborate, best equipped, and most up-to-date kitchen available.

Kitchen technology, especially washing machines, dryers, dishwashers, garbage disposals, ovens, and refrigerators, as well as smaller electric appliances such as double boilers, coffee pots, blenders, and hand mixers, were often highlighted at trade fairs, complete with actresses posing as housewives to demonstrate the efficiency of the kitchen and its appliances. In the case of the ANE in Moscow, non-Russian-speaking spokeswomen and home economists from US kitchen appliance and food companies, such as General Electric, Whirlpool, and General Mills, and Russian-speaking Americans, acted as guides and prepared the foods.

A press release issued by the office of the ANE enthusiastically remarked, "The aroma of fried chicken and freshly-baked pies will lead Soviet crowds to a busy kitchen at the American National Exhibition in Moscow this summer [and] Soviet visitors will see for themselves how an American housewife can dish up a full-course dinner in a matter of minutes." The release noted that visitors would "be invited to sample the cooking—110 varieties of food adding up to seven tons. General Foods Corporation is sending 10,000 pounds of frozen foods—beef pies, fish, turkey and chicken dinners, 32 different fruit and vegetable products, and many other specialties."[28] The guides wore typical American dress, and the kitchens included potted plants and curtains.

Showcasing America's advanced technology in freezing and up-to-date refrigerators and freezers, the General Mills and General Foods kitchen guides prepared frozen Bird's Eye products in a several-times-a-day performance for the Soviet spectators. And if frozen peas and carrots seemed dull, perhaps a little dressing up would help.

Minted Peas and Carrots

The Frozen Food Cook Book (1948)[29]

Cook 1 pkg *Peas and Carrots* without defrosting; drain. Add heaping tablespoon mint jelly and 2 tbsp. butter or margarine; reheat.

Ellen Mickiewicz, a Russian-speaking American who participated as one of the Moscow exhibition guides, noted that "plates of vegetables, fried chicken, layer cakes with candy-color frosting, Boston cream pies, biscuits, and more were arrayed on countertops."[30] At first, Soviet visitors received food samples, but after complaints from Soviet officials, the tastings ended. Therefore, the prepared food was simply displayed on the counters for the rest of the exhibition, for viewing only.

Captive Nations

On July 17, days before Nixon's arrival in Moscow, Congress passed Public Law 86-90, known as Captive Nations Week. The joint resolution began, "Whereas the enslavement of a substantial part of the world's population by Communist imperialism makes a mockery of the idea of peaceful coexistence between nations and constitutes a detriment to the natural bonds of understanding between the people of the United States and other people." Each year since 1950, Congress authorized the president to issue the proclamation "until such time as freedom and independence shall have been achieved for all the captive nations of the world."[31] President Eisenhower asked the American people to pray for the enslaved peoples of Eastern Europe.[32] The Soviets denounced the proclamation as slander, and a special memorandum regarding Soviet press coverage of the exhibition remarked, "The coincidence of Captive Nations Week with Nixon's visit was the principal point of irritation."[33]

Nixon and Khrushchev Meet

Although the Kitchen Debate has become historical Cold War lore, discussions and debates between Khrushchev and Nixon were episodic events that took place over several days in different exhibition locations: the Kremlin, the American Embassy, and Khrushchev's summer home. Nixon and Khrushchev conducted their first exchange in the Kremlin the morning after Nixon's arrival. The meeting progressed amicably while the photographers were present, but after dismissing them, Khrushchev "launched into a tirade against the Captive Nations resolution," arguing that it was "a stupid and frightening decision" asking if "war would be the next step."[34] After this testy beginning, Nixon and Khrushchev drove to the ANE. One of the first exhibits they viewed was a model television studio presented by RCA. Khrushchev began talking for the cameras, which captured the event. Thus, it became the only exchange between Nixon and Khrushchev that was caught on film. Khrushchev announced, "We will say America has been in existence for one hundred and eighty years, and this is the level she has reached. We have existed not quite forty-two years, and in another seven years, we will be on the same level as America. When we catch up with you, in passing you by, we will wave to you."[35]

After walking through the exhibition hall with Nixon, it is understandable that when Khrushchev finally arrived at the entrance to the shiny yellow kitchen in the model house, full of American appliances and gadgets, he was in a terrible mood. With a backdrop of a General Electric washing machine and dryer, the lemon-yellow kitchen of the model home became the center stage for a debate between the vice president of the United States and the premier of the USSR. To begin the infamous debate, Nixon "issued the most unusual call to arms in diplomatic history: 'Let me show you this kitchen.' "[36] Described as looking like a prop from a Doris Day movie, critics commented that it appeared "clean and yellow and apple pie neat." Demonstrators showed "the wonders that could emerge from the lemon-yellow fridge: cupcakes topped with cool creamy frosting [and] fudgy chocolate layer cake."[37]

While the kitchen's female cooks, dressed as typical American housewives, prepared an assortment of processed foods, the two most powerful leaders in the world sparred over the merits of capitalism and communism. It was an hour-long "battle for the hearts, the minds, and—perhaps most importantly—the stomachs of citizens in the cold war world."[38] Pointing to the washing machine and dryer, Nixon noted, "In America, these are designed to make things easier for our women." Khrushchev snorted, "A capitalist attitude." Nixon praised the kitchen's modern time-saving technology. Not moved, Khrushchev retorted, "Newly built Russian houses have all this equipment right now." Khrushchev seemed exasperated by all the gadgets contained in the kitchen. "Don't you have a machine that puts food into the mouth and pushes it down?" After much arguing, the debate ended with Khrushchev demanding that everything he said be translated into English and broadcast in the United States. Nixon responded, "Certainly it will, and everything I say is to be translated into Russian and broadcast across the Soviet Union. That's a fair bargain." The two leaders shook hands to end the debate. Nixon recalled in his memoirs that Khrushchev said, "We want peace and friendship with all nations, especially with America." Nixon replied, "We want peace, too." The two then returned to the Kremlin for a "lavish luncheon," toasting each other with "champagne" and caviar served on silver dishes.[39]

The bubbly served at the Kremlin luncheon was most likely a domestic, Soviet champagne. (The Soviets did not abide by the agreements among other countries relating to the usage of the word "champagne.") In 1936, the Soviet government, under the leadership of Stalin, passed a resolution to "dramatically increase the production of sparkling wine, setting an ambitious goal of producing millions of bottles quickly." According to historians, this wasn't possible using the traditional (French) bottle-aged method. Thus, Soviet winemaker Anton Frolov-Bagreyev designed a method of fermentation in pressurized tanks, which shortened the normal three-year process into a month. The Soviets could produce between 1,300 and 2,600 gallons in a single batch. By the end of the 1940s, Sovetskoye Shampanskoye was widely available in Moscow and other cities.[40] *CCCP Cook Book: True Stories of Soviet Cuisine* provides a recipe for "Soviet Champagne Cocktail, Working-Class Champagne." The cocktail (which must pack a considerable punch), often served at official parties, included a copious amount of alcohol, including champagne, dry white wines, and cognac, and some optional canned fruit.

Along with the Soviet bubbly, Nixon enjoyed caviar, accompanied by Russian blini, popular buckwheat pancakes prepared with yeast. "To eat your *blini* the Russian way, spread them with melted butter, then put on a slice or two of smoked salmon, or sturgeon, or salt herring—or good fresh caviar, which is the best of all, if you can get it. The standard *blini* pancake is about 3 inches in diameter. Eat at least 10 of them, or you are a sissy in the eyes of any rugged Russian."[41]

BUCKWHEAT BLINI

How to Cook and Eat in Russian (1947)[42]

2 cups milk
1 cup water
1 cake yeast
2 cups sifted buckwheat
3 eggs, separated
2 tbsp. softened butter
1 tsp. sugar
1 tsp. salt

Warm ½ cup of the milk mixed with 1 cup water. Crumble the yeast into this liquid and stir till smooth. Add enough flour to make a thick sponge—about 1 cup. Cover the bowl of dough with a cloth and set in a warm place away from drafts to rise for 2½ or 3 hours. Beat the egg yolks till frothy, then combine them with the rest of the milk, the butter, sugar, and salt. Mix well and add this to the sponge, along with the rest of the flour. Whip the egg whites quite stiff. Fold them carefully into the batter. Let stand 45 minutes without stirring.

Ladle the batter out in small quantities. Use small frying pans very lightly buttered, and fry the pancakes till brown on both sides.

The next evening, the US Embassy hosted a dinner for Khrushchev. According to Nixon, after Khrushchev waxed eloquently about the beauty of the Russian countryside, he insisted that "Pat and I spend the night in his dacha outside Moscow." Caught by surprise, Nixon noted, "Half an hour later we were in a limousine speeding down deserted roads." Nixon notes that the dacha formerly had been a Czarist summer home and "was almost as large as the White House. Surrounded by acres of grounds and gardens, on one side the of the grand house, the forest dropped down to the banks of the Moskva River."[43]

The Moscow River became the staging ground for the last meeting between the two leaders during the excursion at Khrushchev's dacha. Nixon and Khrushchev took a riverboat trip down the Moscow River, during which Khrushchev continued to provoke Nixon by inviting him to see "how the slaves live." People stood along the riverbank, and the boat frequently stopped while Khrushchev inquired if anybody considered that they were captive people. "The crowds shouted 'nyet, nyet.'"[44]

After the boat trip, the two leaders enjoyed a typical, traditional Russian meal. Nixon described the scene:

> We had lunch on the lawn under a canopy of magnificent birch trees; the scene could have been out of Chekhov. One of the first courses was a Siberian delicacy, raw whitefish sliced very thin and spiced with salt, pepper, and garlic. Khrushchev took a generous portion and smiled approvingly when he saw me do the same. "It was Stalin's favorite dish," he remarked as he took a large mouthful. "He said it put steel in his backbone."[45]

The raw fish appetizer mentioned by Nixon might have been *stroganina*, a Russian version of sashimi. It originates from the Russian arctic and usually uses a type of whitefish such as *omul*, *nelma*, or *muksun*.[46] The frozen fish is shaved very thinly and served with salt, pepper, and occasionally onion. Thus, Nixon's reference to garlic may have been an urban Moscow addition, or he could have mistaken garlic for onion. Plenty of vodka usually accompanies *stroganina*.

As well as the *stroganina*, Nixon most likely sampled other tidbits that were popular Russian luncheon dishes, perhaps a Veal and Cucumber Salad.

VEAL AND CUCUMBER SALAD

How to Cook and Eat In Russian (1947)[47]

½ cup mayonnaise
½ cup sour cream

1 tsp. Worcestershire sauce
2 cups cold diced veal
1 cup diced cucumber
½ cup diced dill pickle
1 cup diced tart apple
2 cups diced cold potato

Mix the mayonnaise with the sour cream and Worcestershire sauce. Add all other ingredients and toss carefully. Serve very cold.

In the end, Nixon, the US government, and the exhibition's creators considered the ANE a huge success. Khrushchev, however, was not so sure. "From my point of view there was nothing there that could be put to practical use." Later, Khrushchev took delight in criticizing one appliance. He said, "I think the organizers of this exhibition don't have a serious attitude toward the USSR and are showing us things that are not important. Here's an automatic device for squeezing juice. But for tea, you only need a few drops. Does this kind of automatic device make a housewife's work easier or does it not? In my opinion it does not: it takes less time and labor to simply cut the lemon with a knife." Khrushchev assessed the Americans as well: "In general Nixon conducted himself as the representative of a major capitalist country." He summed up, "A high level of technological thought, inventiveness scientific discoveries, everything new that moves culture forward was on display, but only in photographs. The only real-life item was the kitchen."[48]

On September 10, 1959, CIA director Allen W. Dulles submitted a report to Hugh S. Cumming Jr., director of intelligence and research at the US Department of State, titled "Comparative Summary of Soviet Coverage of the Vice President's Visit." Read now more than sixty years after the ANE and Nixon's continued travels through the Soviet bloc, the report seems predictable and often churlish. "As a postscript, it may be noted that Soviet media have continued intermittent criticism and attempted rebuttal of some of the Vice president's arguments since his return. It should also be borne in mind that the Soviet press and radio accompanied the visit of the Vice President and the showing of our Exhibition in Sokolniki Park with a running drumfire of criticism of American life, attempting to discredit the image of America presented by both." After a highly detailed analysis of Soviet press coverage of Nixon and the ANE and compared to US media coverage of the New York City USSR exhibition, the report states, "The Soviet authorities evidently combined (a) an unusual degree of coverage in the central Moscow newspapers and radio—to the minimum extent necessary to avoid arousing adverse world opinion—with (b) a usual degree of silence and suppression in all other internal media, to limit the impact on the Soviet people. The major contrast, should the President wish to raise the matter with Khrushchev, would be noted in the attention given nation-wide to the respective visits of leaders."[49]

Although historians have eulogized the importance of the kitchen and the Kitchen Debate, the Soviet visitors at the time were not impressed. When asked to "vote" for their favorite exhibits, Disney's Circarama and jazz were at the top of the list. The model house ranked thirteenth out of fifteen choices, and Whirlpool's Miracle Kitchen came in at the bottom. With all their modern technology and dazzling color schemes, the kitchens seemed unconnected and irrelevant to the average Moscow citizen. Many argued that they also were irrelevant to many families living in the US.

In their memoirs, the two leaders expressed opinions about each other. Nixon wrote, "Few foreigners had been invited to meet Khrushchev [and] some came away swearing that he was the devil incarnate; others swearing that he was just a drunk. All thought he was a bully." Nixon also expressed concern that "Russia was still shrouded in much of the sinister mystery of the Stalin era. The Iron Curtain was pulled tight across Europe, and Soviet missiles were feared." Nixon further characterized Khrushchev as "a crude bear of a man [his] rough manners, bad grammar, and heavy drinking caused many Western journalists and diplomats to underestimate him. [H]e had a keen mind and a ruthless grasp of power politics."[50] Khrushchev felt Nixon showed himself to be "a man of reactionary views, a man hostile to the Soviet Union. In a word, he was a McCarthyite." In the epilogue to his memoirs, Khrushchev made this final assessment of Richard Nixon. "To my way of thinking, he's unpredictable, I'd even say unbalanced. I don't know what motivates him, other than his obvious ideological hatred for Communism and everything progressive."[51]

On Sunday evening, July 26, 1959, at 11 p.m., the American people gathered around their television sets as the three major networks (ABC, CBS, and NBC) broadcast a sixteen-minute tape of part of what has become known as the Kitchen Debate.

Booze Diplomacy

Russia has been long famous for its hospitality, which often features a ceremonial meal where guests are judged on their character and dependability by consuming copious amounts of alcohol—usually vodka. In his memoirs, Nixon noted that Westerners who had met Khrushchev thought he was either a "bully" or a "drunk." But he also noted that Khrushchev's "heavy drinking caused many Western journalists and diplomats to underestimate him." In his July 1959 encounters with Khrushchev, Nixon attended several banquets. He often kept a tally of the vodka toasts at these meals as vice president and later as president. In 1994, Nixon observed, "We are great world powers and our interests will inevitably clash, but the greatest mistake we can make is to try to drown down differences in champagne and vodka toasts at 'feel-good' summit meetings."[52] In an article titled "The Vodka Effect: Happy New Year; A Short History of Booze Diplomacy," author Mark Lawrence Schrad notes that these banquets "contain their own rituals: most notably the volleying of round upon round of loquacious toasts between the hosts and their guests." Tradition requires that everybody drink or risk insulting the host. Schrad explains, "Foreigners unaccustomed to these rituals risk a minor faux pas, while those unprepared to consume large quantities of potent distilled spirits often risk even more."[53]

Nixon's biographer James C. Humes remarked, "With the Soviets it was often bombast followed by laughter; saber rattling giving way to smiles; and then the hard work of negotiation succeeded by hard drinking."[54] When negotiating a 1970s US-Soviet nuclear arms deal that went into the early morning hours, one observer noted, "Soviet leader Leonid Brezhnev pushed for greater American concessions while Henry Kissinger was exhausted, and Nixon was drunk."[55]

Nixon Enjoys His Mai Tais

> "This iconic cocktail of the tiki movement demands respect, even if it was also the official cocktail of Richard Nixon's presidency," notes a 2016 online article. It continues, "And yet over the decades, its mix of rums, orgeat (almond syrup), lime juice, rich demerara simple syrup, and orange curaçao has somehow devolved into a mess of syrups and juices, seemingly open to whatever interpretation the bartender feels like."
>
> —Caroline Pardilla, "You Deserve a Mai Tai"[56]

Nixon was a regular customer at Trader Vic's, located in the basement of the Statler-Hilton Hotel (now the Capitol Hilton) in Washington, DC.

He loved a good mai tai, and it "became a somewhat official drink of his administration."[57] The mai tai's origins, however, are in dispute. Victor J. Bergeron (known as Trader Vic) claims to be the originator; others claim that Trader Vic's competitor, Donn Beach of Don the Beachcomber, a popular California tiki bar, first offered the drink. (The mai tai is not a South Pacific drink—as a rum-based drink, its roots are the Caribbean.) In 1953, Marson Steamship Lines hired Bergeron to supervise the cocktails for their Royal Hawaiian and Moana Surfrider Hotels. Legend says that Bergeron began to add pineapple and orange juices to the mai tai for a more Hawaiian tourist–friendly cocktail.

Mai Tai

Liquor.com (2020)[58]

Ingredients:

1½ ounces white rum
¾ ounce orange curaçao
¾ ounce lime juice, freshly squeezed
½ ounce orgeat [almond syrup]
½ ounce dark rum

Garnish: lime wheel; mint sprig

Steps:

1. Add the white rum, curaçao, lime juice and orgeat into a shaker with crushed ice and shake lightly (about 3 seconds).

2. Pour into a double rocks glass.

3. Float the dark rum over the top.

4. Garnish with a lime wheel and mint sprig. [Serves 1]

A nontraditional mai tai is often made from bottled fruit juices, garnished with maraschino cherries and pineapple sticks, and topped with a flashy paper umbrella. A Caribbean-inspired hors d'oeuvre was considered an excellent accompaniment to a mai tai.

Shrimp Canape

Trade Winds Cookery: Tropical Recipes for All America (1956)[59]

Use freshly cooked shrimp. Remove black line. Split shrimp and spread between halves a little Roquefort or Bleu cheese which has been smoothed with a little cream. Skewer halves together with toothpicks. Dip shrimp in flour, then beaten egg, then bread crumbs. Fry in deep fat to a delicate brown.

Trader Vic's tiki bars often served Chinese-inspired food with his rum drinks.

Barbecued Spareribs

The House of Chan Cookbook (1952)[60]

1 clove garlic, mashed
½ cup soya sauce
⅓ cup sugar
1 teaspoon salt
¼ teaspoon pepper
2½ or 3-pound piece young spareribs (whole piece)
1 tablespoon grated orange peel

Mix garlic, soya sauce, sugar, salt, pepper, and orange peel. Trim fat from spareribs; do not chop or break; use the piece whole. Place meat in a shallow dish or pan, pour the garlic sauce over it and spread over meat. Let stand in the refrigerator about ½ to 1 hour. Turn the meat two or three times in that time, spreading the sauce over it thoroughly each time.

To barbecue in the broiler, place the meat curved side down on a rack in a baking pan. Preheat the broiler 15 minutes; place the rib pan 6 to 8 inches from medium flame for about 20 minutes. When the meat is crusty and done on one side, turn it and continue the cooking till the other side is browned. Total cooking time is 40 to 50 minutes, depending on how hot broiler is. 4 servings.

On July 28, 1959, *The New York Times* noted that during his trip to the ANE, Nixon "managed in a unique way to personify a national character proud of peaceful accomplishment, sure of its way of life, confident of its power under threat."[61] Even after friendly toasts with vodka and champagne, relations with the Soviets cooled after an American U2 high-altitude reconnaissance plane was shot down by the Soviets on May 1, 1960, and the Cuban Missile Crisis of October 16 to 28, 1962, pushed the United States and the Soviet Union to the verge of a nuclear war. The relationship between the US and the USSR would not improve until the 1970s.

Epilogue

My mother, who described herself as "pleasingly plump," had a closet full of silhouette shapers, full-body girdles, and a waist-cinching brassiere called a Merry Widow (named for Lana Turner's role in the 1952 movie musical *The Merry Widow*). Television and print media relentlessly portrayed the perfect woman's body as thin, with a wasp-waist. One needed only to leaf through popular women's magazines to see idealized women, illusions with perfect bodies, sometimes even in girdles and cocktail dresses as they cooked and cleaned, make perfectly curated meals with cookbooks chock full of new, modern recipes for the nuclear family. "The dictates of fashion reinforced the message that women existed to please men rather than as beings in their own right who warranted comfort."[1]

If creating a body shape through girdles was an illusion, so too were television's favorite American mothers—June Cleaver (*Leave It to Beaver*) and Margaret Anderson (*Father Knows Best*)—who represented ideal housewives but not from the realities of "lived" lives. The perfect nuclear families presented on these shows did not represent the diversity found in much of American urban or suburban life. In *Rethinking Cold War Culture*, Peter J. Kuznick and James Gilbert write that radio, recorded sound, television, and the movies represented a "communications revolution of the 1950s [that] endlessly portrayed and fictionalized contemporary culture."[2] But even with such programming, television became a formidable power that influenced everyday behavior in people who attempted to live the American way of life.[3]

In the 1950s, the advertising industry acquired ample power. One of the tenets of the American way of life was to respect authority—husbands, government, the medical profession, churches, and the dictates of Madison Avenue. Advertisements of the 1950s gave us a husband spanking his wife

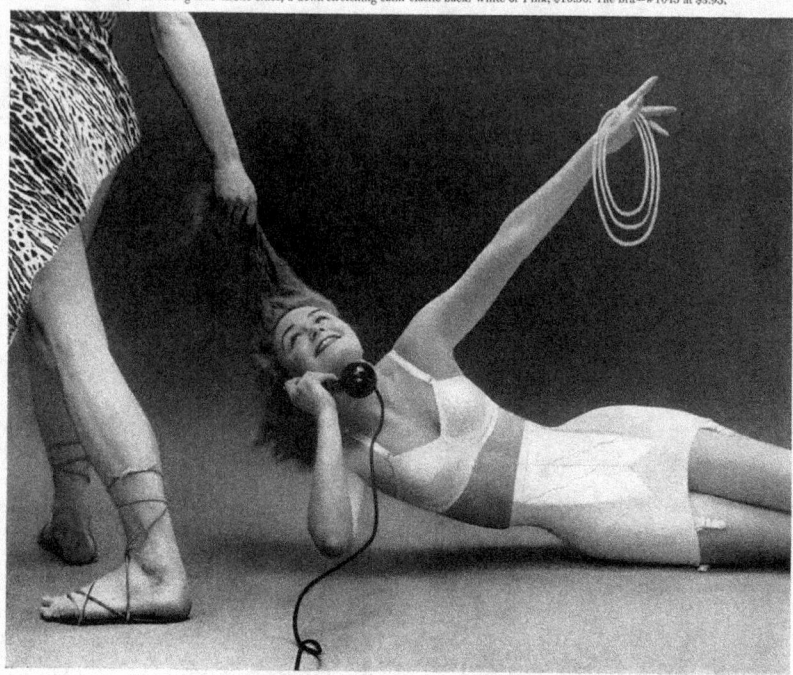

Figure E.1. "You don't need to wear armor to be a charmer." Magazine advertisement in the 1950s for Warner's bras, girdles, and corselettes. Source: Retro AdArchives/Alamy Stock Photo.

for using the wrong brand of coffee, doctors who glamorized the pleasures of smoking ("More doctors smoke Camels than any other cigarette"), and a recommendation to add 7 Up to children's milk ("Mothers know this is a wholesome combination"). Rarely questioned, the authority of the advertising industry and its interpretations of the ideal American family and foods provided challenging and vivid images.

Fear, especially the fear of nuclear war, permeated much of American society. Nuclear weapons changed the way people thought about the

Figure E.2. "If he discovers you're still taking chances on getting flat, stale coffee, woe be unto you!" Chase and Sanborn magazine advertisement, 1950s. Source: Retro AdArchives/Alamy Stock Photo.

world, launching an environment of dread that had not previously existed. Survival could not be guaranteed. The Eisenhower administration understood the power of fear to both paralyze and motivate the population in the United States.[4] Stocked with all the available canned and dehydrated foods, Americans believed they could survive the unthinkable by building bomb shelters. Teaching children to "duck and cover"[5] and never to look directly into the blast of a thermonuclear weapon, the Federal Civil Defense Administration called upon women to take the lead in readiness: "The home is the basic unit of the community; civil defense looks to you, as a woman, to take an active role in protecting your home. No one else can do that job for you."[6] This was the ultimate "job" for the busy housewife.

The US government published numerous booklets for home use including *Your Guide for Defense Against the H-Bomb* (1955), *Home Protection Exercises* (1959), and *The Family Fallout Shelter* (1959). The Federal Defense Administration also urged all families to keep a seven-day supply of food and water, such as Hawaiian Punch, canned soup, Tang drink mix, candy, Kellogg's Corn Flakes, SPAM®, Vienna sausages, and cans of tuna.[7] "Civil defense policies in the '50s and early '60s were based on the flawed notion that most of the nation's population would survive a catastrophic nuclear attack."[8] In retrospect, these preparations seem somewhat useless, given that science now better understands the power of nuclear weapons. Fortunately, as the US wasn't attacked by atomic weapons, we will never know if these measures would have saved lives or if they simply were illusions.

Rooted along with the concern of the USSR's nuclear capability was the basic fear of communism. Pamphlets, books, newspaper and magazine ads, and newsletters circulated throughout the US in the late 1940s and 1950s warning of the red menace. The government issued titles such as *Communist Infiltration in the United States* (1946) and *Facts on Communism* (1959). Concern that there might be communists in the entertainment community led to the 1950s titles *Americans . . . Don't Patronize the Reds. Keep Them Out of Your Living Rooms . . . Out of Radio . . . Off the Screen* and *Red Channels: Report of Communist Influence in Radio and Television*. Civic and religious groups published their versions of the dangers. *It's Fun to Live in America*, produced by Kiwanis International, reminded its readers that the pamphlet was prepared "in the interest of the American way of life." During the early 1950s, the Church League of America regularly published anti-communist and anti-labor literature. Newspaper and magazine advertising often appeared with titles as "How and What to Tell a Communist." The zenith of America's anxiety over communism is observed in the famed McCarthy hearings of 1950–1954. In the end, the US Senate condemned McCarthy in 1954 for his investigations and accusations of subversive activities throughout the government and civilian populations, largely due to the power of live-broadcast television and the journalist Edward R. Murrow. (Murrow's televised takedown of McCarthy is legendary and is an "iconic example of journalistic guts.")[9]

While much of the US was consumed by political angst, cookbooks continued to provide recipes for glistening mounds of Jell-O, crammed full of marshmallows and other processed, not quite natural foods from cans. Women who wished to be "creative" by adding a personal touch, or utilized processed and prepackaged foods, took advantage of Betty Crocker cake mixes or the Wilton Company's inventory of cookie presses and cake decorating tools, products that "make baking and decorating fun and easy."[10] For others, the simple act of opening a can might seem to be actual cooking as they read and followed the directions offered in the *Can-Opener Cook Book*.

Many mainstream cookbooks of the 1950s displayed lavish color photography, and when added to a recipe's descriptive words, the images were designed "to make us act on our consumer impulses—to get up and make something to eat."[11] Now and again, cookbooks serve as motivational texts. Author Megan J. Elias notes, "Sometimes we aspire to make just one recipe; at other times we more broadly reach for the lifestyle and values presented in a book."[12]

Cookbooks tell us how to prepare a dish, but other than helping track the popularity and continuity of certain dishes and styles of preparation, they do not tell us if anybody ate them. What they do demonstrate is flexibility. Some women likely created meals by following all the instructions; others took recipes as a foundation for new and original dishes. Sometimes, the hints come in used cookbooks: a checkmark beside a recipe, a resounding "no" that appears at the end of a recipe, and changes in ingredient amounts all add to the historical narrative.

During the 1950s, through processed foods and fast-food restaurants, "regional distinctions were blurring fast," and the American palate was becoming "homogenized, leading to what came to be regarded as the 'bland American diet' full of tasteless meats, fish, vegetables, and fruits," notes critic John Mariani.[13] Meanwhile, magazines and advertisements promoted appliances and gadgets that promised to make cooking "fun" for the housewife. In the famed Kitchen Debate, Richard Nixon argued that these consumer objects made life easier for the American housewife and thus represented the best of American capitalism and the American way of life. The lemon-yellow kitchen where the discussion between Nixon and Khrushchev took place was an idealized room from an imaginary American model ranch house. It was barricaded and cut in half—a space designed only for spectators, an illusion for everybody who experienced the exhibition. In this kitchen, and the other kitchens represented at the exhibition, "pretend" housewives prepared boxed Betty Crocker Boston cream pies, Birds Eye frozen vegetables, and fried chicken as entertainment for the onlookers.

Looking back at the 1950s, it seems that all recipes started with a can of cream of mushroom soup, and indeed, many did. Advertisers presented these foods as "modern," "nutritious," and "fast and easy." Madison Avenue wanted to create the illusion that being modern and cooking in the 1950s meant emphasizing processed foods. Industry needed to show that trusted women (real or imaginary) would lead the way in using the new products. Madison Avenue, and General Mills, used Betty Crocker as one of many illusions to sell industry's new goods. She was not an actual person but a collage of many faces, impersonated by several actresses. Voted the second most popular woman in America in 1945 (following former first lady of the United States Eleanor Roosevelt), Betty Crocker empowered women as cooks. Perhaps sadly, Betty Crocker was one of the few "people" whom 1950s housewives could trust.

Although Betty Crocker was unique in her longevity and influence, the cooking "world" was full of spokeswomen who were simply illusions. In discussing a recipe that appeared in the April 1954 issue of *Woman's Day*, writer Laura Shapiro noted that the recipe's author, "Mary Blake," a well-known spokeswoman for Carnation Evaporated Milk, did not exist. In the advertisement, Mary Blake told her readers that the recipe was a creation of her good friend Betty Crocker of General Mills. Lending human faces to products made them easier to sell to women, and with this in mind, Libby, McNeill & and Martin, purveyors of Libby's canned foods, created Mary Hale Martin, and Castle and Cook, a seller of tropical fruits, invented Patricia Collier to encourage sales of Dole's canned pineapple. Another famous spokeswoman was Ann Pillsbury, created to hawk the Pillsbury brand. These food corporations wrote advertising copy, answered mail, and wrote speeches for their "spokeswomen." What did these trusted spokeswomen do? They "taught women how to use new electric stoves, mixers, and blenders, how to cook blocks of frozen peas, how to garnish canned ham with pears dipped in food coloring, and how to make Crêpes Suzette with pancake mix."[14] As Shapiro points out, "These women weren't real, per se [but they flourished] in a surreal universe that left purely optional the distinction between fiction and reality."[15] Industry needed to show that trusted women (real or imaginary) would lead the way in using the new products.

However, cookbooks written by proponents of gourmet cooking such as Dione Lucas, James Beard, Louis Diat, Alice B. Toklas, and Freda De Knight challenged the assumptions of Madison Avenue. They encouraged adventurous cooking and using fresh ingredients when possible. Exercise guru Jack LaLanne and health author Adelle Davis also are represented as champions of fresh, non-processed foods and healthy living.

Women did explore other cooking options, and many cookbooks reflected this. Reading beyond the cans and dehydrated foods in boxes, some mainstream cookbooks also offered options. For example, *Betty Crocker's Picture Cookbook* presents recipes that utilized processed foods and recipes from scratch. Even her Potage St. Germaine, the subject of a 1951 critical review of the book, is made from scratch. (It was Crocker's suggested garnish of sliced bologna that enraged the critic.) Nevertheless, the soup's ingredients consisted of dried peas and fresh vegetables. Betty Crocker could have recommended beginning with a can of split pea soup, as other cookbook authors of the era might have done. Although the image presented by a quick reading of recipes is that women always used processed foods in the 1950s, often they did not. Much of the current scholarship does not consider the adaptability and creative spirit of 1950s women and the cookbooks that encouraged them, if in small ways, to return to fresh cooking and experiment with international and gourmet dishes.

Were illusions enough? What did women do if they were unhappy or needed help managing the burden of a household or wanted to return to the workforce against their family's wishes? What if they just wanted somebody to listen? Or perhaps the average suburban woman simply could not live up to the unrealistic expectations expressed by *Life* magazine in 1956, which described her as "this wondrous creature who marries younger than ever, bears more babies, and looks and acts far more feminine than the emancipated girls of the 1920s or even 30s [and] who gracefully concedes the top job rungs to men."[16] Mostly gone were the images of women working outside the home to help win the war, such as the iconic Rosie the Riveter. Now women were enveloped in an illusion of contentment and warmth in the family kitchen, happily cooking meals and taking care of a husband and children.

Popular women's magazines such as *Ladies' Home Journal* and *Cosmopolitan* offered advice columns to address these issues. In 1953, the *Ladies' Home Journal* ran two syndicated columns, "Can This Marriage Be Saved?" and "Tell the Doctor." Answers to readers' questions were predictable (all the advice came from men). If a woman complained about physical abuse or her husband's infidelity, the magazine's advice was to examine herself to see what *she* might have done to provoke violence or infidelity. As the 1950s progressed, these columns took another approach, advising their women readers with any sort of problem to "take a pill."

Betty Friedan described women's malaise of the 1950s as "the problem with no name," a tension, depression, and anxiety that "results from the gaps between the expectations of a fulfilling life and the realities of a stifling existence."[17] Lives in reality haunted by an illusion. To provide remedies, scientists at major pharmaceutical corporations began to develop new drugs to treat depression. Patented in 1952, Miltown (meprobamate) was among the agents at the center of the most significant middle-class drug-abuse phenomenon of the 1950s. Known throughout suburbia as a "dehydrated martini," Miltown became the "happy pill" for "harried housewives and stressed-out [male] commuters."[18] Pharmaceutical companies' advertising agencies peddled tranquilizers like they did refrigerators or cans of SPAM® or other consumer items. Leading news magazines such as *Newsweek*, *Time*, and *Science Digest* and all the popular women's periodicals contained advertisements and articles promoting the use of Miltown and similar drugs.[19] These campaigns were so successful that by 1957 thirty-five million prescriptions had been written for more than seventy types of tranquilizers. One in twenty Americans took Miltown. Pharmacies often ran out and placed signs in their windows saying, "Out of Miltown—more tomorrow." The dark side of this pharmaceutical success was an attempt to reinforce strict 1950s gender roles. Advertising implied that these pills "would allow men to strengthen their authority at home and in the office and would allow women to embrace their duties as wives and mothers."[20]

Contemporary society continues to view the era of the 1950s as nostalgic. (The Internet is full of "nostalgic" 1950s websites.) However, looking past the illusions it can be seen that many gains were made in the 1950s, including a potent anti-polio vaccine; new science technology, such as mankind's first explorations of outer space; advancing consumer technology, such as television, foods, and appliances; a sophisticated mechanized industry; and rock 'n' roll. These are not illusions.

The 1950s brought us some of the best classic films ever made: *All About Eve* (1950), *An American in Paris* (1951), *Singin' in the Rain* (1952), *From Here to Eternity* (1953), *On the Waterfront* (1954), *Rebel Without a Cause* (1955), and *Some Like it Hot* (1959). The 1950s also produced an extraordinary number of fine novels and plays: *The Ballad of the Sad Café* (Caron McCullers, 1951), *The Catcher in the Rye* (J. D. Salinger, 1951), *Wise Blood* (Flannery O'Connor, 1952), *Waiting for Godot* (Samuel Beckett, 1953), *The Crucible* (Arthur Miller, 1953), *Lord of the Flies* (William Golding, 1954), *Doctor Zhivago* (Boris Pasternak, translated into English in 1958), and the perennial children's favorites *Charlotte's Web* (E. B. White, 1952) and *The Cat in the Hat* (Dr. Seuss, 1957). Many composers who contributed to the classical music scene include Aaron Copland, Samuel Barber, Leonard Bernstein, Igor Stravinsky, John Cage, and Milton Babbitt. The US dance world gave us works by Martha Graham, George Balanchine, Jerome Robbins, Agnes de Mille, Merce Cunningham, Katherine Dunham, and many others.

Now, more than seventy years later, many people continue to call the nation's large cities home. However, Americans are still moving to suburban communities with families that now include single parents, immigrants, mixed-race families, families of color, and same-sex families—faces now represented in advertising and television. Immigrants continue to arrive, enlivening the US with their food and culture as they work to get a part of the American way of life. One of the last vestiges of communism and the Cold War, the Berlin Wall, built in 1961, fell in 1989. Aunt Jemima pancake products still exist but now with new packaging and under a new name—the stereotyped, racist image presumably gone. Today, with growing and curious palates, Americans are as likely to eat Thai cuisine as hot dogs and Indian food as a McDonald's hamburger. Meanwhile, the old favorites Velveeta, SPAM®, canned soups, marshmallows, and frozen and dehydrated foods continue to occupy shelves in the nation's supermarkets, reminding us that while the world changes, some things are forever.

༄

Often missed in the study of 1950s foods are the recipes that repeatedly appear in all genres of cookbooks. Recipes for cakes, cookies, candy, ice cream, sauces, puddings and custards, mousses, and more fill many pages of every cookbook published in the 1950s. Of these desserts, one category stands out because it is almost always the only dessert made from scratch—no boxed mixes and no canned ingredients. Fresh pies consist of a homemade crust of flour, water, salt, shortening, and a fresh fruit filling.

Two pies are frequently mentioned: the all-American apple pie and lemon pie. Author Megan J. Elias, in *Food on the Page*, writes about the proliferation of lemon pie desserts found in late nineteenth- and early twentieth-century charity cookbooks. "Because lemon pie is not an especially difficult or expensive dish to make, we can probably take its ubiquity as a sign that it was something people actually made and enjoyed during this period."[21]

Alongside recipes that use mushroom soup in a can, recipes for fresh Lemon Pie, Lemon Cream Pie, Lemon Meringue Pie, Lemon Sponge Pie, and Lemon Tart can be found in every mainstream and many specialty cookbooks published in the 1950s. These recipes use fresh ingredients: eggs, sugar, fresh lemon juice, and perhaps a bit of butter or whipped cream. (These recipes contain no lemon Jell-O, no lemon pudding mix, no canned condensed milk, no bottled lemon juice.) The color of a lemon pie is sunny and bright; its citrus taste is not too sweet, not too tart. In short, a fresh lemon pie can be viewed as optimistic, crisp, and in stark contrast to the heavy meals of processed foods pushed by the advertising industry and the staged lemon-yellow kitchen in Moscow. Recipes for fresh lemon pies remind us that there may have been many illusions in the 1950s, but lemon pie (as well as apple pie and other fresh fruit pies) was not one of them. The following recipe is said to have been a favorite of the Truman family during their years at the White House; therefore, in the words of M. F. K. Fisher, "I serve it forth."[22]

Frozen Lemon Pie

Mrs. Harry S. Truman

Who Says We Can't Cook! by members of the Women's National Press Club[23]

2 eggs, separated
1 cup cream, whipped
⅓ cup lemon juice

½ cup sugar
1 tablespoon lemon rind, grated
½ cup crumbled graham crackers

Beat egg yolks, add lemon juice and rind, and all but two tablespoons sugar. Cook over low heat, stirring constantly. Cool. Beat egg whites with the two tablespoons sugar and fold into cooked mixture, and then fold cream into the mixture. Line greased pan, pie or refrigerator pan, with the crumbs and sprinkle a few on top. Freeze. Serves four or five.

Notes

Introduction

1. It would be several decades before advertisers and advertising agencies would recognize the spending power of the gay community.

2. Mary L. Dudziak, *Cold War Civil Rights: Race and the Image of American Democracy* (Princeton, NJ: Princeton University Press, 2000), 11. For further reading on racial issues in Cold War America, see *Contested Democracy: Freedom, Race, and Power in American History*, eds. Manisha Sinha and Penny Von Eschen (New York: Columbia University Press, 2007); Penny M. Von Eschen, *Race Against Empire: Black Americans and Anticolonialism, 1937–1957* (Ithaca, NY: Cornell University Press, 1997); and Brenda Gayle Plummer, "Race and the Cold War," in *The Oxford Handbook of The Cold War*, eds. Richard H. Immerman and Petra Goedde (Oxford: Oxford University Press, 2013), 503–22.

3. Marilyn Kern-Foxworth, "Minorities: Representations in Advertising," in *The Ad Agency Advertising Encyclopedia*, eds. John McDonough and Karen Egolf, vol. 2 (London: Routledge [Taylor and Francis Group], 2003), 1057.

4. Jessamyn Neuhaus, *Manly Meals and Mom's Home Cooking: Cookbooks and Gender in Modern America* (Baltimore: Johns Hopkins University Press, 2003), 16.

5. Poppy Cannon, *The Can-Opener Cook Book* (A Macfadden-Bartell Book, 1962; originally published in 1951), 146.

6. *Big Boy Barbecue Book* (New York: Tested Recipe Institute, 1956), 5.

7. Arthur M. Schlesinger, *Paths to the Present* (New York: MacMillan, 1949); rev. ed. introduction by Arthur M. Schlesinger Jr. (Boston: Houghton Mifflin, 1964), 230.

8. See David Hackett Fisher, *Albion's Seed: Four British Folkways in America* (New York: Oxford University Press, 1989).

9. *Good Housekeeping's Casserole Cook Book* (Chicago: Consolidated Book Publishers, 1958), 18.

10. Courtesy of National Park Service, Harry S. Truman National Historic Site, HSTR 8962-83. Accessed October 26, 2020. www.nps.gov/museum/exhibits/hstr/image/parkimg/recipes/tuna_casserole.html.

11. Jeffrey Kluger, "Redeeming the Supermarket: The Diet for the 99%," *Time*, November 21, 2012. https://Healthland.time.com/2012/11/21/redeeming-the-supermarket-the-diet-for-the-99/.

12. Sally Edelstein, "Selling the Nuclear Family," *Envisioning the American Dream* (blog), May 22, 2014. http://envisioningtheamericandream.com/2014/05/22/selling-the-nuclear-family.

13. M. F. K. Fisher, *The Art of Eating: 50th Anniversary Edition* (New York: Wiley Publishing, 2004), 353.

Chapter 1

1. Quoted in Mette Bruaas, "Hitler's Hunger Plan," Nobel Peace Center, May 18, 2021. https://www.nobelpeacecenter.org/en/news/hitler-s-hungerplan. Hans Frank's collection of personal diaries is located at the National Archives, Washington, DC, RG 238. See "Diary of Hans Frank, 1939–1945" (collection description), National Archives Collection of World War II War Crimes Records, T992, n.d. https://www.archives.gov/files/research/captured-german-records/microfilm/t992.pdf.

2. John Ellis, *The World War II Databook: The Essential Facts and Figures for All the Combatants* (London: Aurum Press, 1993), 253–54. Quoted in Lizzie Collingham, *The Taste of War: World War II and the Battle for Food* (New York: Penguin Books, 2013), 1. Collingham also notes that 19.5 million is a low estimate that does not include deaths of Chinese prisoners of the Japanese or Soviet prisoners in German hands. Also, there are no estimates for the many (probably millions) of civilians from Africa and Asia who died of starvation.

3. Kevin McDowell, "Japan in Manchuria: Agricultural Emigration in the Japanese Empire, 1932–1945," *Eras Journal* 5 (November 2003), Monash University, Victoria, Australia. https://www.monash.edu/arts/philosophical-historical-international-studies/eras/past-editions/edition-five-2003-november/1094-2.

4. Claude Conyers, "Victory Gardens," in *A Miscellany for Gardeners* (Holmes, NY: Hillbrow Publishing, 2012), 49.

5. Ales Adamovich and Daniil Granin, *A Book of the Blockade*, trans. Hilda Perham (Moscow: Raduga Publishers, 1983), 47.

6. Dick Wittenberg, "This Is What Hunger Does," *The Correspondent*, October 23, 2016. https://thecorrespondent.com/5379/this-is-what-hunger-does/358445802-e6acda55.

7. Quoted in Erwin W. Rugendorff, "The Hunger Disease Study in the Warsaw Ghetto," *Scope of Urology Newsletter* 2 (Summer 2020), William P. Didusch Center for Urologic History, American Urological Association. Official

Nazi order dated April 19, 1941. https://www.urologichistory.museum/collections/the-scope-of-urology-newsletter/issue-2-summer-2020/hunger-disease-study.

8. "Daily Life in the Warsaw Ghetto," Imperial War Museums, London, accessed February 14, 2022. https://www.iwm.org.uk/history/daily-life-in-the-warsaw-ghetto.

9. Gregg Huff, "Causes and Consequence of the Great Vietnam Famine, 1944–1945," *Economic History Review* 71, no. 1 (February 2019): 286–316. https://www.viet-studies.net/kinhte/VietNamFamine1945_HR.pdf. Numbers quoted in Cormac Ó Gráda, "The Famines of WWII," VOXEU, September 2019. https://voxeu.org/article/famines-wwii/.

10. See Lance Brennan, Les Heathcote, and Anton Lucas, "War and Famine around the Indian Ocean during the Second World War," *Ethics in the Global South (Research in Ethical Issues in Organizations*, vol. 18) (Bingley, UK: Emerald Publishing, 2017), 5–70; and Pierre van der Eng, "Food Supply in Java during War and Decolonisation, 1940–1950," University of Hull Centre for South Asian Studies, Occasional Paper 25, 1994.

11. Collingham, *The Taste of War*, 1. See Michael Safi, "Churchill's Policies Contributed to 1943 Bengal Famine—Study," *The Guardian*, March 29, 2019. https://www.theguardian.com/world/2019/mar/29/winston-churchill-policies-contributed-to-1943-bengal-famine-study.

12. Alex von Tunzelmann, *Indian Summer: The Secret History of the End of Empire* (London: Simon and Schuster, 2007), 391. Quoted in Colllingham, *The Taste of War*, 142.

13. Peter Lewis, "Q: What Was the Deadliest Weapon of World War II? A: Starvation, Which Killed 20 Million People," review of *The Taste of War*, Lizzie Collingham, [Daily] MailOnline, January 27, 2011. https://www.dailymail.co.uk/home/books/article-1351152/Q-What.

14. Collingham, *The Taste of War*, 10.

15. Kallie Szczepanski, "Bushido: The Ancient Code of the Samurai Warrior," ThoughtCo, updated September 5, 2019. https://www.thoughtco.com/what-is-bushido-195302.

16. Collingham, *The Taste of War*, 7.

17. "WWII: German Rations and Feeding the Troops of the Third Reich," *Warfare History*, accessed February 14, 2022. https://warfarehistorynetwork.com/2018/12/20/wwii-german-rations-feeding-troops-of-third-reich/.

18. Collingham, *The Taste of War*, 438. See also Caroline Laurence and Joanne Tiddy, *From Bully Beef to Ice Cream: The Diet of the Australian Armed Forces in WWI and WWII* (Daw Park, SA: Repatriation General Hospital, 1989), 35–36, 45–46. This criticism does not consider the difficulty in providing two hot meals per day to soldiers, often under extreme battle conditions.

19. The papers of E. Barrington April 26–May 12, 1945, Department of Documents, Imperial War Museums, London, 88/58/2 (P). Quoted in Collingham, *The Taste of War*, 415.

20. "U.S. Army Field Rations," *Modeling the U.S. Army in WWII* (blog), accessed February 14, 2022. http://www.usarmymodels.com/ARTICLES/Rations/krations.html. See also http://www.Kration.info/original-k-rations.html.

21. Linda Civitello, *Cuisine and Culture: A History of Food and People* (Hoboken, NJ: John Wiley and Sons, 2008), 321.

22. Hershey Community Archives, "Serving Our Country: Hershey Chocolate's Contributions to World War II," April 9, 2010. https://hersheyarchives.org/encyclopedia/serving-the-country-hershey-chocolates-contributions-to-wwii/.

23. George C. Marshall, radio speech on the Food Conservation Program, October 5, 1947. G. C. Marshall Papers (Secretary of State, Speeches), Marshall Foundation.

24. Harry S. Truman, "Radio and Television Address Concluding a Program by the Citizens Food Committee," full transcript online by Gerhard Peters and John T. Woolley, American Presidency Project, accessed February 14, 2022. https://www.presidency.ucsb.edu/node/232383.

25. Robert E. Farrell, ed., *Truman in the White House: The Diary of Eben A. Ayers* (Columbia: University of Missouri Press, 1991), 197. Ayers served as assistant press secretary (1945–1950) to presidents Roosevelt and Truman.

26. Harry S. Truman, "Radio and Television Address Concluding a Program by the Citizens Food Committee."

27. Harry Truman to Bess, October 7, 1947, letter, Family, Business, and Personal Affairs, Papers of Harry S. Truman, Harry S. Truman Library, accessed February 14, 2022. https://www.trumanlibrary.gov/node/368139.

28. Remarks by Secretary of State Marshall, delivered as part of the radio and television address by President Truman, October 5, 1947. https://www.marshallfoundation.org/marshall/the-marshall-plan/marshall-plan-speech.

29. Public Papers of the Presidents of the United States, Harry S. Truman, Containing the Public Messages, Speeches, and Statements of the President, January 1 to December 31, 1947 (Office of the Federal Register, National Archives and Records Service, General Services Administration, Washington, DC: United States Government Printing Office, 1963, 458); see also "How Truman Will Fare in Food-Saving," Newspapers.com, October 7, 1947. https://www.newspapers.com/clip/13028353/truman-meatless-meal/.

30. Recipe for Coffee Mallow in Dennis A. Fitzgerald papers, 1945–1969, series I-Truman, folder 2, box 1, Citizens Food Committee, October 6, 1947, Eisenhower Presidential Library. Used by Permission.

31. Mark Simonson, "Area Saw Meatless Tuesdays, 'Chickless' Thursdays in 1947," *Daily Star* (Oneonta, NY), October 8, 2012. https://www.thedailystar.com/opinion/columns/area-saw-meatless-tuesdays-chickless-thursdays-in-1947/article_3abb58d8-61fb-5326-9bde-d51917fc9f66.html.

32. From a speech delivered by Winston Churchill (1874–1965), May 14, 1947. Quoted in Gerald Zarr, "The Marshall Plan: Rebuilding a Devasted Europe—How George C. Marshall Guided Efforts to Rebuild Post World War II Europe,"

History Magazine, October/November 2012, 37. https://www.usaidalumni.org/wp-content/uploads/2011/05/Marshall_Plan_PDF_Hi-Res.pdf.

33. Zarr, "The Marshall Plan," 38. For a list of Marshall Plan–related websites, see "History of the Marshall Plan." https://www.marshallfoundation.org/marshall/the-marshall-plan/history-marshall-plan/.

34. "Marshall Plan Exhibit Brings Berlin Television," August 1951, press release, RG 286 MOP Ger. 1088-1106, Visual records, U.S. National Archives, College Park, MD. Quoted in Greg Castillo, *Cold War on the Home Front: The Soft Power of Midcentury Design* (Minneapolis: University of Minnesota Press, 2010), xvii.

35. The full text for the Smith-Mundt Act of 1948 is available at https://www.usagm.gov/who-we-are/oversight/legislation/smith-mundt/.

36. The Advertising Council, "A Year of Cold War. Advertising Faced it Realistically," (1948–1949 annual report), 4–5.

37. The name Operation Vittles is attributed to Brigadier General Joseph Smith (1901–1993), who established the basic systems for the early phase of the Berlin Airlift. Quoted in William H. Tunner, *Over the Hump: The Story of General William H. Tunner; The Man Who Moved Anything Anywhere* (New York: Duel, Sloan, and Pierce, 1964), 159. See also Roger G. Miller, To Save a City: The Berlin Airlift, 1948–1949 (College Station: Texas A&M University Press, 1998), 58; and Roger G. Miller, "Operation Vittles: A Name for the Berlin Airlift," Airforce Historical Foundation, *Air Power History* 55, no. 3 (Fall 2008): 46–55. https://www.jstor.org/stable/26275022.

38. For a thorough discussion of the events leading up to the Soviet blockade, see "The Berlin Crisis," Research Project No. 17, rough draft, U.S. Department of State, c. 1948, President's Secretary's Files, Truman Papers. Harry S. Truman Library. https://www.trumanlibrary.gov/library/research-files/berlin-crisis-research-project-no-17-rough-draft-department-state?documentid=NA&pagenumber=1.

39. Quoted in John J. Krugel, "USAF Honors Approaching Anniversary of 'Operation Vittles': Berlin Airlift Dispensed Food, Delivered Blow to Communism," Aero News Network, May 17, 2008. http://www.aero-news.net/index.cfm?do=main.textpost&id=c872b64b-792a-45a2-845a-6acf21707f2f.

40. "Effect of Soviet Restrictions on the U.S. Position in Berlin," Central Intelligence Agency, June 14, 1948. The Berlin Airlift, President's Secretary's Files, Harry S. Truman Library. https://www.trumanlibrary.gov/library/research-files/effect-soviet-restrictions-us-position-berlin.

41. Correspondence between Matthew Woll (chairman, International Labor Relations Department, Free Trade Union Committee, American Federation of Labor) and Harry S. Truman, Letter to President Truman, June 30, 1948, The Berlin Airlift, Harry S. Truman Library. https://www.trumanlibrary.gov/library/research-files/correspondence-between-matthew-woll-and-harry-s-truman.

42. C. V. Glines, "Berlin Airlift: Operation Vittles," *Aviation History*, May 1998, n.p.

43. Colonel Donald C. Foote (TC transportation officer, Berlin Military Post, Berlin, Germany), "'Operation Vittles'—Templehof A Transportation Corps Milestone," Historical Reference Collection of the U.S. Army Center of Military History, GEOG, M Ger. 523, Berlin Airlift, 15.

44. Glines, "Berlin Airlift: Operation Vittles," n.p.

45. Caroline Lieffers and Frederick Mills, "A Cheerful American Cookbook Memorializing the 1948 Berlin Blockade," *Slate*, August 4, 2017. www.slate.com/human-interest/2017/08/a-cookbook-published-by-american-women-during-the-berlin-blockade.html. See also Prudence Bushnell (former US ambassador to Kenya and Guatemala), "Operation Vittles: A Recipe Book. An Airlift. A Song," *American Diplomacy: Insight and Analysis from Foreign Affairs Practitioners and Scholars*, May 2019. https://americandiplomacy.web.unc.edu/2019/05/operation-vittles/.

46. The American Women in Blockaded Berlin, comp., *Operation Vittles Cook Book* (Deutscher Verlag, 1949). http://www.berlinbrats.org/pdfs/49Vittles.pdf.

47. Lieffers and Mills, "A Cheerful American Cookbook."

48. The American Women, *Operation Vittles Cook Book*, 4, 59.

49. Lieffers and Mills, "A Cheerful American Cookbook."

50. The American Women, *Operation Vittles Cook Book*, 3. The author's first name is Marian, but the signature obscures her last name.

51. Zarr, "The Marshall Plan," 41–42.

52. "Milestones in the History of U.S. Foreign Relations, Marshall Plan, 1948," Office of the Historian, U.S. Department of State. https://history.state.gov/milestones/1945-1952/marshall-plan.

53. Tom Standage, *An Edible History of Humanity* (New York: Walker, 2009), 145.

Chapter 2

1. Statement by Henry L. Stimson, Secretary of War in *You're Going to Employ Women*, April 1, 1943, Records of the Adjutant General's Office 1905–1981, Record Group 94 (online version). https://www.docsteach.org/documents/document/youre-going-to-employ-women.

2. Franklin D. Roosevelt, "Executive Order 9139: Establishing the War Manpower Commission," April 18, 1942. Online by *The American Presidency Project*. https://www.presidency.ucsb.edu/node/210517.

3. See Blair D. Hydrick, comp., "A Guide to the Microfilm Edition of Records of the United States Department of Labor, 1918–1965. Part II Women in World War II," Series B, Subjects and Correspondence Files on War Industries. US Department of Labor. https://researchworks.oclc.org/archivegrid/collection/data/122682238.

4. Harold W. Metz, *Is There Enough Manpower?* (Washington, DC: Brookings Institution, 1942), 6–7.

5. *Womanpower Committees During World War II: United States and British Experience*, Women's Bureau Bulletin no. 244 (Washington, DC: US Department of Labor, 1953), 45.

6. Franklin D. Roosevelt, "Executive Order 9182: Establishing the Office of War Information," June 13, 1942, online by *The American Presidency Project*. https://www.presidency.ucsb.edu/documents/executive-order-9182-establishing-the-office-war-information. The act consolidated several agencies and created the Foreign Information Service—the propaganda centerpiece of the oversees branch of the OWI. In his order, Roosevelt noted, "In recognition of the right of the American people and of all other peoples opposing the Axis aggressors to be truthfully informed about the common war effort." Further, section 4(c) of the order stated that the office's charge was to "obtain, study, and analyze information concerning the war effort and advise agencies concerned with the dissemination of such information as to the most appropriate and effective means of keeping the public adequately and accurately informed."

7. "Life on the Newsfronts of the World," *Life*, September 28, 1942, 32.

8. Albert Perry, *What Women Can Do to Win the War* (Chicago: Consolidated Book Publishers, 1942), 3.

9. Amy Bentley, *Eating for Victory: Food Rationing and the Politics of Domesticity* (Urbana: University of Illinois Press, 1998), 13.

10. William H. Chafe, *The American Woman: Her Changing Social, Economic, and Political Roles, 1920–1970* (New York: Oxford University Press, 1972), 148.

11. Judith Sealander, A Guide to the Microfilm Edition of Records of the United States Department of Labor, 1918–1965, introduction, Part I: Reports of the Director, Annual Summaries, Major Conferences, Speeches, and Articles, ed. Dale Grinder, comp. Blair Hydrick (Frederick, MD: University Publications of America, 1986), v–vi. https://pq-static-content.proquest.com/collateral/media2/documents/2640_womenlabor1.pdf.

12. Stephanie Ann Carpenter, "'Regular Farm Girl': The Women's Land Army in World War II," *Agricultural History* 71, no. 2 (1997): 163–85.

13. OWI press release, March 23, 1943, box 200, RG 86, United States National Archives and Records Administration; and quoted in Judy Barrett Litoff and David C. Smith, "To the Rescue of the Crops," The Women's Land Army During World War II (Washington, DC: US National Archives and Records Administration), *Prologue Magazine* 25, no. 4 (Winter 1993): 8.

14. Quoted in Litoff and Smith, "To the Rescue of the Crops," 2.

15. *Your Share: How to Prepare Appetizing Healthful Meals with Foods Available Today. Betty Crocker* (Minneapolis: General Mills, 1943). https://www.archive.org/details/YourShare.

16. *Home Canning Cook Book*, Food for Victory National Nutrition Issue (Los Angeles: Kerr Glass Manufacturing Company, n.d.).

17. Mary MacFadyen, "Keeping Your Family Fit Tops Defense Job for Housewife," *Pittsburgh Press*, February 9, 1942, 14.

18. Alice Winn-Smith, *Thrifty Cooking for Wartime* (New York: Macmillan, 1942); quoted in Jessamyn Neuhaus *Manly Meals and Mom's Home Cooking: Cookbooks and Gender in Modern America* (Baltimore: Johns Hopkins University Press, 2003), 141.

19. William Waller, American Sociologist (1899–1945), quoted in William H. Chafe, *The American Woman: Her Changing Social, Economic, and Political Roles, 1930–1970* (New York: Oxford University Press, 1972), 176.

20. Quoted in A. G. Mezerik, "Getting Rid of Women," *Atlantic*, CLXXV (June 1945), 79–83.

21. Quoted in Chafe, *The American Woman*, 177. See also Lillian Sharpley, "Married Women at Work" (unpublished master's thesis, Columbia University, 1945), 42.

22. Chafe, *The American Woman*, 174.

23. Sherri A. Inness, *American Women and Culinary Culture* (Iowa City: University of Iowa Press, 1995), 167.

24. "The Great Housing Shortage," *Life*, December 24, 1945, 27; quoted in Suellen Hoy, *Chasing Dirt: The American Pursuit of Cleanliness* (New York: Oxford University Press, 1995), 167.

25. Elaine Tyler May, *Homeward Bound: American Families in the Cold War Era*, rev. ed. (New York: Basic Books, 2008), 1.

26. Cindy J. Dorfman, "The Garden of Eating: The Carnal Kitchen in Contemporary American Culture," *Feminist Issues* 12.1 (Spring 1992): 21.

27. In July 1947, George Kennan (1904–2005) published an article in the journal *Foreign Affairs*, in which he outlined a theory of "'containment' [that] provided a conceptual framework for a series of successful initiatives undertaken from 1947 to blunt Soviet expansion." See "Kennan and Containment, 1947," US Department of State, Office of the Historian. https://history.state.gov/milestones/1945-1952/kennan.

28. May, *Homeward Bound*, 16.

29. Bess Truman Quotes (n.d.), BrainyQuote.com. https://www.brainyquote.com/quotes/bess_truman_301441.

30. Courtesy of National Park Service, Harry S. Truman National Historic Site, HSTR 8962-83. https://www.nps.gov/museum/exhibits/hstr/image/parkimg/recipes/cococookies.html.

31. Karen Anderson, *Wartime Women: Sex Roles, Family Relations, and the Status of Women during World War II* (Westport, CT: Greenwood Press, 1981), 60.

32. Emily Yellin, *Our Mother's War: American Women at Home and at the Front during World War II* (New York: Free Press, 2004), 36.

Chapter 3

1. Sherrie A. Inness, "The Enchantment of Mixing Spoons: Cooking Lessons for Girls and Boys," in *Kitchen Culture in America: Popular Representations*

of *Food, Gender, and Race*, ed. Sherrie A. Inness (Philadelphia: University of Pennsylvania Press, 2001), 123.

2. Peggy Hoffman, *Miss B.'s First Cookbook* (Indianapolis: Bobbs-Merrrill, 1950).

3. Julia Kiene, *The Step-by-Step Cook Book for Girls and Boys* (New York: Simon and Schuster, 1956), 10.

4. Helen Evans Brown and Philip S. Brown, *The Boys' Cook Book* (Garden City, NY: Doubleday, 1959), 9–10.

5. Mary Blake, *Fun to Cook Book* (Los Angeles, CA: Carnation Company, Ltd., 1955), 12. Mary Blake served as spokesperson for the Carnation Company and, like her "colleague" Betty Crocker, Mary Blake did not exist.

6. Betty Betz, *The Betty Betz Teen-Age Cookbook* (New York: Henry Holt, 1953), 18.

7. *Little Mother's Cook Book* (Kansas City: Pixie Press, 1952), 18

8. Betz, *The Betty Betz Teen-Age Cookbook*, 128.

9. Kiene, *The Step-by-Step Cook Book*, 34.

10. Brown and Brown, *The Boys' Cook Book*, 153.

11. Brown and Brown, 117.

12. Jerrold Beim, *The First Book of Boys' Cooking* (New York: Franklin Watts, 1957), 63.

13. Beim, 45.

14. Beim, 79.

15. Brown and Brown, *The Boys' Cook Book*, 205–6.

16. Robert H. Loeb Jr., *Date Bait* (Chicago: Wilcox and Follett, 1952), 9.

17. Betz, *The Betty Betz Teen-Age Cookbook*, 1.

18. Esther Rudomin, *Let's Cook without Cooking* (New York: Thomas Y. Crowell, 1955), vi.

19. Mae Blacker Freeman, *Fun With Cooking: Easy Recipes for Beginners* (New York: Random House, 1947), 20.

20. Tracy M., "Candlestick Salad," *By Common Consent* (blog), a non-profit LDS publication, November 25, 2008. https://bycommonconsent.com/2008/11/25/candlestick-salad/.

For a YouTube demonstration on creating the Candlestick Salad, see https://www.youtube.com/watch?v=u9-gCJhR_30.

21. Inness, *Kitchen Culture*, 133.

22. Inness, 126.

23. *Betty Crocker's Cook Book for Boys and Girls* (New York: Wiley Publishing, 1957), 112.

24. Beim, *The First Book of Boys' Cooking*, 33.

25. Helen Jill Fletcher, *The See and Do Cook of Cooking* (New York: H. S. Stuttman, 1959), 94.

26. Brown and Brown, *The Boys' Cook Book*, 45.

27. Roland Barthes, "Steak and Chips," in *Mythologies* (New York: Hill and Wang, 1972), 62. Originally published in 1957.

28. Kristin L. Matthews, "One Nation Over Coals: Cold War Nationalism and the Barbecue," *American Studies* 50, no. 3/4 (Fall/Winter 2009): 6. https://journals.ku.edu/amsj/article/view/4175/3945.

29. James Beard, *Jim Beard's complete book of barbecue & rotisserie cooking* (Indianapolis, IN: Bobbs-Merrill, 1954), 6.

30. Matthews, "One Nation Over Coals," 12.

31. *Better Homes and Gardens Barbecue Book* (Des Moines, IA: Meredith Publishing, 1956), 25.

32. *Big Boy Barbecue Book* (New York: Grosset and Dunlap, 1956), 24.

33. *Big Boy Barbecue Book*, 5.

34. John and Marie Roberson, *The Complete Barbecue Book* (New York: Bramhall House, 1951), 2.

35. Henry Botsford, *What's Cookin' Men? A Handy Cookbook for Men Who Enjoy Outdoor Cooking* (Portland, ME: A.T. Springer and F.L. Tower, 1957).

36. *Big Boy Barbecue Book*, 5.

37. *Life Picture Cook Book* (New York: Time, 1958), 8.

38. *Sunset Barbecue Cook Book* (Menlo Park, CA: Lane Publishing, 1950), 88.

39. Mary Meade, "Barbecuing is New Hobby and Anyone Can Take Part," *Chicago Tribune*, August 13, 1950.

40. Beard, *Jim Beard's complete book*, 12.

41. "And What is Sumer Without a Barbecue?," *American Home*, April 1955, 50. Quoted in Matthews, "One Nation Over Coals," 5.

42. John and Marie Roberson, *The Complete Barbecue Book*, 2.

43. Mrs. Raymond Hargrove, "He's an Outdoor Chef," *Parents' Magazine*, August 1956, 63.

44. Poppy Cannon, *The Can-Opener Cook Book* (A Macfadden-Bartell Book, 1962; originally published in 1951), 146.

45. Freda De Knight, *A Date With A Dish: A Cook Book of American Negro Recipes* (New York: Hermitage Press, 1948), 227–28. https://babel.hathitrust.org/cgi/pt?id=coo.31924001194749&view=1up&seq=1&skin=2021&q1=Boston%20Baked%20Beans.

46. *The General Foods Kitchens Cookbook* (New York: Random House, 1959), 295.

47. *Big Boy Barbecue Book*, 3.

48. Matthews, "One Nation Over Coals," 17.

49. Michael W. Twitty, "Barbecue is an American Tradition—of Enslaved Africans and Native Americans," *Guardian*, July 4, 2015. https://www.theguardian.com/commentisfree/2015/jul/04/barbecue-american-tradition-enslaved-africans-native-americans. For other resources, see Twitty's *The Cooking Gene: A Journey through African-American Culinary History in the Old South* (New York: Amistad [HarperCollins], 2017); Adrian Miller, *Black Smoke: African Americans and the United States of* Barbecue (Chapel Hill: University of North Carolina Press, 2021);

Natasha Geilling, "The Evolution of Barbecue," *Smithsonian Magazine*, July 18, 2013. www.smithsonianmag.com/arts-culture/the-evolution-of-Americas-barbecue-13770775; Blue Pacific Flavors, "From Safer Food to Better Barbecue," February 25, 2021. https://www.bluepacificflavors.com/black-history-month-2021; and Alexander Lee, "The History of the Barbecue: A Native American Method of Tenderizing Meat Goes Global," August 8, 2019. https://www.historytoday.com/archive/historians-cookbook/history-barbecue.

50. Mary Ulmer and Samuel E. Beck, eds., *Cherokee Cooklore: To Make My Bread* (Cherokee, NC: Museum of the Cherokee Indian, 1951). Reprint pub. Mary and Goinback Chiltoskey (dist. Cherokee, NC: Cherokee Publications, 2014), 47. Recipe used by permission.

51. Robert H. Loeb Jr., *Wolf in Chef's Clothing* (Chicago: Wilcox and Follett, 1950), 10. Fourth printing in 1952.

52. *Robertshaw Measured Heat Cook Book* (Youngwood, PA: Robertshaw-Fulton Controls, 1947), 71–74. Quoted in Jessamyn Neuhaus, *Manly Meals and Mom's Home Cooking: Cookbooks and Gender in Modern America* (Baltimore: Johns Hopkins University Press, 2003), 197.

53. Sherri A. Inness, *Dinner Roles: American Women and Culinary Culture* (Iowa City: University of Iowa Press, 2001), 23.

54. Beard, *Jim Beard's Complete Book*, 130.

55. Nate Erickson "The Bullshot is the Bloody Mary's Salty Cousin from Detroit," *Esquire*, February 10, 2019. https://www.esquire.com/food-drink/drinks/a26243113/bullshot-cocktail-beef-broth-recipe/.

56. Frank Shay, *The Best Men Are Cooks* (New York: Coward-McCann, 1941), 84.

57. *Big Boy Barbecue Book*, 36.

58. Jessie Payne, *Paynie's Parties*, comp. Mrs. J. F. Spruill and Mrs. Stokes Adderton (Lexington, NC: Fred O. Sink Printing, 1955), 28. www.davidsoncountyhistoricalmuseum.com/recipesfromthecollection.

Chapter 4

1. Ruth Berolzheimer, ed., *Culinary Arts Institute Encyclopedic Cookbook* (Chicago: Book Production Industries, 1950). This cookbook contains material from other Culinary Arts Institute publications published between 1940 and 1948.

2. Jessamyn Neuhaus, *Manly Meals and Mom's Home Cooking: Cookbooks and Gender in Modern America* (Baltimore: Johns Hopkins University Press, 2012), 4.

3. See Anne L. Bower, *Recipes for Reading: Community Cookbooks, Stories, Histories* (Amherst: University of Massachusetts Press, 1997); Carol Fisher, *The American Cookbook: A History* (Jefferson, NC: McFarland, 2006); and Mary Anna

DuSablon, *America's Collectible Cookbooks: The History, the Politics, the Recipes* (Athens: Ohio University Press, 1994). See also Lavonne Brady Axford, ed., *English Language Cookbooks, 1600–1973* (Detroit: Gale Research Company, 1976); and Eleanor and Bob Brown, *Culinary Americana* (New York: Roving Eye Press, 1961).

4. Other important mainstream, commercial cookbooks include *Better Homes and Gardens New Cook Book* (New York: Meredith Publishing, 1953); Ruth Berolzheimer, ed., *Culinary Arts Institute Encyclopedic Cookbook* (Chicago: Culinary Arts Institute, 1950); and Women of General Foods Kitchens, *The General Foods Kitchens Cookbook* (New York: Random House, 1959).

5. John L. Hess and Karen Hess, *The Taste of America* (Urbana: University of Illinois Press, 2000), 129. Originally published in 1972.

6. For further information on Farmer, see William Rice, "The Updated, Revised, but Otherwise Original, Fannie Farmer Cookbook," *Washington Post*, September 27, 1979. https://www.washingtonpost.com/archive/lifestyle/1979/09/27/the-updated-revised-but-otherwise-original-fannie-farmer-cookbook/6800a850-97eb-42e5-a62c-7aba8b5d2bfb/. See also "Fannie Farmer, the Mother of Level Measurements," *Amazing Women in History*, n.d. https://amazingwomeninhistory.com/fannie-farmer/; Julie Moskin, "Overlooked No More: Fannie Farmer, Modern Cookery's Pioneer," *The New York Times*, June 13, 2018. https://www.nytimes.com/2018/06/13/obituaries/fannie-farmer-overlooked.html; and Laura Shapiro, *Perfection Salad: Women and Cooking at the Turn of the Century*, repr. (Berkeley: University of California Press, 2009), 100–19. Originally published in 1986 by Farrar, Straus, and Giroux.

7. Fannie Merritt Farmer, *The Boston Cooking-School Cook Book* (Boston: Little, Brown, 1896), 412. https://d.lib.msu.edu/fa/8#page/2/mode/2up.

8. Farmer, 431. The 1951 edition contains three recipes for pound cake and each uses fewer eggs and butter than the 1896 version, likely because of an increase of the size of eggs.

9. For further information on Romberg and her cookbooks, see Anne Mendelson, *Stand Facing the Stove: The Story of the Women Who Gave America the Joy of Cooking* (New York: Scribner, 2003). See also, Marion Rombauer Becker, *Little Acorn: The Story Behind The Joy of Cooking, 1931–1966* (Indianapolis, IN: Bobbs-Merrill, 1966); Tim Farrell, "The Genius of the *Joy of Cooking*," *Mental Floss*, January 2, 2010. https://mentalfloss.com/article/23623/genius-joy-cooking; Kim Severson, "Does the World Need Another 'Joy'? Do You?," *The New York Times*, November 1, 2006. https://www.nytimes.com/2006/11/01/dining/01joy.html.

10. Irma S. Rombauer and Marion Rombauer Becker, *The Joy of Cooking* (Indianapolis, IN: Bobbs-Merrill, 1951), introduction.

11. Hess and Hess, *The Taste of America*, 119.

12. Marion Rombauer Becker, "Rombauer, Irma (1877–1962)," posted by Emily Mace, July 26, 2012. https://www.harvardsquarelibrary.org/biographies/irma-rombauer/.

13. Irma S. Rombauer, *The Joy of Cooking: A Compilation of Reliable Recipes with a Casual Culinary Chat*, foreword to the Facsimile Edition by Edgar R. Rombauer (New York: Simon and Schuster, 1998), 1. Originally published 1931.

14. Anne Mendelson, "Irma Rombauer," in *The Oxford Encyclopedia of Food and Drink in America*, ed. Andrew F. Smith, 2nd ed., vol. 3 (New York: Oxford University Press, 2013) 150–52.

15. Rombauer and Rombauer Becker, *The Joy of Cooking*, 175.

16. Rombauer and Rombauer Becker, 175. From the *Joy of Cooking* by Irma S. Rombauer and Marion Rombauer Becker. Copyright © 1931, 1936, 1941, 1942, 1943, 1946, 1951, 1953, 1962, 1963, 1964, 1975 by Simon & Schuster, Inc. Copyright 1997 by Simon & Schuster, Inc., The Joy of Cooking Trust and The MRB Revocable Trust. Reprinted with the permission of Scribner, a division of Simon & Schuster, Inc. All rights reserved.

17. Marion Rombauer Becker, "Irma Rombauer: *The Joy of Cooking*, 1877–1962," posted by Emily Mace, n.d. https://www.harvardsquarelibrary.org/biographies/irma-rombauer/.

18. Rombauer Becker, "Irma Rombauer."

19. Susan Marks, *Finding Betty Crocker: The Secret Life of America's First Lady of Food* (New York: Simon and Schuster, 2005); Laura Shapiro, *Something from the Oven: Reinventing Dinner in 1950s America* (New York: Penguin Books, 2005); Tori Avery, "Who Was Betty Crocker?" *PBS*, February 15, 2013. https://www.pbs.org/food/the-history-kitchen/who-was-betty-crocker.

20. Faces of AAUW, "Marjorie Child Husted: The Real Betty Crocker," Washington, DC: American Association of University Women (AAUW). Accessed November 3, 2022. https://www.aauw.org/resources/faces-of-aauw/betty-crocker/.

21. Marks, *Finding Betty Crocker*, 87.

22. Marks, 135.

23. Helmut Ripperger, "A Sport without a Season," *Publishers' Weekly* 11, August 1951, 549. Quoted in Jessamyn Neuhaus, *Manly Meals and Mom's Cooking: Cookbooks and Gender in Modern America* (Baltimore: Johns Hopkins University Press, 2012), 171.

24. *Betty Crocker's Picture Cook Book* (Minneapolis: General Mills Inc., 1950), 370. Betty Crocker is a registered trademark of General Mills© General Mills. Recipe used by permission.

25. *Betty Crocker's Picture Cook Book*, 430–31.

26. Ernest Dichter, "A Psychological Research Study on the Sales and Advertising for Motivational Research," prepared for Knox Reeves Advertising, Minneapolis, MN, November 1952. Quoted in Katherine Parking, *Food Is Love: Advertising and Gender Roles in Modern America* (Philadelphia: University of Pennsylvania Press, 2007), 37.

27. When purchasing vintage cookbooks, it is often possible to acquire new or pristine copies. However, to get a sense of the person who might have used the

book, it is best to look for a copy in the worst condition: grease marks, writing in the margins, or corrections to ingredients. If you can't look at books in person, offerings on the Internet often describe the condition in detail. Fortunately, in my experience, booksellers do not remove the loose ephemera, usually in the form of clippings from magazines or newspapers, index cards with recipes, or handwritten recipes. These items are invaluable.

28. Mary Hamman, ed., *Picture Cook Book* (New York: Time, 1958), 1.

29. *Favorite Recipes of the Women of Tippecanoe Presbyterian Church*, comp. Dorcas Circle of the Women's Guild (Milwaukee, WI: Dorcas Circle of the Women's Guild, 1949).

30. Women's National Press Club, *Who Says We Can't Cook!* (Washington, DC: McIver Art and Publications, 1955), 3rd printing.

31. Women's National Press Club, 13.

32. Women's National Press Club, 90. Copyright held by The Washington Press Club Foundation. Recipe used by permission.

33. Harvey A. Levenstein, *Revolution at the Table: The Transformation of the American Diet* (Berkeley: University of California Press, 2003), 4. Originally published in 1988 by Oxford University Press.

34. John Egerton, "Foreword: A Gallery of Great Cooks," in *The Jemima Code: Two Centuries of African American Cookbooks*, Toni Tipton Martin (Austin: University of Texas Press, 2015), ix. See also Jeanne Firth and Catarina Passidomo, "New Orleans' 'Restaurant Renaissance': Chef Humanitarians, and the New Southern Food Movement," *Food, Culture & Society* 25, no. 2 (2022): 183–200.

35. William C. Whit, "Soul Food as Cultural Creation," *African American Foodways: Explorations of History & Culture*, ed. Anne L. Bower (Urbana: University of Illinois Press, 2007), 47. See also Judith A. Carney and Richard Nicholas Rosomoff, *In the Shadow of Slavery: Africa's Botanical Legacy in the Atlantic World* (Berkeley: University of California Press, 2009), 7, 135, 136–37. For information on how some of these foods arrived in the new world, see Jessica B. Harris, *High on the Hog: A Culinary Journey from Africa to America* (New York: Bloomsbury, 2011).

36. Judith Ann Carney, *Black Rice: The African Origins of Rice Cultivation in the Americas* (Cambridge, MA: Harvard University Press, 2001), xii. See also two books by Michael W. Twitty, *The Cooking Gene: A Journey Through African American Culinary History in the Old South* (New York: Amistad [HarperCollins], 2018); and *Rice* (Chapel Hill: University of North Carolina Press, 2021).

37. Robert L. Hall, "Food Crops, Medicinal Plants, and the Atlantic Slave Trade," in *African American Foodways: Explorations of History & Culture*, ed. Anne L. Bower (Urbana: University of Illinois Press, 2007), 23–24.

38. Whit, "Soul Food as Cultural Creation," 52.

39. Mrs. Abby Fisher, *What Mrs. Fisher Knows about Old Southern Cooking, Soups, Pickles, Preserves, Etc.* (San Francisco: Women's Co-Operative Printing Office, 1881); see also the Facsimile Edition with historical notes by Karen Hess (Bedford,

MA: Applewood Books, 1995), 78–79, 90. https://www.google.com/books/edition/What_Mrs_Fisher_Knows_about_Old_Southern/WlFaENz0YHwC?hl=en&gbpv=1.

40. Laura Schenone, *A Thousand Years Over a Hot Stove: A History of American Women Told Through Food, Recipes, and Remembrances* (New York: W. W. Norton, 2003), 74.

41. Ruth Berolzheimer, ed., *The United States Regional Cook Book* (Chicago: Culinary Arts Institute, 1947), 161–62.

42. Egerton, "Foreword: A Gallery of Great Cooks," in *The Jemima Code*, xi.

43. Barbara Haber, "Foreword: Why Cookbooks Matter," in Martin, *The Jemima Code*, xv.

44. Martin, *The Jemima Code*, 71.

45. Edith Ballard Watts, *Jesse's Book of Creole and Deep South Recipes*, with John Watts (New York: Viking Press, 1954); see also repr. (New York: Weathervane Books, distributed by Crown Publishers, 1985), 55.

46. Jessie Hargrave Payne, *Paynie's Parties* (Lexington, NC: Fred O. Sink Printing House, 1955), 5, 6. www.davidsoncountyhistoricalmuseum.com/recipesfromthecollection.

47. Payne, *Paynie's Parties*, 10.

48. Sue Bailey Thurman, ed. and comp., *The Historical Cookbook of the American Negro*, National Council of Negro Women (Washington, DC: Corporate Press, 1958); see repr. with a foreword by Dorothy J. Height and an introduction by Anne L. Bower (Boston: Beacon Press, 2000).

49. Thurman, *The Historical Cookbook*, 2. Recipe attributed to council regions III and IV. Recipe used by permission.

50. Freda De Knight, *A Date with a Dish: Cook Book of American Negro Recipes* (New York: Hermitage Press, 1948), xii. https://babel.hathitrust.org/cgi/pt?id=coo.31924001194749&view=1up&seq=1.

51. Janet Theophano, *Eat My Words: Reading Women's Lives through the Cookbooks They Wrote* (New York: Palgrave, 2002), 60.

52. Gertrude Blair, "There's Magic in a Cook Book," in De Knight, *A Date with a Dish*, x.

53. De Knight, *A Date with a Dish*, 190–91.

54. Hodding Carter, "Introduction" in Martin, *The Jemima Code*, 8–9.

55. For a list of important authors and food historians who are writing about the African diaspora, see Kayla Stewart, "28 Essential Cookbooks by Black Chefs, Authors and Historians," *Food Network*, June 2, 2022. https://www.foodnetwork.com/how-to/packages/shopping/articles/essential-cookbooks-black-chefs-authors-historians.

Chapter 5

1. John C. Keats, *Crack in the Picture Window* (Cambridge, MA: Riverside Press, 1956), 83.

2. Poppy Cannon, *The Bride's Cookbook* (New York: Henry Holt, 1954), ix.

3. Mary Blake, *Carnation Cook Book* (Milwaukee: Carnation Company, 1942), 73–74.

4. Poppy Cannon, *The Can-Opener Cook Book* (A MacFadden-Bartell Book, 1962; originally published in 1951), 303.

5. Blake, *Carnation Cook Book*, 74.

6. Diane Boucher, *The 1950s American Home* (London: Shire Publications, 2013), 178.

7. *Choice Recipes and Menus Using Canned Foods* (New York: American Can Co., n.d.), 9.

8. *Choice Recipes*, [47].

9. Cannon, *The Can-Opener Cook Book*, 7.

10. Anne Marshall, *Cooking with Condensed Soups* (Camden, NJ: Campbell Soup Co., 1952), 39, 41.

11. *Better Homes and Gardens New Cook Book* (De Moines, IA: Meredith Publishing, 1953), 346.

12. Jasper White, *50 Chowders: One Pot Meals—Clam, Corn & Beyond* (New York: Scribner, 2000), 25.

13. Cannon, *The Can-Opener Cook Book*, 49.

14. Mary Drake Mcfeely, *Can She Bake a Cherry Pie? American Women and the Kitchen in the Twentieth Century* (Amherst: University of Massachusetts Press, 2000), 98–99.

15. Jean MacGregor Whelan, "Soup in the Can is Sauce for the Casserole," *Parents' Magazine*, March 1951, 64–65.

16. *Chiquita Banana's Recipe Book* (New York: United Fruit Company, 1956), 3.

17. Nedda Casson Anders, *Casserole Specialties* (New York: Gramercy Publishing, 1955), 8.

18. Louella G. Shouer, "Casserole Collection," *Ladies' Home Journal*, April 1951, 226–28.

19. Cannon, *The Can-Opener Cook Book*, 117.

20. *Good Housekeeping's Casserole Book* (Chicago: Consolidated Book Publishers, 1958), 42. Recipe used by permission of Hearst Magazine Media, Inc.

21. Anders, *Casserole Specialties*, 29.

22. Blanch C. Firman, *Peggy Put the Kettle On: Recipes and Entertainment Ideas for Young Wives* (New York: Exposition Press, 1951), 99.

23. Christopher Holmes Smith, "Freeze Frames: Frozen Foods and Memories of the Postwar American Family," in *Kitchen Culture in America: Popular Representations of Food, Gender, and Race*, ed. Sherrie A. Inness (Philadelphia: University of Pennsylvania Press, 2001), 187.

24. Quoted in Harvey Levenstein, *Paradox of Plenty: A Social History of Eating in Modern America*, California Studies in Food and Culture (Oakland: University of California Press, 2003), 109.

25. "The Strange History of Frozen Food: From Clarence Birdseye to the Distinguished Order of Zerocrats," *Eater*, August 21, 2014. https://www.eater.com/2014/8/21/6214423/the-strange-history-of-frozen-food-from-clarence-birdseye-to-the.

26. Andrew F. Smith, *Eating History: Thirty Turning Points in the Making of American Cuisine* (New York: Columbia University Press, 2011), 171.

27. Nicola Humble, *Cake: A Global History* (London: Reaktion, 2010), 70.

28. Nadia Berenstein, "The History of Push-Button Cuisine," *Lucky Peach*, August 2016. A list of Berenstein's online writings can be found at http://nadiaberenstein.com/writing.

29. David S. Ensor, ed., *Aerosol Science and Technology: History and Reviews* (Research Triangle Park, NC: Research Triangle Institute (RTI) Press, 2011), 328.

30. Berenstein, "The History of Push-Button Cuisine."

31. Eleanor Early, *American Cookery* (formerly *The Boston Cooking School Magazine*) (Boston [n.p.], 1942). Quoted in Jane Stern and Michael Stern, *Square Meals: A Cookbook by Jane and Michael Stern* (New York: Alfred A. Knopf, 1985), 243.

32. Robert D. Buzzell and Robert E. M. Nourse, *Product Innovation in Food Processing, 1954–1964* (Boston: Division of Research, Graduate School of Business Administration, Harvard University, 1967), 42.

33. Laura Shapiro, *Something from the Oven: Reinventing Dinner in the 1950s* (New York: Penguin Books, 2004), 174.

34. Mark Bittman, *Animal, Vegetable, Junk: A History of Food, from Sustainable to Suicidal* (Boston: Houghton Mifflin Harcourt, 2021), 135.

35. Jeff Wells, "14 Cheesy Facts about Velveeta," *Mental Floss*, April 6, 2016. www.mentalfloss.com/article/68222/14-cheesy-facts-about-velveeta. See also Sara Rath, "Velveeta," *The Oxford Encyclopedia of Food and Drink in America*, ed. Andrew F. Smith, 2nd ed., vol. 3 (Oxford: Oxford University Press, 2013), 540.

36. Irma S. Rombauer and Marion Rombauer Becker, *The Joy of Cooking* (Indianapolis, IN: Bobbs-Merrill, 1951), 96.

37. Michael Reise, *The 20 Minute Cookbook* (New York: Crown Publishers, 1953), 136–37.

38. Reise, 137.

39. *The Wonder Bread Cookbook* (Berkeley, CA: Ten Speed Press, 2007). https://archive.org/details/wonderbreadcookb0000unse. See also Jim Chevallier, "Bread" and Marty Martindale, "Bread: Sliced Bread," in *The Oxford Encyclopedia of Food and Drink in America* 1 (2013): 198–204.

40. June Towne, "Take a Package of Marshmallows," *American Home*, September 1956, 88. Quoted in Sherri A. Inness, *Dinner Roles: American Women and Culinary Culture* (Iowa City: University of Iowa Press, 2001), 149.

41. Lessie Bowers, *Plantation Recipes* (New York: Robert Speller and Sons, 1959), 123.

42. *Tramping and Trailing with the Girl Scouts* (New York: Girl Scouts, 1927), 71. https://babel.hathitrust.org/cgi/pt?id=wu.89017190521&view=1up&seq=5&skin=2021&q1=%22Some%20More%22.

43. Edith Ballard Watts with John Watts, *Jesse's Book of Creole and Deep South Recipes* (New York: Viking Press, 1954; repr. New York: Weathervane Books, 1985), 133.

44. Whitney Filloon, "The Sweet, Gooey History of Marshmallow Fluff: How the Sticky Confection became Fluternutter-Famous," *Eater*, February 9, 2017. https://www.eater.com/2017/2/9/14551084/marshmallow-fluff-history.

45. "Mamie's Million Dollar Fudge," Eisenhower Presidential Library. https://www.eisenhowerlibrary.gov/sites/default/files/file/mamie_million_dollar_fudge.pdf. See also Southern Living Editors, "Mamie Eisenhower's Chocolate Fudge Recipe," *Southern Living*, June 26, 2022. https://www.southernliving.com/recipes/mamie-eisenhower-chocolate-fudge-recipe.

46. Jane and Michael Stern, *Square Meals*, xi. "Fudge Whippo" is a mystery. However, a few years later, both Pillsbury and Betty Crocker produced aerosol cake frostings, which are still available in some markets.

Chapter 6

1. Laura Shapiro, *Something from the Oven: Reinventing Dinner in the 1950s* (New York: Penguin Books, 2004), 57.

2. Ruth Langland Holbert, *Take it Easy Before Dinner* (New York: Thomas Y. Crowell, 1945), 27.

3. Carolyn Wyman, *SPAM®: A Biography* (San Diego: Harcourt Brace, 1999), 19. Wyman notes, "This ode to wartime Spam weariness (Spamschmerz) was widely promulgated and credited to many different soldiers as well as to the ever-popular Anonymous."

4. Andrew Martin, "Spam Turns Serious and Hormel Turns Out More," *The New York Times*, November 15, 2008. www.nytimes.com/2008/11/15/business/15spam.html.

5. For a SPAM®-related clip of Artie Shaw and his orchestra with Burns and Allen, see https://www.youtube.com/watch?v=U9viYhQdYYQ.

6. Strobe Talbott, ed., *Khrushchev Remembers* (Boston: Little, Brown, 1970); and quoted in Carolyn Wyman, "Spam," in *The Oxford Encyclopedia of Food and Drink in America*, ed. Andrew F. Smith, 2nd ed., vol. 3 (New York: Oxford University Press, 2013), 343.

7. Wyman, *SPAM®*, 26.

8. Wyman, "Spam," 343.

9. Jill M. Sullivan and Danielle D. Keck, "The Hormel Girls," *American Music* 25.3 (Fall 2007): 289.

10. "Spam Cakes!" Magazine advertisement for SPAM® and Bisquick SPAM® is a registered trademark of Hormel Foods, LLC, and is used with permission from Hormel Foods Corporation.

11. SPAM "Around the World" dinner casserole (1959). SPAM® is a registered trademark of Hormel Foods, LLC, and is used with permission from Hormel Foods Corporation.

12. Andrew F. Smith, "Spam," in *Fast Food and Junk Food: An Encyclopedia of What We Love to Eat*, vol. 2 (Santa Barbara, CA: Greenwood, 2012), K–Z, 657–58.

13. The three-minute Monty Python SPAM® sketch can be viewed at http://www.dailymotion.com/video/x9fly1. The official reaction of Hormel company when it learned that "spam" referred to sending unsolicited commercial email (UCE) is noted in Marguerite Patten, *SPAM: The Cookbook* (London: Octopus Publishing Group, 2018), 63: "We do not object to the use of this slang term to describe UCE, although we do object to the use of our product image in association with that term. Also, if the term is to be used, it should be used in all lower-case letters to distinguish it from our trademark SPAM, which should be used with all uppercase letters."

14. Magazine advertisements for SPAM Cakes and SPAM 'n Noodles Romanoff SPAM® is a registered trademark of Hormel Foods, LLC, and recipes are used with permission from Hormel Foods Corporation.

15. Dwight Jon Zimmerman, "A War Won with Spam (and a Few Other Things)," *DefenseMediaNetwork*, May 19, 2011. https://www.defensemedianetwork.com/stories/war-won-spam-things/.

16. Sarah Grey, "A Social History of Jell-O Salad: The Rise and Fall of an American Icon," *Serious Eats*, August 19, 2010; updated August 10, 2018. https://www.seriouseats.com/2015/08/history-of-jell-o-salad.html.

17. James Beard, *James Beard's American Cookery* (Boston: Little, Brown, 1972), 34.

18. John L. Hess and Karen Hess, *The Taste of America* (Chicago: University of Illinois Press, 2000), 125. Originally published in 1972.

19. *Gourmet of the Delta*, collected by St. John's Woman's Auxiliary, Leland, MS, and St. Paul's Woman's Auxiliary, Hollandale, MS (Jackson, MS: Hederman Brothers, 1958), 109. Recipe used by permission.

20. Poppy Cannon, *The Bride's Cookbook* (New York: Henry Holt, 1954), 93–94.

21. Marion Young Taylor, *Martha Deane's Cooking for Compliments* (New York: M. Barrows, 1954), 71. Marion Young Taylor appeared on WOR's radio program as Martha Deane.

22. Michael Reise, *The 20 Minute Cookbook* (New York: Crown Publishers, 1953), 218.

23. Ronald Radosh and Joyce Milton, *The Rosenberg File*, 2nd ed. (New Haven, CT: Yale University Press, 1997), 69. Quoted in Nathan Abrams, "'More

Than One Million Mothers Know It's the REAL Thing'": The Rosenbergs, Jell-O, Old-Fashioned Gefilte Fish, and 1950s America," in *Edible Ideologies: Representing Food and Meaning*, eds. Kathleen LeBesco and Peter Naccaerato (Albany: State University of New York Press, 2008), 83.

24. Walter Schneir and Miriam Schneir, *Invitation to an Inquest: A New Look at the Rosenberg-Sobell Case* (New York: Dell, 1968), 347. Quoted in Abrams, 83. See also *Secret Agents: The Rosenberg Case, McCarthyism and Fifties America*, eds. Marjorie B. Garber and Rebecca L. Walkowitz, CultureWork series, Center for Literacy and Cultural Studies at Harvard (New York: Routledge, 1995).

25. Carolyn Wyman, *Jell-O: A Biography* (San Diego: Harcourt, 2001).

26. Laura Shapiro, *Perfection Salad: Women and Cooking at the Turn of the Century* (Berkeley: University of California Press, 2009), 227.

27. For a complete history of Coca-Cola, see Mark Pendergrast, *For God, Country and Coca-Cola: The Unauthorized History of the Great American Soft Drink and the Company That Makes It*, 3rd ed., rev. and enl. (New York: Basic Books, 2013).

28. Sidra Sitch, *Made in the U.S.A.: An Americanization in Modern Art, the 50s and 60s* (Oakland: University of California Press, 1987), 93.

29. [Cover] *Time*, May 15, 1950. The caption reads: "World & Friend. Love that piaster, that lira, that tickey, and that American way of life"

30. Andrew F. Smith, *Fast Food and Junk Food: An Encyclopedia of What We Love to Eat* vol. 1 (Santa Barbara, CA: Greenwood [ABR-CLIO]), 137–41.

31. Mark Pendergrast "Coca-Cola," *The Oxford Encyclopedia of Food and Drink in America*, ed. Andrew F. Smith, 2nd ed., vol. 1 (New York: Oxford University Press, 2013), 427.

32. Pendergrast, 428.

33. Pendergrast, *For God, Country and Coca-Cola*, 203.

34. Pendergrast, 206.

35. Becky Mercuri, "7UP," in *The Oxford Encyclopedia of Food and Drink in America*, ed. and rev. Andrew F. Smith, 2nd ed., vol. 3 (New York: Oxford University Press, 2013), 242.

36. Andrew F. Smith, "7UP," *Fast Food and Junk Food*, vol. 2, 627.

37. Smith, *Fast Food and Junk Food*, 544.

38. Ruth Tobias, "Ginger Ale," in *The Oxford Encyclopedia of Food and Drink in America*, ed. Andrew F. Smith, 2nd ed., vol. 2 (New York: Oxford University Press, 2013), 107.

39. *a guide to pink elephants: 200 most requested mixed drinks on alcohol resistant cards* (New York: Richards Rosen, 1952), 160.

40. *Loyalty Cook Book: Native Daughters of the Golden West*, comp. Willow Borba, 4th ed. (Sebastopol, CA: Willow Borba, 1953), 265. Recipe attributed to Estelle Dresser, Santa Anna Parlor.

41. Andrew F. Smith, "A&W Root Beer Stands," and "Hires' Root Beer," in *The Oxford Encyclopedia of Food and Drink in America*, 2nd ed., vol. 1 (New York: Oxford University Press, 2013), 188. See Andrew F. Smith, "Root Beer," in *Fast Food and Junk Food*, vol. 2, 600.

42. Helen Evans Brown and Philip S. Brown, *The Boys' Cook Book* (Garden City, NY: Doubleday, 1959), 45.

43. Jean and Clarke Mattimore, *Cooking by the Clock* (New York: Ace Books, 1948), 188.

44. Betty MacDonald, *Onions in the Stew* (Philadelphia: J. B. Lippincott, 1954), 178.

Chapter 7

1. Irma S. Rombauer and Marion Rombauer Becker, *The Joy of Cooking* (Indianapolis, IN: Bobbs-Merrill, 1951), 919.

2. Elaine Tyler May, *Homeward Bound: American Families in the Cold War Era*, rev. ed. (New York: Basic Books, 2008), 1, 13.

3. Freda De Knight, *A Date With A Dish: A Cook Book of American Negro Recipes* (New York: Hermitage Press, 1948), 7. https://babel.hathitrust.org/cgi/pt?id=coo.31924001194749&view=1up&seq=1.

4. Hal Boyle, *San Bernadino Sun*, December 27, 1955. Quoted in Catlin Morris, "Mid-Century Parties: 1950s," *Apartment Therapy*, December 9, 2010. https://www.apartmenttherapy.com/midcentury-deco-133567.

5. Peggy Harvey, *When the Cook's Away* (Chicago: Henry Regnery, 1952), 3–4.

6. Sylvia Lovegren, *Fashionable Food: Seven Decades of Food Fads* (Chicago: University of Chicago Press, 2005), 207.

7. Richard Williams, "Never Again!," *House Beautiful*, October 1951; quoted in Lovegren, *Fashionable Food*, 207.

8. *Trader Vic's Book of Food & Drink* (Garden City, NY: Doubleday, 1946), 181–82. Lucrezia Borgia (1480–1519), daughter of Pope Alexander VI, became notorious for her role in political intrigue as well in some suspicious poisonings and murders.

9. Jane Trahey, ed., *A Taste of Texas* (New York: Random House, 1949), 17.

10. Trahey, 17.

11. *Betty Crocker's Picture Cook Book* (Minneapolis: General Mills, 1950), 42. Betty Crocker is a registered trademark of General Mills© General Mills. Recipe used by permission.

12. Ruth Ellen Church, *Mary Meade's Magic Recipes for the Electric Blender* (Indianapolis, IN: Bobbs-Merrill Company, 1952), 86.

13. Church, 86.

14. Edith Barber, ed., *Silver Jubilee Super Market Cook Book* (New York: Super Market Publishing, 1955), 66.

15. De Knight, *A Date with a Dish*, 89.

16. *Gourmet of the Delta*, collected by St. John's Woman's Auxiliary, Leland, MS, and St. Paul's Woman's Auxiliary, Hollandale, MS (Jackson, MS: Hederman Brothers, 1958), 8S. Recipe used by permission.

17. De Knight, *A Date with a Dish*, 90–91.

18. Trahey, *A Taste of Texas*, 18.

19. "Love It or Hate It—The Great Cilantro Debate," *Cleveland Clinic*, October 27, 2020. https://health.clevelandclinic.org/do-you-love-or-hate-cilantro-the-reason-may-surprise-you/.

20. Trahey, *A Taste of Texas*, 165.

21. Trahey, 19.

22. Jean and Clark Mattimore, *Cooking by the Clock* (New York: Ace Books, 1948), 192–93.

23. James A. Beard and Sam Aaron, *How to Eat Better for Less Money* (New York: Permabooks, 1957), 154.

24. Do a Google search for "guacamole." See also, Sucheta Rawal, "This Mexican Chef Has News For You: Margaritas and Tres Leches Aren't Mexican," *Huffpost*, October 6, 2022. https://www.huffpost.com/entry/angel-medina-mexican-cuisine_l_632cd38ee4b0d12b54033b43. In this article, Chef Angel Medina notes that cilantro is not native to Mexico.

25. Marcia Keegan, *Southwest Indian Cookbook* (Santa Fe, NM: Clear Light Publishing, 2010), 45; Cheryl Alters Jamison and Bill Jamison, *Tasting New Mexico: Recipes Celebrating One Hundred Years of Distinctive Home Cooking* (Santa Fe, NM: Museum of New Mexico Press, 2011), 51. This book also contains an excellent history of New Mexican cookery.

26. William Grimes, *Straight Up or on the Rocks: The Story of the American Cocktail* (New York: North Point Press [Farrar, Straus, and Giroux], 2001), 113.

27. Rombauer and Rombauer Becker, *The Joy of Cooking*, 1.

28. *a guide to pink elephants* (New York: Richards Rosen Associates, 1952), 75.

29. William Grimes, *Straight Up or on the Rocks*, 113–14. Grimes's reference to dominoes originates with the Cold War theory that if one nation or region fell to communism, it's neighbor would soon follow—just as dominoes knock each other over, one by one.

30. *a guide to pink elephants*, 158.

31. Jean I. Simpson and Demetria M. Taylor, *The Frozen Food Cook Book* (New York: Simon and Schuster, 1948), 277.

32. Church, *Mary Meade's Magic Recipes*, 104.

33. Church, 104.

34. David Wondrich, "Atomic Cocktail," *Esquire*, November 5, 2007. Lyrics of song by Slim Gaillard, 1945. https://www.esquire.com/food-drink/recipes/a3715/atomic-cocktail-drink-recipe.

35. "Atomic Cocktail Recipe," *Foodviva.com*. https://cocktails.foodviva.com/champagne-recipes/atomic-cocktail/.

36. Paul Lewandowski, "Oppenheimer, Martinis, and the Atom Bomb," *War on the Rocks: National Security for Insiders. By Insiders*, September 1, 2015. www.warontherocks.com/2015/09/trinity-oppenheimer-martinis-and-the-atom-bomb.

37. *The General Foods Kitchens Cookbook* (New York: Random House, 1959), 85.

38. *Silver Jubilee Super Market Cook Book*, 33.

39. *The General Foods Kitchens Cookbook*, 104. Recipe used by permission of Kraft Heinz Foods Company.

40. Olga and Pavel Syutkin, *CCCP Cook Book: True Stories of Soviet Cuisine*, trans. Ast A. Moore (London: Fuel Publishing, 2015), 96. The recipe for beef stroganoff includes beef, onions, butter, flour, sour cream, a small amount of tomato paste and "a splash of Worcester sauce to taste."

41. Alexandra Kropotkin, *How to Cook and Eat in Russian* (New York: G. P. Putnam's Sons, 1947), v, vi.

42. Elizavetta Dmitrovna, *Samovar: A Russian Cook Book* (Richmond, VA: Dietz Press, 1946), 41–42. Recipe used by permission.

43. *Jersey Shore Cooks and Artists* (Point Pleasant, NJ: Point Pleasant Hospital Guild, 1950), 67.

44. Poppy Cannon, *The Can-Opener Cook Book* (A MacFadden-Bartell Book, 1962; originally published in 1951), 103.

45. Eleanor Early, *New York Holiday* (New York: Rinehart, 1950), 299.

46. Megan J. Elias, *Food on the Page: Cookbooks and American Culture* (Philadelphia: University of Pennsylvania Press, 2017), 22.

47. Edith Ballard Watts with John Watts, *Jesse's Book of Creole & Deep South Recipes* (New York: Weathervane Books, 1954; 1985 edition distributed by Crown Publishers), 49.

48. Mildred O. Knopf, *The Perfect Hostess Cook Book* (New York: Alfred A. Knopf, 1955), 69. A recipe for Cream Sauce is provided on page 203.

49. Rombauer and Rombauer Becker, *The Joy of Cooking*, 919.

Chapter 8

1. Poppy Cannon, *The Can-Opener Cook Book* (A MacFadden-Bartell Book, 1962; originally published in 1951), 14.

2. James Beard, *Jim Beard's Complete Book of Barbecue & Rotisserie Cooking* (New York: Maco Magazine, 1954), 132.

3. *How You Can Give Hawaiian Parties* (San Francisco: Hawaiian Pineapple Company, 1959), 3.

4. Mary Blake, *Carnation Cook Book* (Milwaukee, WI: Carnation Company, 1948), 75.

5. Blake, *Carnation Cook Book*, 75. CARNATION® is a trademark of Société des Produits Nestlé S. A. Vevy, Switzerland. Recipe used by permission.

6. *Gourmet of the Delta*, collected by St. John's Woman's Auxiliary, Leland, MS, and St. Paul's Woman's Auxiliary, Hollandale, MS (Jackson, MS: Hederman Brothers, 1958), 52. Recipe used by permission.

7. Edith Barber, *Silver Jubilee Super Market Cook Book*, rev. ed. (New York: Super Market Publishing, 1955), 28.

8. Barber, 29.

9. *Gourmet of the Delta*, 41. Recipe used by permission.

10. *Betty Crocker's Good and Easy Cook Book* (Minneapolis: General Mills, 1954; repr. Skyhouse Publishing, 2017), 118.

11. *Betty Crocker's Good and Easy Cook Book*, 220.

12. Margaret Visser, *The Rituals of Dinner: The Origins, Evolution, Eccentricities, and Meaning of Table Manners* (New York: Grove Weidenfeld, 1991), 84.

13. Visser, 85.

14. The title for this section comes from *The Gourmet Cookbook* (New York: Gourmet, 1956), 685.

15. *Better Homes and Gardens*, February 1953; quoted in Sylvia Lovegren, *Fashionable Food: Seven Decades of Food Fads* (Chicago: University of Chicago Press, 2005), 206.

16. Megan J. Elias, *Food on the Page: Cookbooks and American Culture* (Philadelphia: University of Pennsylvania Press, 2017), 23.

17. Carol Brock, "For the Hostess," *Good Housekeeping*, March 1952, 136.

18. Ruth Chier Rosen, *Wick and Lick: A Gazette of Chafing Dish Specialities* (New York: Richard Rosen Associates, 1954), 70.

19. Rosen, 108.

20. John and Marie Roberson, *The Chafing Dish Cookbook* (Englewood Cliffs, NJ: Prentice-Hall, 1958), 233.

21. Rosen, *Wick and Lick*, 130.

22. Rosen, 132.

23. *Betty Crocker's Picture Cook Book* (Minneapolis: General Mills, 1950), 50.

24. Roberson, *The Chafing Dish Cookbook*, 1.

25. Although 1950s hosts and party revelers seemed oblivious to the origins of their food, Hawaiian food was relatively well documented by the turn of the twentieth century. For example, Sara Tyson Rorer (1849–1937) published *Mrs. Rorer's New Cookbook: A Manual of House-Keeping* (Philadelphia: Arnold and

Company, 1902), which contained thirty-five recipes for Hawaiian foods in a section called "A Group of Hawaiian Recipes" (691–701). Her adventurous ingredients included breadfruit, taro root, guava, sago, mango, green gingerroot, tamarind, and coconut. http://www.archive.org/details/mrsrorersnewcook00roreuoft/mode/2up.

26. Jason Henderson and Adam Foshko, *California Tiki: A History of Polynesian Idols; Pineapple Cocktails and Coconut Palm Trees* (Charleston, SC: History Press, 2018), 29–30.

27. Alice Kim, "Christian Missionaries in Hawaii," *Hawai'i Digital Newspaper Project*, January 21, 2015. https://sites.google.com/a/hawaii.edu/ndnp-hawaii/Home/historical-feature-articles/christian-missionaries-in-hawaii.

28. History.com Editors, "Americans Overthrow Hawaiian Monarchy," *This Day in History*, February 9, 2010; updated January 14, 2020. https://www.history.com/this-day-in-history/americans-overthrow-hawaiian-monarchy. See also, "Annexation of Hawaii, 1898," US Department of State Archive, January 20, 2001, to January 20, 2009. https://2001-2009.state.gov/r/pa/ho/time/gp/17661.htm; Keanu Sai, "The Illegal Overthrow of the Hawaiian Kingdom Government," *neaToday* (National Education Association), April 2, 2018. https://www.nea.org/advocating-for-change/new-from-nea/illegal-overthrow-hawaiian-kingdom-government; and "44b. Hawaiian Annexation," *U.S. History Online Textbook*, accessed February 19, 2022. https://ushistory.org/us/44b.asp.

29. Charles Stinson, "*Shark Reef* Teams up with the *Blood Beast*," Los Angeles Times, December 5, 1958, A9.

30. James A Michener (1907–1997) was an American author known for careful, scrupulous background research for his books. Michener's other tropically themed books include *Return to Paradise* (1950) and *Hawaii* (1959). *Tales of the South Pacific* is his Pulitzer Prize-winning collection of stories based on his experiences during World War II while stationed with the US Navy on the island Espiritu Santo in the New Hebrides Islands (Vanuatu).

31. From the film *The Blue Gardenia* (1953), a Warner Bros. feature that stars Anne Baxter, Richard Cote, Ann Southern, and Raymond Burr. The statement is made by Raymond Burr's character Harry Prebble and is quoted in Aaron Sagers's "Passport to Summer: Perfect Tiki Movies and Tiki Drinks Pairings," *Den of Geek*, August 5, 2019. www.denofgeek.com/culture/tiki-movies-drinks-pairings/.

32. Brett Llenos Smith, "10 Best Rums for an El Floridita," June 2, 2022. https://www.tastingtable.com/882666/best-rums-for-an-el-floridita/.

33. *Trader Vic's Book of Food & Drink* (Garden City, NY: Doubleday, 1946), 92. Reprinted with permission from Trader Vic's. Other Cuban drink recipes include the Havana Beach (rum and pineapple juice) and Havana Club Rickey (lime juice and Puerto Rican rum). The Cuba Presidente (rum, vermouth, curaçao, and grenadine) and the Coronel Batista (vermouth and rum) both reference Fulgencio Batista, elected president of Cuba 1940 to 1944 and later a US-backed military dictator from 1952 to 1959.

34. Kaori O'Connor, "Luau," in *The Oxford Encyclopedia of Food and Drink in America*, ed. Andrew F. Smith, 2nd ed., vol. 2 (New York: Oxford University Press, 2013), 490–91.

35. *How You Can Give Hawaiian Parties*, 4–5.

36. *How You Can Give Hawaiian Parties*, 9.

37. *How You Can Give Hawaiian Parties*, 17.

38. Robynne L. Maii, "Hawai'ian Food," in *The Oxford Encyclopedia of Food and Drink in America*, ed. Andrew F. Smith, 2nd ed., vol. 2 (New York: Oxford University Press, 2013), 159–61.

39. *A Hawaiian Luau*, Presented by the Dole Company, c. 1950.

40. Tuto Kay, *Wiki Wiki Kau Kau* (Honolulu: Watkins and Strugis, 1954), Pork Hawaiian, 57; Pineapple Sticks, 69.

41. Joseph Lanza, *Elevator Music: A Surreal History of Muzak, Easy-Listening, and Other Moodsongs*, rev. ed. (Ann Arbor: University of Michigan Press, 2004), 120.

42. "Exotica," *Hip Wax*, accessed February 19, 2022. http://www.hipwax.com/music/exotica.html. This article provides an exhaustive list of available recordings.

Chapter 9

1. Jean Hamilton Campbell and Gloria Kameran, *Simple Cooking for the Epicure* (New York: Viking Press, 1949), 1.

2. Jessamyn Neuhaus, *Manly Meals and Mom's Home Cooking: Cookbooks and Gender in Modern America* (Baltimore: Johns Hopkins University Press, 2003; paperback ed., 2012), 165.

3. Florence Arfmann, comp., *The Time Reader's Book of Recipes* (New York: E. P. Dutton, 1951), 213. While the recipes may have been adapted to American palates, the drawings that accompany the offerings reinforce the exotic nature of non-Anglo cuisines by featuring racist drawings of Africans and South Pacific Islanders as well as a Southern "mammy."

4. Clementine Paddleford, *How America Eats* (New York: Charles Scribner's Sons, 1960), v. An extraordinary writer, Paddleford is known for reporting on Winston Churchill's dinner after he gave a speech in March 1946 where he coined the term "iron curtain," a term that resonated throughout the Cold War. She described Churchill's soufflé as "a rapturous, half-hushed sigh as it settled softly to melt and vanish in a moment like smoke or a dream." Quoted in Janet Duncan, "Clementine Paddleford: Food Writer, World Traveler, Hometown Gal," *Mercury* (Manhattan, KS), January 30, 2021. https://globalnewsandentertainment.com/clementine-paddleford-food-writer-world-traveler-hometown-gal-features/.

5. Fred Wasser, "The Matzo Ball Matriarch of American Jewish Food," Weekend Edition Sunday, *NPR*, April 12, 2009. https://www.npr.org/templates/story/story.php?storyId=102913413.

6. Layla Schlack, "The *Settlement Cookbook*: 116 Years and 40 Editions Later," *Taste*, June 21, 2017. https://tastecooking.com/the-settlement-cookbook-116-years-and-40-editions-later.

7. Other books written about Jewish cooking during the 1950s include Mildred G. Bellin's *The Jewish Cook Book* (New York: Tudor Publishing, 1958).

8. Nedda Casson Anders, *Casserole Specialties* (New York: Gramercy Publishing, 1955), inside jacket cover.

9. Mme. Germaine Carter, *The Home Book of French Cookery* (Garden City, NY: Doubleday, c. 1950s), inside front cover flap. Foreword by Sir Thomas Rapp indicates that the work is a translation.

10. Edna Beilenson, comp., *The Melting Pot: A Cookbook of All Nations* (Mt. Vernon, NY: Peter Pauper Press, 1958), 5–12.

11. Ruth Chier Rosen, *Pardon My Foie Gras: The Choice Cuisine of France* (New York: Richards Rosen Associates, 1956), 2.

12. Christopher Kimball, "Gourmet to All That," *The New York Times*, October 7, 2009. https://nytimes.com/2009/10/08/opinion/08kimball.html.

13. Jan Longone, "The Life and Death of Gourmet: The Magazine of Good Living, January 1941–November 2009," lecture, November 18, 2014, University of Michigan, Ann Arbor. https://deepblue.lib.umich.edu/bitstream/handle/2027.42/120259/Gourmet_14.pdf%3Fsequence=1&isAllowed=y.

14. Dorothy Roe, "US Women Can't Cook, Says Chef," *Hartford Courant*, October 7, 1945.

15. Louis Diat, *Louis Diat's French Cooking for Americans* (Philadelphia: J. B. Lippincott, 1946), 138. Copyright © 1946 by Louis Diat. Recipe used by permission of HarperCollins Publishers.

16. Dione Lucas, *The Cordon Bleu Cook Book* (Boston: Little, Brown, 1947), x.

17. Lucas, 97. Recipe used by permission.

18. Jim Scheppke, "James Beard (1903–1985)," *Oregon Encyclopedia*, updated November 8, 2020. https://www.oregonencyclopedia.org/articles/beard_james_1903_1985_/#.YX12Sy-cb_Q.

19. James A. Beard and Alexander Watt, *Paris Cuisine* (Boston: Little, Brown, 1952), xv.

20. Beard and Watt, 7. First opened in 1832 and now a historic monument, the restaurant L'Escargot still exists on 38 Rue Montorgueil.

21. Staff Home Economists, *The Gourmet Foods Cookbook*, dir. Melanie De Proft (Chicago: Culinary Arts Institute, 1955), 3.

22. Rosen, *Pardon My Foie Gras*, 33.

23. Ada Boni, *The Talisman Italian Cook Book*, trans. Matilde La Rosa (New York: Crown Publishers, 1950), x.

24. Irma S. Rombauer and Marion Rombauer Becker, *The Joy of Cooking* (Indianapolis, IN: Bobbs-Merrill, 1951), 82.

25. Paddleford, *How America Eats*, 446.

26. *The General Foods Kitchens Cookbook* (New York: Random House, 1959), 26. Recipe used by permission Kraft Heinz Foods Company.

27. Matt Blitz, "Chef Boyardee Was A Real Person Who Brought Italian Food to America," updated September 30, 2016. https://www.foodandwine.com/chefs/chef-boyardee-real-person.

28. Yong Chen, *Chop Suey, USA: The Story of Chinese Food in America* (New York: Columbia University Press. Arts and Traditions of the Table: Perspectives on Culinary History, 2014), 1.

29. See Gaye Tuchman and Harry Gene Levine, "New York Jews and Chinese Food: The Social Construction of an Ethnic Pattern," in *The Taste of American Place: A Reader on Regional and Ethnic Foods*, eds. Barbara G. Shortridge and James R. Shortridge (Lanham, MD: Rowman and Littlefield, 1998), 163–84; and Jamie Lauren Keiles, "The History of Jews, Chinese food, and Christmas, explained by a Rabbi," *Vox*, updated December 25, 2020. https://www.vox.com/the-goods/2018/12/21/18151903/history-jews-chinese-food-christmas-kosher-american.

30. "Chinese Exclusion Act," *history.com*, August 24, 2018; updated September 13, 2019. https://www.history.com/topics/immigration/chinese-exclusion-act-1882.

31. "Chinese Immigration and the Chinese Exclusion Acts," Office of the Historian, United States Department of State, n.d. https://history.state.gov/milestones/1866-1898/chinese-immigration.

32. "Chinese Revolution," Office of the Historian, United States Department of State, n.d. https://history.state.gov/milestones/1945-1952/chinese-rev.

33. *Betty Crocker's Picture Cook Book* (New York: McGraw-Hill, 1950), 394. Betty Crocker is a registered trademark of General Mills © General Mills. Recipe used by permission.

34. Barbara G. Shortridge and James R. Shortridge, eds., *The Taste of American Place: A Reader on Regional and Ethnic Foods* (Lanham, MD: Rowman and Littlefield, 1998), 131.

35. See Sherrie A. Inness, *Secret Ingredients: Race, Gender, and Class at the Dinner Table* (New York: Palgrave Macmillan, 2006), 40–60.

36. Doreen Yen Hung Feng, *The Joy of Chinese Cooking* (New York: Grosset and Dunlap, 1952), 11–12.

37. Isabelle Chang, *What's Cooking at Changs'* (New York: Liveright, 1959; rev. 1970), 9.

38. For further information on Buwei Yang Chao, see Mayukh Sen, *Taste Makers: Seven Immigrant Women Who Revolutionized Food in America* (New York: W.W. Norton, 2022), 1–26; Janet Theophano, "Home Cooking: Boston Baked Beans and Sizzling Rice Soup as Recipes for Pride and Prejudice" in *Kitchen Culture in America: Popular Representations of Food, Gender, and Race*, ed. Sherrie A. Inness (Philadelphia: University of Pennsylvania Press, 2001), 143–53.

39. Buwei Yang Chao, *How To Cook and Eat in Chinese*, 3rd ed. (New York: John Day Company, Asia Press ed., 1949), xix. https://openlibrary.org/books/OL6064948M/How_to_cook_and_eat_in_Chinese.

40. Chao, 52–53.

41. Mei-Mei Ling, *Chop Suey: A Collection of Simplified Chinese Recipes Adapted for the American Home* (Honolulu, HI: South Sea Sales, 1953), iii.

42. Myrtle Lum Young, *Fun with Chinese Recipes* (New York: Vantage Press, 1958), 5.

43. Chang, *What's Cooking at Changs'*, 34, 97–98.

44. *The ABC of Casseroles* (Mt. Vernon, NY: Peter Pauper Press, 1954), 28. © 1954 by Peter Pauper Press, Inc. Used by permission.

45. Feng, *The Joy of Chinese Cooking*, 12.

46. Richard J. Hooker, *Food and Drink in America: A History* (Indianapolis, IN: Bobbs-Merrill, 1981) 287.

47. *Pictorial Review Standard Cook Book: Methods of Preparing and Cooking Over 20000 Appetizing Dishes* (New York: Pictorial Review, 1932), 216–17.

48. See Andrew Coe, *Chop Suey: A Cultural History of Chinese Food in the United States* (New York: Oxford University Press, 2009); and Yong Chen, *Chop Suey, USA: The Story of Chinese Food in America* (New York: Columbia University Press, 2014).

49. Ling, *Chop Suey*, 17.

50. Robb Walsh, *The Tex-Mex Cookbook: A History in Recipes and Photos* (Berkeley: Ten Speed Press, 2004), xvi.

51. Diana Kennedy, *The Cuisines of Mexico* (New York: Harper and Row, 1972), 4.

52. Alison Cook, "La Reina Diana," *Texas Monthly*, June 1985; and quoted in Gustavo Arellano, *Taco USA: How Mexican Food Conquered America* (New York: Scribner, 2012), 100.

53. See José R. Ralat, *American Tacos: A History and Guide* (Austin: University of Texas Press, 2020), 10. For a history of Mexican and Mexican American foods, see Jeffrey M. Pilcher, *Planet Taco: A Global History of Mexican Food* (New York: Oxford University Press, 2012).

54. Waverly Root and Richard de Rochemont, *Eating in America: A History* (New York: William Morrow, 1976), 281.

55. Sarah Pruitt, "Tracing the History of Tex-Mex," *History*, June 16, 2015; updated September 2, 2020. https://www.history.com/news/tracing-the-history-of-tex-mex.

56. Michael Reise, *The 20 Minute Cookbook* (New York: Crown Publishers, 1953), 82.

57. Ruth Berolzheimer, ed., *Culinary Arts Institute Encyclopedic Cookbook* (Chicago: Culinary Arts Institute, 1950), 357.

58. See David Thomsen and Derek Wilson, *¡Burritos!* (Salt Lake City, UT: Gibbs-Smith Publisher, 1998).

59. Kennedy, *The Cuisines of Mexico*, 131. See Rick Bayless, *Authentic Mexican: Regional Cooking from the Heart of Mexico* (New York: William Morrow, 20th anniversary ed., 2007), 141–42.

60. Madhur Jaffrey, *An Invitation to Indian Cooking* (New York: Alfred A. Knopf, 1973; latest repr. 2021), 5. For a history of Indian food in America, see Joel Denker, *The World on a Plate: A Tour through the History of America's Ethnic Cuisine* (Lincoln: University of Nebraska Press, 2003), 115–34. See also Colleen Taylor Sen, *Curry: A Global History*. Edible Series, ed. Andrew F. Smith (London: Reaktion Books, 2009).

61. See Sarah Lohman, *Eight Flavors: The Untold Story of American Cuisine* (New York: Simon and Schuster, 2016), chap. 4 "Curry Powder," 86–117.

62. Florence Brobeck, *Cooking with Curry* (New York: Gramercy Publishing, 1952), 7.

63. Brobeck, 14.

64. *Culinary Arts Institute Encyclopedic Cookbook*, 362.

65. Dharam Jit Sing, *Classic Cooking from India* (Boston: Houghton Mifflin Company, 1956), 175. See Lizzie Collingham, "Korma: East India Company Merchants, Temples, and the Nawabs of Lucknow," in *Curry: A Tale of Cooks and Conquerors* (New York: Oxford University Press, 2006), 81–100; and Mari Uyehara, "The Real Story of Curry," *Food & Wine*, September 14, 2022. https://www.foodandwine.com/cooking-techniques/real-story-of-curry.

66. Maurice R. Davis, *World Immigration* (New York: Macmillan, 1936), 496. Quoted in Hooker, *Food and Drink in America*, 285.

Chapter 10

1. David M. Potter, *People of Plenty: Economic Abundance and the American Character* (Chicago: University of Chicago Press, 1954), 177.

2. Lawrence R. Samuel, *The American Way of Life: A Cultural History* (Madison, NJ: Fairleigh Dickinson University Press, 2017), viii.

3. Wendy Wall, "Anti-Communism in the 1950s," Gilder Lehrman Institute of American History Advanced Placement, United States History Study Guide, n.d., accessed February 17, 2022. https://ap.gilderlehrman.org/history-by-era/fifties/essays/anti-communism-1950s.

4. M. M. Manring, *Slave in a Box: The Strange Career of Aunt Jemima* (Charlottesville: University of Virginia Press, 1998), 1.

5. Maurice Manring, "Aunt Jemima," in *The Oxford Encyclopedia of Food and Drink in America*, ed. Andrew F. Smith, 2nd ed. (New York: Oxford University Press, 2013), 97.

6. Marilyn Kern-Foxworth, "African-Americans: Representations in Advertising," in *The Advertising Age Encyclopedia of Advertising*, eds. John McDonough and Karen Egolf, vol. 1 (London: Routledge, 2003), 15.

7. For information on each of the women who portrayed Aunt Jemima, see Marilyn Kern-Foxworth, *Aunt Jemima, Uncle Ben, and Rastus: Blacks in Advertising, Yesterday, Today, and Tomorrow* (Westport, CT: Praeger, 1994), 66–70.

8. Christina Ward, *American Advertising Cookbooks: How Corporations Taught us to Love SPAM®, Bananas, and Jell-O®* (Port Townsend, WA: Process Media, n.d.), 37.

9. M. M. Manring, *Slave in a Box*, 7. In 2021 Aunt Jemima's parent company, Pepsi-Co, announced it was changing the brand name to Pearl Milling Company and would also change the familiar Aunt Jemima packaging. See Chauncey Alcorn, "Pearl Milling Company's New Ads Remind Customers it Used to Be Aunt Jemima—Without Mentioning the Racist Brand," *CNN Business*, September 3, 2021. https://www.cnn.com/2021/08/31/business/pearl-milling-company-aunt-jemima/index.html.

10. Mary Drake Mcfeely, *Can She Bake a Cherry Pie: American Women and the Kitchen in the Twentieth Century* (Amherst: University of Massachusetts Press, 2000), 2–3.

11. Dianne Harris, *Little White Houses: How the Postwar Home Constructed Race in America* (Minneapolis: University of Minnesota Press, 2013), 195.

12. Lee Rainwater, Richard D. Coleman, and Gerald Handel, *Workingman's Wife: Her Personality, World and Life Style* (New York: Oceana Publications, 1959; repr. New York: Arno, 1979), 83–84; and quoted in Lizabeth Cohen, *A Consumers' Republic: The Politics of Mass Consumption in Postwar America* (New York: Vintage Books, 2004), 148. See also Cohen's endnote 77, page 452, for an excellent list of publications that examine 1950s consumer shopping.

13. Karal Ann Marling, *As Seen on TV: The Visual Culture of Everyday Life in the 1950s* (Cambridge, MA: Harvard University Press, 1994), 134–35.

14. Thomas Hine, *Populuxe* (New York: Alfred A. Knopf, 1987), 99.

15. Quoted in Cohen, *A Consumers' Republic*, 294.

16. Marling, *As Seen on TV*, 129.

17. Mary and George Catlin, *Building Your New House* (New York: A. A. Wyn, 1946), 151.

18. Ruth Schwartz Cowan, *More Work for Mother: The Ironies of Household Technology from the Open Hearth to the Microwave* (New York: Basic Books, 1983), 212.

19. For information on the use of color in advertising, see Faber Birren, *Selling with Color* (New York: McGraw Hill, 1945). https://archive.org/details/sellingwithcolor00birrrich/page/n1/mode/2up?ref=ol&view=theater.

20. Marion Tracy, *Cooking Under Pressure* (New York: Viking Press, 1950), 3.

21. *How to Get the Most Out of Your New DeLuxe Sunbeam Automatic Mixmaster Mixer* (Chicago: Sunbeam Corporation, 1957), 2.

22. *Modern Magic in Food Preparation with the Waring Blendor* (New York: Waring Products Corporation, 1953).

23. Alexandre Lange, "The Woman Who Invented the Kitchen: She Couldn't Cook," *Slate*, October 28, 2012. https://slate.com/human-interest/2012/10/lillian-gilbreths-kitchen-practical-how-it-reinvented-the-modern-kitchen.html.

24. Harris, *Little White Houses*, 202.

25. Harris, 203.
26. Harris, 197.
27. Marling, *As Seen on TV*, 220.
28. Harris, *Little White Houses*, 193.
29. *Better Home and Gardens Decorating Book* (Des Moines, IA: Meredith Publishing, 1956), 357, 351.
30. Ai Hisano, *Visualizing Taste: How Business Changed the Look of What You Eat* (Cambridge, MA: Harvard University Press, 2019), 40.
31. Andrew F. Smith, *Eating History: Thirty Turning Points in the Making of American Cuisine* (New York: Columbia University Press, 2011), 171.
32. M. F. K. Fisher, *The Art of Eating, 50th Anniversary Edition* (Hoboken, NJ: Wiley Publishing, 2004), 643–44.
33. See Jessamyn Neuhaus, *Housework and Housewives in Modern American Advertising* (New York: Palgrave Macmillan, 2011), chap. 3, 107–73.
34. Marguerite Gilbert McCarthy, *The Queen is in the Kitchen: A Cookbook of Informal Meals of all Kinds* (New York: Scribner, 1954). McCarthy's book contains a chapter titled "Television, the Permanent Dinner Guest."
35. "1950s: TV and Radio," *Encyclopedia.com*, accessed February 17, 2022. https://www.encyclopedia.com/history/culture-magazines/1950s-tv-and-radio.
36. *Better Home and Gardens Decorating Book*, 144, 147.
37. Margaret Haerens, "1950s," in *American Food by the Decades*, ed. Sheri Liberman (Santa Barbara, CA: Greenwood [ABC-CLIO], 2011), 123.
38. Andrew F. Smith, "Cheez Whiz," in *Fast Food and Junk Food: An Encyclopedia of What we Love to Eat*, vol. 1 (Santa Barbara, CA: Greenwood [ABC-CLIO], 2012), 112.
39. *Food Favorites from the KRAFT Television Theatre: Selected by Popular Request* (KRAFT Foods Company, 1951), 2. Recipe used by permission Kraft Heinz Foods Company.
40. John and Marie Roberson, *Complete Small Appliance Cookbook* (New York: A. A. Wyn, 1953), 267.
41. Abigail Carroll, *Three Squares: The Invention of the American Meal* (New York: Oxford University Press, 1995), 184.
42. Ruth Berolzheimer, ed., *Culinary Arts Institute Encyclopedic Cookbook* (Chicago: Culinary Arts Institute, 1950), 876
43. "Pretzel's Progress: Sticks Displace Sentimental Twists in a Campaign for Champagne Trade," *Kiplinger's*, February 1947, 36.
44. The story of this picnic is told in a children's book by Leslie Kimmelman, *Hot Dog!: Eleanor Roosevelt Throws a Picnic* (Ann Arbor, MI: Sleeping Bear Press, 2014).
45. Smith, "Hot Dog," 1:352.
46. Mildred O. Knopf, *The Perfect Hostess Cook Book* (New York: Alfred A. Knopf, 1955), 128–29.

47. *Cooking with the Experts: Over 400 Simple, Easy-to-Follow, Taste-Tempting Recipes Selected by Television's Best Cooks*, ed. William I. Kaufman (New York: Random House, 1955), 127.

48. Marsha F. Cassidy, *What Women Watched: Daytime Television in the 1950s* (Austin: University of Texas Press, 2005), 1.

49. Mark Evanier, "Misery Meets Reality TV: Queen for a Day," *Dr. Gerald Stein* (blog), August 27, 2010. https://drgeraldstein.wordpress.com/tag/mark-evanier.

50. "More Work for Housewives," *Time*, February 2, 1953, 47. Quoted in Cassidy, *What Women Watched*, 8.

Chapter 11

1. "Keeping Your Family Fit in Wartime," World War II Ration Book Recipes, n.d., n.p.

2. Mary MacFadyen, "Keeping Your Family Fit Tops Defense Job for Housewife," *Pittsburgh Press*, February 9, 1942.

3. *Home Canning Book* (n.p.: Kerr Glass Works Manufacturing Corporation, 1942).

4. "Keeping Your Family Fit in Wartime."

5. Paul Freedman, *American Cuisine and How it Got This Way* (New York: W. W. Norton, 2019), 188–89.

6. Freedman, 189.

7. Jessica J. Mudry, *Measured Meals: Nutrition in America* (Albany: State University of New York, 2009), 37. For a complete description of Atwater's work and the calorimeter, see pages 30–46.

8. Mudry, 50.

9. Mudry, 56.

10. M. L. Wilson (chief, Nutrition and Food Conservation Branch) and W. H. Sebrell (associate chief, Nutrition and Food Conservation Branch), United States Department of Agriculture, Food Distribution Administration, Washington DC, May 1943. Records of the Office of Labor (War Food Administration), Washington, D.C., National Archives.

11. Mudry, *Measured Meals*, 68.

12. Agriculture Information Bulletin No. 160, *Essentials of An Adequate Diet: Facts for Nutrition Programs*, November 1956, Agricultural Research Service, United States Department of Agriculture, Washington, DC. https://naldc.nal.usda.gov/download/1789401/PDF.

13. Agriculture Information Bulletin No. 160, 1.

14. The term *fast-food* was first recognized as an adjective by lexicographers with the publication of the 1951 edition of the *Merriam-Webster Dictionary*.

15. See Andrew F. Smith, "McDonalds," in *Fast Food and Junk Food: An Encyclopedia of What We Love to Eat*, vol. 2 (Santa Barbara, CA: Greenwood [ABC-CLIO], 2012), 445–48.

16. Andrew F. Smith, *Eating History: Thirty Turning Points in the Making of American Cuisine* (New York: Columbia University Press, 2011), 223.

17. Andrew P. Haley, "Restaurant Culture," in *The Routledge History of American Foodways*, eds. Michael D. Wise and Jennifer Jensen Wallach (New York: Routledge, 2016), 224.

18. Katherine J. Parkin, *Food is Love: Advertising and Gender Roles in Modern America* (Philadelphia: University of Pennsylvania Press, 2006), 177.

19. *Betty Crocker's Picture Cook Book* (Minneapolis: General Mills, 1950), 31–35.

20. Irma S. Rombauer, *The Joy of Cooking* (New York: Simon and Schuster, 1931; Facsimile Edition, foreword by Edgar R. Rombauer Jr., 1998), xiii.

21. Irma S. Rombauer, *Streamlined Cooking* (Indianapolis, IN: Bobbs-Merrill, 1939), 195.

22. Irma S. Rombauer and Marion Rombauer Becker, *The Joy of Cooking* (Indianapolis, IN: Bobbs-Merrill, 1951), 931–37.

23. *Better Homes and Gardens New Cook Book* (New York: Meredith Publishing, 1953), 6–36.

24. *The General Foods Kitchens Cookbook* (New York: Random House, 1959), 166.

25. *The General Foods Kitchens Cookbook*, 166–67.

26. *The General Foods Kitchens Cookbook*, 389–406.

27. *The General Foods Kitchens Cookbook*, 397–98. Recipe used by permission Kraft Heinz Foods Company.

28. Donald G. Cooley, "Diet for Glamour and Sex Appeal," in *Eat and Get Slim*, ed. Douglas Lurton, new 1954 edition (Concord, NH: Your Health Publications, 1954), 8.

29. Postum is a substitute for coffee that consists of wheat and molasses and mixed with milk. It originated with cereal maker C. W. Post and became available in 1912.

30. Saccharin contains no calories and is three hundred times sweeter than sugar. President Theodore Roosevelt's doctor once ordered a sugar-free diet and Roosevelt became a fan of saccharin. In 1908, the head of the USDA questioned the safety of the product, describing it as "a coal tar product totally devoid of food value and extremely injurious to health." Roosevelt shot back, "Anybody who says saccharin is injurious to health is an idiot." In the 1950s saccharin was joined by a new sugar-free chemical, cyclamate, which was banned in 1977 but reinstated in 2000. See Miss Cellania, "The Sweet and Not-So-Sweet History of Saccharin," *Mental Floss*, November 24, 2016. https://www.mentalfloss.com/article/83730/sweet-and-not-so-sweet-history-saccharin.

31. Ann Williams-Heller, "Busy Woman's 7-Day Reducing Diet," in *Eat and Get Slim*, ed. Douglas Lurton, new 1954 edition (Concord, NH: Your Health Publications, 1954), 11.

32. Williams-Heller, *Eat and Get Slim*, 12.

33. Carlton Fredericks, *Eat, Live and Be Merry* (New York: Institute of Nutrition Research, printed by Paxton-Slade Publishing, 1951), 42.

34. Jack LaLanne, *Your Health Cook Book* (Oakland, CA: Fontes Printing, 1954), 208–9.

35. Adelle Davis, *Let's Cook it Right* (New York: Harcourt, Brace, 1947), 329.

36. See R. E. Shank, review of *Let's Eat Right to Keep Fit* in *American Journal of Public Health and the Nation's Health* 45, no. 9 (1955): 1176; and a review in *California Medicine* 82, vol. 3 (March 1955): 207–9.

37. Stephen Barrett, "The Legacy of Adelle Davis," *Quackwatch*, October 13, 2006. https://quackwatch.org/consumer-education/davis/.

38. John P. Swann, "The History of Efforts to Regulate Dietary Supplements in the USA," *Drug Testing and Analysis*, November 25, 2015. https://doi.org/10.1002/dta.1919.

39. Arthur S. Flemming, Papers (1939–1975), box 10, Food and Drug Administration (1)-(5) [1959–1965, food fads and quackery], Eisenhower Presidential Library.

40. Fredericks, *Eat, Live and Be Merry*, 8.

41. Stephen Barrett, "A Critical Look at Carleton Fredericks," *Quackwatch*, March 25, 2012; revised January 27, 2020. https://quackwatch.org/11Ind/fredericks/.

42. LaLanne, *Your Health Cook Book*, 97–98.

43. Dr. Hans Kraus and Ruth P. Hirschland, "Muscular Fitness and Health," *Journal of the American Association for Health, Physical Education, and Recreation* 24, no. 10 (1953): 12.

44. Robert H. Boyle "The Report that Shocked the President," *Sports Illustrated*, August 1956, 1955. https://vault.si.com/vault/1955/08/15/the-report-that-shocked-the-president. In August 1957, Dorothy Stull wrote "A Measure of Fitness," also for *Sports Illustrated*, that detailed the work of the President's Council, with a subheading "Encouraging progress has been made since the President's Conference last year but there are still more words than deeds."

45. Dwight D. Eisenhower, "Executive Order 10673—Fitness of American Youth," *The American Presidency Project*, accessed February 17, 2022. https://www.presidency.ucsb.edu/documents/executive-order-10673-fitness-american-youth.

46. Claudia Luther, "Jack LaLanne Obituary: Jack LaLanne Dies at 96; Spiritual Father of U.S. Fitness Movement," *Los Angeles Times*, January 23, 2011. https://www.latimes.com/local/obituaries/la-me-jack-lalanne-20110124-story.html.

47. Vincent LoBrutto, *TV in the USA: A History of Icons, Idols and Ideas* (Santa Barbara, CA: Greenwood [ABC-CLIO], 2018), 69.

48. Luther, "Jack LaLanne Obituary."

49. LaLanne, *Your Health Cook Book*, vegetable salad, 24; fruit salad, 32.
50. LaLanne, 154.
51. Jack LaLanne, *Foods for Glamour* (Englewood Cliffs, NJ: Prentice-Hall, 1961), 89.
52. Jack LaLanne, *Way to Good Health* (Englewood Cliffs, NJ: Prentice-Hall, 1960), 139.
53. LaLanne, *Your Health Cook Book*, 153.
54. LaLanne, *Way to Good Health*, 48.
55. Michael Tortorello, "The Great Cranberry Scare of 1959," *New Yorker*, November 24, 2015. https://www.newyorker.com/tech/annals-of-technology/the-great-cranberry-scare.

Chapter 12

1. Ellen Mickiewicz, "Efficacy and Evidence: Evaluating U.S. Goals at the American National Exhibition in Moscow, 1959," *Journal of Cold War Studies* 13, no. 4 (Fall 2011): 138. http://www.mitpressjournals.org/doi/pdf/10.1162/JCWS_a_00171.

2. Victoria de Grazia, *Irresistible Empire: America's Advance through Twentieth-Century Europe* (Cambridge, MA: Belknap Press of Harvard University Press, 2005), 454.

3. Kenneth Osgood, *Total Cold War: Eisenhower's Secret Propaganda Battle at Home and Abroad* (Lawrence: University Press of Kansas, 2006), 45.

4. See "Report to the President," President's Committee on International Information Activities, June 30, 1953. Of particular interest is the Committee's objections to the use of the terms "cold war" and "psychological warfare." https://history.state.gov/historicaldocuments/frus1952-54v02p2/d370. See also "Finding Aid: U.S. President's Committee on International Information Activities (Jackson Committee)," Records, 1950–1953, Eisenhower Presidential Library. https://www.eisenhowerlibrary.gov/sites/default/files/finding-aids/pdf/us-presidents-committee-on-international-information-activities.pdf.

5. See "Finding Aid: U.S. President's Advisory Committee on Government Organizations," Records, 1953–1961, Eisenhower Presidential Library. https://www.eisenhowerlibrary.gov/sites/default/files/finding-aids/pdf/us-presidents-advisory-committee-government-organization.pdf.

6. *Overseas Information Programs of the United States: Hearing Before a Subcommittee of the Committee on Foreign Relations, Second Session on Overseas Information Programs of the United States, Part 3, January 15, 1954*, United States Sen., 83rd Cong. (Washington, DC: US Government Printing Office, 1954). The report was filed June 15, 1953. https://books.google.ws/books?id=KtpITyQKN3kC&printsec=frontcover&source=gbs_ge_summary_r&cad=0#v=onepage&q&f=false.

7. Nicholas J. Cull, *The Cold War and the United States Information Agency: American Propaganda and Public Diplomacy, 1945–1989* (New York: Cambridge University Press, 2008; repr. 2013), 81–82.

8. Report to the National Security Council by the Executive Secretary (Lay), Statement of Policy by the National Security Council, Mission of the United States Information Agency, October 24, 1953. https://history.state.gov/historicaldocuments/frus1952-54v02p2/d357. See also the Intelligence Advisory Committee—Survey of U.S. Information Agency's Intelligence Needs, April 23, 1954. https://www.eisenhowerlibrary.gov/sites/default/files/research/online-documents/declassified/fy-2011/1954-04-23.pdf.

9. Mickiewicz, "Efficacy and Evidence," 142.

10. At times these displays missed the mark by not taking local customs or economic status into consideration. For example, the 1955 trade fair held in Ethiopia—primarily an agrarian country—showcased a fully equipped Ford Thunderbird, televisions, and a General Electric kitchen that highlighted cakes baked from boxed mixes—food that was not part of the daily diet of Ethiopians. The next year the fair held in Damascus, Syria, once again featured a fully-equipped American kitchen that must have puzzled the attendees as it had nothing to do with traditional Syrian cooking methods.

11. Shane Hamilton, *Supermarket USA: Food and Power in the Cold War Farms Race* (New Haven, CT: Yale University Press, 2018), 166. See also Tracey Deutsch, *Building a Housewife's Paradis: Gender, Politics, and American Grocery Stores in the Twentieth Century* (Chapel Hill: University of North Carolina Press, 2010), 191–93; and de Grazia, *Irresistible Empire*, 381.

12. Greg Castillo, *Cold War on the Home Front: The Soft Power of Midcentury Design* (Minneapolis: University of Minnesota Press, 2010), 121.

13. Robert H. Haddow, *Pavilions of Plenty: Exhibiting American Culture Abroad in the 1950s* (Washington, DC: Smithsonian Institution Press, 1997). Quoted in Cull, *The Cold War and the United States Information Agency*, 114.

14. The Russian-to-English translation of this narrative is somewhat rough. Nevertheless it constitutes the opening paragraph in the official USSR booklet for its 1959 exhibition in New York. Official guide, *USSR Exhibition New York 1959*, 1.

15. Castillo, *Cold War on the Home Front*, viii.

16. Max Frankel, "Soviet's Hopes on View: Coliseum Exhibition Depicts Nation Not as it Is, but as it Wishes to Be," *The New York Times*, June 30, 1959.

17. Frederick C. Barghoorn, *The Soviet Cultural Offensive: The Role of Cultural Diplomacy in Soviet Foreign Policy* (Princeton, NJ: Princeton University Press, 1960), 92.

18. Circarama consisted of eleven movie screens linked to eleven synchronized projectors, showing 16-mm films. Its name is a play "on Cinerama, the three-film, three-projector process used to show some Hollywood features on wide, curving screens in specially-equipped movie houses." Created by American Motors Corporation, in 1955, it was utilized by Walt Disney in his theme

parks. See Werner Weiss, "The Bell System Presents America the Beautiful in Circarama," *Yesterland* (blog), updated May 26, 2017. https://www.yesterland.com/circarama.html.

19. Karal Ann Marling, *As Seen on TV: The Visual Culture of Everyday Life in the 1950s* (Cambridge, MA: Harvard University Press, 1996), 245.

20. Irene Cieraad, "The Radiant American Kitchen: Domesticating Dutch Nuclear Energy," in *Cold War Kitchen: Americanization, Technology, and European Users*, eds. Ruth Oldenziel and Karin Zachmann (Cambridge, MA: MIT Press, 2009), 113.

21. Susan E. Reid, "Soviet Responses to the American Kitchen," in *Cold War Kitchen*, 89.

22. Douglas Martin, "Charles Pollock, Designer of Popular Office Chair Dies at 83," *The New York Times*, August 24, 2013. https://www.nytimes.com/2013/08/25/nyregion/charles-pollock-designer-of-popular-office-chair-dies-at-83.html.

23. A four-minute, twenty-three-second excerpt of *Glimpses of the USA* is available on YouTube. https://www.youtube.com/watch?v=Ob0aSyDUK4A.

24. The Soviets refused to allow visitors to accept sample products, such as lipsticks. After witnessing the long lines for free makeovers at the Helena Rubenstein model beauty salon, the Soviets discontinued the makeovers. See Marling, *As Seen on TV*, 247–48.

25. Walter L. Hixson, *Parting the Curtain: Propaganda, Culture, and the Cold War, 1945–1961* (New York: St. Martin's Griffin, 1998), 167. Quoted in Castillo, *Cold War on the Home Front*, vii.

26. Quoted in "When Herman Miller took on the USSR," *Phaidon*, 2019. Review of *Herman Miller: A Way of Living*, eds. Amy Auscherman, Sam Grawe, and Leon Ramsmeier (London: Phaidon, 2019). https://www.phaidon.com/agenda/design/articles/2019/july/24/when-herman-miller-took-on-the-ussr/.

27. "Moments in U.S. Diplomatic History: Nixon vs. Khrushchev—the 1959 Kitchen Debate," Association for Diplomatic Studies and Training, July 13, 2015. https://adst.org/2015/07/nixon-vs-khrushchev-the-1959-kitchen-debate/.

28. Office of the American National Exhibition in Moscow, "Cooking Display in Moscow to Feature American Dishes," press release, May 13, 1959, folder 1, box 1, RG 306 entry 54, National Archives II, College Park, MD. Quoted in Shane Hamilton and Saran Phillips, *The Kitchen Debate and Cold War Consumer Politics: A Brief History with Documents* (Boston: Bedford/St. Martin's, 2014), 39–40.

29. Jean I. Simpson and Demetria M. Taylor *The Frozen Food Cook Book* (New York: Simon and Schuster, 1948), 325.

30. Mickiewicz, "Efficacy and Evidence," 156.

31. Joint Resolution—July 17, 1959, Pub. L. No 86-90, Stat. 73 (1959). https://www.govinfo.gov/content/pkg/STATUTE-73/pdf/STATUTE-73-Pg212.pdf.

32. Bennett Koving, *Of Walls and Bridges: The United States & Eastern Europe* (New York: New York University Press, 1991), 164.

33. Hugh S. Cumming Jr. (Department of State) to Allen W. Dulles (director, Central Intelligence Agency), memorandum and summary of the Soviet press, radio, and TV coverage of the vice president's visit to the USSR, September 10, 1959. https://www.cia.gov/readingroom/docs/CIA-RDP80B01676R002600110007-7.pdf.

34. Richard M. Nixon, *The Memoirs of Richard Nixon* (New York: Grosset and Dunlap, 1978), 207. While sources do not always agree on the location of these remarks, the transcript places this discussion inside the television studio. https://watergate.info/1959/06/24/kitchen-debate-nixon-khrushchev.html.

35. Nixon, *The Memoirs of Richard Nixon*, 208. Accounts of Khrushchev's comments differ in other sources, some claim that these remarks were made in the model house kitchen.

36. Quoted in Castillo, *Cold War on the Home Front*, x.

37. Bee Wilson, *Consider the Fork: A History of How we Cook and Eat* (New York: Basic Books, 2012), 212.

38. Hamilton and Phillips, *The Kitchen Debate*, 1.

39. Nixon, *The Memoirs of Richard Nixon*, 209.

40. Jessica Gingrich, "How Stalin and the Soviet Union Created a Champagne for the Working Class," *Gastro Obscura*, November 5, 2019. https://www.atlasobscura.com/articles/champagne-in-soviet-union.

41. Alexandra Kropotkin, *How to Cook and Eat in Russian* (New York: G. P. Putnam's Sons, 1947), 9–10.

42. Kropotkin, *How to Cook and Eat in Russian*, 117.

43. Nixon, *The Memoirs of Richard Nixon*, 208.

44. Hixson, *Parting the Curtain*, 181.

45. Nixon, *The Memoirs of Richard Nixon*, 210.

46. "Stroganina," *Tasteatlas* (blog), accessed August 12, 2021. https://www.tasteatlas.com/stroganina.

47. Kropotkin, *How to Cook and Eat in Russian*, 59.

48. Sergei Khrushchev, ed., *Memoirs of Nikita Khrushchev*, trans. George Shriver, supplementary material trans. Stephen Shenfield (University Park: Pennsylvania State University Press, 2007), 183–84. http://kiatipis.org/Writers/N/Nikita.Khrushchev/Memoirs-of-Nikita-Khrushchev%5BVol3%5D.pdf.

49. Allen W. Dulles (director, Central Intelligence Agency) to Hugh S. Cumming Jr. (director of intelligence and research, Department of State), memorandum and summary of Soviet press, radio, and television coverage of the vice president's visit to the USSR, September 10, 1959. https://www.cia.gov/readingroom/docs/CIA-RDP80B01676R002600110007-7.pdf.

50. Nixon, *The Memoirs of Richard Nixon*, 203.

51. Nikita Khrushchev, *Khrushchev Remembers: The Last Testament* (Boston: Little, Brown, 1974), 367, 530. In 1950, Wisconsin Senator Joseph McCarthy claimed he had lists of known Communist members within the federal government, including the State Department. After bitter hearings, chaired by McCarthy,

the Senate voted to censure him in December 1954. The term *McCarthyism* was coined in 1950 and perhaps Khrushchev was referring to its meaning as making personal attacks on individuals, using indiscriminate allegations with insufficient regard to evidence.

52. Richard Nixon, "Moscow, March '94: Chaos and Hope," *The New York Times*, March 25, 1994. https://www.nytimes.com/1994/03/25/opinion/moscow-march-94-chaos-and-hope.html.

53. Mark Lawrence Schrad, "The Vodka Effect: Happy New Year; A Short History of Booze Diplomacy," *Politico*, December 30, 2013. https://www.politico.com/magazine/story/2013/12/vodka-russia-foreign-policy-101613/.

54. James C. Humes, *Nixon's Ten Commandments of Leadership* (New York: Touchstone Edition, 1998), 49. Originally published as *Nixon's Ten Commandments of Statecraft* (1997).

55. Schrad, "The Vodka Effect."

56. Caroline Pardilla, "You Deserve a Mai Tai—a Real One, That Is." *Eater*, November 10, 2016. https://www.eater.com/21348867/best-mai-tai-recipe-history.

57. "Tiki Bars," *Quartz Weekly Obsession* (blog), July 24, 2018. https://qz.com/emails/quartz-obsession/1335796/.

58. "Traditional Mai Tai," *Liquor.com* (blog), updated November 8, 2020. https://www.liquor.com/recipes/traditional-mai-tai/. See also Amy Zavatto, "The History and Secrets of the Mai Tai," *Liquor.com* (blog), August 10, 2020. https://www.liquor.com/articles/mai-tai/.

59. Norma A. Davis, *Trade Winds Cookery: Tropical Recipes for All America* (Richmond, VA: Dietz Press, 1956), 63–64. Used by permission.

60. Sou Chan, *The House of Chan Cookbook* (Garden City, NY: Doubleday, 1952), 29–30.

61. Associated Press, "Soviet TV Shows Tape of Debate," *The New York Times*, July 28, 1959.

Epilogue

1. Glenna Matthews, *"Just a Housewife": The Rise and Fall of Domesticity in America* (New York: Oxford University Press, 1987), 210.

2. Peter J. Kuznick and James Gilbert, "U.S. Culture and the Cold War," *Rethinking Cold War Culture*, eds. Peter J. Kuznick and James Gilbert (Washington, DC: Smithsonian Books, 2010), 6.

3. See Stephanie Coontz, *The Way We Never Were: American Families and the Nostalgia Trap*, rev. and updated ed. (New York: Basic Books, 2016), chap. 1, 1–21.

4. Ira Chernus, "Eisenhower: Faith and Fear in the Fifties," *Ira Chernus* (blog), accessed February 23, 2022. https://spot.colorado.edu/~chernus/Research/

EFaithAndFear.htm. See also Chernus, "Operation Candor: Fear, Faith, and Flexibility," *Diplomatic History* 29.5 (November 2005): 779–809.

5. "Duck and Cover" is a short film devised for US classrooms in 1951 and can be viewed on YouTube. For further information on civil defense and women, see Laura McEnaney, *Civil Defense Begins at Home: Militarization Meets Everyday Life in the Fifties* (Princeton, NJ: Princeton University Press, 2000).

6. Federal Civil Defense Administration, "Women in Civil Defense" (Washington, DC: US Government Print Office, 1952), 1.

7. See Sarah Pruitt, "At Cold War Nuclear Fallout Shelters, These Foods Were Stocked for Survival," *History.com*, February 26, 2020. https://www.history.com/news/cold-war-fallout-shelter-survival-rations-food.

8. Pruitt, "At Cold War Nuclear Fallout Shelters."

9. Jack Mirkinson, "60 Years Ago, Edward R. Murrow Took Down Joseph McCarthy," *Huffpost*, March 10, 2014. https://www.huffpost.com/entry/edward-murrow-joseph-mccarthy-60-years-later_n_4936308.

10. See "Wilton Brands," Wilton, accessed February 7, 2022. https://www.wilton.com/about-wilton/.

11. Megan J. Elias, *Food on the Page: Cookbooks and American Culture* (Philadelphia: University of Pennsylvania Press, 2017), 4.

12. Elias, *Food on the Page*, 4.

13. John Mariani, *America Eats Out* (New York: William Morrow, 1991), 161. Southern cooking is an exception to the blurring of regional styles. Immediately after the Civil War and through the 1950s, many Southern regional cookbooks became available. In addition to offering Southern food, they also reflected a nostalgia for a lifestyle, specifically a plantation lifestyle, which no longer existed.

14. Mariani, *America Eats Out*, 30.

15. Laura Shapiro, "I Guarantee: Betty Crocker and the Woman in the Kitchen," in *From Betty Crocker to Feminist Food Studies: Critical Perspectives on Women and Food*, eds. Arlene Voski Avakian and Barbara Haber (Amherst: University of Massachusetts Press, 2005), 29–31.

16. "The American Woman; Her Achievements and Troubles," *Life*, Special Holiday Issue, December 24, 1956. https://books.google.com/books?id=00EEAAAAMBAJ&printsec=frontcover#v=onepage&q&f=false.

17. Allan V. Horwitz, review of David Herzbert's *Happy Pills in America: From Miltown to Prozac* (2009); J. John Mann's *The Age of Anxiety: A History of America's Turbulent Affair with Tranquilizers* (2009); and Edward Shorter's *Before Prozac: The Troubled History of Mood Disorders*, *New England Journal of Medicine* 360 (February 19, 2009): 841–44. https://www.nejm.org/doi/full/10.1056/nejmbkrev0809177.

18. Horwitz, review of *Happy Pills*, 841–44.

19. Jonathan M. Metzl, "'Mother's Little Helper': The Crisis of Psychoanalysis and the Miltown Resolution," *Gender & History* 15.2 (August 2003): 241.

20. Horwitz, review of *Happy Pills*, 841–44.

21. Elias, *Food on the Page*, 18–19.

22. M. F. K. Fisher, *Serve it Forth* (1937), in *The Art of Eating, 50th Anniversary Edition* (Hoboken, NJ: Wiley Publishing, 2004), 6.

23. Women's National Press Club, *Who Says We Can't Cook!* (Washington, DC: McIver Art and Publications, 1955), 157. Recipe submitted by WNPC member Beth Short. Copyright held by The Washington Press Club Foundation. Recipe used by permission.

Index

7 Up, *57*, 131–32, 294
The 20 Minute Cookbook (Reise), 109–10, 127, 206–7
50 Chowders: One Pot Meals—Clam, Corn & Beyond (White), 95

A&W Root Beer, 136
Aaron, Sam: *How to Eat Better for Less Money* (with Beard), 147
The ABC of Casseroles, 189–90, 202
Abplanalp, Robert, 104
Adamovich, Ales, 16
Adderton, Stokes, 84–85
The Adventures of Rin Tin (television program, 1954–59), 241
The Adventures of Wild Bill Hickok (television program, 1951–58), 241, 251
advertising: American way of life and, 19, 217, *218*, 293–95, *294–95*; appliances and, 3, 9, 39–40, 42–43, 99, 227–28, 229–30, 297–98; barbecue in, 57–58, *57*; car industry and, 223–25, *224*; colors in, 121–22, 229–31; convenience foods in, 3, 91–96, *93*, *100*, 101–2, *102*, 104, *105*, 110, 115, 117, 120–21, *130*, 131–32, *134*, *182*, 298; criticism of, 268–69; fictional spokeswomen in, 298–99 (*see also* Betty Crocker (character); Mary Blake (character)); foreign foods in, *204*, *208*, *211*, 212; gender roles and, 1, 2–3, 5, 39–41, 42–43, 220, 223–28, *224*; Hawaiian Islands and, 175; health and nutrition in, *7*, 248–49, 254, *255–56*; nuclear family in, 9, 57–58; pharmaceutical companies and, 300; power of, 10; snack foods and, 233–34, *234*, 241; stereotypical images of African Americans in, 3–4, 83, 220–22, *222*, 301, 330n3; suburban life and, 42, 131; sugary cereals and, 250–52; television programs and, 3, 224, 233–35, 239–43, 251; television sets and, *232*; wartime propaganda and, 34–36, *35*; as weapon of Cold War, 25; weight loss and, 254, *255–56*; World War II and, 110
Advertising Council, 25, 34, 248–49
aerosols, 103–6, *105*, 108
African Americans: Southern regional cooking and, 81–89; stereotypical images of, 3–4, 83, 220–22, *222*, 301, 330n3; suburbs and, 41, 301. See also *A Date with a Dish* (De Knight, 1948); women of color

African Americans *(continued)*
  agriculture, 2, 18, 37–38, 82. *See also* US Department of Agriculture (USDA)
alcohol, cocktails and drinks: carbonated beverages and, 116, 134–35, 136; champagne, 284; in cookbooks, 61–62, 71, 134–35, 136, 149–53; entertaining and, 148–53; gelatin salads and, 126, 134–35; mai tais, 289–90; Russian drinks, 148–49, 150, 284, 288–89; temperance legislation and, 129; in tiki bars and restaurants, 175, 180–83
Allen, Gracie, 117
Allen, Roy, 136
Alton, Robert, 177
American Association of University Women (AAUW), 73
American Can Company, 94, 99
American Communist Party, 218. *See also* communism and anti-communism
American Cuisine and How it Got this Way (Freeman), 247
American exceptionalism, 275
American Express, 278
American Federation of Labor (AFL), 26
The American Frugal Housewife (Child, 1833), 124
American Home Economics Association, 247
American Home (magazine), 94
American Medical Association (AMA), 262, 265
American National Exhibition (Moscow, 1959): Captive Nations Week and, 282–83; funding of, 277–78; *Glimpses of the USA* (1959 film) and, 62, 280; goals and design of, 273–75, 278–81, *279*; Kitchen Debate at, 8, *132*, 133, 217–18, 283–84, 288, 297–98; kitchen design and, 278, 279, 281–82, 288; Nixon and, 278, 281, 282–89, 292
American way of life: advertising and, 19, 217, *218*, 293–95, *294–95*; anti-communism and, 217–20, *219*, 296–97; barbecue and, 57–58, 62; gender roles and, 2, 41–44, *43*; immigrants and, 301; suburban life and, *40*, 41; television programs and, *242*, 293; trade fairs and exhibitions and, 275. *See also* American National Exhibition (Moscow, 1959)
The American Woman's Cook Book for Housewives (Berolzheimer), 245
Amery, Leo, 17
Anders, Nedda: *Casserole Specialties*, 96–97, 98–99, 190
Andres, Charles O., 39
Ann Pillsbury (character), 298
Annie Oakley (television program, 1954–57), 241
Anybody Can Cook (French), 126
appetizers, 141–48, 173
appliances: advertising and, 3, 9, 39–40, 42–43, 99, 227–28, 229–30, 297–98; American National Exhibition and, 280, 281–82; gender roles and, 39–40, 226–28, *226*; production of, 8, 99, 226–27. *See also* chafing dishes; electric blenders; refrigerators and freezers
Arctic Cooler (recipe), 135
Arfmann, Florence: *The Time Reader's Book of Recipes*, 187
Arness, James, 177
Atomic Cocktail (recipe), 152–53
"Atomic Cocktail" (song), 152
Atwater, Wilbur Olin, 247–48

Aunt Jemima (character), 3–4, 83, 220–22, *222*, 301
automobiles, 223–25, *224*, 252–53
avocado, 145–48
Avocado Canapes, II (recipe), 146–47
Avocado Mousse, 50

baby boom, 41
Backe, Herbert Friedrich Wilhelm, 14
Bailey, Jack, 241
Baked Sweet Potatoes Marshmallow (recipe), 112
Ballard Watts, Edith: *Jesse's Book of Creole and Deep South Recipes*, 83–84, 112, 158–59
barbecue: entertaining and, 163; masculinity and, 5, 48–49, 52–58, *57*, 62–63; roots of, 59–60, *59*; theme parties and, 173; women and, 54–59, *57*; young boys and, 48–49. See also *Jim Beard's complete book of barbecue & rotisserie cooking*
Barbecue Sauce (recipe), 63
Barbecued Fish (recipe), 60
Barbecued Spareribs (recipe), 291
Barber, Edith: *The Silver Jubilee Super Market Cook Book*, 143, 154, 166
Barghoorn, Frederick C., 277
Barq's, 136
Barrington, Eric, 19
Barthes, Roland, 52
Batista, Fulgencio, 329n32
Baxter, Les, 186
Bayless, Rick, 209
Beach, Donn (aka Ernest Raymond Beaumont Gantt), 174–75
Beard, James A., 124, 188, 191, 193–94, 239–40, 299; *Casserole Cookbook*, 193; *How to Eat Better for Less Money* (with Aaron), 147; *Jim Beard's complete book of barbecue & rotisserie cooking*, 53, 55, 61, 62, 163, 193; *Paris Cuisine* (with Watt), 194
Beebe, Lucius, 191
Beef Roly Poly, 62–63
beef stroganoff, 29, 123, 155–58, 161
Beef Stroganoff (recipe), 156–57
Beim, Jerrold: *The First Book of Boys' Cooking*, 49, 52
Belgium, 18
Berenstein, Nadia, 103, 106
Bergeron, Victor Jules, Jr. (Trader Vic), 174–75, 181, 191, 289–90
Berlin, 25–31, *27*, *29*, 275
Berlin, Irving, 31
Berolzheimer, Ruth: *The American Woman's Cook Book for Housewives*, 245; *Culinary Arts Institute Encyclopedic Cookbook*, 67, 207, 210–11, 236; *The United States Regional Cook Book* (1947), 83, 209
Bess Truman's Cocoanut Cookies (recipe), 44
The Best Men Are Cooks (Shay), 62
Better Homes and Gardens (magazine), 103. See also *The Holiday Cook Book* (Better Home and Gardens, 1959)
Better Homes and Gardens Barbecue Book, 53, 173
Better Homes and Gardens Cook Book, 140, 150
Better Homes and Gardens Decorating Book, 228–29, 230, 232
Better Homes and Gardens New Cook Book: casseroles in, 96; color illustrations in, 230; convenience foods in, *118*, 125; on entertaining, 169; foreign foods in, 196; on garnishes, 95; on health and nutrition, 258

The Betty Betz Teen-Age Cookbook (Betz), 48, 50, 111
Betty Crocker (character), 4, 74, 76, 77, 298
The Betty Crocker Magazine of the Air (radio program), 74
Betty Crocker's Cook Book for Boys and Girls, 51
Betty Crocker's Good and Easy Cook Book, 167
Betty Crocker's Junior Baking Book, 46
Betty Crocker's New Boys and Girls Cookbook, 51
Betty Crocker's New Picture Cookbook, 5
Betty Crocker's Picture Cook Book: alcoholic drinks in, 150; on appetizers, 141, 142, 173; casseroles in, 96; color illustrations in, 76, 230; foreign foods in, 188–89, 196, 199–200; on health and nutrition, 257; marshmallows in, 111; popularity and approach of, 4, 68, 73–77, 299
Betz, Betty: *The Betty Betz Teen-Age Cookbook*, 48, 50, 111
beverages, 52. *See also* alcohol, cocktails and drinks; carbonated beverages
Biardot, Alphonse, 197
Big Boy Barbecue Book, 54, 60, 62–63
Big Jim McLain (1952 film), 177
Bird of Paradise (1932 film), 177
The Bird of Paradise (1951 film), 177
Bird's Eye, *100*, 282
Birdseye, Clarence, 100
blackface, 220
Blair, Gertrude, 87
Blake, Mary. *See* Mary Blake (character)
Block, Aaron, 104
The Blue Gardenia (1953 film), 180

Blueberry Boy-Bait, 50
Bobbs-Merrill Company, 70
Boiardi, Ettore [Chef Boyardee], 197–98
Boni, Ada: *The Talisman Italian Cook Book*, 195
Boone, Pat, 224
booze diplomacy, 288–89
Borba, Willow: *Loyalty Cook Book: Native Daughters of the Golden West*, 135, 207, 234
Borden Foods, 239–40
Boston baked beans, 55, 56–57
Boston Baked Beans Gone to Heaven, 56
Boston Cooking-School Cook Book (Farmer), 68–70, 69–70
Botsford, Henry: *What's Cookin' Men? A Handy Cookbook for Men Who Enjoy Outdoor Cooking*, 61
Bower, Anne L., 86
Bowers, Lessie, 111
boxed cake mixes, 76, *77*, 101–3, *102*, 131–32, 280
Boyer, Charles, 180
Boyle, Hal, 140
The Boys' Cook Book (Brown and Brown), 49, 50, 136
Bradham, Caleb, 132
Brazzi, Rossano, 180
The Bride's Cookbook (Cannon), 64, 92–93, 126
Brobeck, Florence: *Cooking with Curry*, 210
Brown, Helen Evans: *The Boys' Cook Book*, 49, 50, 136; *Helen Brown's West Coast Cook Book*, 209
Brown, Philip S.: *The Boys' Cook Book*, 49, 50, 136
brunch, 164–65
Buck, Pearl, 201
Buckwheat Blini (recipe), 285

buffet dinners and formal dinner parties, 153–61, *154*. *See also* chafing dishes
Bullshot (recipe), 61–62
Bunny Salad, 85
Burger King (previously Insta-Burger King), 254
Burns, George, 117
burrito, 208–9
Burton, Paul, 254
Butterscotch Pudding (recipe), 127

C. W. Post, 250, 251
Cagney, James, 177
Calfee, Ken and Lu, 240
California Dip, 236
California Medicine (journal), 262
calories, 247–48
Campbell, Jean Hamilton: *Simple Cooking for the Epicure*, 187, 196
Campbell Soup Company (Campbell's), 94–95, 197
Candler, Asa, 129
Candlestick Salad, 50–51
canned foods: advertising and, *93*; barbecue and, 55–57; colors and, 230; in cookbooks for young girls and boys, 50–51; fear of nuclear weapons and, 296; foreign foods and, 189–90, 197, 203–4, *204*, *208*; gelatin salads and, 125–26; military rations and, 18, 19–20; uses of, 4, 42, 93–99, 298. *See also* SPAM
Cannibal Steak, 49
Cannon, Poppy: on appetizers, 147; on beef stroganoff, 157–58; on Boston baked beans, 56; on canned foods, 4, 6, 92–93, 94, 95, 97; on entertaining, 163, 166; on gelatin salads, 126; on lobster Thermidor, 160; on macaroni and cheese, 109. See also *The Bride's Cookbook* (Cannon, 1954); *The Can-Opener Cook Book* (Cannon)
The Can-Opener Cook Book (Cannon), 4, 6, 147
Cantrell, Thomas Joseph, 133
Captive Nations Week (Public Law 86–90), 282–83
carbonated beverages, 116, 129–36, *130*, *132*, *134*, 294
Cardini, Jack, 240
Carl's Jr., 254
Carnation Company, 298. *See also* Mary Blake (character)
Carnation Cook Book, 92, 93, 164, 189
Carney, Judith Ann, 82
cars, 223–25, *224*, 252–53
Carson, Rachael, 262
Carter, Hodding, 89
Casserole à la King, 97
Casserole Cookbook (Beard), 193
Casserole of Savory Spanish Rice (recipe), 98–99
Casserole Specialties (Anders), 96–97, 98–99, 190
casseroles: canned foods and, 4, 95–99; as comfort food, 8–9; foreign foods and, 6, 189–90, 207; snack foods in, 238; SPAM® and, 116, 121–22
Castillo, Greg, 275
Castle and Cook, 298
Catlin, Mary and George, 226
CCCP Cook Book: True Stories of Soviet Cuisine (Syutkin and Syutkin), 284
Central Intelligence Agency (CIA), 26
cereals, 6–7, 231, 250–52
Chafe, William H., 36
The Chafing Dish Cookbook (Roberson and Roberson), 171, 173
chafing dishes, 169–73, *172*, 227
champagne, 284

Chan, Sou: *The House of Chan Cookbook*, 291
Chaney, Lon, 177
Chang, Isabelle, 200, 202
Chao, Buwei Yang: *How to Cook and Eat in Chinese*, 200–201, 202
Chao, Rulan, 200
Chao, Yuen Ren, 200
Charisse, Cyd, 177
charity cookbooks (fundraising cookbooks), 78–81, 188
Charleston Receipts (cookbook), 82–83
cheese balls, 142
Cheet-os (later Cheetos), 233
Cheez Whiz, 233–34, 241
Chef-Boy-Ar-Dee, 197–98
Chen, Yong, 198
Cherokee Cooklore, 60
Cherry Coke Salad (recipe), 126
Cherry Jubilee (recipe), 172–73
Chevrolet, 224
Chicago Sunday Tribune (newspaper), 74
Chicago Tribune (newspaper), 28
Chicken à la King (recipe), 165
chicken divan, 158, 161
Chicken Noodle Casserole, 92
Child, Julia: *Mastering the Art of French Cooking*, 5
Child, Lydia Maria Francis: *The American Frugal Housewife*, 124
children. *See* young girls and boys
Chili Con Carne (recipe), 206–7
China, 13–14, 16, 198, 219
Chinese cuisine, 5–6, 198–204, *204*, 213, 291
Chinese Exclusion Act (1882), 198
chips and dip, 236
Chiquita Banana's Recipe Book (United Fruit Company), 96
chocolate, 20–21, 28
Chocolate Popcorn Balls (recipe), 236

Choice Recipes and Menus using Canned Foods (American Can Co., n.d.), 94
Chop Suey: A Collection of Simplified Chinese Recipes Adapted for the American Home (Ling), 202–3
Chop Suey (recipe), 202–3
Chow Mein Loaf (recipe), 199–200
chowders, 95
Christmas Candle Cake, 103, 231
Chun King, 203–4, *204*
Church, Ruth Ellen: *Mary Meade's Magic Recipes for the Electric Blender*, 126, 142, 147, 151
Church League of America, 296
Churchill, Winston, 23, 330n4
cilantro, 145, 147–48
Cinnamon Muffins (recipe), 79
cioppino, 196
Clam Appetizer Dip (recipe), 234–35
Classic Cooking from India (Singh), 212
classical music, 301
Clayton, A. C., 70
Coca-Cola, 129–31, *130*, 134
Cocktail Meat Balls in Wine Sauce (recipe), 143–44
cocktail parties, 140–53
cocktails. *See* alcohol, cocktails and drinks
coffee, 36
Coffee Mallow (recipe), 23
Cohn, Roy, 128
Collier, Patricia, 183–84
Collingham, Lizzie, 17–18, 306n2
color illustrations, 4, 76, 77–78, 230–31, 297
colors, 227, 229–31, 233, 288
Colorvision Cake, 231
Combination Salad [Fruit Salad] (recipe), 267
communism and anti-communism: alcoholic drinks and, 149–50; American way of life and, 217–

20, *219*, 296–97; anti-Chinese sentiment and, 198; barbecue and, 53, 55; Captive Nations Week and, 282–83; gender roles and, 42–43; Marshall Plan and, 2, 3, 24–25; Rosenberg trial and, 128, 220; Soviet blockade of West Berlin and, 25–31; suburban life and, 140. *See also* American National Exhibition (Moscow, 1959)

The Complete Barbecue Book (Roberson and Roberson), 54

Complete Small Appliance Cookbook (Roberson and Roberson), 228

Concentration (television program, 1958–1973), 241

Condé Nast, 191

convenience foods: advertising and, 3, 91–96, *93, 100,* 101–2, *102,* 104, *105,* 110, 115, 117, 120–21, *130,* 131–32, *134, 182,* 298; aerosols, 103–6, *105,* 108; American National Exhibition and, 279, 280, 281–82; boxed cake mixes, 76, *77,* 101–3, *102,* 131–32, 280; carbonated beverages, 116, 129–36, *130, 132, 134,* 294; colors and, 230, 231, 233; in cookbooks for young girls and boys, 50–51; criticism of, 6–7, 137; dehydrated foods, 103, 106–8, 296; foreign foods and, 189–90; marshmallows, 110–13; nutritional value of, 249; presliced bread, 110; processed cheese, 108–10; production of, 2; stereotypical images of African Americans and, 3–4, 83, 220–22, *222,* 301. *See also* canned foods; frozen foods; Jell-O; snack foods

Cook, Dorothy, 240

cookbooks: alcoholic drinks in, 61–62, 71, 134–35, 136, 149–53; appliances and, 228; barbecue and, 48–49, 53–58, 59–60, 163; charity cookbooks, 78–81, 188; color illustrations in, 4, 76, 77–78, 230–31, 297; convenience foods in, 92–99, 109–10, 111–12, 125–26; on entertaining, 140–48; foreign foods and gourmet cooking in, 6, 187–90, 299 (*see also specific cuisines*); gender roles and, 42, 68 (*see also* young girls and boys); Hawaiian-themed party (luau) in, 163–64; on health and nutrition, 255–60, 266–69; indexes of, 71, 96, 209; mainstream cookbooks, 68–78; for men, 60–63; Operation Vittles and, 28–31, *29*; pies in, 302; popularity and approaches of, 4–5, 297; snack foods in, 234; as source of information, 67–68; Southern regional cooking and, 81–89 (see also *A Date with a Dish* (De Knight, 1948)); for young girls and boys, 45–52, 63–64, 111–12

Cooke, Mrs. John, 124, 128–29

Cookin' for the Helluvit (Tibbens), 61

Cooking by the Clock (Mattimore and Mattimore), 136, 147

cooking shows, 192, 193, 239–40

Cooking Under Pressure (Tracy), 227

Cooking with Condensed Soups (Marshall), 94–95

Cooking with Curry (Brobeck), 210

Cooking with the Experts (Kaufman), 240

cookware, 97

Cooley, Donald G., 260, 261

Coquilles St. Jacques en Escalopes (Baked Scallops) (recipe), 193

Cordon Bleu Cook Book (Lucas), 192–93

coriander, 145

Corman, Roger, 177
Corning Glass Works, 97
Cosmopolitan (magazine), 300
Cowan, Ruth Schwartz, 226
Crabmeat Delight, 170
Crack in the Picture Window (Keats), 91
Crackerjack, 233
crackers, 234, 241, 254
cranberry industry, 269
Crane, Joseph Stephen, 175
Crawford, Frederick, 39
Cream of Wheat, 221
Crocker, Betty. *See* Betty Crocker (character)
Cugat, Xavier, 177, 186
The Cuisines of Mexico (Kennedy), 205
Culinary Arts Institute (Chicago), 96, 209, 228, 245
Culinary Arts Institute Encyclopedic Cookbook (Berolzheimer), 67, 96, 207, 210–11, 236
cultural diplomacy, 274–75
Cumming, Hugh S., Jr., 287
Cunningham, Marion, 70
Curried Cream of Chicken Soup, 92–93
curry, 209–13, *211*
Cuth, Charles, 133
cyclamate, 338n30

D rations, 20–21
Daigneau, Kenneth, 117
Dainty Food Manufacturers, 107
daiquiris, 181
Dancer Fitzgerald Sample (advertising agency), 231
Darren, James, 177
Date Bait (Loeb), 48, 50, 64
A Date with a Dish (De Knight), 56–57, 86–89, 140, 143, 144–45, 234

Davis, Adelle, 262, 299
Davis, Norma A.: *Trade Winds Cookery: Tropical Recipes for All America*, 291
Davis, R. G., 220–21
Day, Doris, 180
De Knight, Freda, 299; *A Date with a Dish*, 56–57, 86–89, 140, 143, 144–45, 234
Dee, Sandra, 177
dehydrated foods, 19, 103, 106–8, 230, 236, 296
del Río, Dolores, 177
Denmark, 18
Dennis, B. J., 89
Denny, Martin, 186
Denny's, 254
depression, 300
Design for Living (radio program), 263
Deviled Egg and Shrimp Casserole (recipe), 166–67
Diat, Louis, 191–92, 299
Dichter, Ernest, 76, 101
Dinah Shore Show (television program, 1956–1963), 224
The Dione Lucas Cooking Show (television program, 1953–1956), 192
Dione Lucas's Gourmet Club (television, program, 1958–1960), 192
dips, 236
Dishes Men Like, 234
Disney, 277–78, 288
Dmitrovna, Elizavetta: *Samovar: A Russian Cook Book*, 156–57
Dobson, Harmon, 254
Dole, James, 181
Dole, Samuel, 176, 181
Dole Company, 163–64, 174, 181, *182*, 183–84, 186, 298

Dominion Imperial, 235
Domino Sugar, 7
Dried-Beef Curry on Rice (recipe), 210–11
drinks. *See* alcohol, cocktails and drinks
Duckling with Peas (Canard aux Petits Pois Bonne Femme) (recipe), 191–92
Dulles, Allen W., 287
Dulles, John Foster, 274
Dunkin' Donuts, 254
Dupont, 104
Durante, Jimmy, 177

Eames, Charles and Ray, 62, 280
Earl, Harley, 225
Early, Eleanor, 106, 158
East Germany (German Democratic Republic), 28
Eat, Live and Be Merry (Fredericks), 261, 263
Eat and Get Slim (periodical), 261
Ebony (magazine), 87
Economic Cooperation Act (1948), 24
Ed Sullivan Show (television program, 1948–1971), 224
Egerton, John, 81
Eggless-Butterless-Milkless Cake (recipe), 259–60
Eisenhower, Dwight D.: American National Exhibition and, 273–75; anti-communism and, 219; "Atoms for Peace" speech by, 278; Captive Nations Week and, 282–83; Federal-Aid Highway Act (1956) and, 139; on health and fitness, 6, 264–65; on religion, 218; on SPAM, 123
Eisenhower, Mamie, 112, 229, 269
Ek-Aur Chingra Korma (recipe), 212
electric blenders, 126, 142, 147, 151, 227–28

Elena's Secrets of Mexican Cooking (Zelayeta), 147–48
Elias, Megan J., 158, 297, 302
Elizabeth, Queen consort of the United Kingdom, 237
Elson, Edward, 218
enslaved Africans, 60, 81–83. *See also* African Americans; racism
entertaining, 139–40; brunch and luncheon, 164–67; chafing dishes, 169–73, *172*, 227; cocktail parties, 140–53; formal dinner parties and buffet dinners, 153–61, *154* (*see also* chafing dishes); good neighbor gatherings, 168–69; teas, 167–68, *168*; theme parties, 163–64, 173–74, 184–86. *See also* barbecue
Esquire (magazine), 61–62
Essentials of An Adequate Diet: Facts for Nutrition Programs (USDA), 249–50
Ethiopia, 341n10
eugenics, 247
European Recovery Program (Marshall Plan), 2, 3, 23–25, 31–32, 117
euthenics, 247
exercise, 7, 264–69, *266*, 299
exhibitions, 229, 273–75. *See also* American National Exhibition (Moscow, 1959); Soviet Exhibition (New York City, 1959)
exotica music, 185–86

Farmer, Fannie Merritt, 68–70
fast-food restaurants, 6, 252–54, *253*
Father Knows Best (television program, 1954–60), *242*
Favorite Recipes of the Women of Tippecanoe Presbyterian Church, 79
Federal Defense Administration, 296

Federal Republic of Germany (West Germany), 28–31, 275
Federal-Aid Highway Act (1956), 139
femininity, 44
Feng, Doreen Yen Hung, 200
Fergusson, Erna: *Mexican Cookbook*, 147, 208–9
Fillet of Sole en Papillote (recipe), 195
Firmin, Blanche C.: *Peggy Put the Kettle On*, 64, 99, 125
The First Book of Boys' Cooking (Beim), 49, 52
Fisher, M. F. K., 9–10, 113, 191, 230, 302
Flaming Cabbage, 173
Fletcher, Helen Jill: *The See and Do Book of Cooking*, 52, 56
Fluff-Duff, 48
Fonda, Henry, 177
food: melting pot as cooking pot, 5–6, 10 (*see also* foreign foods); political and social issues and, 1–3 (*see also* gender roles); as weapon in World War II, 13–21, *15*; as weapon of Cold War, 2, 21–32, *27*, *29*, 295–96. *See also* convenience foods; entertaining
Food and Drug Administration (FDA), 106, 262–63, 269
Food Favorites from the KRAFT Television Theatre, 234–35
food pyramid, 250
Foods for Glamor (LaLanne, 1961), 267
Ford, Henry, 253
Ford Motor Company, 225, 278
foreign foods: acceptance and popularity of, 5–6, 187–90; Chinese cuisine, 5–6, 198–204, *204*, 213, 291; French cuisine, 5, 190–95; German cuisine, 189; Italian cuisine, 6, 195–98; Mexican cuisine, 5–6, 145–48 (*see also* Tex-Mex cuisine); Russian cuisine and drinks, 148–50, 156–57, 284–87, 288–89 (*see also* vodka); South Asian cuisine, 209–13, *211*; Tex-Mex cuisine, 205–9, *208*, 213
formal dinner parties and buffet dinners, 153–61, *154*. *See also* chafing dishes
Fortune (magazine), 4
Four Levels of Nutritive Content and Cost (Stiebeling), 248
France, 16–17, 18, 25–28. *See also* French cuisine
Franco American Company, 197
Frankel, Max, 277
frankfurter (hot dog), 51, 189, 237–38, *238*, 239
Frankfurters in Casserole (recipe), 239
Franny Frog's Lily Dessert, 48
Fredericks, Carlton, 261, 263
freedom, 217–18, 275
Freeman, Paul, 247
freeze drying, 107
freezers. *See* frozen foods; refrigerators and freezers
French, Gwen: *Anybody Can Cook*, 126
French cuisine, 5, 190–95
French's, *211*
Frey, Emil, 108
Friedan, Betty, 300
Fritos Corn Chips, 233
Frolov-Bagreyev, Anton, 284
The Frozen Food Cook Book (Simpson, and Taylor), 150, 282
frozen foods: advertising and, *100*; American National Exhibition and, 281–82; colors and, 230; foreign foods and, 197, 204; uses of, 4, 42, 99–101. *See also* TV dinners
Frozen Lemon Pie (recipe), 302–3

Fuller, Buckminster, 277–78
Fun to Cook Book (Blake), 47
Fun with Chinese Recipes (Young), 202
fundraising cookbooks (charity cookbooks), 78–81, 188

Gaillard, Slim, 152
garnishes, 85, 92–93, 95
Garret, Amelia A., 119
The Garry Moore Show (television program, 1958–67), 241
The Gastronomical Me (Fisher), 9–10
Gaynor, Mitzi, 180, *180*
gelatin, 124. *See also* Jell-O
Gelatin Easter Egg Salad (recipe), 240
gender roles: advertising and, 1, 2–3, 5, 39–41, 42–43, 220, 223–28, *224*; American way of life and, 2, 41–44, *43*; appliances and, 226–28, *226*; cookbooks and, 42, 68 (*see also* young girls and boys); health and nutrition and, 257, 268; household duties and, 38–39, 39–44, *43*; tranquilizers and, 300; young girls and boys and, 45–52, *46–47*, 63. *See also* men and masculinity; women
General Electric (GE), 278, 281
General Foods, 278, 279, 280, 282
The General Foods Kitchens Cookbook: alcoholic drinks in, 150; on barbecue, 59; casseroles in, 96; color illustrations in, 230–31; on entertaining, 153, 154, *154*, 155, 165, *168*, 172; foreign foods in, 197; on health and nutrition, 258–60; marshmallows in, 111
General Mills: American National Exhibition and, 278, 279, 280, 281–82; boxed cake mixes and, 76, *77*, 101–2, 280; cereals and, 231, 251–52; dehydrated foods and, 106–7. *See also* Betty Crocker (character)
General Motors (GM), 225, 278
Genesee Pure Food Company, 125
Genuine Mexican and Spanish Cookery Recipes for American Homes (Richardson), 147
George VI, King of the United Kingdom, 237
German cuisine, 189
German Democratic Republic (East Germany), 28
Germany, 25–31, *29*, 275
GI Bill (Servicemen's Readjustment Act) (1944), 41
Gidget (1959 film), 177
Gilbert, James, 293
Gilbreth, Lillian, 228
Gin Cocktail, 70
ginger ale, 133–34, *134*
Gingerale Salad (recipe), 135
Girl Scouts, 111–12
Glimpses of the USA (1959 film), 62, 280
Good Housekeeping (magazine), 91, 119, 123, 170
Good Housekeeping Cook Book (1955), 54, 55
Good Housekeeping Cook Book (1944), 4
Good Housekeeping's Casserole Book, 96, 98, 190
good neighbor gatherings, 168–69
Gordon, Brick: *The Groom Boils and Stews: A Man's Cook Book for Men*, 61
Gourmet (magazine), 191
The Gourmet Foods Cookbook (Culinary Arts Institute), 194
Gourmet of the Delta, 126, 143, 165, 166–67
Graham, Billy, 218

Graney, Mimi, 112
Granin, Daniil, 16
Grape-Nuts, 254, *255*
Great Britain, 17, 23–24, 25–28
Great Depression, 36, 74, 248
Green, Nancy, 220–21
Green Cheese Ball (recipe), 142
Greenglass, David, 128
Grey, Sarah, 124
Grigg, Charles Leiper, 131
Grimes, William, 148–49
The Groom Boils and Stews: A Man's Cook Book for Men (Gordon), 61
growth hormones, 262
guacamole, 145–47
Guacamole (recipe), 146
Guide to Easier Living (Wright and Wright), 229, 233
a guide to pink elephants (Rosen), 135, 149–50

H. W. Lay and Company, 233
Haakon VII, King of Norway, 31
Haber, Barbara, 83
Haddow, Robert H., 275
Hall, Rosie, 221
Halvorsen, Gail Seymour, 28
Ham and Eggs (recipe), 164
Ham Banana Rolls with Cheese Sauce, 96
Hamman, Mary: *Picture Cook Book*, 78, 164
Hammerstein, Oscar II, 179–80
Handwerker, Nathan, 237
Harper, Ethel Ernestine, 221
Harris, Dianne, 229
Harris, Jessica B., 89
Harvey, Peggy: *When the Cook's Away*, 190
Hawaiian Islands, 175–83, *178–80*. See also Hawaiian-themed party (luau); tiki bars and restaurants

A Hawaiian Luau, 163–64, 174, 184
Hawaiian Pineapple Company (later Dole Company), 163–64, 174, 181, *182*, 183–84, 186, 298
Hawaiian-themed party (luau), 163–64, 174, 184–86
health and nutrition: in advertising, 7, 248–49, 254, *255–56*; calories and, 247–48; cookbooks on, 255–60, 266–69; exercise and, 7, 264–69, *266*, 299; fast-food restaurants and, 252–54; gender roles and, 257; home economics movement and, 247; nutrition guidelines and, 248–50, 257–59; obesity and, 6, 260; quackery and, 262–63; sugary cereals and, 6–7, 250–52; weight loss and, 254, *255–56*, 261–62; World War II and, 246–47, 248–49
Helen Brown's West Coast Cook Book (Brown, 19), 209
Hemingway, Ernest, 181
Hershey, Milton, 20
Hershey Company, 20–21, 24
Hess, John L., 68–69, 125
Hess, Karen, 68–69, 82, 125
Heyerdahl, Thor, 179, *179*
Hires, Charles E., 135–36
Hires Root Beer, 135–36
Hirschland, Ruth P., 264
Hisano, Ai, 230
Hiss, Alger, 220
The Historical Cookbook of the American Negro (Thurman), 85–86
Hoffman, Peggy: *Miss B.'s First Cookbook*, 46, 48, 111
The Holiday Cook Book (Better Home and Gardens), 103
Hollywood movies, 176–80, *178–80*, 301
Home Canning Book (Kerr Glass Works), 246
home economics movement, 247

Hope, Bob, 31
Hormel, Jay, 117
Hormel Foods. *See* SPAM®
Hormel Girls Drum and Bugle Corps (Spamettes), 120
hot dog (frankfurter), 51, 189, 237–38, *238*, 239
House Beautiful (magazine), 141
The House of Chan Cookbook (Chan), 291
House Un-American Activities Committee (HUAC), 128, 177
household duties, 38–39, 39–44, *43*
house-to-house dinner parties, 168
housing, 34. *See also* suburban life
How America Eats (Paddleford), 196, 210
How to Cook and Eat in Chinese (Chao), 200–201, 202
How to Cook and Eat in Russian (Kropotkin), 156, 157, 285, 286–87
How to Eat Better for Less Money (Beard and Aaron), 147
How to Select Foods: What the Body Needs (Hunt), 248
How You Can Give Hawaiian Parties (Hawaiian Pineapple Company), 183–84
Howdy Doody (television program, 1947–60), 241
Humes, James C., 289
Hunt, Caroline, 248
Husted, Marjorie Child, 74

I Love to Eat (television program, 1946–1947), 193, 239–40
IBM, 277–78, 278
indexes, 71, 96, 209
India, 17
Inness, Sherrie A., 45, 51, 61
Insta-Burger King (later Burger King), 254

Is There Enough Manpower (Metz), 33–34
Island Beach Boy Morsels (Bacon Wrapped Chunks) (recipe), 184
Italian cuisine, 6, 195–98

Jackson, C. D., 274
Jackson, William H., 274
Jaffrey, Madhur, 209
Jamison, Cheryl Alters and Bill: *Tasting New Mexico: Recipes Celebrating One Hundred Years of Distinctive Home Cooking*, 148
Japan, 13–14, 16–18
Java, 17
Jell-O: in America's history and culture, 128–29; uses of, 48, 116, 119, 120–21, 124–28; weight loss and, 254, *256*
Jell-O: A Biography (Wyman), 128
Jersey Shore Cooks and Artists, 157, 158
Jesse's Book of Creole and Deep South Recipes (Ballard Watts), 83–84, 112, 158–59
Jiffy Pop, 235–36
Jiffy Stew (recipe), 52
Jim Beard's complete book of barbecue & rotisserie cooking (Beard), 53, 55, 61, 62, 163, 193
Johnson, Alice Frein, 79–80
Johnson, Elmer, 79
Johnson, Myrna, 103
Johnson, Sibyl, 240
Jourdan, Louis, 177
Journal of the American Association for Health, Physical Education, and Recreation, 6, 264
The Joy of Cooking (Rombauer and Rombauer Becker): on brunch and luncheon, 166; on casseroles, 96; on drinks, 149, 150; on entertaining,

The Joy of Cooking (continued) 139, 140; on foreign foods, 6, 156, 189, 196, 212; on health and nutrition, 257, 258–59; on macaroni and cheese, 109; popularity and approach of, 68, 70–72, 76, 149; rationing and, 245; writing and editions of, 71–73

K rations, 19–20
Kameran, Gloria: *Simple Cooking for the Epicure*, 187, 196
Kander, Lizzie Black: *The Settlement Cook Book* (1901), 68, 188, 258. See also *The New Settlement Cook Book* (1954) and *The New Settlement Cook Book* (1991/1997)
Karcher, Carl, 254
Kaufman, William I.: *Cooking with the Experts*, 240
Keats, John C., 91
Keck, Danielle D., 120
Keegan, Marcia: *Southwest Indian Cookbook*, 148
Keel, Howard, 177
Kellogg, John Harvey, 251
Kellogg, Will Keith, 251
Kellogg's, 7, 241, 250–51
Kelvinator, 39–40
Kendall, Donald M., *132*
Kennan, George, 42–43
Kennedy, Diana, 205, 209
Kennedy, John F., 265, 269
Kennedy, Scoop, 240
Kentucky Fried Chicken, 254
Kern-Foxworth, Marilyn, 221
Kerr Glass Works, 246
Khrushchev, Nikita, 8, 119, *132*, 133, 217–18, *219*, 283–88
Kiene, Julia: *The Step-by-Step Cook Book for Girls and Boys*, 46
Kingsford Chemical Company, 54

Kiplinger's (magazine), 237
Kitchen Debate, 8, *132*, 133, 217–18, 283–84, 288, 297–98
kitchen design, 8, 42, 228–30, 278, 279, 281–82, 288
Kiwanis International, 296
Kluger, Jeffrey, 9
Knopf, Mildred O.: *The Perfect Hostess Cook Book*, 159–60, 239
Knox, Charles B., 124
Kon-Tiki (1951 film), 179
Kon-Tiki (Heyerdahl), 179
Korean War, 198, 219
Kraft, James L., 108
Kraft Foods Company, 108, 112–13, 170, 233–35, *234*, 241
KRAFT Television Theatre (television program, 1947–58), 233–35, 241
Kraus, Hans, 264
Kroc, Ray, 253
Kroger, 112–13
Kropotkin, Alexandra: *How to Cook and Eat in Russian*, 156, 157, 285, 286–87
Kubla Khan, 204
Kuznick, Peter J., 293

La Florida Daiquiri No. 3 (recipe), 181
Ladies' Home Journal, 300
LaLanne, Jack, 6–7, 262, 264, 265–69, *266*, 299
Lamas, Fernando, 180
Lanza, Joseph, 185
Lapin, Aaron S. "Bunny," 104
Lawford, Peter, 177
Leeb, Wilhelm von, 16
Lemon, Jack, 177
lemon pie, 302–3
Leningrad, 16
Let's Cook it Right (Davis), 262
Let's Cook Without Cooking (Rudomin), 50

Let's Eat Right to Keep Fit (Davis), 262
Levitt, William J., 40–41
Lewis, Aylene, 221
Lewis, Edna, 89
Lewis, Jesse Willis, 83–84
Lewis, Peter, 17
Libby's (Libby, McNeill & Libby), 298
Lieffers, Caroline, 30
Life (magazine), 34, 260, 299
Liliuokalani, Queen of the Hawaiian Islands, 176
Ling, Mei-Mei: *Chop Suey: A Collection of Simplified Chinese Recipes Adapted for the American Home*, 202–3
Lipton, 106–7
Lipton Dehydrated Onion Soup Mix, 236
Little Mother's Cook Book, 47
Little White Houses (Harris), 229
lobster, 158–60
Lobster Newburg (recipe), 170
lobster thermidor, 159–61
Lobster Thermidor (recipe), 158–60
Loeb, Robert H. Jr.: *Date Bait*, 48, 50, 64; *Wolf in Chef's Clothing*, 60–61
Loft Candy Company, 133
Lord and Thomas (advertising agency), 221
Los Angeles Times, 177
Louis Diat's French Cooking for Americans (Diat), 191–92
The Love Trader (1930 film), 177
Lovegren, Sylvia, 141
Loy, Percy, 204
Loyalty Cook Book: Native Daughters of the Golden West (Borba), 135, 207, 234
luau (Hawaiian-themed party), 163–64, 174, 184–86
Lucas, Dione, 192–93, 240, 299

Luce, Henry, 34
luncheon, 164–67

macaroni and cheese, 108–10
MacDonald, Betty, 137
MacFadyen, Mary, 38–39, 246
Mack, Walter, 133
Macy's, 280–81
Magic Chef, 39–40
Mai Tai (recipe), 289–90
Mamie's Million Dollar Fudge (recipe), 113
mammy stereotype, 3–4, 83, 220–22, 222, 330n3
Management-Labor Policy Committee, 33
Mao Zedong, 198
Mariani, John, 205, 297
Marling, Karal Ann, 225, 230
Mars Company, 20, 21
Marshall, Anne: *Cooking with Condensed Soups*, 94–95
Marshall, George C., 21, 22, 23–24, 31
Marshall Plan (European Recovery Program), 2, 3, 23–25, 31–32, 117
Marshmallow Fluff, 112–13
marshmallows, 110–13
Martin, Mary, 179–80
Martini—Medium Dry (recipe), 149
Mary Blake (character), 298, 313n5. See also Carnation Company; *Fun to Cook Book* (Blake)
Mary Meade's Magic Recipes for the Electric Blender (Church), 126, 142, 147, 151
Mary's Cornbread (recipe), 30–31
The Master Chef's Outdoor Grill Cookbook, 54
Mastering the Art of French Cooking (Child), 5
Matthews, Kristin L., 53, 60

Mattimore, Jean and Clarke: *Cooking by the Clock*, 136, 147
May, Elaine Tyler, 41, 42–43, 139
Mayer, Oscar, 237–38, *238*
McCarthy, Joseph, 128, 198, 219, 297, 343–44n51
McDonald, Richard and Maurice, 252–53
McDonald Brothers Burger Bar Drive-In (later McDonald's), 252–53, *253*
Mcfeely, Mary Drake, 95
McGraw-Hill, 278
McKinley Tariff Act (1890), 176
McLaughlin, John, 133
McNutt, Paul V., 33
Meade, Julia, 224
Meade, Mary, 55
Meat Ball Sauce (recipe), 144
meatballs, 195–96
meatless Tuesdays, 22–23
The Melting Pot: A Cookbook of All Nations, 189, 190
men and masculinity: barbecue and, 5, 48–49, 52–58, *57*, 63; cars and, 223–24, *224*; cookbooks and, 60–63. *See also* gender roles; young girls and boys
meprobamate, 300
Metz, Harold W., 33–34
Mexican Cookbook (Fergusson), 147, 208–9
Mexican Cook-Book: Mexican Dishes for American Kitchens (Scott), 147
Mexican cuisine, 5–6, 145–48. *See also* Tex-Mex cuisine
Mexican Tamale Pie (recipe), 207
Meyerhoff, Arthur, Jr., 104
Michener, James A., 179
Mickiewicz, Ellen, 282
military rations, 18–21, 106, 117, 119
Mills, Frederick, 30

Miltown (meprobamate), 300
mineral oil, 261–62
Minted Peas and Carrots (recipe), 282
Miracle Cherry Pie (recipe), 155
Miracle Kitchen (Whirlpool), 229, 278, 279, 288
Miss B.'s First Cookbook (Hoffman), 46, 48, 111
Mister Roberts (1955 film), 177
The Mixer, Hand Mixer, and Blender Cookbook (Culinary Arts Institute), 228
Modern Magic in Food Preparation with the Waring Blendor (Waring Products Corporation), 147, 227–28
Monkey Pudding, 48
Monroe Cheese Company, 108
Montalban, Ricardo, 177
Monty Python's Flying Circus (BBC television program), 122
More Work for Mother (Cowan), 226
Moreno, Rita, 177
Mrs. Rorer's New Cookbook (Rorer), 328n25
Mudry, Jessica, 249
Murrow, Edward R., 122, 297
Mushrooms Under Glass (recipe), 71–72

Nabisco, 241, 251, 252
nachos, 206
Nadine's Boston Baked Beans (recipe), 56
Native Americans, 5–6, *59*, 60
Nazi Germany, 13–14, 16, 18
Nelson, George, 280
Netherlands, 18
Neuhaus, Jessamyn, 68
Nevada Test Site, *151–52*, 152
New England Clam Chowder, 95
The New Fannie Farmer Boston Cooking-School, 68–70

Index | 363

The New Settlement Cook Book (The Settlement Cook Book Company, 1954), 188, 258
The New Settlement Cook Book: The First Classic Collection of Ethnic Recipes (Pierce, 1991/1997), 68, 258
New York State Journal of Medicine (journal), 264
The New York Times (newspaper), 23, 74, 117, 191, 292
New York Travel (Early), 158
New Yorker (magazine), 277
Newsweek (magazine), 300
Nixon, Richard M.: American National Exhibition and, 8, *132*, 217–18, 278, 281, 282–89, 292, 297–98; cranberry industry and, 269; Kitchen Debate and, 133; mai tais and, 289–90; President's Council on Youth Fitness and, 6, 264–65
Nobel Peace Prize, 31
Norway, 18
novels, 301
nuclear family, 9, 41, 57–58, 131, 257, 293. *See also* gender roles
nuclear weapons, 152–53, *152*, 295–96
nutrition guidelines, 248–50, 257–59

obesity, 6, 260
O'Connor, Kaori, 183
Office of War Information (OWI), 34, 74, 248–49, 311n6
"Old Aunt Jemima" (song), 220
On an Island with You (1948 film), 177
Operation Vittles, 27–31, *29*
"Operation Vittles" (song), 31
Operation Vittles Cook Book (American Women in Blockaded Berlin), 28–31, *29*
Oppenheimer, J. Robert, 153

Oppenheimer Martini (recipe), 153
orange juice, 99
Our Nation's Rations (radio program, 1945), 74

P. Duff and Sons, 101
Packaged Macaroni Dinner (recipe), 109–10
Paddleford, Clementine, 187, 191, 196, 210
Pagan Love Song (1950 film), 177
Paget, Debra, 177
PAM (nonstick cooking spray), 104
Pardilla, Caroline, 289
Pardon My Foie Gras (Rosen, 1956), 190, 194–95
Paris Cuisine (Beard and Watt, 1952), 194
Parkin, Katherine J., 254
The Pat Boone Chevy Showroom (television program, 1957–1960), 224
Patricia Collier (character), 298
Paulucci, Jeno, 203
Payne, Jessie Hargrave: *Paynie's Parties*, 84–85
Pearl Milling Company, 335n9
Peggy Put the Kettle On (Firmin), 64, 99, 125
Pemberton, John Stith, 129
people of color, 41, 42. *See also* African Americans; women of color
Pepsi-Cola, 7, 132–33, *132*, 134, 278, 335n9
The Perfect Hostess Cook Book (Knopf), 159–60, 239
Perry, Albert, 34–36
pesticides, 262
pharmaceutical companies, 300
Picture Cook Book (Hamman), 78, 164
Pierce, Charles: *The New Settlement Cookbook* (1991/1997), 68, 188, 258

pies, 302–3
pigs in a blanket, 51
Pillsbury, *102*, 298
pineapple, 175, 181, *182*, 185, 186. See also Hawaiian Pineapple Company (later Dole Company)
Pineapple Sticks (recipe), 185
Pinza, Enzo, 179–80
pizza, 197
plays, 301
Poland, 16
Polynesian recipes and parties, 173–74. *See also* luau (Hawaiian-themed party); tiki bars and restaurants
popcorn, 235–36
Pork Hawaiian (recipe), 185
Post, Charles William, 251
Post Grape-Nuts, 7
Postum Cereal Company (later General Foods Corporation), 125, 250
Potage St. Germaine (recipe), 75
Potato Chip Institute, 238
potato chips, 236, 238
potluck dinners, 168–69
Potter, David M., 217
Pound Cake (recipe), 70
Powell, Eleanor, 177
Powell, William, 177
President's Advisory Committee on Government Organization, 274
President's Committee on International Information Activities, 274
President's Council on Physical Fitness, 265
President's Council on Youth Fitness, 6, 264–65
presliced bread, 110
pressure cooker, 227
pretzels, 236–37, 238
Principles of Nutrition and Nutritive Value of Food (Atwater), 248

Pringles, 107
Private Enterprise Unit, 25
processed cheese, 108–10, 206
processed foods. *See* convenience foods
psychological warfare, 274–75
Publisher's Weekly (magazine), 4
Purple Cow, 52
Pyrex, 97

quackery, 262–63
Quail on Toast (recipe), 85
Quaker Oats, 221
Queen for a Day (radio program, 1945–1957; television program, 1956–64), 241

R. T. French Company, 107
racism, 3–4, 41, 83, 220–22, *222*, 301, 330n3
radio, 120, 263
Ralston Purina Company, 252, 254
Randolph, Mary: *The Virginia House Wife*, 209
rarebit (Welsh rabbit), 171
Rastus (character), 3–4, 221
rationing: in Great Britain, 23; implementation of, 14, 36, 245–47, *246*; in Poland, 16; processed cheese and, 108–9; sugar and, 20–21, 36, 125, 131, 133, 233, 248–49; transportation and, 34, 36. *See also* military rations
Rawhide (television program, 1959–65), 241
recipes: Artic Cooler, 135; Atomic Cocktail, 152–153; Avocado Canapes, II, 146–147; Baked Sweet Potatoes Marshmallow, 112; Barbecued Fish, 60; Barbecue Sauce (for chicken), 63; Barbecued Spareribs, 291; Beef Stroganoff [I],

157; Beef Stroganoff [II], 157; Bess Truman's Cocoanut Cookies, 44; Buckwheat Blini, 285; Bullshot, 61–62; Butterscotch Pudding, 127; Casserole of Savory Spanish Rice, 98–99; Cherry Coke Salad, 126; Cherry Jubilee, 172–173; Chicken à la King, 165; Chili Con Carne, 206–207; Chocolate Popcorn Balls, 236; Chop Suey, 203; Chow Mein Loaf, 199–200; Cinnamon Muffins, 79; Clam Appetizer Dip, 235; Cocktail Meat Balls in Wine Sauce, 143–144; Coffee Mallow, 23; Combination Salad [fruit salad], 267; Coquilles St. Jacques en Escalopes, 193; Deviled Eggs and Shrimp Casserole, 166–167; Dried-Beef Curry on Rice; 210–211; Duckling with Peas, 191–192; Eggless-Butterless-Milkless Cake, 259–260; Ex-Aur Chingra Korma [shrimp curry], 212; Fillet of Sole en Papillote, 195; Frankfurters in Casserole, 239; Frozen Lemon Pie, 302–303; Gelatin Easter Egg Salad, 240; Gingerale Salad, 135; Green Cheese Ball, 142; Guacamole, 146; Ham and Eggs, 164; Island Beach Boy Morsels, 184; Jiffy Stew, 52; La Florida Daiquiri No. 3, 181; Lobster Newburg, 170; Lobster Thermidor [I], 158–159; Lobster Thermidor [II], 159–160; Mai Tai, 290; Maimie's Million Dollar Fudge, 113; Martini-Medium Dry, 149; Mary's Cornbread, 30–31; Mexican Tamale Pie, 207; Minted Peas and Carrots, 282; Miracle Cherry Pie, 155; Mushrooms Under Glass, 72–73; Nadine's Boston Baked Beans, 56; Oppenheimer Martini, 153; Packaged Macaroni Dinner, 109–110; Pineapple Sticks, 185; Pork Hawaiian, 185; Potage St. Germaine, 75; Pound Cake, 70; Quail on Toast, 85; Red Snapper, 88–89; Red-Cooked Meat Proper: Plain, 201; Russian Cocktail, 152–153; Shrimp Canape, 291; Shrimp Jambalaya, 84; "Some More," 111–112; Southern Hopping John, 86; SPAM "Around the World" Dinner Casserole, 122; SPAM Noodles Romanoff, 123; Strawberry Punch, 150; Stuffed Bell Peppers [vegetable salad], 266–267; Sukiyaki, 80–81; Tiny Wiener Appetizers, 144–145; Tomato-Crab Bake, 98; Tuna Casserole, 8–9; Veal and Cucumber Salad, 286–287; Veal Parmigiana, 197; Welch Rabbit, 171; Whisky Sour, 136

Recipes and Party Ideas Starring Potato Chips (Potato Chip Institute, 1959), 238

Recommended Dietary Allowances (RDAs), 248, 258

Red Snapper (recipe), 88–89

Red-Cooked Meat Proper: Plain (recipe), 201

Reddi-wip (whipped cream), 104, *105*

refrigerators and freezers, 99, 125, 227, 282. *See also* frozen foods

Reise, Michael: *The 20 Minute Cookbook*, 109–10, 127, 206–7

religion, 218, *242*

Rethinking Cold War Culture (Kuznick and Gilbert), 293

Richards, Ellen Swallow, 247

Richardson, Myrtle: *Genuine Mexican and Spanish Cookery Recipes for American Homes*, 147

Ripperger, Helmut, 74–76

River Road Recipes (Junior League of Baton Rouge, Inc.), 125, 158
Roberson, John and Marie: *The Chafing Dish Cookbook*, 171, 173; *The Complete Barbecue Book*, 54; *Complete Small Appliance Cookbook*, 228
Robinson, Anna, 221
Rockefeller, Nelson, 274
Rocket Salad, 51
Rodgers, Richard, 179–80
Rombauer, Irma S., 257–58. See also *The Joy of Cooking* (Rombauer and Rombauer Becker)
Rombauer Becker, Marion, 70–71, 189
Roosevelt, Eleanor, 237
Roosevelt, Franklin D., 33, 34, 38, 39, 237, 245, 248–49
Roosevelt, Theodore, 338n30
Root, Waverly, 205
root beer, 135–36
Rorer, Sara Tyson: *Mrs. Rorer's New Cookbook*, 328n25
Rosen, Ruth Chier: *a guide to pink elephants*, 135, 149–50; *Pardon My Foie Gras*, 190, 194–95; *Wick and Lick*, 170–71, 172–73
Rosenberg, Bill, 254
Rosenberg, Julius and Ethel, 128, 220
Rosie the Riveter, 34
Roto-Broil Corporation of America, 228
Rubin, Leon, 104
Rudomin, Esther: *Let's Cook Without Cooking*, 50
Russell, Malinda, 89
Russian Cocktail (recipe), 150
Russian cuisine and drinks, 148–50, 156–57, 284–87, 288–89. See also vodka
Rutt, Chris, 220
Ry-Krisp, 254

saccharin, 261, 338n30
salads, 49–51, 116, 124, 125–27, 134–35, 261, 265–67
Samovar: A Russian Cook Book (Dmitrovna), 156–57
Samuelsson, Marcus, 89
Saturday Review (magazine), 74
sauces, 190
Saypol, Irving, 128
Schenone, Laura, 82
Schlesinger, Arthur M. Sr., 5, 10
Schrad, Mark Lawrence, 289
Science Digest (magazine), 300
Scott, Natalie: *Mexican Cook-Book: Mexican Dishes for American Kitchens*, 147
Scribner, 71
The See and Do Book of Cooking (Fletcher), 52, 56
Selective Service Act (1917), 39
seltzer (soda water), 136
Selznick, David O., 177
Servicemen's Readjustment Act (GI Bill) (1944), 41
The Settlement Cook Book: The Way to a Man's Heart (Kander, 1901), 68, 188, 258. See also *The New Settlement Cook Book* (1954) and *The New Settlement Cook Book* (1991/1997)
Shapiro, Laura, 107, 298, 299
Shaw, Artie, 117
Shay, Frank: *The Best Men Are Cooks*, 62
She Gods of Shark Reef (1958 film), 177, *178*
Ships Ahoy (1942 film), 177
Shrimp Canape (recipe), 291
Shrimp Jambalaya (recipe), 84
Sica, Vittorio De, 180
side dishes, 55–57
Silent Spring (Carson), 262

Index | 367

Silver Jubilee Super Market Cook Book (Barber), 143, 154, 166
Simple Cooking for the Epicure (Campbell and Kameran), 187, 196
Simpson, Jean I.: *The Frozen Food Cook Book*, 150, 282
Singh, Dharam Jit: *Classic Cooking from India*, 212
Sino-Japanese War, 13–14, 16
Sirkin, Abraham M., 281
sitcoms, 242–43
Skelton, Red, 177
Skinner and Eddy, 106–7
Smith, Andrew F., 135, 233–34, 254
Smith, Joseph, 309n37
Smith-Mundt Act (1948), 24–25
snack foods, 233–39, *238*, 241, 254
soap operas, 241–42
soda fountains, 116, 129–30, 132–34
"Some More" [S'mores] (recipe), 111–12
South Asian cuisine, 209–13, *211*
South Pacific (1958 film), 180, *180*
South Pacific (musical), 179–80
Southern Hopping John (recipe), 86
Southern regional cooking, 81–89, 345n13. See also *A Date with a Dish* (De Knight)
Southwest Indian Cookbook (Keegan), 148
Sovetskoye Shampanskoye, 284
Soviet Cultural Offensive (Barghoorn), 277
Soviet Exhibition (New York City, 1959), 273, *276*, 277–78
Soviet Union: blockade of West Berlin and, 25–31; Marshall Plan and, 24; siege of Leningrad and, 16. See also American National Exhibition (Moscow, 1959); communism and anti-communism; Russian cuisine and drinks

SPAM®, 6, 24, 91, 116–23, *118*, 231
spam (junk email), 122
SPAM "Around the World" Dinner Casserole (recipe), 122
SPAM 'n Noodles Romanoff (recipe), 123
Spamettes (Hormel Girls Drum and Bugle Corps), 120
Spellman, Francis Joseph, 218
Sports Illustrated (magazine), 264
Spruill, J. F., 84–85
Sputnik crisis, 277
Square Meals (Stearn and Stearn), 113
Stalin, Joseph, 26
Standage, Tom, 31
Sta-Whip, 104
Stearns, Jessie, 80
Steichen, Edward, 277–78
The Step-by-Step Cook Book for Girls and Boys (Kiene), 46
Stephen, George, 54
Stern, Jane and Michael, 113
Stiebeling, Hazel, 248
Stimson, Henry L., 33
stir-frying, 199
Strawberry Bavarian Cream, 48
Streamlined Cooking (Rombauer), 257–58
Stuffed Bell Peppers [Vegetable Salad] (recipe), 266–67
Stull, Dorothy, 339n44
Subcommittee on Overseas Information Programs of the Committee on Foreign Relations, 274
suburban life: advertising and, 42, 131; anti-communism and, 140; origins and evolution of, 2–3, 39, 40–41, *40*, 301. See also entertaining
sugar: cereals and, 6–7, 250–52; criticism of, 6–7, 268–69; as

368 | Index

sugar *(continued)*
 healthy, 7, *7*; rationing of, 20–21, 36, 125, 131, 133, 233, 248–49
sugar industry, 176
Sugar Information Inc., 7
Sukiyaki (recipe), 80–81
Sullivan, Jill M., 120
Sumac, Yma, 186
Sunbeam Corporation, 227
Sunset Barbecue Cook Book, 54–55
Super Market Institute, 275
supermarkets, 275, 278
Swanson, Carl A., 100–101
Swanson Company, 100–101, 230, 233
Sweater Girl Salad, 61
sweeteners, 261
Syria, 341n10
Syutkin, Olga and Pavel, 284

Taco Tia (later Taco Bell), 254
tacos, 207
Tales of the South Pacific (Michener), 179
The Talisman Italian Cook Book (Boni), 195
tamales, 207
Tariff Act (1890), 176
The Taste of American Place (Shortridge and Shortridge), 200
A Taste of Texas (Trahey), 141–42, 145, 146–47, 209
Tasting New Mexico: Recipes Celebrating One Hundred Years of Distinctive Home Cooking (Jamison and Jamison), 148
Taylor, Demetria M.: *The Frozen Food Cook Book*, 150, 282
Taylor, Elizabeth, 180
technology, 300–301. *See also* appliances
Telegraph Agency of the Soviet Union (TASS), 281

television: in Europe, 24; first presidential address on, 22. *See also* snack foods; TV dinners
television programs: advertising and, 3, 224, 233–35, 239–43, 251; American way of life and, *242*, 293; cooking shows, 192, 193, 239–40; exercise programs, 7, 268; wild West in, 49
television sets, 231–33, *232, 279*
television trays, 233
Texas Kabobs, 94
Tex-Mex cuisine, 205–9, *208*, 213
theme parties, 163–64, 173–74, 184–86
Theophano, Janet, 87, 200–201
Thomas, Benjamin, 129
Thompson, Llewellyn, 280
three bean salad, 55
Thurman, Sue Bailey: *The Historical Cookbook of the American Negro*, 85–86
Tibbens, Paul K.: *Cookin' for the Helluvit*, 61
tiki bars and restaurants, 174–76, 180–83, 186, 289–90
Time (magazine), 9, 129, 252, 300
The Time Reader's Book of Recipes (Arfmann), 187
Tiny Wiener Appetizers (recipe), 144
Tipton-Martin, Toni, 89
To the Queen's Taste (television program, 1947–1953), 192
Tobias, Ruth, 133
Toklas, Alice B., 299
tomato aspic, 50, 125
Tomato-Crab Bake (recipe), 98
Tommy Dorsey Band, 177
Tozzi, Giorgio, 180
Tracy, Marion: *Cooking Under Pressure*, 227

trade fairs, 229, 273–75, 341n10. *See also* American National Exhibition (Moscow, 1959); Soviet Exhibition (New York City, 1959)
Trade Winds Cookery: Tropical Recipes for All America (Davis), 291
Trader Vic (Victor Jules Bergeron Jr.), 174–75, 181, 191, 289–90
Trader Vic's Book of Food & Drink (Trader Vic), 181
Trahey, Jane: *A Taste of Texas*, 141–42, 145, 146–47, 209
Tramping and Trailing with the Girl Scouts, 111–12
tranquilizers, 300
Truman, Bess (Elizabeth Virginia "Bess" Truman), 8–9, 22, 44
Truman, Harry S., 4, 8, 22–23, 39, 218
Tully, Richard Walton, 177
Tuna Casserole (recipe), 8–9
Tupper, Earl, 58
Tupperware, 58–59, *58*
TV dinners, 100–101, 230, 232–33
TV-Time Popcorn, 235, 241
Twitty, Michael W., 60, 89

Uncle Ben (character), 3–4, 221
Underwood, Charles, 220
United States Information Agency (USIA), 274, 278, 280
The United States Regional Cook Book (Berolzheimer), 83, 209
Universal Appliances, 39–40
US Coast Guard Women's Reserve (SPARS), 36–37
US Department of Agriculture (USDA), 14, 104, 107, 248–50, 257–59
US Department of Commerce, 278
US Department of Labor, 33
US Department of State, 24–25, 198, 287

US Embassy, 278
US Office of Price Administration, 36, 245
US State Department, 219, 278
US War Department, 14

Van Camp's, *208*
Veal and Cucumber Salad (recipe), 286–87
Veal Parmigiana (recipe), 196–97
vegetarian dishes, 267. *See also* salads
Velveeta, 108, 206
Venable, Willis, 129
Vichyssoise, 191
victory gardens, 14
Vidor, King, 177
Vietnam, 16–17
The Virginia House Wife (Randolph), 209
Visser, Margaret, 169
Visualizing Taste (Hisano), 230
vodka, 61–62, 149–50, 286, 288–89

Wagon Train (television program, 1957–1965), 241
Wait, Pearle, 124–25
Walker, George, 225
Wall, Wendy, 218
Waller, William, 39
Walsh, Robb, 205
War Advertising Council, 34–36
War Manpower Commission (WMC), 33, *35*
Waring Products Corporation, 147, 227–28
Washburn, Abbott, 274
Washburn-Crosby Company (later General Mills), 4, 74, 251. *See also* Betty Crocker (character)
Watt, Alexander, 194
Watts, John, 83–84
Wayne, John, 177

Weber Kettle, 54
weight loss, 254, *255–56*, 261–62
Welch Rabbit (recipe), 171
Welsh rabbit (rarebit), 171
West Bend, 235
West Berlin, 25–31, *27, 29*, 275
West Germany (Federal Republic of Germany), 275
Westinghouse, 39–40, 278, 279
Whataburger, 254
What's Cookin' Men? A Handy Cookbook for Men Who Enjoy Outdoor Cooking (Botsford), 61
When the Cook's Away (Harvey), 190
Whirlpool, 229, 278, 279, 281, 288
Whisky Sour (recipe), 136
Whit, William C., 82
White, Jasper, 95
White Castle, 252
White Shadows in the South Seas (1928 film), 177
Whitehead, Joseph, 129
Who Says We Can't Cook! (Women's National Press Club), 79–81, 302–3
Wick and Lick (Rosen), 170–71, 172–73
Wieners Royale, 61
Wiki Wiki Kau Kau, 185
Wild Salad, 49–50
Williams, Esther, 177
Williams, Richard, 141
Williams-Heller, Ann, 261
Wilson, Edith, 221
Wilton Enterprises, 103
Wolf in Chef's Clothing (Loeb), 60–61
Womanpower Committees During World War II (1953), 34
Woman's Day (magazine), 298
women: barbecue and, 54–59, *57*; brunch and luncheon for, 164–67; cars and, 225; employment of, 2, 33–44, *35, 37*; as idealized housewives, 293, 299–300; teas for, 167–68, *168*; weight loss and, 254, *255–56*, 261. *See also* gender roles; women of color; young girls and boys
Women Accepted for Volunteer Emergency Service (WAVES), 36–37
Women Airforce Service Pilots (WASP), 36–37, *37*
Women in War Jobs, 34–36
women of color, 34, 42, 223. *See also* African Americans
Women's Advisory Committee (WAC), 33
Women's Army Corps (WAC), 36–37
Women's Bureau, 33, 34
Women's Christian Temperance Union, 129–31
Women's Home Companion (magazine), 117–19
Women's Land Army (WLA), 37–38
women's magazines, 77–78, 91–92, 117–19, 293, 300. *See also* advertising; *specific magazines*
Women's National Press Club: *Who Says We Can't Cook!*, 79–81, 302–3
Wonder Bread, 110
Wong, Robert, 204
Woodward, Frank, 125
World War II: advertising and, 110; aerosols and, 104; appliances and, 99; Betty Crocker (character) and, 74; convenience foods and, 115, 116, 117, 119, 122, 133; dehydrated foods and, 107; food as weapon in, 13–21, *15*; health and, 246–47, 248–49; military rations in, 18–21, 106, 117, 119; women's employment and, 2, 33–39, *35, 37*, 44. *See also* rationing
Wright, Mary and Russel: *Guide to Easier Living*, 229, 233
Write, Frank, 136

Wyman, Carolyn, 117, 128

Young, Myrtle Lum: *Fun with Chinese Recipes*, 202
young girls and boys, 45–52, 46–47, 63, 111–12

Your Health Cook Book (LaLanne), 265–67

Zelayeta, Elena: *Elena's Secrets of Mexican Cooking*, 147–48
Zimmerman, Max Mandell, 275